A Concise History

Volume One

SECOND EDITION

DARLENE CLARK HINE
Northwestern University

WILLIAM C. HINE
South Carolina State University

STANLEY HARROLD
South Carolina State University

Upper Saddle River, New Jersey 07458

Library of Congress Cataloging-in-Publication Data
Hine, Darlene Clark.
African Americans : a concise history / Darlene Clark Hine, William C. Hine, Stanley Harrold.—2nd ed.
p. cm.
"Combined volume."
Includes bibliographical references and index.
ISBN 0-13-192583-0 (combined volume)
1. African Americans—History. I. Hine, William C. II. Harrold, Stanley. III. Title.
E185.H534 2006
973'.0496073—dc22

2005049286

Vice President/Editorial Director: Charlyce Jones Owen
Associate Editor: Emsal Hasan
Editorial Assistant: Maureen Diana
Director of Production and Manufacturing: Barbara Kittle
Senior Managing Editor: Joanne Riker
Production Liaison: Louise Rothman
Prepress and Manufacturing Manager: Nick Sklitsis
Prepress and Manufacturing Buyer: Benjamin Smith
Director of Marketing: Heather Shelstad
Electronic Artist: Mirella Signoretto
Composition and Full-Service Project Management: GGS Book Services, Atlantic Highlands
Cover Design: Bruce Kenselaar
Printer/Binder: Courier Companies, Inc.
Cover Printer: Courier Companies, Inc.

Credits and acknowledgments borrowed from other sources and reproduced, with permission, in this textbook appear on appropriate page within text.

Pearson Education LTD.
Pearson Education Australia PTY, Limited
Pearson Education Singapore, Pte. Ltd
Pearson Education North Asia Ltd
Pearson Education, Canada, Ltd
Pearson Educación de Mexico, S.A. de C.V.
Pearson Education–Japan
Pearson Education Malaysia, Pte. Ltd

10 9 8 7 6 5 4 3 2 1
ISBN 0-13-192585-7

To

Carter G. Woodson & Benjamin Quarles

Contents

CHAPTER 7 • Free Black People in Antebellum America 123

CHAPTER 8 • Opposition to Slavery, *1800–1833* 145

Preface

"One ever feels his two-ness,—an American, a Negro; two souls, two thoughts, two unreconciled strivings; two warring ideals in one dark body." So wrote W. E. B. Du Bois in 1897. African-American history, Du Bois maintained, was the history of this double-consciousness. Black people have always been part of the American nation that they helped to build. But they have also been a nation unto themselves, with their own experiences, culture, and aspirations. African-American history cannot be understood except in the broader context of American history. American history cannot be understood without African-American history.

Since Du Bois's time our understanding of both African-American and American history has been complicated and enriched by a growing appreciation of the role of class and gender in shaping human societies. We are also increasingly aware of the complexity of racial experiences in American history. Even in times of great racial polarity some white people have empathized with black people and some black people have identified with white interests.

It is in light of these insights that we tell the story of African Americans. That story begins in Africa, where the people who were to become African Americans began their long, turbulent, and difficult journey, a journey marked by sustained suffering as well as perseverance, bravery, and achievement. It includes the rich culture—at once splendidly distinctive and tightly intertwined with a broader American culture—that African Americans have nurtured throughout their history. And it includes the many-faceted quest for freedom in which African Americans have sought to counter white oppression and racism with the egalitarian spirit of the Declaration of Independence that American society professes to embody.

Nurtured by black historian Carter G. Woodson during the early decades of the twentieth century, African-American history has blossomed as a field of study since the 1950s. Books and articles have appeared on almost every facet of black life. Yet this survey is the first comprehensive college textbook of the African-American experience. It draws on recent research to present black history in a clear and direct manner, within a broad social, cultural, and political framework. It also provides thorough coverage of African-American women as active builders of black culture.

African Americans: A Concise History balances accounts of the actions of African-American leaders with investigations of the lives of the ordinary men and women in black communities. This community focus helps make this a history of a people rather than an account of a few extraordinary individuals. Yet the book does not neglect important political and religious leaders, entrepreneurs, and entertainers. And it gives extensive coverage to African-American art, literature, and music.

African-American history started in Africa, and this narrative begins with an account of life on that continent to the sixteenth century and the beginning of the forced migration of millions of Africans to the Americas. Succeeding chapters present the struggle of black people to maintain their humanity during the slave trade and as slaves in North America during the long colonial period.

The coming of the American Revolution during the 1770s initiated a pattern of black struggle for racial justice in which periods of optimism alternated with times of repression. Several chapters analyze the building of black community institutions, the antislavery movement, the efforts of black people to make the Civil War a war for emancipation, their struggle for equal rights as citizens during Reconstruction, and the strong opposition these efforts faced. There is also substantial coverage of African-American military service, from the War for Independence through American wars of the nineteenth and twentieth centuries.

During the late nineteenth century and much of the twentieth century, racial segregation and racially motivated violence that relegated African Americans to second-class citizenship provoked despair, but also inspired resistance and commitment to change. Chapters on the late nineteenth and early twentieth centuries cover the great migration from the cotton fields of the South to the North and West, black nationalism, and the Harlem Renaissance. Chapters on the 1930s and 1940s—the beginning of a period of revolutionary change for African Americans—tell of the economic devastation and political turmoil caused by the Great Depression, the growing influence of black culture in America, the racial tensions caused by black participation in World War II, and the dawning of the civil rights movement.

The final chapters tell the story of African Americans during the second half of the twentieth century and beginning of the twenty-first century. They portray the successes of the civil rights movement at its peak during the 1950s and 1960s and the efforts of African Americans to build on those successes during the more conservative 1970s, 1980s, and 1990s. Finally, there are discussions of black life at the turn of the twenty-first century and of the continuing impact of African Americans on life in the United States.

In all, *African Americans: A Concise History* tells a compelling story of survival, struggle, and triumph over adversity. It will leave students with an appreciation of the central place of black people and black culture in this country and a better understanding of both African-American and American history.

New to the Second Edition

For the second edition, we have broadened the text's international perspective, expanded coverage of interaction among African Americans and other ethnic groups, and added new material on African Americans in the western portion of the United States. We have also added a new chapter on the evolution of black politics since the 1980s.

In early chapters there is additional material concerning the growth of the Atlantic slave trade and on black life in New Spain's northern borderlands. There is also an extended comparison of slavery in the American South with slavery in Latin America. African-American interaction with American Indians in the colonial era receives increased attention. We also have more information on African Americans on the western frontier during and after Reconstruction including their often uneasy, if not hostile, relationships with Native Americans. The discussion of black towns in the west has been enhanced. We have added material on black Roman Catholics by including a discussion of the nineteenth-century Healy family.

In chapters dealing with the twentieth century there is a new international account of black migration from the Caribbean. There are also international approaches to the African-American reaction to the Italian invasion of Ethiopia in 1935, to black entertainer and political activist Paul Robeson, and to the HIV/AIDS crisis in Africa and the United States. Our discussion of the Supreme Court's decision in *Brown v. Topeka Board of Education* has been revised and consolidated. The new chapter on late-twentieth twentieth century politics portrays African Americans developing from a special interest group into the core of the Democratic Party. Our final chapter includes broadened coverage of contemporary culture, immigration and ethnic tension, black feminism, black mega-churches, and hip hop.

Special Features

The special features and pedagogical tools integrated within *African Americans: A Concise History* are designed to make the text accessible to students. They include a variety of tools to reinforce the narrative and help students grasp key issues.

- **Brief chronologies** provide students with a snapshot of the temporal relationship among significant events.
- **End-of-chapter timelines** establish a chronological context for events in African-American history by relating them to events in American history and in the rest of the world.
- **Review questions** encourage students to analyze the material they have read and to explore alternative perspectives on that material.
- **Recommended Reading** and **Additional Bibliography** lists direct students to more information about the subject of each chapter.

Supplementary Instructional Materials

The supplements that accompany *African Americans: A Concise History* provides instructors and students with resources that combine sound scholarship, engaging content, and a variety of pedagogical tools to enrich the classroom experience and students' understanding of African-American history.

Instructor's Manual with Tests

The Instructor's Manual with Tests provides summaries, outlines, learning objectives, lecture and discussion topics, and audio/visual resources for each chapter. Test materials include multiple choice, essay, identification and short-answer, chronology, and map questions. To help with the assignment of supplementary material offered with the text, the Test Item File includes test questions in multiple choice, true/false and essay format for this material.

History Notes (Volumes I and II)

This student study aid includes a summary for each chapter, reviews key points and concepts, and provides multiple choice, essay, chronology, and map questions.

Documents Set (Volumes I and II)

The *Documents Set* supplements the text with additional primary and secondary source material covering the social, cultural, and political aspects of African-American history. Each reading includes a short historical summary and several review questions. The documents are included on the student CDROM and many are referenced throughout the text with special call outs to call attention to related textual material.

African American Stories

This collection of brief biographical sketches of the many African-American figures represented in the text serves as an indispensable companion to *African Americans.* Students can use this as a reference to learn more about the people who have helped to shape both American and African American history.

Prentice Hall and Penguin Bundle Program

Prentice Hall and Penguin are pleased to provide adopters of *African Americans: A Concise History* with an opportunity to receive significant discounts when orders for *African Americans: A Concise History* are bundled together with Penguin titles in American history. Contact your local Prentice Hall representative for details.

Research Navigator™

This unique resource helps your students make the most of their research time. From finding the right articles and journals, to citing sources, drafting and writing effective papers, and completing research assignments, **Research Navigator**™ simplifies and streamlines the entire process. Access to **Research Navigator**™ is available with every copy of the *OneSearch guide.* For more information, contact your local Prentice Hall representative.

Acknowledgments

Each of us enjoyed the support of family members, particularly Barbara A. Clark, Robbie D. Clark, Emily Harrold, Judy Harrold, Carol A. Hine, Peter J. Hine, Thomas D. Hine, and Alma J. McIntosh.

We gratefully acknowledge the essential help of the superb editorial and production team at Prentice Hall: Charlyce Jones Owen, Vice President and Editorial Director for the Humanities, whose vision got this project started and whose unwavering support saw it through to completion; Editorial Assistant, Maureen Diana; Louise Rothman, Production Editor, who saw it efficiently through production; Stephen Forsling, Photo Researcher; Heather Shelstad, Director of Marketing; Emsal Hasan, Associate Editor, who pulled together the book's supplementary material; and Nick Sklitsis, Manufacturing Manager, Benjamin Smith, Manufacturing Buyer, and Joanne Riker, Managing Editor, who kept the whole team on schedule.

About the Authors

Darlene Clark Hine

Darlene Clark Hine is Board of Trustees Professor of African American Studies and Professor of History at Northwestern University. She is past-president of the Organization of American Historians (2001–2002) and of the Southern Historical Association (2002–2003). Hine received her BA at Roosevelt University in Chicago, and her MA and Ph.D. from Kent State University, Kent, Ohio. Hine has taught at South Carolina State University, Purdue University, and at Michigan State University. In 2000–2001 she was a fellow at the Center for Advanced Study in the Behavioral Sciences at Stanford University, and in 2002–2003 she was a fellow at Radcliffe Institute for Advanced Studies. She is the author and/or editor of fifteen books, most recently, with David Barry Gaspar, *Beyond Bondage: Free Women of Color in the Americas* (Urbana: University of Illinois Press, 2004), and *The Harvard Guide to African American History* (Cambridge: Harvard University Press, 2000) coedited with Evelyn Brooks Higginbotham and Leon Litwack. She coedited a two-volume set with Earnestine Jenkins, A *Question of Manhood: A Reader in Black Men's History and Masculinity* (Bloomington: Indiana University Press, 1999, 2001); and with Jacqueline McLeod, *Crossing Boundaries: Comparative History of Black People in Diaspora* (Bloomington: Indiana University Press, 2000pk). With Kathleen Thompson she wrote *A Shining Thread of Hope: The History of Black Women in America* (New York: Broadway Books, 1998), and edited with Barry Gaspar, *More Than Chattel: Black Women and Slavery in the Americas* (Bloomington: Indiana University Press, 1996). She won the Dartmouth Medal of the American Library Association for the reference volumes coedited with Elsa Barkley Brown and Rosalyn Terborg-Penn, *Black Women in America: An Historical Encyclopedia* (New York: Carlson Publishing, 1993). She is the author of *Black Women in White: Racial Conflict and Cooperation in the Nursing Profession,* 1890–1950 (Bloomington: Indiana University Press, 1989). Her forthcoming book is entitled *Black Professional Class and Race Consciousness: Physicians, Nurses, Lawyers, and the Origins of the Civil Rights Movement, 1890–1955.*

William C. Hine

William C. Hine received his undergraduate education at Bowling Green State University, his master's degree at the University of Wyoming, and his Ph.D. at Kent State University. He is a professor of history at South Carolina State University. He has had articles published in several journals, including *Agricultural History, Labor History,* and the *Journal of Southern History*. He is currently writing a history of South Carolina State University.

Stanley Harrold

Stanley Harrold, Professor of History at South Carolina State University, received his bachelor's degree from Allegheny College and his master's and Ph.D. degrees from Kent State University. He is coeditor with Randall M. Miller of *Southern Dissent,* a book series published by the University Press of Florida. He received during the 1990s two National Endowment for the Humanities Fellowships to pursue research dealing with the antislavery movement. His books include: *Gamaliel Bailey and Antislavery Union* (Kent, Ohio: Kent State University Press, 1986), *The Abolitionists and the South* (Lexington: University Press of Kentucky, 1995), *Antislavery Violence: Sectional, Racial, and Cultural Conflict in Antebellum America* (co-edited with John R. McKivigan, Knoxville: University of Tennessee Press, 1999), *American Abolitionists* (Harlow, U.K.: Longman, 2001); *Subversives: Antislavery Community in Washington, D.C., 1828–1865* (Baton Rouge: Louisiana State University Press, 2003), and *The Rise of Aggressive Abolitionism: Addresses to the Slaves* (Lexington: University Press of Kentucky, 2004). He has published articles in *Civil War History, Journal of Southern History, Radical History Review, and Journal of the Early Republic.*

• CHAPTER ONE •

AFRICA

THE BIRTHPLACE OF HUMANITY

Paleoanthropologists—scientists who study the evolution and prehistory of humans—have concluded that the origins of humanity lie in the savannah regions of Africa. All people today, in other words, are very likely descendants of beings who lived in Africa millions of years ago.

Fossil and genetic evidence suggests that both humans and the forest-dwelling great apes (gorillas and chimpanzees) descended from a common apelike ancestor who lived in Africa about five to ten million years ago. The African climate was growing drier at that time, as it has continued to do into the present. Forests gave way to spreading savannahs dotted with isolated copses of trees.

The earliest known *hominids* (the term designates the biological family to which humans belong) were the *australopithecines*, who emerged about four million years ago. These creatures walked upright but otherwise retained many apelike characteristics and probably did not make stone tools. The first stone tools are associated with the emergence—about 2.4 million years ago—of *Homo habilis*, the earliest creature designated as within the *homo* (human) lineage. Individuals of the *Homo habilis* species had larger brains than the australopithecines. They butchered meat with stone cutting and chopping tools and built shelters with stone foundations. Like people in hunting and gathering societies today, they probably lived in small bands in which women foraged for plant food and men hunted and scavenged for meat.

Recently scientists have found *Homo habilis* fossils in the Caucasus region of southeastern Europe. A more advanced human, *Homo erectus*, spread even farther from Africa, reaching eastern Asia and Indonesia. *Homo erectus*, who emerged in Africa about 1.6 million years ago, is associated with the first evidence of human use of fire.

Paleoanthropologists agree that modern humans, *Homo sapiens*, evolved from *Homo erectus*, but they disagree on how. According to a multiregional model, modern humans evolved throughout Africa, Asia, and Europe from ancestral regional populations of *Homo erectus* and archaic *Homo sapiens*. According to the out-of-Africa model, modern humans emerged in Africa some 200,000 years ago and began migrating to the rest of the world about 100,000 years ago, eventually replacing all other existing hominid populations. Both of these models are consistent with recent genetic evidence, and both indicate that all living peoples are closely related. The "Eve" hypothesis, which supports the out-of-Africa model, suggests that all modern humans are descended from a single African woman. The multiregional model maintains that a continuous exchange of genetic material allowed archaic human populations in Africa, Asia, and Europe to evolve simultaneously into modern humans.

Ancient Civilizations and Old Arguments

The earliest civilization in Africa and one of the two earliest civilizations in world history is that of ancient Egypt, which emerged in the Nile River valley in the fourth millennium BCE. Mesopotamian civilization, the other of the two, emerged in the valleys of the Tigris and Euphrates Rivers in southwest Asia with the rise of the city-states of Sumer. In both regions, civilization appeared at the end of a long process in which hunting and gathering gave way to agriculture. The settled village life that resulted from this transformation permitted society to become increasingly hierarchical and specialized. Similar processes gave rise to civilization in the Indus valley in India around 2300 BCE, in China—with the founding of the Shang dynasty—around 1500 BCE, and in Mexico and Andean South America during the first millennium BCE.

The race of the ancient Egyptians and the nature and extent of their influence on later Western civilizations have long been a source of controversy that reflects more about racial politics of recent history than it reveals about the Egyptians themselves. It is not clear whether they were an offshoot of their Mesopotamian contemporaries, whether they were representatives of a group of peoples whose origins were in both Africa and southwest Asia, or whether the ancestors of both the Egyptians and Mesopotamians were black Africans. What is clear is that the ancient Egyptians exhibited a mixture of racial features and spoke a language related to the languages spoken by others in the fertile regions of North Africa and southwest Asia.

In this context the argument over whether the Egyptians were black or white is unlikely to be resolved. They were both or neither and certainly did not regard themselves in a way related to modern racial terminology. The argument began in the nineteenth century when African Americans and white liberals sought to refute claims by racist pseudoscientists that people of African descent were inherently inferior to whites. Unaware of the achievements of West African civilization, those who believed in human equality used evidence that the Egyptians were black to counter assertions that African Americans were incapable of civilization.

Recently there has been a more scholarly debate between Afrocentricists led by Martin Bernal and traditionalists led by Mary Lefkowitz. Bernal, in his book *Black Athena*, argues that black Egyptians colonized ancient Greece, which is usually regarded as the birthplace of the values associated with Western civilization. According to Bernal, the Egyptians supplied the Greeks with the basis of their scientific method and, therefore, Africans are the progenitors of Western civilization. Lefkowitz and her colleagues respond that modern racial categories have no relevance to the world of the ancient Egyptians, no evidence indicates the Egyptians colonized Greece, and the Greeks developed the origins of the Western empirical method of inquiry on their own. Yet although scholars question many of Bernal's claims, they have always recognized Egypt's contribution to the spread of civilization throughout the Mediterranean region. In religion, commerce, and art—if not in philosophy—Egypt strongly influenced the development of Greece and subsequent Western civilizations.

Egyptian Civilization

Egypt was, as the Greek historian Herodotus observed 2,500 years ago, the "gift of the Nile." A gentle annual flooding regularly irrigates the banks of this great river, leaving behind a new deposit of fertile soil. It was the Nile that allowed Egyptians to cultivate wheat and barley and herd goats, sheep, pigs, and cattle in an otherwise desolate region. The Nile also provided the Egyptians with a transportation and communications artery, while its desert surroundings protected them from foreign invasion. Egypt was unified into a single kingdom in about 3150 BCE and was ruled by a succession of thirty-one dynasties until its incorporation into the Roman Empire in the first century BCE. Historians have divided this immensely long span into several epochs. During the early dynastic period (3100–2700 BCE) and Old Kingdom (2700–2200 BCE), Egypt's kings consolidated their authority and claimed the status of gods. After a period of instability following the end of the Old Kingdom, royal authority was reestablished during the Middle Kingdom (2050–1650). During the New Kingdom (1550–1100), Egypt expanded beyond the Nile valley to establish an empire over coastal regions of southwest Asia as well as Libya and Nubia in Africa. It was in this period that Egypt's kings began using the title *pharaoh,* which means "great house." During the Post-Empire period (1100–30 BCE), Egypt fell prey to a series of outside invaders. With the invasion of Alexander the Great's Macedonian army in 331 BCE, Egypt's ancient culture crumbled under the pressure of Greek ideas and institutions.

The way of life that took shape during the Old Kingdom, however, had resisted change for most of ancient Egypt's history. Kings presided over a strictly hierarchical society. Beneath them were classes of warriors, priests, merchants, artisans, and peasants. A class of scribes, who were masters of Egypt's complex hieroglyphic writing, staffed a comprehensive bureaucracy.

Egyptian society was also strictly patrilineal and patriarchal. Royal incest was customary, with each king choosing a sister to be his queen. Kings maintained numerous concubines; other men could also take additional wives if the first wife failed to produce children. Egyptian women nonetheless held a high status compared with women in much of the rest of the ancient world. They owned property independently of their husbands, oversaw household slaves, controlled the education of their children, held public office, served as priests, and operated businesses. There were several female rulers, one of whom, Hatshepsut, reigned for twenty years (1478–1458 BCE). She is depicted in carvings and monuments wearing the regalia of male rulers, including the traditional false beard.

A complex polytheistic religion shaped every facet of Egyptian life. Although there were innumerable gods, two of the more important were the sun god Re (or Ra), who represented the immortality of the Egyptian state, and Osiris, the god of the Nile, who embodied each individual's personal immortality. In Egyptian myth Osiris was murdered by his evil brother Seth and resurrected by his sister and wife Isis. This myth, originally an allegory for the seasonal rebirth of vegetation brought by the Nile's annual flooding, came to symbolize the possibility of individual immortality. Egyptians came to regard Osiris as the judge of the worthiness of souls.

Personal immortality and the immortality of the state merged in the person of the king, as expressed in Egypt's elaborate royal funerary architecture. The most dramatic

The ruined pyramids of Meroë on the banks of the upper Nile River are not as old as those at Giza in Egypt and differ from them stylistically. But they nonetheless attest to the cultural connections between Meroë and Egypt.
Timothy Kendall

examples of that architecture, the Great Pyramids at Giza near the modern city of Cairo, were built more than 4,500 years ago to protect the bodies of three prominent kings of the Old Kingdom so that their souls might successfully enter the life to come. The pyramids also dramatically symbolized the power of the Egyptian state and have endured as embodiments of the grandeur of Egyptian civilization.

Kush, Meroë, and Axum

To the south of Egypt in the upper Nile River valley, in what is today the nation of Sudan, lay the ancient region known as Nubia. As early as the fourth millennium BCE, the indisputably black people who lived there interacted with the Egyptians. Recent archaeological evidence suggests that grain production and the concept of monarchy may have arisen in Nubia and subsequently spread northward to Egypt. But Egypt's population was always much larger than that of Nubia, and during the second millennium BCE, Egypt used its military power to make Nubia an Egyptian colony and control Nubian copper and gold mines. Egyptians also imported ivory, ebony, leopard pelts, and slaves from Nubia and required the sons of Nubian nobles to live in Egypt as hostages.

The hostages served as ambassadors of Egyptian culture when they returned home. As a result, Egyptian religion, art, hieroglyphics, and political structure became firmly established in Nubia. Then, with the decline of Egypt's New Kingdom at the end of the second millennium BCE, the Nubians established an independent kingdom known as Kush, which had its capital at Kerma on the upper Nile River. During the eighth century BCE, the Kushites took control of upper Egypt, and in about 750 the Kushite king Piankhy added lower Egypt to his realm. Piankhy made himself pharaoh and founded Egypt's twenty-fifth dynasty, which ruled until the Assyrians, who invaded Egypt from southwest Asia, drove the Kushites out in 663 BCE.

Kush itself remained independent for another thousand years. Its kings continued for centuries to call themselves pharaohs and had themselves buried in pyramid tombs covered with Egyptian hieroglyphics. They and the Kushite nobility practiced the Egyptian religion and spoke the Egyptian language. But a resurgent Egyptian army destroyed Kerma in 540 BCE and the Kushites moved their capital southward to Meroë. The new capital was superbly located for trade with East Africa, with regions to the west across the Sudan, and with the Mediterranean world by way of the Nile River. Trade made Meroë wealthy, and the development of a smelting technology capable of exploiting local deposits of iron transformed the city into Africa's first industrial center.

As Meroë's economic base expanded, the dependence of Kushite civilization on Egyptian culture declined. By the second century CE, the Kushites had developed their own phonetic script to replace hieroglyphics. An architecture derived from that of Egypt gave way to an eclectic style that included Greek, Indian, and sub-Saharan African motifs, as well as Egyptian.

Because of its commerce and wealth, Kush attracted powerful enemies, including the Roman Empire, which by 31 BCE controlled all the lands bordering the Mediterranean Sea. A Roman army, for example, invaded Kush in 23 BCE. But it was actually the decline of Rome and its Mediterranean economy that were the chief factors in Kush's destruction. As the Roman Empire grew weaker and poorer, its trade with Kush declined, and Kush, too, grew weaker. During the early fourth century CE, Kush fell to the neighboring Noba people, who in turn fell to the nearby kingdom of Axum, whose warriors destroyed Meroë.

Located in what is today Ethiopia, Axum emerged as a nation during the first century BCE as Semitic people from the Arabian Peninsula, who were influenced by Hebrew culture, settled among a local black population. By the time it absorbed Kush during the fourth century CE, Axum had become the first Christian state in sub-Saharan Africa. By the eighth century, shifting trade patterns, environmental depletion, and Islamic invaders combined to reduce Axum's power. It nevertheless retained its unique culture and its independence.

West Africa

Like Africa as a whole, West Africa is physically, ethnically, and culturally diverse. Much of West Africa south of the Sahara Desert falls within the great savannah that spans the continent from east to west. West and south of the savannah, however, in Senegambia (modern Senegal and Gambia), stretching along the southwestern coast of West Africa, and in the lands located along the coast of the Gulf of Guinea, there are extensive forests. These two environments—savannah and forest—were home to a great variety of cultures and languages. Patterns of settlement in the region ranged from isolated homesteads and hamlets through villages and towns to cities.

West Africans began cultivating crops and tending domesticated animals between 1000 BCE and 200 CE. Those who lived on the savannah usually adopted settled village life well before those who lived in the forests. The early farmers produced millet, rice, and sorghum while tending herds of cattle and goats. By 500 BCE, beginning with the Nok people of the forest region, some West Africans were producing iron tools and weapons.

From early times, the peoples of West Africa traded among themselves and with the peoples who lived across the Sahara Desert in North Africa. This extensive trade became an essential part of the region's economy and formed the basis for the three great western Sudanese empires that successively dominated the region from before 800 CE to the beginnings of the modern era.

Ancient Ghana

The first known kingdom in the western Sudan was Ghana. Founded by the Soninke people in the area north of the modern republic of Ghana, its origins are unclear. It may have arisen as early as the fourth century CE or as late as the eighth century when Arab merchants began to praise its great wealth. Its name comes from the Soninke word for king, which Arab traders mistakenly applied to the entire kingdom.

Ghana's kings were known in Europe and southwest Asia as the richest of monarchs, and the source of their wealth was trade. The key to this trade was the Asian camel, which was introduced into Africa during the first century CE. With its ability to endure long journeys on small amounts of water, the camel dramatically increased trade across the Sahara between the western Sudan and the coastal regions of North Africa.

Ghana traded in several commodities. From North Africa came silk, cotton, glass beads, horses, mirrors, dates, and, especially, salt, which was a scarce necessity in the torridly hot western Sudan. In return, Ghana exported pepper, slaves, and, especially, gold. The slaves were usually war captives, and the gold came from mines in the Wangara region to the southwest of Ghana. The Soninke did not mine the gold themselves, but the kings of Ghana grew rich by taxing it as it passed through their lands.

Before the fifth century CE, when the Roman Empire dominated the Mediterranean region, Roman merchants and Berbers—the indigenous people of western North Africa—were West Africa's chief partners in the trans-Sahara trade. After the fifth century, as Roman power declined and Islam spread across North Africa, Arabs replaced the Romans. Arab merchants settled in Saleh, the Muslim part of Kumbi Saleh, Ghana's capital. By the twelfth century, this was an impressive city, with stone houses and tombs, and as many as twenty thousand people. Visitors remarked the splendor of Kumbi Saleh's royal court. Saleh had several mosques, and some Soninke converted to Islam, although it is unclear whether the royal family was among them. Moslems certainly dominated the royal bureaucracy and in the process introduced Arabic writing to the region.

A combination of commercial and religious rivalries finally destroyed Ghana during the twelfth century. The Almorvids, who were Islamic Berbers, had been Ghana's principal competitors for control of the trans-Sahara trade. In 992 Ghana's army captured Awdaghost, the Almorvid trade center northwest of Kumbi Saleh. Driven as much by religious fervor as by economic interest, the Almorvids retaliated decisively in 1076 by conquering Ghana. The Soninke regained their independence in 1087, but a little over a century later fell to the Sosso, a previously tributary people, who destroyed Kumbi Saleh.

The Empire of Mali, 1230–1468

Following the defeat of Ghana by the Almorvids, many western Sudanese peoples competed for political and economic power. This contest ended in 1235 when the Mandinka, under their legendary leader Sundiata (c. 1210–1260), defeated the Sosso at the Battle of Kirina. In the wake of this victory, Sundiata went on to forge the Empire of Mali.

Mali, which means "where the emperor resides" in Mende, the language of the Mandinka, was socially, politically, and economically similar to Ghana. It was larger than Ghana, however—stretching 1,500 miles from the Atlantic coast to the region east of the Niger River—and was centered farther south, in a region of greater rainfall and more abundant crops. Sundiata gained direct control of the gold mines of Wangara, making his empire wealthier than Ghana had been. As a result, Mali's population grew, reaching a total of eight million.

Sundiata was also an important figure in western Sudanese religion. According to legend, he wielded magical powers to defeat his enemies. This suggests that he practiced an indigenous faith. But Sundiata was also a Muslim and helped make Mali—at least superficially—a Muslim state. West Africans had been converting to Islam since Arab traders began arriving in the region centuries before, although many converts continued to practice indigenous religions as well. By Sundiata's time, most merchants and bureaucrats were Muslims, and the empire's rulers gained stature among Arab states by converting to Islam.

To administer their vast empire at a time when communication was slow, Mali's rulers relied heavily on personal and family ties with local chiefs. Commerce, bureaucracy, and scholarship also played a role in holding the empire together. Mali's most important city was Timbuktu, which had been established during the eleventh century beside the Niger River near the southern edge of the Sahara Desert. Two other cities—Walata in the northwest and Gao in the east—also functioned as economic and cultural centers.

By the thirteenth century, Timbuktu was a major hub for trade in gold, slaves, and salt. It attracted merchants from throughout the Mediterranean world and became a center of Islamic learning. There were several mosques in the city, 150 Islamic schools, a law school, and many book dealers. It supported a cosmopolitan community and impressed visitors with its absence of religious and ethnic intolerance. Even though Mali enslaved war captives and traded slaves, an Arab traveler noted in 1352–1353, "the Negroes possess some admirable qualities. They are seldom unjust, and have a greater abhorrence of injustice than any other people."

The Mali Empire reached its peak during the reign of Mansa Musa (1312–1337). One of the wealthiest rulers the world has known, Musa made himself and Mali famous when in 1324 he undertook a pilgrimage across Africa to the Islamic holy city of Mecca in Arabia. With an entourage of sixty thousand, a train of one hundred elephants, and a propensity for distributing huge amounts of gold to those who greeted him along the way, Musa amazed the Islamic world. After Musa's death, however, Mali declined. The empire's leading families vied with each other for wealth and power and its subject peoples began to rebel. In 1468, one of the most powerful of its formerly subject peoples, the Songhai, captured Timbuktu, and their leader, Sunni Ali, founded a new West African empire.

The Empire of Songhai, 1464–1591

Like the Mandinka and Soninke before them, the Songhai were great traders and warriors. The Songhai had seceded from Mali in 1375, and under Sunni Ali, who reigned from 1464 to 1492, they built the last and largest of the western Sudanese empires. Sunni Ali required conquered peoples to pay tribute, but otherwise let them run their own affairs. Nominally a Muslim, he—like Sundiata—was reputedly a great magician who derived power from the traditional spirits.

A devout Muslim, Muhammad Toure used his power to spread the influence of Islam within the empire. During a pilgrimage to Mecca in 1497 he established diplomatic relations with Morocco and Egypt and recruited Moslem scholars to serve at the Sankore Mosque at Timbuktu. Subsequently, the mosque became a widely known center for the study of theology, law, mathematics, and medicine. Despite these efforts, by the end of Muhammad Toure's reign (the aging ruler, senile and blind, was deposed by family members), Islamic culture was still weak in West Africa outside urban areas. Peasants, who made up 95 percent of the population, spoke a variety of languages, continued to practice indigenous religions, and remained loyal to their local chiefs.

Songhai reached its peak of influence under Askia Daud between 1549 and 1582. But the political balance of power in West Africa was changing rapidly, and, lacking new leaders as resourceful as Sunni Ali or Muhammad Toure, Songhai failed to adapt. Since the 1430s, adventurers from the European country of Portugal had been establishing trading centers along the Guinea coast seeking gold and diverting it from the trans-Sahara trade. Their success threatened the Arab rulers of North Africa, Songhai's traditional partners in the trans-Sahara trade. In 1591 the king of Morocco, hoping to regain access to West African gold, sent an army of four thousand (mostly Spanish) mercenaries armed with muskets and cannons across the Sahara to attack Gao, Songhai's capital. Only one thousand of the soldiers survived the grueling march to confront Songhai's elite cavalry at Tondibi on the approach to Gao. But the Songhai forces were armed only with bows and lances, which were no match for firearms, and the mercenaries routed them. Its army destroyed, the Songhai empire fell apart. The center of Islamic scholarship in West Africa shifted eastward from Timbuktu to Hausaland. The Moroccans soon left the region, and West Africa was without a government powerful enough to intervene when the Portuguese, other Europeans, and the African kingdoms of the Guinea Coast became more interested in trading for human beings than for gold.

The West African Forest Region

The area called the forest region of West Africa, which includes stretches of savannah, extends two thousand miles along the Atlantic coast from Senegambia in the northwest to the former kingdom of Benin (modern Cameroon) in the east. (See Map 1–1.) Among the early settlers of the forest region were the Nok, who around 500 BCE, in what is today southern Nigeria, created a culture noted for its iron working technology and its terra-cotta sculptures. But significant migration into the forests began only after 1000 CE, as the western Sudanese climate became increasingly dry.

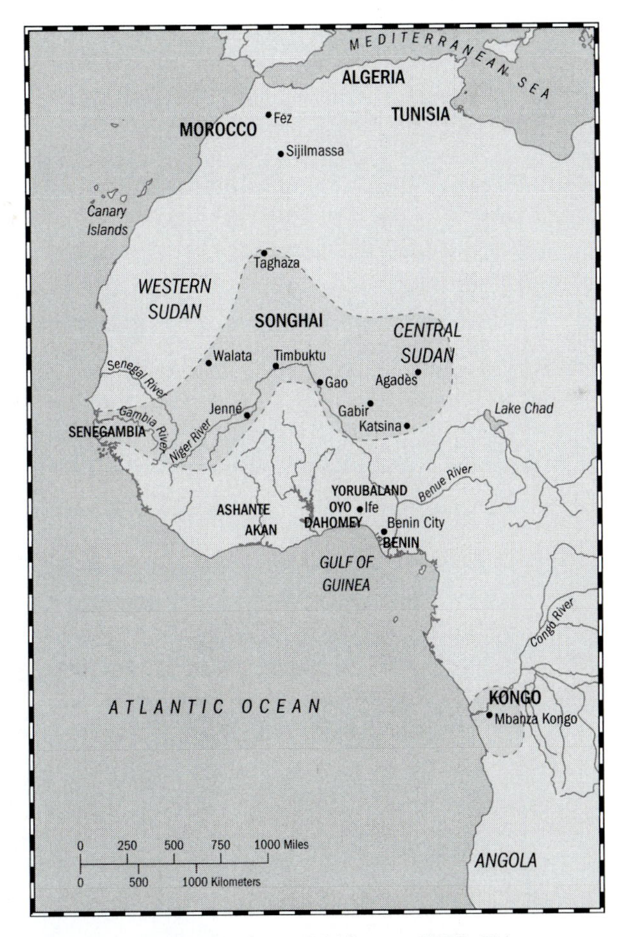

MAP 1–1 West and Central Africa, c. 1500. This map shows the Empire of Songhai (1464–1591), the Kingdom of Kongo (c. 1400–1700), and the major kingdoms of the West African forest region.

Because people migrated southward from the Sudan in small groups over an extended period, the process brought about considerable cultural diversification. A variety of languages, economies, political systems, and traditions came into existence. Some ancient customs survived, such as dividing types of agricultural labor by gender and living in villages composed of extended families. Nevertheless, the forest region became a patchwork of diverse ethnic groups with related, but sometimes quite different, ways of life.

The inhabitants of Senegambia shared a common history and spoke closely related languages, but they were not politically united. Parts of the region had been incorporated within the empires of Ghana and Mali and had been exposed to Islamic influences. Senegambian society was strictly hierarchical, with royalty at the top and slaves at the bottom. Most people were farmers, growing rice, millet, sorghum,

This carved wooden ceremonial offering bowl is typical of a Yoruba art form that has persisted for centuries. It reflects religious practices as well as traditional hairstyle and dress.

Yoruba Offering Bowl from Ekiti Efon-Alaye, (BON46967) Bonhams, London, UK/Bridgeman Art Library, London/New York plantains, beans, and bananas. They supplemented their diet with fish, oysters, rabbits, and monkeys.

To the southeast of Senegambia were the Akan states. They emerged during the sixteenth century as the gold trade provided local rulers with the wealth they needed to clear forests and initiate agricultural economies. To accomplish this, the rulers traded gold from mines under their control for slaves, who did the difficult work of cutting trees and burning refuse. Then settlers received open fields from the rulers in return for a portion of their produce and services. When Europeans arrived, they traded guns for gold. The guns in turn allowed the Akan states to expand, and during the late seventeenth century, one of them, the Ashante, created a well-organized and densely populated kingdom, comparable in size to the modern country of Ghana. By the eighteenth century, this kingdom not only dominated the central portion of the forest region, but also used its army extensively to capture slaves for sale to European traders.

To the east of the Akan states (in modern Benin and western Nigeria) lived the people of the Yoruba culture, who gained ascendancy in the area as early as 1000 CE by trading kola nuts and cloth to the peoples of the western Sudan. The artisans of the Yoruba city of Ife gained renown for their fine bronze, brass, and terra-cotta sculptures. Ife was also notable for the prominent role of women in conducting its profitable commerce. During the seventeenth century, the Oyo people, employing a well-trained cavalry, imposed political unity on part of the Yoruba region. They, like the Ashanti, became extensively involved in the Atlantic slave trade.

Located to the west of the Oyo were the Fon people, who formed the Kingdom of Dahomey, which rivaled Oyo as a center for the slave trade. The king of Dahomey was an absolute monarch who took thousands of wives for himself from leading Fon families as a way to assure the loyalty of potential rivals.

At the eastern end of the forest region was the Kingdom of Benin, which controlled an extensive area in what is today southern Nigeria. The people of this kingdom shared a common heritage with the Yoruba, who played a role in its formation during the thirteenth century. Throughout its history, Benin's politics were marked by a struggle for power between the Oba (king), who claimed divine status, and the kingdom's hereditary nobility.

Benin remained little influenced by Islam or Christianity, but like other coastal kingdoms, it became increasingly involved in the Atlantic slave trade. Beginning in the late fifteenth century, the Oba of Benin allowed Europeans to enter the country to trade for gold, pepper, ivory, and slaves. Initially, the Oba forbade the sale of his own subjects, but his large army—the first in the forest region to be provided with European firearms—captured others for the trade as it conquered neighboring regions. By the seventeenth century, Benin's prosperity depended on the slave trade. As the kingdom declined during the eighteenth century, it began to sell some of its own people to European slave traders.

To Benin's east was Igboland, a densely populated but politically weak region stretching along the Niger River. The Igbo people lived in one of the stateless societies common in West Africa. In these societies, families rather than central authorities governed. Village elders provided local government and life centered on family homesteads. Igboland had for many years exported field workers and skilled artisans to

Benin and other kingdoms. When Europeans arrived, they expanded this trade, which brought many Igbos to the Americas.

Kongo and Angola

Although the forebears of most African Americans came from West Africa, many also came from Central Africa, in particular the region around the Congo River and its tributaries and the region to the south that the Portuguese called Angola. The people of these regions had much in common with those of the Guinea Coast. They divided labor by gender, lived in villages composed of extended families, and accorded semi-divine status to their kings. Like the people of West Africa, they were ensnared in the Atlantic slave trade as it grew to immense proportions after 1500.

During the fourteenth and fifteenth centuries, much of the Congo River system, with its fertile valleys and abundant fish, came under the control of the Kingdom of Kongo. The wealth of this kingdom also derived from its access to salt and iron and its extensive trade with the interior of the continent. Nzinga Knuwu, who was *Mani Kongo* (the Kongolese term for king) when Portuguese expeditions arrived in the region in the late fifteenth century, surpassed other African rulers in welcoming the intruders. His son Nzinga Mbemba tried to convert the kingdom to Christianity and remodel it along European lines. The resulting unrest, combined with Portuguese greed and the effects of the slave trade, undermined royal authority and ultimately led to the breakup of the kingdom and the social disruption of the entire Kongo-Angola region.

West African Society and Culture

West Africa's great ethnic and cultural diversity makes it hazardous to generalize about the social and cultural background of the first African Americans. The dearth of written records from the region south of the Sudan compounds the difficulties. But working with a variety of sources, including oral histories, traditions, and archaeological and anthropological studies, historians have pieced together a broad understanding of the way the people of West Africa lived at the beginning of the Atlantic slave trade.

Families and Villages

By the early sixteenth century, most West Africans were farmers. They usually lived in hamlets or villages composed of extended families and clans called lineages. Generally, one lineage occupied each village, although some large lineages peopled several villages. The members of extended families were descended from a common ancestor, and the lineages claimed descent from a mythical personage. Depending on the ethnic group involved, extended families and lineages were either patrilineal or matrilineal. In patrilineal societies, social rank and property passed in the male line from fathers to sons. In matrilineal societies, rank and property, although controlled by men, passed from generation to generation in the female line. A village chief in a matrilineal society was succeeded by his sister's son, not his own. Elders in the extended family had great power over the economic and social lives of its members. In contrast with ancient Egypt, strictly enforced incest taboos prohibited people from marrying within their extended family.

Villagers' few possessions included cots, rugs, stools, and wooden storage chests. Their tools and weapons included bows, spears, iron axes, hoes, and scythes. Households used grinding stones, woven baskets, and a variety of ceramic vessels to prepare and store food. Villagers in both the savannah and forest regions produced cotton for clothing, but their food crops were quite distinct. West Africans in the savannah cultivated millet, rice, and sorghum as their dietary staples; kept goats and cattle for milk and cheese; and supplemented their diets with peas, okra, watermelons, and a variety of nuts. Yams, rather than grains, were the dietary staple in the forest region. Other important forest region crops included bananas and coco yams, both ultimately derived from far-off Indonesia.

Women

In general, men dominated women in West Africa. As previously noted, it was common for men to take two or more wives, and, to a degree, custom held women to be the property of men. But West African women also enjoyed a relative amount of freedom that impressed Arab and European visitors. In ancient Ghana, women sometimes served as government officials. Later, in the forest region, women sometimes inherited property and owned land—or at least controlled its income. Women—including enslaved women—in the royal court of Dahomey held high government posts. Ashante noblewomen could own property, although they themselves could be considered inheritable property. The Ashante queen held her own court to administer women's affairs.

Sexual freedom in West Africa was, however, more apparent than real. Throughout the region secret societies instilled in men and women ethical standards of personal behavior. The most important secret societies were the women's *Sande* and the men's *Poro.* They initiated boys and girls into adulthood and provided sex education. They also established standards for personal conduct, especially in regard to issues of gender, by emphasizing female virtue and male honor. Other secret societies influenced politics, trade, medical practice, recreation, and social gatherings.

Class and Slavery

Although many West Africans lived in stateless societies, most lived in hierarchically organized states headed by monarchs who claimed divine or semidivine status. These monarchs were far from absolute in the power they wielded, but they commanded armies, taxed commerce, and accumulated considerable wealth. Beneath the royalty were classes of landed nobles, warriors, peasants, and bureaucrats. Lower classes included blacksmiths, butchers, weavers, woodcarvers, tanners, and the oral historians called *griots.*

Slavery had been part of this hierarchical social structure since ancient times. Although it was very common throughout West Africa, slavery was less so in the forest region than on the savannah. It took a wide variety of forms and was not necessarily a permanent condition. Like people in other parts of the world, West Africans held war captives—including men, women, and children—to be without rights and suitable for enslavement. In Islamic regions, masters had obligations to their slaves similar to those of a guardian for a ward and were responsible for their slaves' religious well-being. In non-Islamic regions, the children of slaves acquired legal protections, such as the right not to be sold away from the land they occupied.

Slaves who served either in the royal courts of West African kingdoms or in the kingdoms' armies often exercised power over free people and could acquire property. Also, the slaves of peasant farmers often had standards of living similar to those of their masters. Slaves who worked under overseers in gangs on large estates were far less fortunate. However, even for such enslaved agricultural workers, the work and privileges accorded to the second and third generations became little different from those of free people. Regardless of their generation, slaves retained a low social status, but in many respects slavery in West African societies functioned as a means of assimilation.

Religion

There were two religious traditions in fifteenth-century West Africa: Islamic and indigenous. Islam, which was introduced into West Africa by Arab traders and took root first in the Sudanese empires, was most prevalent in the more cosmopolitan savannah. Even there it was stronger in cities than in rural areas. Islam was the religion of merchants and bureaucrats. It fostered literacy in Arabic, the spread of Islamic learning, and the construction of mosques in the cities of West Africa. Islam is resolutely monotheistic, asserting that Allah is the only God. It recognizes its founder, Muhammad, as well as Abraham, Moses, and Jesus, as prophets, but regards none of them as divine.

West Africa's indigenous religions remained strongest in the forest region. They were polytheistic and animistic, recognizing a great number of divinities and spirits. Beneath an all-powerful, but remote, creator god were pantheons of lesser gods who represented the forces of nature. Other gods were associated with particular mountains, rivers, trees, and rocks. Indigenous West African religion, in other words, saw the force of God in all things.

In part because practitioners of West African indigenous religions perceived the creator god to be unapproachable, they invoked the spirits of their ancestors and turned to magicians and oracles for divine assistance. Like the Chinese, they believed the spirits of their direct and remote ancestors could influence their lives. Therefore, ceremonies designed to sustain ancestral spirits and their power over the earth were a central part of traditional West African religions. These rituals were part of everyday life, making organized churches and professional clergy rare. Instead, family members with an inclination to do so assumed religious duties. These individuals encouraged their relatives to participate actively in ceremonies that involved music, dancing, and animal sacrifices in honor of deceased ancestors. Funerals were especially important because they symbolized the linkage between living and dead.

Art and Music

As was the case in other parts of the world, West African art was intimately related to religious practice. West Africans, seeking to preserve the images of their ancestors, excelled in woodcarving and sculpture in terra-cotta, bronze, and brass. Throughout the region, artists produced wooden masks representing in highly stylized manners ancestral spirits as well as various divinities. Wooden and terra-cotta figurines, sometimes referred to as "fetishes," were also extremely common. West Africans used them in funerals, in rituals related to ancestral spirits, in medical practice, and in coming-of-age ceremonies. In contrast to masks and fetishes, the great bronze sculptures of Benin, which had political functions, were quite realistic in their approach to their subjects, which consisted of kings, warriors, and nobles rather than deities and spirits.

TIMELINE

EVENTS IN AFRICA	WORLD EVENTS
10 million years ago	
5–10 million years ago Separation of hominids from apes **4 million years ago** Emergence of *australopithecines* **2.4 million years ago** Emergence of *Homo habilis* **1.7 million years ago** Emergence of *Homo erectus*	**1.6 million years ago** *Homo erectus* beginning to spread through Eurasia
1.5 million years ago	
100,000–200,000 years ago Appearance of modern humans **6000 BCE** Beginning of Sahara Desert formation	**8000 BCE** Appearance of the first agricultural settlements in southwest Asia
5000 BCE	
5000 BCE First agricultural settlements in Egypt **3800 BCE** Predynastic period in Egypt **c. 3150 BCE** Unification of Egypt	**3500 BCE** Sumerian civilization in Mesopotamia
2500 BCE	
2700–2150 BCE Egypt's Old Kingdom **2100–1650 BCE** Egypt's Middle Kingdom	**2300 BCE** Beginning of Indus Valley civilization
1500 BCE	
1550–700 BCE Egypt's New Kingdom	**1600–1250 BCE** Mycenaean Greek civilization **c. 1500** Beginning of Shang dynasty in China

continued

EVENTS IN AFRICA	WORLD EVENTS
1000 BCE	
750–670 BCE Rule of Kushites over Egypt **540 BCE** Founding of Meroë **c. 500 BCE** Beginning of iron smelting in West Africa **50 CE** Destruction of Kush	**600–336 BCE** Classical Greek civilization
500 CE	
632–750 CE Islamic conquest of North Africa **c. 750–1076 CE** Empire of Ghana; Islam begins to take root in West Africa	**204 BCE–476 CE** Domination of Mediterranean by Roman Republic and Empire **500–1350 CE** European Middle Ages **c. 570 CE** birth of Muhammad
1200 CE	
1230–1468 CE Empire of Mali **c. 1300 CE** Rise of Yoruba states	
1400 CE	
1434 CE Start of Portuguese exploration and establishment of trading outposts on West African coast **c. 1450 CE** Centralization of power in Benin **1464–1591 CE** Empire of Songhai	**1492 CE** Christopher Columbus and European encounter of America **1517** Reformation begins in Europe
1600 CE	
c. 1650 CE Rise of Kingdom of Dahomey and the Akan states	**1610** Scientific Revolution begins in Europe

West African music also served religion. Folk musicians employed such instruments as drums, xylophones, bells, flutes, and mbanzas (predecessor to the banjo) to produce a highly rhythmic accompaniment to the dancing that was an important part of religious rituals. A call-and-response style of singing also played a vital role in ritual.

Vocal music, produced in a full-throated, but often raspy, style, was characterized by polyphonic textures and sophisticated rhythms.

Literature: Oral Histories, Poetry, and Tales

West African literature was part of an oral tradition that passed from generation to generation. At its most formal, this was a literature developed by specially trained poets and musicians who served kings and nobles. But West African literature was also a folk art that expressed the views of the common people.

At a king's court there could be several poet-musicians who had high status and specialized in poems glorifying rulers and their ancestors by linking fact and fiction. Recitations of these poems were often accompanied by drums and horns. Court poets also used their trained memories to recall historical events and precise genealogies. The self-employed poets, called *griots*, who traveled from place to place were socially inferior to court poets, but they functioned in a similar manner. Both court poets and griots were men. It was in the genre of folk literature that women excelled. They joined men in the creation and performance of work songs and led in creating and singing dirges, lullabies, and satirical verses. Often these forms of literature used a call-and-response style similar to that of religious songs.

Just as significant for African-American history were the West African prose tales. Like similar stories told in other parts of Africa, these tales took two forms: those with human characters and those with animal characters who represented humans. The tales involving human characters dealt with such subjects as creation, the origins of death, paths to worldly success, and romantic love. Such tales often involved magic objects and potions.

The animal tales aimed both to entertain and to teach lessons. They focused on small creatures, often referred to as "trickster characters," which are pitted against larger beasts. Among the heroes were the hare, the spider, and the mouse. Plots centered on the ability of these weak animals to outsmart larger and meaner antagonists, such as the snake, leopard, and hyena. In all instances, the animal characters had human emotions and goals. They were presented in human settings, although they retained animal characteristics.

In West Africa, these tales represented the ability of common people to counteract the power of kings and nobles. When the tales reached America, they became allegories for the struggle between enslaved African Americans and their powerful white masters.

CONCLUSION

In recent years, paleoanthropologists, archaeologists, and historians have revealed much about Africa's history and prehistory, but much remains to be learned concerning the past of this vast and diverse continent. The evolution of humans, the role of ancient Egypt in world history, and Egypt's relationship to Nubia and Kush are all topics that continue to attract wide interest.

Yet the history of African Americans begins in West Africa, the region from which the ancestors of most of them were unwillingly wrested. Historians have discovered, as subsequent chapters will show, that West Africans taken to America and their descendants in America were able to preserve much more of their ancestral way of life than scholars once believed possible. West African family organization, work habits, language structures and some words, religious beliefs, legends and stories, pottery styles, art, and music all made it to America. These African legacies, although often attenuated, influenced the way African Americans and other Americans lived in their new land and continue to shape American life.

Review Questions

1. What was the role of Africa in the evolution of modern humanity?
2. Discuss the controversy concerning the racial identity of the ancient Egyptians. What is the significance of this controversy for the history of African Americans?
3. Compare and contrast the western Sudanese empires with the forest civilizations of the Guinea coast.
4. Discuss the role of religion in West Africa. What was the African religious heritage of black Americans?
5. Describe West African society on the eve of the expansion of the Atlantic slave trade. What were the society's strengths and weaknesses?

Recommended Reading

J. F. Ade Ajayi and Michael Crowder, eds. *History of West Africa,* 3d ed. 2 vols. Burnt Mill, UK: Longman, 1984. A collection of essays on a variety of subjects by prominent scholars in the field of West African history.

Robert W. July. *A History of the African People,* 5th ed. Prospect Heights, IL: Waveland, 1998. A comprehensive and current social history with good coverage of West Africa and West African women.

Roland Oliver. *The African Experience: Major Themes in African History from Earliest Times to the Present.* New York: HarperCollins, 1991. Shorter and less encyclopedic than July's book, but innovative in organization. It also provides insightful analysis of cultural relationships.

John Reader. *Africa: A Biography of the Continent.* New York: Knopf, 1998. The most up-to-date account of early African history, emphasizing the ways the continent's physical environment shaped human life there.

Christopher Stringer and Robin McKie. *African Exodus: The Origins of Modern Humanity.* New York: Henry Holt, 1997. A very clearly written account favoring the out-of-Africa model.

John Thornton. *Africa and Africans in the Making of the Atlantic World,* 1400–1689. New York: Cambridge University Press, 1992. A thorough consideration of West African culture and its impact in the Americas.

• CHAPTER TWO •

MIDDLE PASSAGE

The European Age of Exploration and Colonization

The origins of the Atlantic slave trade and its long duration were products of Western Europe's expansion of power that began during the fifteenth century and continued into the twentieth century. For a variety of economic, technological, and demographic reasons, Portugal, Spain, the Netherlands, France, England, and other nations sought to explore, conquer, and colonize in Africa, Asia, and the Americas. Their efforts had important consequences for these areas.

Portugal took the lead during the early 1400s as ships from its ports reached Africa's western coast. Portuguese captains hoped to find Christian allies there against the Muslims of North Africa and to spread Christianity. But they were more interested in trade with African kingdoms, as were the Spanish, Dutch, English, and French who followed them.

Even more attractive than Africa to the Portuguese and their European successors as sources of trade and wealth were India, China, Japan, and the East Indian islands (modern Indonesia and Malaysia). The desire to reach these eastern regions motivated the Spanish monarchy to finance Christopher Columbus's westward voyages that began in 1492.

Columbus, who believed the earth to be much smaller than it actually is, hoped to reach Japan or India by sailing west. His mistake led to the European conquest, settlement, and exploitation of North and South America and the Caribbean islands, where Columbus first landed. Columbus and those who followed him quickly enslaved indigenous Americans (American Indians) as laborers in fields and mines. Almost as quickly, large numbers of indigenous peoples either died of European diseases and overwork or escaped beyond the reach of European power. Consequently, European colonizers needed additional laborers. This demand for a workforce in the Americas caused the Atlantic slave trade.

The Slave Trade in Africa

When Portuguese voyagers first arrived at Senegambia, Benin, and Kongo, they found a thriving commerce in slaves. These kingdoms represented the southern extremity of an extensive trade conducted by Islamic nations that involved the capture and sale of

Europeans and mixed-race North Africans called Berbers, as well as black people from south of the Sahara Desert. Although Arabs nurtured antiblack prejudice, race was not the major factor in this Islamic slave trade. Arab merchants and West African kings, for example, imported white slaves from Europe.

Insofar as it affected West Africa, the Islamic slave trade was conducted by Sudanese horsemen. The horsemen invaded the forest region to capture people who could not effectively resist—often they came from stateless societies. The trade dealt mainly in women and children, who as slaves were destined for lives as concubines and domestic servants in North Africa and southwest Asia. This pattern contrasted with that of the later Atlantic slave trade, which primarily sought young men for agricultural labor in the Americas. The West African men who constituted a minority of those subjected to the trans-Sahara slave trade were more likely to become soldiers for such North African states as Morocco and Egypt than field workers.

The demand for slaves in Muslim countries remained high from the tenth through the fifteenth centuries because many died from disease or were freed and assimilated into Arab society. The trans-Sahara slave trade therefore rivaled the extensive trade in gold across the Sahara and helped make such West African cities as Timbuktu, Walata, Jenne, and Gao wealthy. According to historian Roland Oliver, it was not until 1600 that the Atlantic slave trade reached the proportions of the trans-Sahara slave trade (see Figure 2–1).

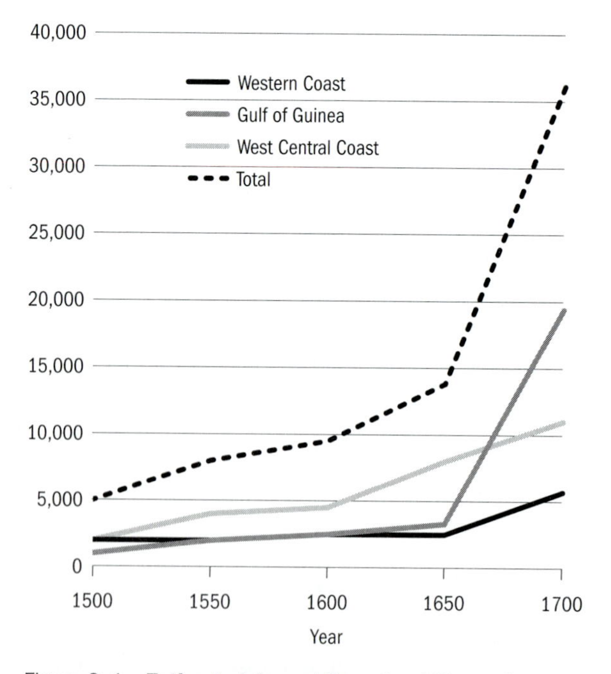

Figure 2–1 **Estimated Annual Exports of Slaves from Western Africa to the Americas, 1500–1700**

Source: John Thornton, *Africa and Africans in the Making of the Atlantic World, 1400–1680* (New York: Cambridge University Press, 1992), 118.

The Origins of the Atlantic Slave Trade

When Portuguese ships first arrived off the Guinea Coast, their captains traded chiefly for gold, ivory, and pepper, but they also wanted slaves. As early as 1441, Antam Goncalvez of Portugal enslaved a Berber and his West African servant and took them home as gifts for a Portuguese prince. During the following decades, Portuguese raiders captured hundreds of Africans for service as domestic servants in Portugal and Spain.

But usually the Portuguese and the other European and white Americans who succeeded them did not capture and enslave people themselves. Instead they purchased slaves from African traders. This arrangement began formally in 1472 when the Portuguese merchant Ruy do Siqueira gained permission from the Oba (king) of Benin to trade for slaves, as well as gold and ivory, within the borders of the Oba's kingdom. Siqueira and other Portuguese found that a commercial infrastructure already existed in West Africa that could distribute European trade goods and procure slaves. The rulers of Benin, Dahomey, and other African kingdoms restricted the Europeans to a few points on the coast, and the kingdoms raided the interior to supply the Europeans with slaves.

Interethnic rivalries in West Africa led to the warfare that produced these slaves during the sixteenth century. Although Africans were initially reluctant to sell members of their own ethnic group to Europeans, they did not at first consider it wrong to sell members of their own race to foreigners. In fact, neither Africans nor Europeans had yet developed the concept of racial solidarity. By the eighteenth century, however, at least the victims of the trade believed that such solidarity *should* exist. Ottobah Cugoano, who had been captured and sold during that century, wrote, "I must own to the shame of my countrymen that I was first kidnapped and betrayed by [those of] my own complexion."

Until the early sixteenth century, Portuguese seafarers conducted the Atlantic slave trade on a tiny scale to satisfy a limited market for domestic servants on the Iberian Peninsula (Portugal and Spain). Other European countries had no demand for slaves because their own workforces were already too large. But the impact of Columbus's voyages drastically changed the trade. The Spanish and the Portuguese—followed by the Dutch, English, and French—established colonies in the Caribbean, Mexico, and Central and South America. As the numbers of American Indians in these regions rapidly declined, Europeans relied on the Atlantic slave trade to replace them as a source of slave labor (see Map 2–1). As early as 1502, African slaves lived on the island of Hispaniola—modern Haiti and the Dominican Republic. During the sixteenth century, gold and silver mines in Spanish Mexico and Peru and especially sugar plantations in Portuguese Brazil produced an enormous demand for labor. The Atlantic slave trade grew to huge and tragic proportions to meet that demand (see Table 2–1).

Growth of the Atlantic Slave Trade

Because Europe provided an insatiable market for sugar, cultivation of this crop in the Americas became extremely profitable. Sugar plantations employing slave labor spread from Brazil to the Caribbean islands (West Indies). Later the cultivation of tobacco,

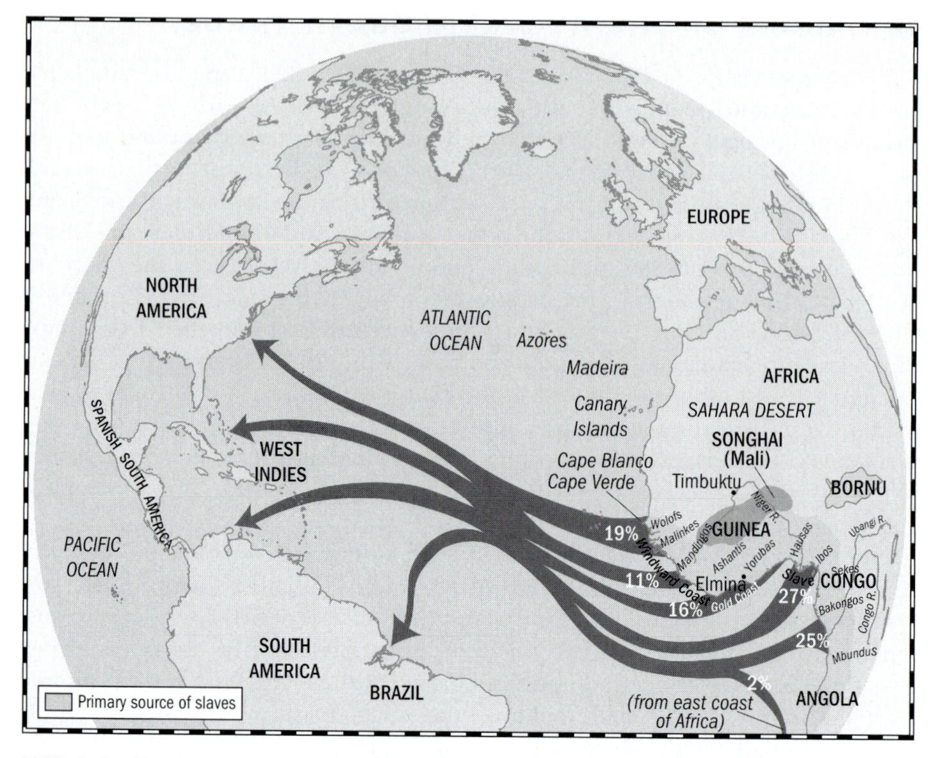

MAP 2–1 The Atlantic and Islamic Slave Trades. Not until 1600 did the Atlantic slave trade reach the proportions of the Islamic slave trade. This map shows the principal sources of slaves, primary routes, and major destinations.

Table 2–1
Estimated Slave Imports by Destination, 1451–1870

Destination	Total Slave Imports
British North America	500,000
Spanish America	2,500,000
British Caribbean	2,000,000
French Caribbean	1,600,000
Dutch Caribbean	500,000
Danish Caribbean	28,000
Brazil	4,000,000
Old World	200,000

Source: Hugh Thomas, *The Slave Trade: The Story of the Atlantic Slave Trade, 1440–1870* (New York: Simon & Schuster, 1997), 804.

rice, and indigo in British North America added to the demand for African slaves, although far more Africans went to Brazil than ever reached North America. By 1510 Spain had joined Portugal in the enlarged Atlantic slave trade, and a new, harsher form of slavery had become established in the Americas. Unlike slavery in Africa, Asia, and Europe, slavery in the Americas was based on race; most of the enslaved were males, and they were generally employed as agricultural laborers rather than soldiers or domestic servants. The enslaved also became *chattel*—meaning personal property—of their masters and lost their customary rights as human beings. Men and boys predominated in part because Europeans believed they were stronger laborers than women and girls. Another factor was that West Africans preferred to have women do agricultural work and therefore tended to withhold them from the Atlantic trade.

Portugal and Spain dominated the Atlantic slave trade during the sixteenth century. They shipped about two thousand Africans per year to their American colonies, with by far the most going to Brazil. From the beginning of the trade until its nineteenth-century abolition, approximately 6,500,000 of the approximately 11,328,000 Africans taken to the Americas went to Portugal's and Spain's colonies. Both of these monarchies granted monopolies over the trade to private companies. In Spain this monopoly became known in 1518 as the *Asiento* (meaning contract). The profits from the slave trade were so great that by 1550 the Dutch, French, and English were becoming involved. During the early seventeenth century, the Dutch drove the Portuguese from the West African coast and became the principal European slave-trading nation. For the rest of that century, most Africans came to the Americas in Dutch ships—including a group of twenty in 1619 who until recently were considered to have been the first of their race to reach British North America.

The Dutch also shifted the center of sugar production to the West Indies. England and France followed, with the former taking control of Barbados and Jamaica and the latter taking Saint Domingue (Haiti), Guadeloupe, and Martinique. With the development of tobacco as a cash crop in Virginia and Maryland during the 1620s and with the continued expansion of sugar production in the West Indies, the demand for African slaves grew. The result was that England and France competed with the Dutch to control the Atlantic slave trade. After a series of wars, England emerged supreme. It had driven the Dutch out of the trade by 1674. Victories over France and Spain led in 1713 to English control of the *Asiento*, which allowed English traders the exclusive right to supply slaves to all of Spain's American colonies. After 1713 English ships dominated the slave trade, carrying about twenty thousand slaves per year from Africa to the Americas. At the peak of the trade during the 1790s, they transported fifty thousand per year.

The profits from the Atlantic slave trade, together with those from the sugar and tobacco produced in the Americas by slave labor, were invested in England and consequently helped fund the industrial revolution during the eighteenth century. In turn, Africa became a market for cheap English manufactured goods. Eventually, two triangular trade systems developed. In one, traders carried English goods to West Africa and exchanged the goods for slaves. Then the traders carried the slaves to the West Indies and exchanged them for sugar, which they took back to England on the third leg of the triangle. In the other triangular trade, white Americans from Britain's New England colonies carried rum to West Africa to trade for slaves. From Africa they took the slaves to the West Indies to exchange for sugar or molasses—sugar syrup—which they then took home to distill into rum.

The African-American Ordeal from Capture to Destination

Recent scholarship indicates that the availability of large numbers of slaves in West Africa resulted from the warfare that accompanied the formation of states in that region. Captives suitable for enslavement were a by-product of these wars. Senegambia and nearby Sierra Leone, then Oyo, Dahomey, and Benin became, in turn, centers of the trade. Meanwhile, on the west coast of Central Africa, slaves became available as a result of the conflict between the expanding Kingdom of Kongo and its neighbors. The European traders provided the aggressors with firearms but did not instigate the wars. Instead they used the wars to enrich themselves.

Sometimes African armies enslaved the inhabitants of conquered towns and villages. At other times, raiding parties captured isolated families or kidnapped individuals. As warfare spread to the interior, captives had to march for hundreds of miles to the coast where European traders awaited them. The raiders tied the captives together with rope or secured them with wooden yokes about their necks. It was a shocking experience, and many captives died from hunger, exhaustion, and exposure during the journey. Others killed themselves rather than submit to their fate, and the captors killed those who resisted.

Once the captives reached the coast, those destined for the Atlantic trade went to fortified structures called *factories*. Portuguese traders constructed the first factory at Elmina on the Guinea Coast in 1481—the Dutch captured it in 1637. Such factories contained the headquarters of the traders, warehouses for their trade goods and supplies, and dungeons or outdoor holding pens for the captives. In these pens, slave traders divided families and—as much as possible—ethnic groups to prevent rebellion. The traders stripped the captives naked and inspected them for disease and physical defects. Those considered fit for purchase were then branded like cattle with a hot iron bearing the symbol of a trading company.

The Crossing

After being held in a factory for weeks or months, captives faced the frightening prospect of leaving their native land for a voyage across an ocean that many of them had never before seen. Sailors rowed them out in large canoes to slave ships offshore. One English trader recalled that during the 1690s "the negroes were so wilful and loth to leave their own country, that they often leap'd out of the canoos, boat and ship, into the sea, and kept under water till they were drowned."

Once at sea, the slave ships followed the route established by Columbus during his voyages to the Americas: from the Canary Islands off West Africa to the Windward Islands in the Caribbean. Because ships taking this route enjoyed prevailing winds and westward currents, the passage normally lasted between two and three months. But the time required for the crossing varied widely. The larger ships were able to reach the Caribbean in forty days, but voyages could take as long as six months.

Both human and natural causes accounted for such delays. During the three centuries that the Atlantic slave trade endured, Western European nations were often at war with each other, and slave ships became prized targets. As early as the 1580s, English "sea dogs," such as John Hawkins and Sir Francis Drake, attacked Spanish ships to steal their valuable human cargoes. Outright piracy peaked between 1650 and 1725 when demand for slaves in the West Indies greatly increased. There were also such potentially disastrous natural forces as doldrums—long windless spells at sea—and hurricanes, which could destroy ships, crews, and cargoes.

The Slavers

Slave ships were usually small and narrow. A ship's size, measured in tonnage, theoretically determined how many slaves it could carry, with the formula being two slaves per ton. A large ship of three hundred tons, therefore, was expected to carry six hundred slaves. But captains often ignored the formula. Some kept their human cargo light, calculating that smaller loads lowered mortality and made revolt less likely. But most captains were "tight packers," who squeezed human beings together in hope that large numbers would offset increased deaths. For example, the 120-ton *Henrietta Marie*, a British ship that sailed from London on its final voyage in 1699, should have been fully loaded with 240 slaves. Yet it carried 350 from West Africa when it set out for Barbados and Jamaica. Another ship designed to carry 450 slaves usually carried 600.

The cargo space in slave ships was generally only five feet high. Ships' carpenters halved this vertical space by building shelves, so slaves might be packed above and below on planks that measured only 5.5 feet long and 1.3 feet wide. Consequently, slaves had only about 20 to 25 inches of headroom. To add to the discomfort, the crews chained male slaves together in pairs to help prevent rebellion and lodged them away from women and children.

Not surprisingly, mortality rates were high because the crowded, unsanitary conditions encouraged seaboard epidemics. Between 1715 and 1775, slave deaths on French ships averaged 15 percent. The highest recorded mortality rate was 34 percent. By the nineteenth century, the death rate had declined to 5 percent. Overall, one-third of the Africans subjected to the trade perished between their capture and their embarkation on a slave ship. Another third died during the middle passage or during "seasoning" on a Caribbean island.

A Slave's Story

In his book *The Interesting Narrative of the Life of Olaudah Equiano or Gustavus Vassa*, published in 1789, former slave Olaudah Equiano provides a vivid account of his capture, sale, and voyage to America in 1755. Equiano was an Igbo, the dominant group in what is today southern Nigeria. When he was ten years old, African slave raiders captured him and forced him to march along with other captives to the Niger River or one of its tributaries, where they traded him to other Africans. His new captors took him to the coast and sold him to European slave traders whose ships sailed to the West Indies.

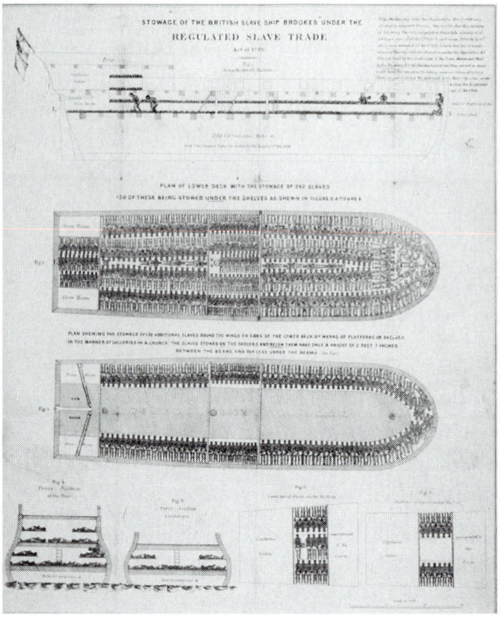

Plan of the British slave ship *Brookes*, 1788. This plan, which may even undercount the human cargo the *Brookes* carried, shows how tightly Africans were packed aboard slave ships.
Courtesy of the Library of Congress

Equiano's experience at the coastal slave factory convinced him he had entered a sort of hell, peopled by evil spirits. The stench caused by forcing many people to live in close confinement made him sick to his stomach and emotionally agitated. His African and European captors tried to calm him with liquor. But because he was not accustomed to alcohol, he became disoriented and more convinced of his impending doom. When the sailors lodged him with others below deck on the ship, he was so sick that he lost his appetite and hoped to die. Instead, because he refused to eat, the sailors took him on deck and whipped him. Later Equiano witnessed the flogging of one of the white crew members. The man died, and the sailors threw his body into the sea just as they disposed of dead Africans.

During the time the ship was in port awaiting a full cargo of slaves, Equiano spent much time on its deck. After putting to sea, however, he usually remained below deck with the other slaves where "each had scarcely room to turn himself." There, the smells of unwashed bodies and of the toilet tubs, "into which the children often fell and were almost suffocated," created a loathsome atmosphere. The darkness, the chafing of chains on human flesh, the shrieks and groans of the sick and disoriented created "a scene of horror almost inconceivable."

When slaves were allowed to get some fresh air and exercise on deck, the crew strung nets to prevent them from jumping overboard. Even so, Equiano observed two Africans, who were chained together, evade the nets and jump into the ocean, preferring drowning to staying on board. Equiano shared their desperation. He recalled that as the ship left the sight of land, "I now saw myself deprived of all chance of returning to my native country, or even the least glimpse of hope of [re]gaining the shore." Equiano insisted that "many more" would have jumped overboard "if they had not been prevented by the ship's crew."

A Captain's Story

Another perspective on the middle passage is provided by white slave-ship captain John Newton, who was born in London in 1725. In 1745 Newton, as an indentured servant, joined the crew of a slaver bound for Sierra Leone. Indentured servants lost their freedom for a specified number of years, either because they sold it or because they were being punished for debt or crime. In 1748, on the return voyage to England, Newton survived a fierce Atlantic storm and, thanking God, became an evangelical Christian. Like most people of his era, Newton saw no contradiction between his newfound faith and his participation in the enslavement and ill treatment of men, women, and children. When he became a slaver captain in 1750, he read Bible passages to his crew twice each Sunday and forbade swearing on board his vessel. But he treated his slave cargoes as harshly as any other slaver captain.

Newton was twenty-five years old when he became captain of the *Duke of Argyle*, an old 140-ton vessel that he converted into a slaver after it sailed from Liverpool on August 11, 1750. Near the Cape Verde Islands, off the coast of Senegambia, carpenters began making the alterations required for packing many Africans below deck. Newton also put the ship's guns and ammunition in order to protect against pirates or African resistance. On October 23 the *Duke of Argyle* reached Frenchman's Bay, Sierra Leone, where Newton observed other ships from England, France, and New England anchored offshore. Two days later, Newton purchased two men and a woman from traders at the port, but he had to sail to several other ports to accumulate a full cargo. Leaving West Africa on May 23, 1751, for the open sea, the ship reached Antigua in the West Indies on July 3 to deliver its slaves.

Provisions for the Middle Passage

Slave ships left Liverpool and other European ports provisioned with food supplies for their crews. These included beans, cheese, beef, flour, and grog, a mixture of rum and water. When the ships reached the Guinea Coast in West Africa, their captains began purchasing pepper, palm oil, lemons, limes, yams, plantains, and coconuts. Because slaves were not accustomed to European foods, the ships needed these staples of the African diet. Meat and fish were rare luxuries on board, and crews did not share them with slaves. Equiano recalled that, at one point during the passage, crew members caught far more fish than they could eat but threw what was left overboard, instead of giving it to the Africans who were exercising on deck. "We begged and prayed for some as well as we could," Equiano noted, "but in vain." The sailors whipped those Africans who filched a few fish for themselves.

The crew usually fed the slaves twice per day in shifts. Cooks prepared vegetable pulps, porridge, and stews for the crew to distribute in buckets as the slaves assembled on deck during good weather or below deck during storms. At the beginning of the voyage, each slave received a wooden spoon for dipping into the buckets, which were shared by about ten individuals. But in the confined confusion below deck, slaves often lost their spoons. In such cases, they had to eat from the buckets with their unwashed hands, a practice that spread disease.

Although slaver captains realized it was in their interest to feed their human cargoes well, they often skimped on supplies to make room for more slaves. Some captains calculated how the eventual profits from an increased human cargo would offset the losses from inevitable deaths during a voyage. Therefore, the food on a slave ship was often too poor and insufficient to prevent malnutrition and weakened immune systems among people already traumatized by separation from their families and homelands. As a result, many Africans died during the middle passage from diseases amid the horrid conditions that were normal aboard the slave ships. Others died from depression: they refused to eat, despite the crews' efforts to force food down their throats.

Sanitation, Disease, and Death

Diseases such as malaria, yellow fever, measles, smallpox, hookworm, scurvy, and dysentery constantly threatened African cargoes and European crews during the middle passage. Death rates were astronomical on board the slave ships before 1750. Mortality dropped after that date because ships became faster and ships' surgeons knew more about hygiene and diet. There were also early forms of vaccinations against smallpox, which may have been the worst killer of slaves on ships. But, even after 1750, poor sanitation led to many deaths. It is important to remember that before the early twentieth century, no civilization had developed a germ theory of disease. Physicians blamed human illnesses on poisonous atmospheres and imbalances among bodily fluids.

Usually slavers provided only three or four toilet tubs below deck for enslaved Africans to use during the middle passage. They had to struggle among themselves to get to the tubs, and children had a particularly difficult time. Those who were too ill to reach the tubs excreted where they lay, and diseases such as dysentery, which are spread by human waste, thrived. Dysentery, known by contemporaries as the bloody flux, vied with smallpox to kill the most slaves aboard ships. Alexander Falconbridge reported that during one dysentery epidemic, "The deck, that is, the floor of [the slaves'] rooms, was so covered with blood and mucus which had proceeded from them in consequence of the flux, that it resembled a slaughter-house. It is not in the power of human imagination, to picture to itself a situation more dreadful or disgusting."

Resistance and Revolt at Sea

Because many enslaved Africans refused to accept their fate, slaver captains had to be vigilant. Rebellions took place while a ship prepared to set sail, the African coast was in sight, and the slaves could still hope to return home. But some revolts occurred on the open sea where it was unlikely the Africans, even if their revolt succeeded, would be able to return to their homes or regain their freedom. Both sorts of revolt indicate that not even capture, forced march to the coast, imprisonment, branding, and sale could break the spirit of many captives. These Africans preferred to face death rather than accept bondage.

Failed slave mutineers could expect harsh punishment, although profit margins influenced sentences. Other slaves resisted their captors by drowning or starving themselves. Thomas Phillips, captain of the slaver *Hannibal* during the 1690s, commented, "We had about 12 negroes did wilfully drown themselves and others starved themselves to death; for 'tis their belief that when they die they return home to their own country and friends again." To deal with starvation, they used hot coals or a metal device called a *speculum oris* to force individuals to open their mouths for feeding.

Cruelty

The Atlantic slave trade required more capital than any other maritime commerce during the seventeenth and eighteenth centuries. The investments for the ships, the exceptionally large crews they employed, the navigational equipment, the armaments, the purchase of slaves in Africa, and the supplies of food and water to feed hundreds of passengers were phenomenal. The aim was to carry as many Africans in healthy condition to the Americas as possible in order to make the large profits that justified such expenditures. Yet, as we have indicated, conditions aboard the vessels were abysmal.

Scholars have debated how much deliberate cruelty the enslaved Africans suffered from ships' crews. The West Indian historian Eric Williams asserts that the horrors of the middle passage have been exaggerated. Many writers, Williams contends, are led astray by the writings of those who, during the late eighteenth and early nineteenth centuries, sought to abolish the slave trade. In Williams's view—and that of other historians as well—the difficulties of the middle passage were similar to those experienced by European indentured servants who suffered high mortality rates on the voyage to America.

From this perspective the primary cause of death at sea on all ships carrying passengers across the Atlantic Ocean to the Americas was epidemic disease, against which medical practitioners had few tools before the twentieth century. Overcrowding by slavers was only a secondary cause for the high mortality rates.

Such observations help place conditions aboard the slave ships in a broader perspective. Cruelty and suffering are, to some degree, historically relative in that practices acceptable in the past are now considered inhumane. Yet cruelty aboard slavers must also be placed in a cultural context. Cultures distinguish between what constitutes acceptable behavior to their own people, on the one hand, and to strangers, on the other. For Europeans, Africans were indeed cultural strangers, and what became normal in the Atlantic slave trade was in fact exceptionally cruel in comparison to how Europeans treated each other. Slaves below deck, for example, received only one-half the space allocated on board to European soldiers, free emigrants, indentured servants, and convicts. Europeans regarded slavery itself as a condition suitable only for non-Christians. And as strangers, Africans were subject to brutalization by European crew members who often cared little about the physical and emotional damage they inflicted.

African Women on Slave Ships

For similar reasons, African women did not enjoy the same protection against unwanted sexual attention from European men that European women received. Consequently, sailors during long voyages attempted to sate their sexual appetites with enslaved women. African women caught in the Atlantic slave trade were worth half the price of African men in Caribbean markets, and as a result, captains took fewer of them on board their vessels. Perhaps because the women were less valuable commodities, crew members felt they had license to abuse them sexually. The separate below-deck compartments for women on slave ships also made them easier targets than they otherwise might have been.

Historian Barbara Bush speculates that the horrid experience of the middle passage may have influenced black women's attitudes toward sexuality and procreation. This, in turn, may help explain why slave populations in the Caribbean and Latin America failed to reproduce themselves: exhaustion, terror, and disgust can depress sex drives.

Landing and Sale in the West Indies

As slave ships neared their West Indian destinations, the crew prepared the human cargo for landing and sale. They allowed the slaves to shave, wash with fresh water, and take more vigorous exercise. Those bound for the larger Caribbean islands or for the British colonies of southern North America were often given some weeks to rest in the easternmost islands of the West Indies. French slave traders typically rested their slave passengers on Martinique. The English preferred Barbados. Sale to white plantation owners followed, and then began a period of what the planters called "seasoning," a period of up to two years of acculturating slaves and breaking them in to plantation routines.

The process of landing and sale that ended the middle passage was often as protracted as the events that began it in Africa. After anchoring at one of the Lesser Antilles Islands—Barbados, St. Kitts, or Antigua—English slaver captains haggled with the agents of local planters over numbers and prices. They then determined whether to sell all their slaves at their first port of call, sell some of them, sail to another island, or sail to such North American ports as Charleston, Williamsport, or Baltimore.

Often, captains and crew had to do more to prepare slaves for sale than allow them to clean themselves and exercise. The ravages of cruelty, confinement, and disease could not be easily remedied. According to legend, young African men and women arrived in the Americas with gray hair, and captains used dye to hide such indications of age before the slaves went to market. Slaves were also required to oil their bodies to conceal blemishes, rashes, and bruises. Ships' surgeons used hemp to plug the anuses of those suffering from dysentery in order to block the bloody discharge the disease caused.

The humiliation continued as the slaves went to market. Once again they suffered close physical inspection from potential buyers, which—according to Equiano—caused "much dread and trembling among us" and "bitter cries." Unless a single purchaser agreed to buy an entire cargo of slaves, auctions took place either on deck or in sale yards on shore. However, some captains employed "the scramble." In these barbaric spectacles, the captain established standard prices for men, women, and children, herded the Africans together in a corral, and then allowed buyers to rush pell-mell among them to grab and rope together the slaves they desired.

This nineteenth-century engraving suggests the humiliation Africans endured as they were subjected to physical inspections before being sold.
Courtesy of the Library of Congress

SEASONING

Seasoning followed sale. On Barbados, Jamaica, and other Caribbean islands, planters divided slaves into three categories: Creoles (slaves born in the Americas), old Africans (those who had lived in the Americas for some time), and new Africans (those who had just survived the middle passage). For resale, Creole slaves were worth three times the value of unseasoned new Africans, whom planters and Creole slaves called "salt-water Negroes" or "Guinea-birds." Seasoning was the beginning of the process of making new Africans more like Creoles.

In the West Indies, this process involved not only an apprenticeship in the work routines of the sugar plantations on the islands. It was also a means of preparing many slaves for resale to North American planters, who preferred "seasoned" slaves to "unbroken" ones who came directly from Africa. In fact, most of the Africans who ended up in the British colonies of North America before 1720 had gone first to the West Indies. By that date, the demand for slave labor in the islands had become so great that they could spare fewer slaves for resale to the North American market. Thereafter, as a result, slave imports into the tobacco-, rice-, and later cotton-growing regions of the American South came directly from Africa and had to be seasoned by their American masters.

In either case, seasoning was a disciplinary process intended to modify the behavior and attitude of slaves and make them effective laborers. As part of this process, the slaves' new masters gave them new names: Christian names, generic African names, or names from classical Greece and Rome (such as Jupiter, Achilles, or Plato).

The seasoning process also involved slaves learning European languages. Masters on the Spanish islands of the Caribbean were especially thorough in this regard. Consequently, the Spanish of African slaves and their descendants, although retaining some African words, was easily understood by any Spanish-speaking person. In the French and English Caribbean islands and in parts of North America, however, slave society produced Creole dialects that in grammar, vocabulary, and intonation had distinctive African linguistic features. These Africanized versions of French and English, including the Gullah dialect still prevalent on South Carolina's sea islands and the Creole spoken today by most Haitians, were difficult for those who spoke more standardized dialects to understand.

Seasoning varied in length from place to place. Masters or overseers broke slaves into plantation work by assigning them to one of several work gangs. The strongest men joined the first gang, or "great gang," which did the heavy fieldwork of planting and harvesting. The second gang, including women and older men, did lighter fieldwork, such as weeding. The third gang, composed of children, worked shorter hours and did such tasks as bringing food and water to the field gangs. Other slaves became domestic servants. New Africans served apprenticeships with old Africans from their same ethnic group or with Creoles.

Planters had to rely on old Africans and Creoles to train new recruits because white people were a minority in the Caribbean. Later, a similar demographic pattern developed in parts of the cotton-producing American South. As a result, in both regions African custom shaped the cooperative labor of slaves in gangs. But the use of old Africans and Creoles as instructors and the appropriation of African styles of labor should not suggest leniency. Although the plantation overseers, who ran day-to-day operations, could be white, of mixed race, or black, they invariably imposed strict discipline. Drivers, who directed the work gangs, were almost always black, but they carried whips and frequently punished those who worked too slowly or showed disrespect. Planters assigned recalcitrant new Africans to the strictest overseers and drivers.

Planters housed slaves undergoing seasoning with the old Africans and Creoles who were instructing them. The instructors regarded such additions to their households as economic opportunities because the new Africans provided extra labor on the small plots of land that West Indian planters often allocated to slaves. Slaves could sell surplus root vegetables, peas, and fruit from their gardens and save to purchase freedom for themselves or others. Additional workers helped produce larger surpluses to sell at local markets, thereby cutting the amount of time required to accumulate a purchase price.

New Africans also benefited from this arrangement. They learned how to build houses in their new land and to cultivate vegetables to supplement the food the planter provided. Even though many Africans brought building skills and agricultural knowledge with them to the Americas, old Africans and Creoles helped teach them how to adapt what they knew to a new climate, topography, building materials, and social organization.

The End of the Journey: Masters and Slaves in the Americas

By what criteria did planters assess the successful seasoning of new Africans? The first criterion was survival. Already weakened and traumatized by the middle passage, many Africans did not survive seasoning. Historian James Walvin estimates that one-third died during their first three years in the West Indies. African men died at a greater rate than African women, perhaps because they did the more arduous fieldwork.

Timeline

SLAVE TRADE	WORLD EVENTS
900	
900–1100 Trans-Sahara trade peaks	**935** Finalization of the Koran text **979** Sung dynasty unites China **1236** Mongols invade Russia **1337** French-English Hundred Years War begins
1400	
1441 Antam Goncalvez of Portugal captures Africans	**1445** Gutenberg prints first book in Europe
1450	
1472 Ruy do Siqueira contracts with the Oba of Benin	**1453** Fall of Constantinople to the Turks **1468** Fall of the Empire of Mali **1492** Columbus's first voyage to the Americas
1500	
1502 African slaves are reported to be on Hispaniola **1518** Spanish *Asiento* begins **1533** Sugar production begins in Brazil	**1517** Protestant Reformation **1519** Spanish conquest of Aztecs

continued

SLAVE TRADE	WORLD EVENTS
1550	
1571 Portuguese colonize Angola	**1591** Fall of the Empire of Songhai
1600	
1610 Dutch drive Portuguese from Africa's west coast	**1607** Founding of Jamestown
1619 Africans reported to be in British North America	**1620** Pilgrims reach New England
1650	
1662 Portuguese destroy Kongo Kingdom	**1688** England's Glorious Revolution
1674 England drives the Dutch out of the slave trade	
1700	
1713 England begins its domination of the slave trade	**1728** Russian exploration of Alaska begins
c. 1745 Olaudah Equiano born	
1750	
1752 British Royal African Company disbands	**1776** American Declaration of Independence
	1789 United States Constitution ratified
1800	
1807 Great Britain abolishes the Atlantic slave trade	**1815** Napolean defeated at the Battle of Waterloo
1808 United States abolishes the Atlantic slave trade	

A second criterion was that the Africans had to adapt to new foods and a new climate. The foods included salted codfish traded to the West Indies by New England merchants, Indian corn (maize), and varieties of squash not available in West Africa. The Caribbean islands like West Africa were tropical, but North America was much cooler. Even within the West Indies, an African was unlikely to find a climate exactly like the one he or she had left behind.

A third criterion was learning a new language. Planters did not require slaves to speak the local language, which could be English, French, Spanish, Danish, or Dutch, perfectly. But slaves had to speak a Creole dialect well enough to obey commands. A final criterion was psychological. When new Africans ceased to be suicidal, planters assumed they had accepted their status and their separation from their homeland.

It would have suited the planters if their slaves had met all these criteria. Yet that would have required the Africans to have been thoroughly desocialized by the middle passage, and they were not. As traumatic as that voyage was—for all the shock of capture, separation from loved ones, and efforts to dehumanize them—most of the Africans who entered plantation society in the Americas had not been stripped of their memories or their culture. When their ties to their villages and families were broken, they created bonds with shipmates that simulated blood relationships. Such bonds became the basis of new extended families. So similar were these new synthetic families to those that had existed in West Africa that slaves considered sexual relations among shipmates and former shipmates incestuous.

As this suggests, African slaves did not lose all their culture during the middle passage and seasoning in the Americas. Their value system never totally replicated that of the plantation. Despite their ordeal, the Africans who survived the Atlantic slave trade and slavery in the Americas were resilient. Seasoning did modify behavior, yet the claim that it obliterated African Americans' cultural roots is incorrect.

The Ending of the Atlantic Slave Trade

The cruelties associated with the Atlantic slave trade contributed to its abolition in the early nineteenth century. During the late 1700s, English abolitionists led by Thomas Clarkson, William Wilberforce, and Granville Sharp began a religiously oriented moral crusade against both slavery and the slave trade. Because the English had dominated the Atlantic trade since 1713, Britain's growing antipathy became crucial to the trade's destruction. But it is debatable whether moral outrage alone prompted this humanitarian effort. By the late 1700s, England's economy was less dependent on the slave trade and the entire plantation system than it had been previously. To maintain its prosperity, England needed raw materials and markets for its manufactured goods. Slowly but surely its industrialists realized it was more profitable to invest in industry and other forms of trade and to leave Africans in Africa.

So morals and economic self-interest were combined when Great Britain abolished the Atlantic slave trade in 1807 and tried to enforce that abolition on other nations through a naval patrol off the coast of Africa. The U.S. Congress joined Britain in outlawing the Atlantic trade the following year. Although American, Brazilian, and Spanish slavers continued to defy these prohibitions for many years, the forced migration from Africa to the Americas dropped to a tiny percentage of what it had been at its peak. Ironically, it was the coastal kingdoms of Guinea and western Central Africa that fought most fiercely to keep the trade going because their economies had become dependent on it. This persistence gave the English, French, Belgians, and Portuguese an excuse to establish colonial empires in Africa during the nineteenth century in the name of suppressing the slave trade.

Conclusion

Over more than three centuries, the Atlantic slave trade brought more than eleven million Africans to the Americas. Several millions more died in transit. Of those who survived, most came between 1701 and 1810, when more Africans than Europeans were reaching the New World. Most Africans went to the sugar plantations of the Caribbean and Brazil. Only 500,000 reached the British colonies of North America, either directly or after seasoning in the West Indies. From them have come the more than thirty million African Americans alive today.

This chapter has described the great forced migration across the Atlantic that brought Africans into slavery in the Americas. We still have much to learn about the origins of the trade, its relationship to the earlier trans-Sahara trade, and its involvement with state formation in West and western Central Africa. Historians continue to debate just how cruel the trade was, the ability of transplanted Africans to preserve their cultural heritage, and why Britain abolished the trade in the early nineteenth century.

We are fortunate that a few Africans, such as Olaudah Equiano, who experienced the middle passage, recorded their testimony. Otherwise, we would find its horror even more difficult to comprehend. But, just as important, Equiano, in overcoming his fears, in surviving the slave trade and ten years of enslavement, and in finally regaining his freedom, testifies to the human spirit that is at the center of the African-American experience.

Review Questions

1. How did the Atlantic slave trade reflect the times during which it existed?
2. Think about Olaudah Equiano's experience as a young boy captured by traders and brought to a slave ship. What new and strange things did he encounter? How did he explain these things to himself? What kept him from descending into utter despair?
3. How could John Newton reconcile his Christian faith with his career as a slave-ship captain?
4. What human and natural variables could prolong the middle passage across the Atlantic Ocean? How could delay make the voyage more dangerous for slaves and crew?
5. How could Africans resist the dehumanizing forces of the middle passage and seasoning and use their African cultures to build black cultures in the New World?

Recommended Reading

Barbara Bush. *Slave Women in Caribbean Society, 1650–1838.* Bloomington: University of Indiana Press, 1990. The book contains an insightful discussion of African women, their introduction to slavery in the Americas, and their experience on sugar plantations.

Basil Davidson. *The African Slave Trade: Revised and Expanded Edition.* Boston: Little, Brown, 1980. Originally published in 1961, this book has been superseded in some respects by more recent studies. But it places the trade in both African and European contexts.

Herbert S. Klein. *The Atlantic Slave Trade.* New York: Cambridge University Press, 1999. This is the most thorough and most current study of the subject.

Edward Reynolds. *Stand the Storm: A History of the Atlantic Slave Trade.* London: Allison and Busby, 1985. Reynolds concentrates on African societies and the responses of those subjected to the Atlantic slave trade.

John Thornton. *Africa and Africans in the Making of the Atlantic World, 1400–1800,* 2d ed. New York: Cambridge University Press, 1998. Thornton emphasizes the contributions of Africans, slave and free, to the economic and cultural development of the Atlantic world during the slave-trade centuries.

• CHAPTER THREE •

BLACK PEOPLE IN COLONIAL NORTH AMERICA

1526–1763

The Peoples of North America

In the North American colonies during the seventeenth and eighteenth centuries, African immigrants gave birth to a new African-American people. Born in North America and forever separated from their ancestral homeland, they preserved a surprisingly large core of their African cultural heritage. Meanwhile, a new natural environment and contacts with people of American Indian and European descent helped African Americans shape a way of life within the circumstances that slavery forced on them. To understand the early history of African Americans, we must first briefly discuss the other peoples of colonial North America.

American Indians

Historians and anthropologists group the original inhabitants of North America together as American Indians. (Sometimes the terms *Amerinds* and *Native Americans* are also used, with the latter term including Inuits [Eskimos].) But when the British began to colonize the coastal portion of this huge region during the early seventeenth century, the indigenous peoples who lived there had no such all-inclusive name. They spoke many different languages, lived in diverse environments, and considered themselves distinct from one another. Like other Indian peoples of the Western Hemisphere, they are believed to have descended from Asians who had migrated eastward across a land bridge connecting Siberia and Alaska at least twelve thousand years ago. Europeans called them Indians as a result of Christopher Columbus's mistaken assumption in 1492 that he had landed on islands near the "Indies," by which he meant near Southeast Asia.

In Mexico, Central America, and Peru, American Indian peoples developed complex, densely populated civilizations with hereditary monarchies, formal religions, armies, and social classes. The peoples of what is today the United States were influenced by cultural developments in Mexico and by the northerly spread of the cultivation of maize (corn). As early as 1000 BCE, the Adena culture had attained the social organization required to construct large burial mounds. Between the tenth and fourteenth centuries CE, what is known as the Mississippian culture established a sophisticated civilization, marked by extensive trade routes, division of labor, and urban centers. The largest such center was Cahokia—located near modern St. Louis—which at its peak had a population of about thirty thousand.

Climatic change and warfare destroyed the Mississippian culture during the fourteenth century, and only remnants of it existed when Europeans and Africans arrived in North America. By that time, a diverse variety of Indian cultures existed in what is today the eastern portion of the United States. People resided in towns and villages, supplementing their agricultural economies with fishing and hunting. They held land communally, generally allowed women a voice in ruling councils, and—although warlike—regarded battle as an opportunity for young men to prove their bravery rather than as a means of conquest. Gravely weakened by diseases that settlers unwittingly brought from Europe, the woodlands Indians of North America's coastal regions were ineffective in resisting British settlers during the seventeenth century. Particularly in the Southeast, the British developed an extensive trade in Indian slaves.

But because the Indians were experts at living harmoniously with the natural resources of North America, they influenced the way people of African and European descent came to live there as well. Indian crops, such as corn, potatoes, pumpkins, beans, and squash, became staples of the newcomers' diets. On the continent's southeastern coast, British cultivation of tobacco, an Indian crop, secured the economic survival of the Chesapeake colonies and led directly to the enslavement in them of Africans. The Indian canoe became a means of river transportation for black and white people, and Indian moccasins became common footwear for everyone.

The relationships between black people and Indians during colonial times were complex. Although Indian nations often provided refuge to escaping black slaves, Indians sometimes became slaveholders and on occasion helped crush black revolts. Some black men assisted in the Indian slave trade and sometimes helped defend European colonists against Indian attacks. Nevertheless, people of African and Indian descent frequently found themselves in similarly oppressive circumstances in Britain's American colonies. Although white officials attempted to keep them apart, social and sexual contacts between the two groups were frequent. Some interracial black-Indian settlements—and a few black-Indian-white settlements—have persisted to the present.

The Spanish Empire

Following Christopher Columbus's voyage in 1492, the Spanish rapidly built a colonial empire in the Americas. Mining of gold and silver, as well as the production of sugar, tobacco, and leather goods, provided a firm economic foundation. But few Spanish people came to the Western Hemisphere, and Spain's colonial economy rested on the forced labor of the Indian population and, when the Indian population declined from disease and overwork, increasingly on enslaved Africans. Overseers in the mines and fields often brutally worked Africans and Indians to death. But because the Spanish were few, some of the African and Indians who survived were able to gain freedom and become tradesmen, small landholders, and militiamen. Often they were of mixed race and identified with their former masters rather than with the oppressed people beneath them in society. African, Indian, and Spanish customs intermingled in what became a multicultural colonial society. Its center was in the West Indian islands of Cuba and Santo Domingo, Mexico, and northern South America. On its northern periphery were lands that are now part of the United States: Florida, Texas, Arizona, New Mexico, and California.

Africans came early to these borderlands. In 1526 Luis Vasquez de Ayllon brought one hundred African slaves with him from Hispaniola (modern Haiti and the Dominican Republic) in an attempt to establish a Spanish colony near what is now Georgetown, South Carolina. A decade later, slaves, who were either African or of African descent, accompanied Hernando de Soto on a Spanish expedition from Florida to the Mississippi River. In 1565 Africans helped construct the Spanish settlement of St. Augustine in Florida, which is now the oldest city in the continental United States. In 1528 a Spanish expedition that departed Cuba to search for gold in western Florida and the Gulf Coast included a slave of African descent named Esteban. Following a shipwreck, Esteban reached the coast of Texas. After a brief captivity among the local Indians, he and other survivors made their way southward to Mexico City.

The British and Jamestown

The British, like the Africans and the American Indians, were not a single nation. The British Isles—consisting principally of Britain and Ireland and located off the northwest coast of Europe—were the homeland of the English, Welsh, Scots, and Irish. At that time, the Kingdom of England was, compared to Spain, a poor country notable mainly for producing wool.

England's claim to the east coast of North America rested on the voyage of John Cabot, who sailed in 1497, just five years after Columbus's first westward voyage. But, unlike the Spanish who rapidly created an empire in the Americas, the English were slow to establish themselves in the region Cabot had discovered. This was partly because of the harsher North American climate, with winters much colder than in England, but also because the English monarchy was too poor to finance colonizing expeditions and because the turmoil associated with the Protestant Reformation absorbed the nation's energies.

It took the English naval victory over the Spanish Armada in 1588 and money raised by joint-stock companies to produce in 1607 at Jamestown the first permanent British colony in North America. This settlement, established by the Virginia Company of London, was located in the Chesapeake region the British called Virginia—after Queen Elizabeth I (r. 1558–1603), the so-called Virgin Queen of England who never married. The company hoped to make a profit at Jamestown by finding gold, trading with the Indians, cutting lumber, or raising crops, such as rice, sugar, or silk, that could not be produced in Britain.

None of these schemes was economically viable. There was no gold, and the climate was unsuitable for rice, sugar, and silk. Because of disease, hostility with the Indians, and especially economic failure, the settlement barely survived into the 1620s. By then, however, the experiments begun in 1612 by the English settler John Rolfe to cultivate a mild strain of tobacco that could be grown on the North American mainland began to pay off. Tobacco was in great demand in Europe where smoking was becoming popular. Soon growing tobacco became the economic mainstay in Virginia and the neighboring colony of Maryland.

The sowing, cultivating, harvesting, and curing of tobacco were labor intensive. Yet colonists in the Chesapeake could not follow the Spanish example and enslave the Indians to produce the crop. Rampant disease had reduced the local Indian population, and those who survived eluded British conquest by retreating westward.

Unlike the West Indian sugar planters, however, the North American tobacco planters did not immediately turn to Africa for laborers. British advocates of colonizing North America had always promoted it as a solution to unemployment, poverty, and crime in England. The idea was to send England's undesirables to America, where they could provide the cheap labor tobacco planters needed. Consequently, until 1700, white labor produced most of the tobacco in the Chesapeake colonies.

Africans Arrive in the Chesapeake

By the early months of 1619, there were, nevertheless, thirty-two people of African descent—fifteen men and seventeen women—living in the English colony at Jamestown. Nothing is known concerning when they had arrived or from where they had come. They were all "in the service of sev[er]all planters." The following August a Dutch warship, carrying seventeen African men and three African women, moored at Hampton Roads at the mouth of the James River. The Dutch warship, with the help of an English ship, had attacked a Portuguese slaver, taken most of its human cargo, and brought these twenty Angolans to Jamestown. The Dutch captain traded them to local officials in return for provisions.

The Angolans became servants to the Jamestown officials and to favored planters. The colony's inhabitants, for two reasons, regarded the new arrivals and those black people who had been in Jamestown earlier to be *unfree,* but not slaves. First, unlike the Portuguese and the Spanish, the English had no law for slavery. Second, at least the Angolans, who bore such names as Pedro, Isabella, Antoney, and Angelo, had been converted by the Portuguese to Christianity. According to English custom and morality in 1619, Christians could not be enslaved. So, once these individuals had worked off their purchase price, they could regain their freedom. In 1623, Antoney and Isabella married. The next year they became parents of William, whom their master had baptized in the local Church of England. William may have been the first black person born in English America. He was almost certainly born free.

During the following years, people of African descent remained a small minority in the expanding Virginia colony. By 1649 the total Virginia population of about 18,500 included only 300 black people. The English, following the Spanish example, called them "negroes." (The word "negro" means black in Spanish.) In neighboring Maryland, which was established as a haven in 1632 for persecuted English Catholics, the black population also remained small. In 1658 only 3 percent of Maryland's population was of African descent.

Black Servitude in the Chesapeake

From the 1620s to the 1670s, black and white people worked in the tobacco fields together, lived together, and slept together (and also did these things with American Indians). As members of an oppressed working class, they were all unfree indentured servants.

Indentured servitude had existed in Europe for centuries. In England, parents indentured—or, in other words, apprenticed—their children to "masters," who controlled their lives and had the right to their labor for a set number of years. In return, the masters supported the children and taught them a trade or profession.

As the demand for labor to produce tobacco in the Chesapeake expanded, indentured servitude came to include adults who sold their freedom for two to seven years in return for the cost of their voyage to North America. Instead of training in a profession, the servants could improve their economic standing by remaining as free persons in America after completing their period of servitude.

When Africans first arrived in Virginia and Maryland, they entered into similar contracts, agreeing to work for their masters until the proceeds of their labor recouped the cost of their purchase. Such indentured servitude could be harsh in the tobacco colonies because masters sought to get as much labor as they could from their servants before the indenture ended. Most indentured servants died from overwork or disease before regaining their freedom. But those who survived, black people as well as white people, could expect eventually to leave their masters and seek their fortunes as free persons.

During the seventeenth century, free black men living in the Chesapeake participated fully in the commercial and legal life of the colony. They owned land, farmed, lent money, sued in the courts, served as jurors and as minor officials, and at times voted.

Prior to the 1670s the English in the Chesapeake did not draw a strict line between white freedom and black slavery. Yet the ruling elite had from the early 1600s treated black servants differently from white servants. Over the decades, the region's British population gradually came to assume that persons of African descent were inalterably alien. This sentiment did not become universal among the white poor during the colonial period. But it was a foundation for what historian Winthrop D. Jordan calls the "unthinking decision" among the British in the Chesapeake to establish chattel slavery, in which slaves were legally private property on a level with livestock, as the proper condition for Africans and those of African descent.

Race and the Origins of Black Slavery

Between 1640 and 1700, the British tobacco-producing colonies stretching from Delaware to northern Carolina underwent a social and demographic revolution. An economy based primarily on the labor of white indentured servants became an economy based on the labor of black slaves. In Virginia, for example, the slave population in 1671 was less than 5 percent of the colony's total non-Indian population. White indentured servants outnumbered black slaves by three to one. By 1700, however, slaves constituted at least 20 percent of Virginia's population. Probably most agricultural laborers were now slaves.

Among the economic and demographic developments that led to the enslavement of people of African descent in the tobacco colonies was the precedent for enslaving Africans set in the British Caribbean sugar colonies during the second quarter of the seventeenth century. Also, Britain was gaining more control over the Atlantic slave trade at a time when fewer English men and women were willing to indenture themselves in return for passage to the Chesapeake. Poor white people found better opportunities for themselves in other regions of British North America, driving up the price of European indentured servants in the tobacco colonies. Meanwhile, British control of the slave trade made African laborers cheaper in those colonies.

These changing circumstances provide the context for the beginnings of black slavery in British North America. Yet race and class played the crucial role in shaping the *character* of slavery in the British mainland colonies. From the first arrival of Africans in the Chesapeake, those English who exercised authority made decisions that qualified the apparent social mobility the Africans enjoyed. The English had historically made distinctions between how they treated each other and how they treated those who were physically and culturally different from them. Such discrimination had been the basis of their colonial policies toward the Irish, whom the English had been trying to conquer for centuries, and the American Indians. Because they considered Africans even more different from themselves than either the Irish or the Indians, the English assumed from the beginning that Africans were generally inferior to themselves.

Therefore, although black and white servants residing in the Chesapeake during the early seventeenth century had much in common, their masters immediately made distinctions between them based on race. The few women of African descent who arrived in the Chesapeake during those years worked in the tobacco fields with the male servants, whereas most white women were assigned domestic duties. By the 1640s, black people could not bear arms, and during the same decade, local Anglican priests (although not those in England itself) maintained that persons of African descent could not become Christians.

These distinctions suggest that the status of black servants had never been the same as that of white servants. But only starting in the 1640s do records indicate a predilection toward making black people slaves rather than servants. During that decade, courts in Virginia and Maryland began to reflect an assumption that it was permissible for persons of African descent to serve their master for life rather than for a set term.

The Emergence of Chattel Slavery

Legal documents and statute books reveal that, during the 1660s, other aspects of chattel slavery emerged in the Chesapeake colonies. Bills of sale began to stipulate that the children of black female servants would also be servants for life. In 1662 the House of Burgesses decreed that a child's condition—free or unfree—followed that of the mother. This ran counter to English common law, which assumed that a child's status derived from the father. The change permitted masters to exploit their black female servants sexually without having to acknowledge the children who might result from such contacts. Just as significant, by the mid-1660s statutes in the Chesapeake colonies assumed servitude to be the natural condition of black people.

With these laws, slavery in British North America emerged in the form that it retained until the American Civil War: a racially defined system of perpetual involuntary servitude that compelled almost all black people to work as agricultural laborers. Slave codes enacted between 1660 and 1710 further defined American slavery as a system that sought as much to control persons of African descent as to exploit their labor. Slaves could not testify against white people in court, own property, leave their master's estate without a pass, congregate in groups larger than three or four, enter into contracts, marry, or, of course, bear arms. Profession of Christianity no longer protected a black person from enslavement nor was conversion a cause for manumission. In 1669 the House of Burgesses exempted from felony charges masters who killed a slave while administering punishment.

By 1700, just as the slave system began to expand in the southern colonies, enslaved Africans and African Americans had been reduced legally to the status of domestic animals except that, unlike animals (or masters when it came to abusing slaves), the law held slaves to be strictly accountable for their transgressions.

Bacon's Rebellion and American Slavery

The series of events that led to the enslavement of black people in the Chesapeake tobacco colonies preceded their emergence as the great majority of laborers in those colonies. The dwindling supply of white indentured servants, the growing availability of Africans, and preexisting white racial biases affected this transformation. But the key event in bringing it about was the rebellion led by Nathaniel Bacon in 1676.

Bacon was an English aristocrat who had recently migrated to Virginia. The immediate cause of his rebellion was a disagreement between him and the colony's royal governor William Berkeley over Indian policy. Bacon's followers were mainly white indentured servants and former indentured servants who resented the control exercised by the tobacco-planting elite over the colony's resources and government. That Bacon also appealed to black slaves to join his rebellion indicates that poor white and black people still had a chance to unite against the master class.

Before such a class-based, biracial alliance could be realized, Bacon died of dysentery, and his rebellion collapsed. But the uprising convinced the colony's elite that continuing to rely on white agricultural laborers, who could become free and get guns, was dangerous. By switching from indentured white servants to an enslaved black labor force that would never become free or control firearms, the planters hoped to avoid class conflict among white people. Increasingly thereafter, white Americans perceived that both their freedom from class conflict and their prosperity rested on denying freedom to black Americans.

Plantation Slavery, 1700–1750

Between 1700 and 1770, some 80,000 Africans arrived in the tobacco colonies, and even more African Americans were born into slavery there. Tobacco planting spread from Virginia and Maryland to Delaware and North Carolina and from the coastal plain to the foothills of the Appalachian Mountains. In the process, American slavery began to assume the form it kept for the next 165 years.

By 1750, 144,872 slaves lived in Virginia and Maryland, accounting for 61 percent of all the slaves in British North America. Another 40,000 slaves lived in the rice-producing regions of South Carolina and Georgia, accounting for 17 percent. Unlike the sugar colonies of the Caribbean, where whites were a tiny minority, whites remained a majority in the tobacco colonies and a large minority in the rice colonies. Also, most southern whites did not own slaves. Nevertheless, the economic development of the region depended on enslaved black laborers.

The conditions under which those laborers lived varied. Most slaveholders farmed small tracts of land and owned fewer than five slaves. These masters and their slaves worked together and developed close personal relationships. Other masters owned thousands of acres of land and rarely saw most of their slaves. During the early eighteenth century, the great planters divided their slaves among several small holdings. They did this to avoid concentrating potentially rebellious Africans in one area. As the proportion of newly arrived Africans in the slave population declined later in the century, larger concentrations of slaves became more common.

Before the mid-eighteenth century, nearly all slaves—both men and women—worked in the fields. On the smaller farms, they worked with their master. On larger estates, they worked for an overseer, who was usually white. Like other agricultural workers, enslaved African Americans normally worked from sunup to sundown with breaks for food and rest. Even during colonial times, they usually had Sunday off.

From the beginnings of slavery in North America, masters tried to make slaves work harder and faster while the slaves sought to conserve their energy, take breaks, and socialize with each other. African men regarded field labor as women's work and tried to avoid it if possible. But, especially if they had incentives, enslaved Africans could be efficient workers. One incentive to which both slaves and masters looked forward was the annual harvest festival. These festivals were held in both Africa and Europe and became common throughout the British colonies early in the eighteenth century.

Not until after 1750 did some black men begin to hold such skilled occupations on plantations as carpenter, smith, carter, cooper, miller, sawyer, tanner, and shoemaker. By 1768 one South Carolina planter noted that "in established Plantations, the Planter has Tradesmen of all kinds in his Gang of Slaves, and 'tis a Rule with them, never to pay Money for what can be made upon their Estates, not a Lock, a Hinge, or a Nail if they can avoid it." Black women had less access to such occupations. When they did not work in the fields, they were domestic servants in the homes of their masters, cooking, washing, cleaning, and caring for children. Such duties could be extremely taxing, because, unlike fieldwork, they did not end when the sun went down.

Low-Country Slavery

South of the tobacco colonies, on the coastal plain, or low country, of Carolina and Georgia a distinctive slave society developed (see Map 3–1). The influence of the West Indian plantation system was much stronger here than in the Chesapeake, and rice, not tobacco, became the staple crop.

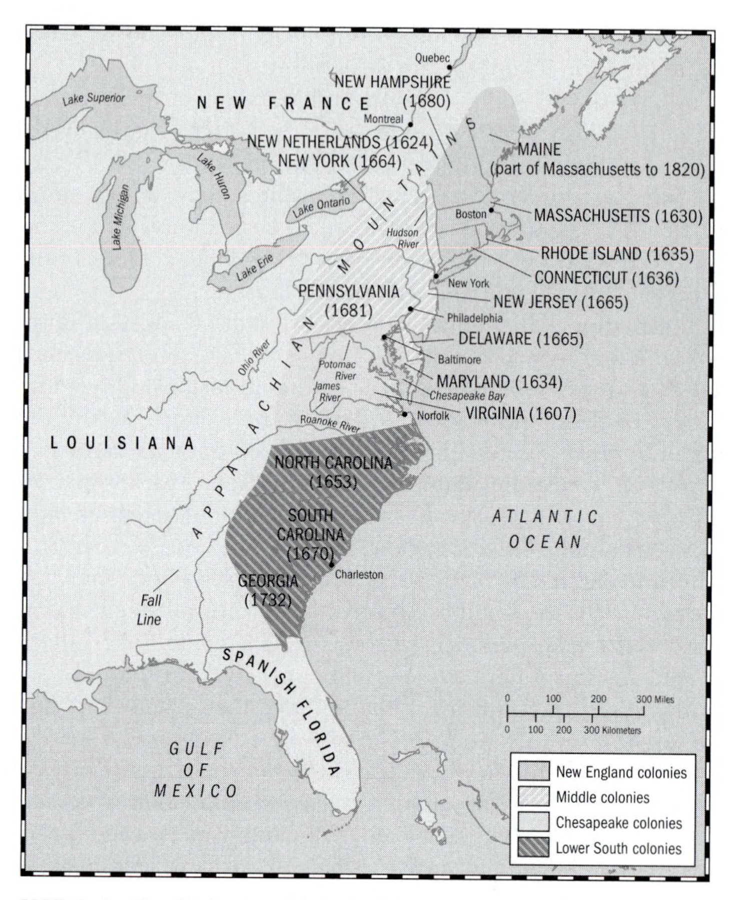

MAP 3–1 The Regions of Colonial North America in the Eighteenth Century

The first British settlers who arrived in 1670 at Charleston (in what would later become South Carolina) were mainly immigrants from Barbados, rather than England. Many of them had been slaveholders on that island and brought slaves with them. Therefore, in the low country, black people were never indentured servants. They were chattel from the start. The region's subtropical climate discouraged white settlement and encouraged dependence on black labor the way it did in the sugar islands. During the early years of settlement, nearly one-third of the immigrants were African, most of them males. By the early eighteenth century, more Africans were arriving than white people.

By 1740 the Carolina low country had 40,000 slaves, who constituted 90 percent of the population in the region around Charleston. In all, 94,000 Africans arrived at Charleston between 1706 and 1776, which made it North America's leading port of entry for Africans during the eighteenth century. A Swiss immigrant commented in 1737 that the region "looks more like a negro country than like a country settled by white people."

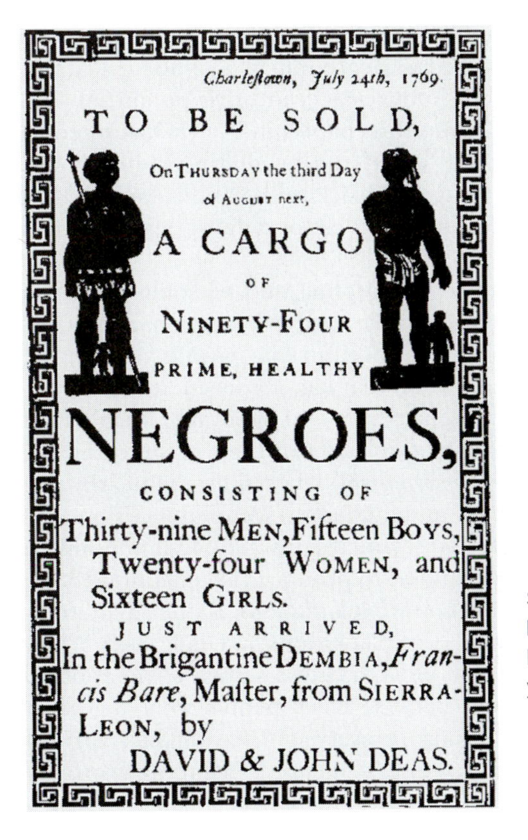

Sales like the one announced in this 1769 broadside were common since slavery had been established in the low country ninety years earlier. South Carolina and Georgia remained dependent on imported slaves for much longer than did the Chesapeake and the North.
Courtesy, American Antiquarian Society

Starting around 1700, the low-country planters concentrated on growing rice. Rice had been grown in West Africa for thousands of years, and many of the enslaved Africans who reached Carolina had the skill required to cultivate it in America. Although tobacco could be profitably produced on small farms, rice required large acreages. Therefore, large plantations on a scale similar to those on the sugar islands of the West Indies became the rule in the low country. During the 1750s, rice cultivation and slavery spread into Georgia's coastal plain. By 1773 Georgia had as many black people—15,000—as white people.

As on Barbados, absentee plantation owners became the rule in South Carolina and Georgia because planters preferred to live in Charleston or Savannah where sea breezes provided relief from the heat. Enslaved Africans on low-country plantations suffered from a high mortality rate from diseases, overwork, and poor treatment just as did their counterparts on Barbados and other sugar islands. Therefore, unlike the slave population in the Chesapeake colonies, the slave population in the low country did not grow by reproducing itself—rather than through continued arrivals from Africa—until shortly before the American Revolution.

This low-country slave society produced striking paradoxes in race relations during the eighteenth century. As the region's black population grew, white people became increasingly fearful of revolt, and by 1698 Carolina had the strictest slave code in North America. In 1721, Charleston organized a "Negro watch" to enforce a curfew on its black population, and watchmen could shoot recalcitrant Africans and African Americans on sight. Yet, as the passage that begins this chapter indicates, black people in Carolina faced the quandary of being both feared and needed by white people. Even as persons of European descent grew fearful of black revolt, the colony in 1704 authorized the arming of enslaved black men when needed for defense against Indian and Spanish raids.

Of equal significance was the appearance in Carolina and to some extent in Georgia of distinct classes among people of color. Like the low-country society itself, such classes were more similar to those in the Caribbean sugar islands than in the mainland colonies to the north. A creole population that had absorbed European values lived in close proximity to white people in Charleston and Savannah. Members of this creole population were frequently mixed-race relatives of their masters and enjoyed social and economic privileges denied to slaves who labored on the nearby rice plantations. Yet this urban mixed-race class was under constant white supervision.

In contrast, slaves who lived in the country retained considerable autonomy in their daily routines. The intense cultivation required to produce rice encouraged the evolution of a "task system" of labor on the low-country plantations. Rather than working in gangs as in the tobacco colonies, slaves on rice plantations had daily tasks. When they completed these tasks, they could work on plots of land assigned to them or do what they pleased without white supervision. Because black people were the great majority in the low-country plantations, they also preserved more of their African heritage than did black people who lived in the region's cities or in the more northerly British mainland colonies.

Slave Life in Early America

Eighteenth-century housing for slaves was minimal and often temporary. In the Chesapeake, small log cabins with dirt floors, brick fireplaces, wooden chimneys, and few, if any, windows were typical. African styles of architecture were more common in coastal South Carolina and Georgia. In these regions, slaves built the walls of their houses with tabby—a mixture of lime, oyster shells, and sand—or, occasionally, mud. In either case, the houses had thatched roofs.

At first, slave dress was minimal during summer. Men wore breechcloths, women wore skirts, leaving their upper bodies bare, and children went naked until puberty. Later men wore shirts, trousers, and hats while working in the fields. Women wore shifts (loose, simple dresses) and covered their heads with handkerchiefs. In winter, masters provided more substantial cotton and woolen clothing and cheap leather shoes. In the early years, much of the clothing, or at least the cloth used to make it, came from England. Later, as the account of George Mason's Gunston Hall plantation indicates, homespun made by slaves replaced English cloth. From the seventeenth century onward, slave women brightened clothing with dyes made from bark, decorated clothing with ornaments, and created African-style headwraps, hats, and hairstyles. In this manner, African Americans retained a sense of personal style compatible with West African culture.

Food consisted of corn, yams, salt pork, and occasionally salt beef and salt fish. Slaves also caught fish and raised chickens and rabbits. When farmers in the Chesapeake began planting wheat during the eighteenth century, slaves baked biscuits. In the South Carolina low country, rice became an important part of African-American diets, but even there corn was the staple. During colonial times, slaves occasionally supplemented this limited diet with vegetables, such as cabbage, cauliflower, black-eyed peas, turnips, collard greens, and rutabagas, that they raised in their own gardens.

Miscegenation and Creolization

When Africans first arrived in the Chesapeake during the early seventeenth century, they interacted culturally and physically with white indentured servants and with American Indians. This mixing of peoples changed all three groups. Interracial sexual contacts—miscegenation—produced people of mixed race. Meanwhile, cultural exchanges became an essential part of the process of creolization that led African parents to produce African-American children. When, as often happened, miscegenation and creolization occurred together, the change was both physical and cultural. However, the dominant British minority in North America during the colonial period defined persons of mixed race as black. Although enslaved mulattoes—those of mixed African and European ancestry—enjoyed some advantages over slaves who had a purely African ancestry, mulattoes as a group did not receive enhanced legal status.

Miscegenation between blacks and whites and blacks and Indians was extensive throughout British North America during the seventeenth and eighteenth centuries. But it was less extensive and accepted than it was in the European sugar colonies in the Caribbean, in Latin America, or in French Canada, where many French men married Indian women. British North America was exceptional because many more white women migrated there than to Canada or the Caribbean, so that white men did not have to take black or Indian wives and concubines. Sexual relations between Africans and Indians were also more limited than they were elsewhere because the coastal Indian population had drastically declined before large numbers of Africans arrived.

The Origins of African-American Culture

The second generation of people of African descent in North America did lose their parents' native languages and their ethnic identity as Igbos, Angolas, or Senegambians. But they retained a generalized West African heritage and passed it on to their descendants. Among the major elements of that heritage were family structure and notions of kinship, religious concepts and practices, African words and modes of expression, musical style and instruments, cooking methods and foods, folk literature, and folk arts.

The preservation of the West African extended family was the basis of African-American culture. Because most Africans imported into the British colonies during the late seventeenth and early eighteenth centuries were males, most black men of that era could not have wives and children. It was not until the Atlantic slave trade declined briefly during the 1750s that sex ratios became more balanced and African-American family life began to flourish. Without that family life, black people could not have maintained as much of Africa as they did.

Even during the middle passage, enslaved Africans created "fictive kin relationships" for mutual support, and in dire circumstances, African Americans continued to improvise family structures. By the mid-eighteenth century, however, extended black families based on biological relationships were prevalent. Black people retained knowledge of their kinship ties to second and third cousins over several generations and wide stretches of territory. These extended families were rooted in Africa, but were also a result of—and a reaction to—slavery. West African incest taboos encouraged slaves to pick mates who lived on different plantations from their own. The sale of slaves away from their immediate families also tended to extend families over wide areas. Once established, such far-flung kinship relationships made it easier for others, who were forced to leave home, to adapt to new conditions under a new master. Kinfolk also sheltered escapees.

Extended families influenced African-American naming practices, which reinforced family ties. Africans named male children after close relatives. This custom survived in America because boys were more likely to be separated from their parents by being sold than girls were. Having one's father's or grandfather's name preserved one's family identity. Also when, early in the eighteenth century, more African Americans began to use surnames, they clung to the name of their original master. This reflected a West African predisposition to link a family name with a certain location. Like taking a parent's name, it helped maintain family relationships despite repeated scatterings.

Bible names did not become common among African Americans until the mid-eighteenth century. This was because masters often refused to allow their slaves to be converted to Christianity. As a result, African religions—both indigenous and Islamic—persisted in parts of America well into the nineteenth century. The indigenous religions in particular maintained a premodern perception of the unity of the natural and the supernatural, the secular and the sacred, and the living and the dead. Black Americans continued to perform an African circle dance known as the "ring shout" at funerals, and they decorated graves with shells and pottery in the West African manner. They looked to recently arrived Africans for religious guidance, held bodies of water to be sacred, remained in daily contact with their ancestors through spirit possession, and practiced divination and magic. When they became ill, they turned to "herb doctors" and "root workers." Even when many African Americans began to convert to Christianity during the mid-eighteenth century, West African religious thought and practice shaped their lives.

The Great Awakening

The major turning point in African-American religion came in conjunction with the religious revival known as the Great Awakening. This extensive social movement of the mid- to late-eighteenth century grew out of growing dissatisfaction among white Americans with a deterministic and increasingly formalistic style of Protestantism that seemed to deny most people a chance for salvation. During the early 1730s in western Massachusetts, a Congregationalist minister named Jonathan Edwards began an emotional and participatory ministry aimed at bringing more people into the church. Later that decade, George Whitefield, an Englishman who with John Wesley founded the Methodist Church, carried a similarly evangelical style of Christianity to the mainland colonies. In his sermons, Whitefield appealed to emotions, offered salvation to all who believed in Christ, and—although he did not advocate emancipation—preached to black people as well as white people.

Some people of African descent had converted to Christianity before Whitefield's arrival in North America. But two factors had prevented widespread black conversion. First, most masters feared that converted slaves would interpret their new religious status as a step toward freedom and equality. Second, many slaves, as we noted previously, continued to derive spiritual satisfaction from their ancestral religions and were not attracted to Christianity.

With the Great Awakening, however, a process of general conversion began. African Americans did indeed link the spiritual equality preached by evangelical ministers with a hope for earthly equality. They tied salvation for the soul with liberation for the body. They recognized that the preaching style Whitefield and other evangelicals adopted had much in common with West African "spirit possession." As in West African religion, eighteenth-century revivalism in North America emphasized personal rebirth, singing, movement, and emotion. The practice of total body immersion during baptism in rivers, ponds, and lakes that gave the Baptist church its name paralleled West African water rites.

Because it drew African Americans into an evangelical movement that helped shape American society, the Great Awakening increased mutual black-white acculturation. Revivalists appealed to the poor of all races and emphasized spiritual equality. Evangelical Anglican, Baptist, Methodist, and Presbyterian churches welcomed black people. Members of these biracial churches addressed each other as *brother* and *sister*. Black members took communion with white members, served as church officers, and both groups were subject to the same church discipline. By the late eighteenth century, black men were being ordained as priests and ministers and—often while still enslaved—preached to white congregations. They thereby influenced white people's perception of how services should be conducted.

Other factors, however, favored the development of a distinct African-American church. From the start, white churches seated black people apart from white people, belying claims to spiritual equality. Black members took communion *after* white members. Masters also tried to use religion to instill in their chattels such self-serving Christian virtues as meekness, humility, and obedience. Consequently, African Americans established their own churches when they could. Dancing, shouting, clapping, and singing became especially characteristic of their religious meetings. Black spirituals probably date from the eighteenth century, and like African-American Christianity itself, they blended West African and European elements.

African Americans also retained the West African assumption that the souls of the dead returned to their homeland and rejoined their ancestors. Reflecting this family-oriented view of death, African-American funerals were often loud and joyous occasions with dancing, laughing, and drinking. Perhaps most important, the emerging black church reinforced black people's collective identity and helped them persevere in slavery.

Language, Music, and Folk Literature

Although African Americans did not retain their ancestral languages, those languages contributed to the pidgins and creolized languages that became Black English by the nineteenth century. It was in the low country, with its large and isolated black populations, that African-English creoles lasted the longest. The Gullah and Geechee dialects of the sea islands of South Carolina and Georgia, which combine African words and some African grammatical elements with a basically English structure, are still spoken today. In other regions, where black people were less numerous, the creoles were less enduring. Nevertheless, they contributed many words to American—particularly southern—English. Among them are *yam, banjo* (from mbanza), *tote, goober* (peanut), *buckra* (white man), *cooter* (tortoise), *gumbo* (okra), *nanse* (spider), *samba* (dance), *tabby* (a form of concrete), and *voodoo.*

Music was another essential part of West African life, and it remained so among African Americans, who preserved an antiphonal, call-and-response style of singing with an emphasis on improvisation, complex rhythms, and a strong beat. They sang while working and during religious ceremonies. Early on, masters banned drums and horns because of their potential for long-distance communication among slaves. But the African banjo survived in America, and African Americans quickly adopted the violin and guitar. At night, in their cabins or around communal fires, slaves accompanied these instruments with bones and spoons. Music may have been the most important aspect of African culture in the lives of American slaves. Eventually African-American music influenced all forms of American popular music.

West African folk literature also survived in North America. African tales, proverbs, and riddles—with accretions from American Indian and European stories—entertained, instructed, and united African Americans. Just as the black people on the sea islands of South Carolina and Georgia were most able to retain elements of African language, so did their folk literature remain closest to its African counterpart. Africans used tales of how weak animals like rabbits outsmarted stronger animals like hyenas and lions to symbolize the power of the common people over unjust rulers. African Americans used similar tales to portray the ability of slaves to outsmart and ridicule their masters.

The African-American Impact on Colonial Culture

African Americans also influenced the development of white culture. As early as the seventeenth century, black musicians performed English ballads for white audiences in a distinctively African-American style. They began to shape American music. In the northern and Chesapeake colonies, people of African descent helped determine how all Americans celebrated. By the eighteenth century, slaves in these regions organized black election or coronation festivals that lasted for several days. Sometimes called *Pinkster* and ultimately derived from Dutch-American pre-Easter celebrations, these festivities included parades, athletics, food, music, dancing, and mock coronations of kings and governors. Although dominated by African Americans, they attracted white observers and a few white participants.

The African-American imprint on southern diction and phraseology is especially clear. Generations of slaveholders' children, who were often raised by black women, were influenced by African-American speech patterns and intonations. Black people

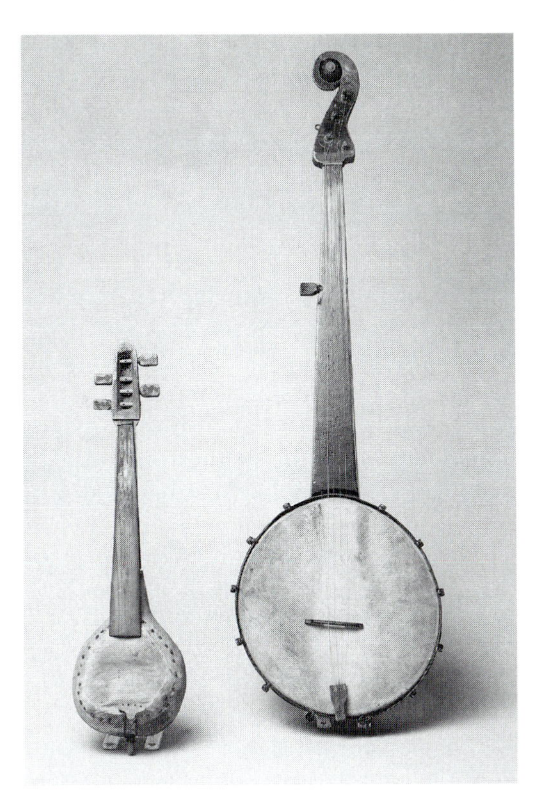

This photograph depicts two versions of the African *mbanza*. They feature leather stretched across a gourd, a wooden neck, and strings made of animal gut. In America, such instruments became known as banjos.
Corbis/Bettmann

also influenced white notions about portents, spirits, and folk remedies. Seventeenth- and eighteenth-century English lore about such things was not that different from West African lore, and white Americans consulted black conjurers and "herb doctors." Black cooks in early America influenced both white southern and African-American eating habits. Preferences for barbecued pork, fried chicken, black-eyed peas, and collard and mustard greens owed much to West African culinary traditions.

African Americans also used West African culture and skills to shape the way work was done in the American South during and after colonial times. Africans accustomed to collective agricultural labor imposed the "gang system" on most American plantations. Masters learned that their slaves would work harder and longer in groups. Their work songs were also an African legacy, as was the slow, deliberate pace of their labor. By the mid-eighteenth century, masters often employed slaves as builders. As a result, African styles and decorative techniques influenced southern colonial architecture. Black builders introduced African-style high-peaked roofs, front porches, woodcarvings, and elaborate ironwork.

Slavery in the Northern Colonies

The British mainland colonies north of the Chesapeake had histories, cultures, demographics, and economies that differed considerably from those of the southern colonies. Organized religion was much more important in the foundation of most of the northern colonies than those of the South (except for Maryland). In New England, where the Pilgrims settled in 1620 and the Puritans in 1630, religious utopianism shaped colonial life. The same was true in the West Jersey portion of New Jersey, where members of the English pietist Society of Friends, or Quakers, began to settle during the 1670s, and Pennsylvania, which William Penn founded in 1682 as a Quaker colony. Quakers, like other pietists, emphasized nonviolence and a divine spirit within all humans, both of which beliefs disposed some of them to become early opponents of slavery.

Even more important than religion in shaping life in northern British North America were a cooler climate, sufficient numbers of white laborers, lack of a staple crop, and a diversified economy. All these circumstances made black slavery in the colonial North less extensive than and different from its southern counterparts.

By the end of the colonial period during the 1770s, only 50,000 African Americans lived in the northern colonies in comparison to 400,000 in the southern colonies. In the North, black people were 4.5 percent of the total population, compared with 40 percent in the South. But, as in the South, the northern black population varied in size from place to place. By 1770 enslaved African Americans constituted 10 percent of the population of Rhode Island, New Jersey, New York, and Pennsylvania. New York City had a particularly large black population, 20 percent of its total by 1750.

Like all Americans during the colonial era, most northern slaves were agricultural laborers. But, in contrast to those in the South, slaves in the North typically lived in their master's house and worked with their master, his family, and one or two other slaves on a small farm. In northern cities, which were often homeports for slave traders, enslaved people of African descent worked as artisans, shopkeepers, messengers, domestic servants, and general laborers.

Consequently, most northern African Americans led different lives from those in the South. Mainly because New England had so few slaves, but also because of Puritan religious principles, slavery there was least oppressive. White people had no reason to suspect that the small and dispersed black population posed a threat of rebellion. The local slave codes were milder and, except for the ban on miscegenation, not rigidly enforced. New England slaves could legally own, transfer, and inherit property. From the early seventeenth century onward, Puritans converted to Christianity the Africans and African Americans who came among them, recognizing their spiritual equality before God.

In the middle colonies of New York, New Jersey, and Pennsylvania, where black populations were larger and hence perceived by white people to be more threatening, the slave codes were stricter and penalties harsher. But even in these colonies, the curfews imposed on Africans and African Americans and restrictions on their ability to gather together were less well enforced than they were further south.

Slavery in Spanish Florida and French Louisiana

Just as slavery in Britain's northern colonies differed from slavery in its southern colonies, slavery in Spanish Florida and French Louisiana—areas that would later become parts of the United States—had distinctive characteristics. People of African descent, brought to Florida and Louisiana during the sixteenth, seventeenth, and eighteenth centuries, had different experiences from those who arrived in the British colonies. They and their descendants learned to speak Spanish or French rather than English, and they became Roman Catholics rather than Protestants. In addition, the routes to freedom were more plentiful in the Spanish and French colonies than they were in Britain's plantation colonies.

The Spanish monarchy regarded the settlement it established at St. Augustine in 1565 as primarily a military outpost, and plantation agriculture was not significant in Florida under Spanish rule. Therefore, the number of slaves in Florida remained small, and black men were needed more as soldiers than as field workers. As militiamen, they gained power that eluded slaves in most of the British colonies, and as members of the Catholic Church, they acquired social status. By 1746 St. Augustine had a total population of 1,500, including about 400 black people. When the British took control of Florida in 1763, these local people of African descent retreated along with the city's white inhabitants to Cuba. It was with the British takeover that plantation slavery began to grow in Florida.

When the French in 1699 established their Louisiana colony in the lower Mississippi River valley, their objective, like that of the Spanish in Florida, was primarily military. In 1720 few black people (either slave or free) lived in the colony. During the following decade, Louisiana imported about six thousand slaves, most of whom were male and from Senegambia. Although conditions were harsh and many died, by 1731 black people outnumbered white people in the colony. Some of the Africans worked on plantations growing tobacco and indigo. But most lived in the port city of New Orleans, where many became skilled artisans, lived away from their masters, became Roman Catholics, and gained freedom. Unfortunately, New Orleans early in its history also became a place where it was socially acceptable for white men to exploit black women sexually. This custom eventually created a sizable mixed-race population with elaborate social gradations based on the amount of white ancestry a person had and the lightness of his or her skin. Unlike the case in Florida, Louisiana's distinctive black and mixed-race population did not leave when the colony became part of the United States in 1803.

African Americans in New Spain's Northern Borderlands

What is today the southwestern portion of the United States was from the sixteenth century to 1821 the northernmost part of New Spain. Centered on Mexico, this Spanish colony reached into Texas, California, New Mexico, and Arizona. The first people of African descent who entered this huge region were members of Spanish exploratory expeditions. As we mentioned earlier, the best known of them was Esteban, an enslaved *Moor*, which was the Spanish term for a dark-skinned Muslim, who survived a shipwreck on the Texas coast in 1529 and joined Spanish explorer Alva Núñez Cabeza de Vaca in an arduous seven-year trek from Texas to Mexico City. Esteban, a skilled interpreter, later explored regions in what are today New Mexico and Arizona.

During the colonial era, however, New Spain's North American borderlands had far fewer black people than there were in the British colonies. In part this was because the total non-Indian population in the borderlands was extremely small. As late as 1792, for example, only around 3,000 colonists lived in Texas, including about 450 described as black or mulatto. There were even fewer colonists in New Mexico and California where people of mixed African, Indian, and Spanish descent were common. Black men in the borderlands gained employment as sailors, soldiers, tradesmen, cattle herders, and day laborers. Some of them were slaves, but others had limited freedom. In contrast to the British colonies, in New Spain's borderlands most slaves were Indians. They worked as domestics and as agricultural laborers or were marched south to Mexico where they labored in gold and silver mines.

Also in contrast to the British mainland colonies, where no formal aristocracy existed but where white insistence on racial separation gradually grew in strength, there were in New Spain's borderlands both hereditary rank and racial fluidity. In theory throughout the Spanish Empire in the Americas, "racial purity" determined social status, with Spaniards of "pure blood" at the top and Africans and Indians at the bottom. In Texas, for example, free black people and Indians suffered legal disabilities. They paid special taxes and could not own guns or travel freely. But almost all of the Spaniards who moved north from Mexico were themselves of mixed race, and people of African and Indian descent could more easily acquire status than was the case in the British colonies. In 1783 Spain's royal government began to allow black people and Indians to elevate themselves legally by paying between seven hundred and one thousand pesos, a substantial sum at the time. By this means they could acquire hereditary rank and great power over those who labored for them.

Black Women in Colonial America

The lives of black women in early North America varied according to the colony in which they lived. The differences between Britain's New England colonies and its southern colonies are particularly clear. In New England, where religion and demographics made the boundary between slavery and freedom permeable, black women distinguished themselves in a variety of ways. The thoroughly acculturated Lucy Terry Prince of Deerfield, Massachusetts, published poetry during the 1740s and had gained her freedom by 1756. Other black women succeeded as bakers and weavers. But in the South, where most black women of the time lived, they had few opportunities for work beyond the tobacco and rice fields and domestic labor in the homes of their masters.

During the late seventeenth and the eighteenth centuries, approximately 90 percent of southern black women worked in the fields, as was customary for women in West Africa. White women sometimes did fieldwork as well, but masters considered black women to be tougher than white women and therefore able to do more hard physical labor. Black women also mothered their children and cooked for their families, a chore that involved lugging firewood and water and tending fires as well as preparing meals. Like other women of their time, colonial black women suffered from inadequate medical attention while giving birth. But because black women worked until the moment they delivered, they were more likely than white women to experience complications in giving birth and to bear low-weight babies.

As the eighteenth century passed, more black women became house servants. Yet most jobs as maids, cooks, and body servants went to the young, the old, or the infirm. Black women also wet-nursed their master's children. None of this was easy work; those who did it were under constant white supervision and were particularly subject to the sexual exploitation that characterized chattel slavery.

European captains and crews molested and raped black women during the middle passage. Masters and overseers similarly used their power to force themselves on female slaves. The results were evident in the large mixed-race populations in the colonies and in the psychological damage it inflicted on African-American women and their mates. In particular, the sexual abuse of black women by white men disrupted the emerging black families in North America because black men usually could not protect their wives from it.

Black Resistance and Rebellion

Slavery in America was always a system that relied ultimately on physical force to deny freedom to African Americans. From its start, black men and women responded by resisting their masters as well as they could.

Such resistance ranged from sullen goldbricking (shirking assigned work) to sabotage, escape, and rebellion. Before the late eighteenth century, however, resistance and rebellion were not part of a coherent antislavery effort. Slave resistance and revolt did not aim to destroy slavery as a social system. Africans and African Americans resisted, escaped, and rebelled not as part of an effort to free all slaves. Instead, in the case of resistance, they aimed to force masters to make concessions within the framework of slavery and, in the case of escape and rebellion, to relieve themselves, their friends, and their families from intolerable disgrace and suffering.

African men and women newly arrived in North America were most open in defying their masters. They frequently refused to work and often could not be persuaded by punishment to change their behavior. "You would really be surpris'd at their Perseverance," one frustrated master commented. "They often die before they can be conquered." Africans tended to escape in groups of individuals who shared a common homeland and language. When they succeeded, they usually became "outliers," living nearby and stealing from their master's estate. In some instances, escaped slaves, known as *maroons*—a term derived from the Spanish word *cimarron*, meaning wild—established their own settlements in inaccessible regions.

The most durable of such maroon communities in North America existed in the Spanish colony of Florida. In 1693 the Spanish king officially made this colony a refuge for slaves escaping from the British colonies, although he did not free slaves who were already there. Many such escapees joined the Seminole Indian nation and thereby gained protection during the period between 1763 and 1783 when the British ruled Florida and after 1821 when the United States took control. It was in part to destroy this refuge for escaped slaves that the United States fought the Seminole War from 1835 to 1842.

As slaves became acculturated, forms of slave resistance changed. To avoid punishment, African Americans replaced open defiance with more subtle day-to-day obstructionism. They malingered, broke tools, mistreated domestic animals, destroyed crops, poisoned their masters, and stole. Not every slave who acted this way, of course, was consciously resisting enslavement, but masters assumed that they were. Acculturation also brought different escape patterns. Increasingly, it was the more assimilated slaves who escaped. They were predominantly young men who left on their own and relied on their knowledge of American society to pass as free.

Rebellions were far rarer in colonial North America than resistance or escape. More and larger rebellions broke out during the early eighteenth century in Jamaica and Brazil. This discrepancy resulted mainly from demographics: in the sugar-producing colonies, black people outnumbered white people by six or eight to one, whereas in British North America, black people were a majority only in the low country. The more slaves outnumbered white people, the more likely they were to rebel.

Nevertheless, there were waves of rebellion in British North America during the years from 1710 to 1722 and 1730 to 1741. Men born in Africa took the lead in these revolts, and the two most notable ones occurred in New York City in 1712 and near Charleston, South Carolina, in 1739. In New York, twenty-seven Africans, taking revenge for "hard usage," set fire to an outbuilding. When white men arrived to put out the blaze, the rebels attacked them with muskets, hatchets, and swords. They killed nine of the white men and wounded six. Shortly thereafter, local militia units captured the rebels, six of whom killed themselves. The other twenty-one were executed—some brutally. In 1741 a conspiracy to revolt in the same city led to another mass execution. Authorities put to death thirty black people and four white people, convicted of helping them.

Even more frightening for most white people was the rebellion that began at Stono Bridge within twenty miles of Charleston in September 1739. Under the leadership of a man named Jemmy or Tommy, twenty slaves, who had recently arrived from Angola, broke into a "weare-house, & then plundered it of guns & ammunition." They killed the warehousemen, left their severed heads on the building's steps, and fled toward Florida. Other slaves joined the Angolans until their numbers reached one hundred. They sacked plantations and killed approximately thirty more white people. But when they stopped to celebrate their victories and beat drums to attract other slaves, planters on horseback aided by Indians routed them, killing forty-four and dispersing the rest. Many of the rebels, including their leader, remained at large for up to three years, as did the spirit of insurrection. In 1740 Charleston authorities arrested 150 slaves and hanged ten daily to quell that spirit.

TIMELINE

AFRICAN-AMERICAN EVENTS	AMERICAN EVENTS
1450	
	1492 Columbus reaches the West Indies
	1497 John Cabot's voyage to North America for England

continued

AFRICAN-AMERICAN EVENTS	AMERICAN EVENTS
1500	
1526 African slaves arrive at failed Spanish colony in present-day South Carolina One hundred African slaves arrive in present-day South Carolina **1529** Esteban shipwrecked on Texas coast	**1519** Spanish conquest of Aztecs **1532** Spanish conquest of Incas
1550	
1565 Africans help establish St. Augustine	**1565** St. Augustine established **1587** Roanoke colony established
1600	
1619 Twenty-two Africans reported to be living in Jamestown. Twenty more arrive **1624** First documented African-American child born at Jamestown	**1607** Jamestown established **1612** Tobacco cultivated in Virginia by John Rolfe
1650	
1640–1670 Evidence of emergence of black slavery in Virginia **1693** Spanish Florida welcomes escaped slaves from the British colonies	**1670** Carolina established **1676** Bacon's Rebellion **1699** Louisiana established
1700	
1712 New York City slave revolt **1739** Stono slave revolt **1741** New York City revolt conspiracy	**c. 1700** Rice cultivation begun in the Carolina low country **1732** Georgia chartered **c. 1738** The Great Awakening begins
1750	
1776 Declaration of Independence	**1754–1763** French and Indian War
1800	

In South Carolina and other southern colonies, white people never entirely lost their fear of slave revolt. Whenever slaves rebelled or were rumored to rebel, the fear became intense. As the quotation that begins this chapter indicates, the unwillingness of many Africans and African Americans to submit to enslavement pushed white southerners into a siege mentality that became a determining factor in American history.

Conclusion

Studying the history of black people in early America is both painful and exhilarating. It is painful to learn of their enslavement, the emergence of racism in its modern form, and the loss of so much of the African heritage. But it is exhilarating to learn how much of that heritage Africans and African Americans were able to preserve, how they rebelled against and resisted their oppression and forged strong family bonds, and how an emerging African-American culture began to influence all aspects of American society.

The varieties of black life during the colonial period also help us understand the complexity of African-American society later in American history. Although they had much in common, black people in the Chesapeake, in the low country, in Britain's northern colonies, in Spanish Florida, in French Louisiana, and in New Spain's borderlands had different experiences, relationships with white people and Indians, and prospects. Those who lived in the fledgling colonial towns and cities differed from those who were agricultural laborers. The lives of those who worked on small farms were quite different from the lives of those who served on large plantations.

Finally, African-American history during the colonial era raises fundamental issues about contingency and determinism in human events. Did economic necessity, racism, and class interest make the development of chattel slavery in the Chesapeake inevitable? Or had things gone otherwise (e.g., if Bacon's Rebellion had not occurred or had turned out differently), might African Americans in that region have retained more rights and more access to freedom? What then would have been the impact on the colonies to the north and south of the Chesapeake?

Review Questions

1. Based on your reading of this chapter, do you believe racial prejudice among British settlers in the Chesapeake led them to enslave Africans? Or did the unfree condition of the first Africans to arrive at Jamestown lead to racial prejudice among the settlers?
2. Why did vestiges of African culture survive in British North America? Did these vestiges help or hinder African Americans in dealing with enslavement?
3. Compare and contrast eighteenth-century slavery as it existed in the Chesapeake, in the low country of South Carolina and Georgia, and in the northern colonies.
4. What were the strengths and weaknesses of the black family in the eighteenth century?
5. How did enslaved Africans and African Americans preserve a sense of their own humanity?

Recommended Reading

Ira Berlin. *Many Thousands Gone: The First Two Centuries of Slavery in North America.* Cambridge, MA: Belknap Press, 1998. Berlin presents an impressive synthesis of black life in slavery during the seventeenth and eighteenth centuries that emphasizes the ability of black people to shape their lives in conflict with the will of masters.

Winthrop D. Jordan. *White over Black: American Attitudes toward the Negro, 1550–1812.* Chapel Hill: University of North Carolina Press, 1968. This classic study provides a probing and detailed analysis of the cultural and psychological forces that led white people to enslave black people in early America.

Peter Kolchin. *American Slavery, 1619–1877.* New York: Hill and Wang, 1993. This is the best brief study of the development of slavery in America. It is particularly useful on African-American community and culture.

Philip D. Morgan. *Slave Counterpoint: Black Culture in the Eighteenth-Century Chesapeake and Lowcountry.* Chapel Hill: University of North Carolina Press, 1998. Comparative history at its best, this book illuminates the lives of black people in important parts of British North America.

Oscar Reiss. *Blacks in Colonial America.* Jefferson, NC: McFarland, 1997. Although short on synthesis and eccentric in interpretation, this book is packed with information about black life in early America.

Peter H. Wood. *Black Majority: Negroes in Colonial South Carolina from 1670 through the Stono Rebellion.* New York: Norton, 1974. This is the best account available of slavery and the origins of African-American culture in the colonial low country.

Donald R. Wright. *African Americans in the Colonial Era: From African Origins through the American Revolution,* 2d ed. Arlington Heights, IL: Harlan Davidson, 2000. Wright provides a brief but well-informed survey of black history during the colonial period.

• C H A P T E R   F O U R •

RISING EXPECTATIONS

AFRICAN AMERICANS AND THE STRUGGLE FOR INDEPENDENCE, 1763–1783

THE CRISIS OF THE BRITISH EMPIRE

The great struggle for empire between Great Britain and France created the circumstances within which an independence movement and rising black hopes for freedom developed in America. Starting in 1689 the British and French fought a series of wars in Europe, India, North America, Africa, and the Caribbean Sea. This great conflict climaxed during the French and Indian War that began in North America in 1754, spread in 1756 to Europe, where it was called the Seven Years' War, and from there to other parts of the world.

By 1763 Britain had forced France to withdraw from North America. Britain took Canada from France and Florida from France's ally Spain. In compensation, Spain received New Orleans and the huge French province of Louisiana in central North America.

After the war ended, British officials decided Americans should be taxed to pay their share of the costs of empire and their commerce should be more closely regulated. In England it seemed entirely reasonable that the government should proceed in this manner, but white Americans had become accustomed to governing themselves, trading with whom they pleased, and paying only local taxes. They were well aware that with the French and Spanish gone, they no longer needed British protection. Therefore, many of them resisted when the British Parliament asserted its power to tax and govern them.

During the 1760s Parliament repeatedly passed laws that many Americans considered oppressive. The Proclamation Line of 1763 aimed to placate Britain's Indian allies by forbidding American settlement west of the crest of the Appalachian Mountains. The Sugar Act of 1764 levied import duties designed, for the first time in colonial history, to raise revenue for Britain rather than simply to regulate American trade. In 1765 the Stamp Act, also passed to raise revenue, heavily taxed printed materials, such as deeds, newspapers, and playing cards.

In response, Americans at the Stamp Act Congress held in New York City in October 1765 took their first step toward united resistance. By agreeing not to import British goods, the congress forced Parliament in 1766 to repeal the Stamp Act. But the

Sugar Act and Proclamation Line remained in force, and Parliament soon indicated that it remained determined to exercise greater control in America.

In 1767 it forced the New York assembly to provide quarters for British troops and enacted the Townshend Acts, named after the British finance minister, which taxed glass, lead, paint, paper, and tea imported into the colonies from Britain. Resistance to these taxes in Boston led the British government to station two regiments of troops there in 1768. The volatile situation this created led in 1770 to the Boston Massacre when a small detachment of British troops fired into an angry crowd, killing five Bostonians. Among the dead was a black sailor named Crispus Attucks, who had taken the lead in accosting the soldiers and became a martyr to the Patriot cause.

The Tea Act gave the British East India Company a monopoly over all tea sold in the American colonies. At the time, Americans drank a great deal of tea and Parliament hoped the tea monopoly would save the company from bankruptcy. But American merchants assumed the act was the first step in a plot to bankrupt them. Because it had huge tea reserves, the East India Company could sell its tea much more cheaply than colonial merchants could. Other Americans believed British leaders would use it as a precedent to raise additional taxes.

In December 1773 Boston's radical Sons of Liberty dumped a shipload of tea into the harbor. Britain then sent more troops to Boston in early 1774 and punished the city economically. This action sparked resistance throughout the colonies and led eventually to American independence. Patriot leaders organized the Continental Congress, which met in Philadelphia in September 1774 and demanded the repeal of all "oppressive" legislation.

In April 1775 Minutemen clashed with British troops at Lexington and Concord near Boston. This was the first battle in what became a war for independence. Shortly thereafter, Congress appointed George Washington commander in chief of the Continental Army. Before he took command, however, the American and British forces at Boston fought a bloody battle at Bunker Hill. After a year during which other armed clashes occurred and the British rejected a compromise, Congress in July 1776 declared the colonies to be independent states, and the war became a revolution.

The Declaration of Independence and African Americans

The Declaration of Independence that the Continental Congress adopted on July 4, 1776, was drafted by a slaveholder in a slaveholding country. When Thomas Jefferson wrote "that all men are created equal; that they are endowed by their Creator with certain unalienable rights; that among these are life, liberty, and the pursuit of happiness," he was not supporting black claims for freedom. Men like Jefferson and John Adams, who served on the drafting committee with Jefferson, frequently distinguished between the rights of white men of British descent and a lack of rights for people of color. So convinced were Jefferson and his colleagues that black people could not claim the same rights as white people that they felt no need to qualify their words proclaiming universal liberty.

Yet, although Jefferson and the other delegates did not mean to encourage African Americans to hope the American War for Independence could become a war against slavery, that is what African Americans believed. Black people were in attendance when Patriot speakers made unqualified claims for human equality and natural rights; they read accounts of such speeches and heard white people discuss them. In response African Americans began to assert that such principles logically applied as much to them as to the white population. They forced white people to confront the contradiction between the new nation's professed ideals and its reality. Most white people did not deny that black people were human beings. White citizens therefore had to choose between accepting the literal meaning of the Declaration, which meant changing American society, or rejecting the revolutionary ideology that supported their claims for independence.

The Impact of the Enlightenment

At the center of that ideology was the European Enlightenment. The roots of this intellectual movement, also known as the Age of Reason, lay in Renaissance secularism and humanism dating back to the fifteenth century. But it was Isaac Newton's *Principia Mathematica,* published in England in 1687, that shaped a new way of perceiving human beings and their universe.

In his essay "Concerning Human Understanding," published in 1690, John Locke maintained that human society—like the physical universe—ran according to natural laws. He contended that at the base of human laws were natural rights all people shared. Human beings, according to Locke, created governments to protect their natural individual rights to life, liberty, and private property. If a government failed to perform this basic duty and became oppressive, he insisted, the people had the right to overthrow it. Locke saw no contradiction between these principles and human slavery, but during the eighteenth century, that contradiction became increasingly clear.

Most Americans became acquainted with Locke's ideas through pamphlets that a radical English political minority produced during the early eighteenth century. This literature portrayed the British government of the day as a conspiracy aimed at depriving British subjects of their natural rights, reducing them to slaves, and establishing tyranny. After the French and Indian War, during the 1760s, Americans, both black and white, interpreted British policies and actions from this same perspective.

The influence of such pamphlets is clear between 1763 and 1776 when white Patriot leaders charged that the British government sought to enslave them by depriving them of their rights as Englishmen. When they made these charges, they had difficulty denying that they themselves deprived African Americans of their natural rights. George Washington, for example, declared in 1774 that "the crisis is arrived when we must assert our rights, or submit to every imposition, that can be heaped upon us, till custom and use shall make us tame and abject, as the blacks we rule over with such arbitrary sway."

African Americans in the Revolutionary Debate

During the 1760s and 1770s when powerful slaveholders such as George Washington talked of liberty, natural rights, and hatred of enslavement, African Americans listened. Most of them had been born in America, they had absorbed English culture, they were united as a people, and they knew their way in colonial society. Those who lived in or near towns and cities had access to public meetings and newspapers. They were aware of the disputes with Great Britain and the contradictions between demanding liberty for oneself and denying it to others. They understood that the ferment of the 1760s had shaken traditional assumptions about government, and many of them hoped for more changes.

The greatest source of optimism for African Americans was the expectation that white Patriot leaders would realize their revolutionary principles were incompatible with slavery. Those in England who believed white Americans must submit to British authority pointed out the contradiction. Samuel Johnson, the most famous writer in London, asked, "How is it that we hear the loudest yelps for liberty among the drivers of negroes?" But white Americans made similar comments. As early as 1763, James Otis of Massachusetts warned that "those who every day barter away other mens['] liberty, will soon care little for their own." Thomas Paine, whose pamphlet *Common Sense* rallied Americans to endorse independence in 1776, asked them to contemplate "with what consistency, or decency they complain so loudly of attempts to enslave them, while they hold so many hundred thousands in slavery; and annually enslave many thousands more."

It was in New England—the heartland of anti-British radicalism—that African Americans formally made their case for freedom. African Americans in Massachusetts, New Hampshire, and Connecticut also petitioned their colonial or state legislatures for gradual emancipation. These petitions indicate that the black men who signed them were familiar with revolutionary rhetoric. African Americans learned this rhetoric as they joined white radicals to confront British authority.

In 1765 black men demonstrated against the Stamp Act in Boston. They rioted against British troops there in 1768 and joined Crispus Attucks in 1770. Black Minutemen stood with their white comrades at Lexington and Concord. In 1773 black petitioners from Boston told a delegate to the colonial assembly, "We expect great things from men who have made such a noble stand against the designs of their *fellow-men* to enslave them. . . . The divine spirit of *freedom,* seems to fire every human breast."

Black Enlightenment

Besides influencing radical political discourse during the revolutionary era, the Enlightenment also shaped the careers of America's first black intellectuals. Because it emphasized human reason, the Enlightenment led to the establishment of colleges and libraries in Europe and America. These institutions usually served a tiny elite, but newspapers and pamphlets made science and literature available to the masses. The eighteenth century was also an era in which amateurs could make serious contributions to human knowledge. Some of these amateurs, such as Thomas Jefferson and Benjamin Franklin, were rich and well educated. They made discoveries in botany and electricity while pursuing political careers. What is striking is that some African Americans, whose advantages were far more limited, also became scientists and authors.

Because they had easier access to evangelical Protestantism than to secular learning, most African Americans who gained intellectual distinction during the late eighteenth century owed more to the Great Awakening than to the Enlightenment. The best known of these is Jupiter Hammon, a Long Island slave who published religious poetry in the 1760s. There were also Josiah Bishop and Lemuel Haynes, black ministers to white church congregations in Virginia and New England. But Phillis Wheatley and Benjamin Banneker, who were directly influenced by the Enlightenment, became the most famous black intellectuals of their time.

Phillis Wheatley

Wheatley came to Boston from Africa—possibly near the Gambia River—in 1761 aboard a slaver. She was seven or eight years old, small, frail, and nearly naked. John Wheatley, a wealthy merchant, purchased her as a servant for his wife. Although Phillis spoke no English when her ship docked, she was soon reading and writing in that language and studying Latin. She pored over the Bible and became a fervent Christian. She also read the fashionable poetry of British author Alexander Pope and became a poet herself by the age of thirteen.

For the rest of her short life, Wheatley wrote poems to celebrate important events. Like Pope's, Wheatley's poetry reflected the aesthetic values of the Enlightenment. She aimed to blend thought, image, sound, and rhythm to provide a perfectly balanced composition. In 1773 the Wheatleys sent her to London where her first book of poems—the first book ever by an African-American woman and the second by any American woman—was published under the title *Poems on Various Subjects, Religious and Moral.* The Wheatleys freed Phillis after her return to Boston, although she continued to live in their house until both of them died. In 1778 she married John Peters, a black grocer, but was soon mired in illness and poverty. Two of her children died in infancy, and she herself died in December 1784 giving birth to her third child, who died with her.

Wheatley was an advocate and symbol of the adoption of white culture by black people. Before her marriage, she lived almost exclusively among white people and absorbed their values. For example, although she lamented the sorrow her capture had caused her parents, she was grateful to have been brought to America:

> *'Twas mercy brought me from my Pagan land,*
> *Taught my benighted soul to understand*
> *That there's a God, that there's a Saviour too:*
> *Once I redemption neither sought nor knew.*

But Wheatley did not simply copy her masters' views. Although the Wheatleys were loyal to Britain, she became a fervent Patriot. She attended Boston's Old North Church, a hotbed of anti-British sentiment, and wrote poems supporting the Patriot cause. In early 1776, for example, she lavishly praised George Washington, "fam'd for thy valour, for thy virtues more," and received effusive thanks from the general.

Wheatley also became an advocate and symbol of John Locke's ideas concerning the influence of environment on human beings. White leaders of the Revolution and intellectuals debated whether black people were inherently inferior in intellect to white people or whether this perceived black inferiority was the result of enslavement. Some slaveholders, such as Thomas Jefferson, who held racist assumptions about

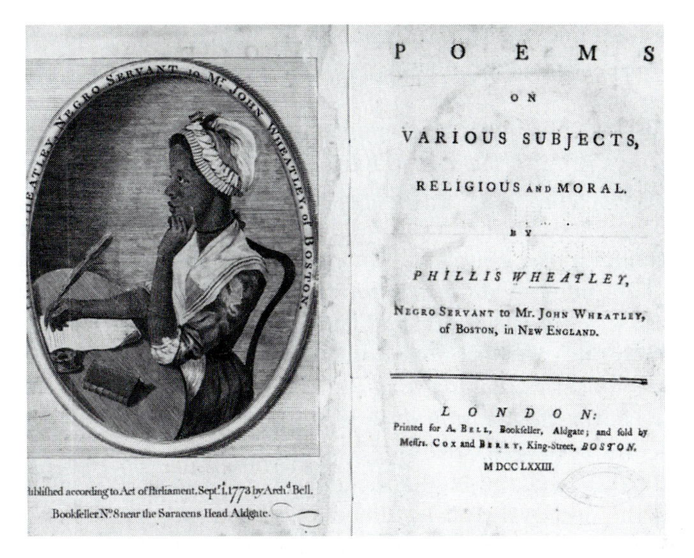

P O E M S
ON
VARIOUS SUBJECTS,
RELIGIOUS AND MORAL.
BY
PHILLIS WHEATLEY,
NEGRO SERVANT to MR. JOHN WHEATLEY,
of BOSTON, in NEW ENGLAND.

LONDON:
Printed for A. BELL, Bookfeller, Aldgate; and fold by
Meffrs. COX and BERRY, King-Street, BOSTON.
M DCC LXXIII.

A frontispiece portrait of Phillis Wheatley precedes the title page of her first book of poetry, which was published in 1773. The portrait suggests Wheatley's small physique and studious manner.
Courtesy of the Library of Congress

innate black inferiority, dismissed Wheatley's work as "below the dignity of criticism." But those who favored an environmental perspective considered Wheatley an example of what people of African descent could achieve if freed from oppression. She made her own views clear:

> *Some view our sable race with scornful eye,*
> *"Their colour is a diabolic dye."*
> *Remember,* Christians, Negroes, *black as* Cain,
> *May be refin'd, and join th' angelic train.*

Benjamin Banneker

In the breadth of his achievement, Benjamin Banneker is even more representative of the Enlightenment than Phillis Wheatley. Like hers, his life epitomizes a flexibility concerning race that the revolutionary era briefly promised to expand.

Banneker was born free in Maryland in 1731 and died in 1806. The son of a mixed-race mother and an African father, he inherited a farm near Baltimore from his white grandmother. As a child, Banneker, whose appearance was described by a contemporary to be "decidedly Negro," attended a racially integrated school. His farm gave him a steady income and the leisure to study literature and science.

With access to the library of his white neighbor George Ellicott, Banneker "mastered Latin and Greek and had a good working knowledge of German and French." By the 1770s he had a reputation as a man "of uncommonly soft and gentlemanly manners and of pleasing colloquial powers." Like Jefferson, Franklin, and others of his time, Banneker was fascinated with mechanics and in 1770 constructed his own clock. However, he gained international fame as a mathematician and astronomer. Because of his knowledge in these disciplines, he became a member of the survey commission for Washington, D.C. This made him the first black civilian employee of the U.S. government. Between 1791 and 1796, he published an almanac based on his observations and mathematical calculations.

Like Wheatley, Banneker had thoroughly assimilated white culture and was keenly aware of the fundamental issues of human equality associated with the American Revolution. In 1791 he sent Thomas Jefferson, who was then U.S. secretary of state, a copy of his almanac to refute Jefferson's claim in *Notes on the State of Virginia* that black people were inherently inferior intellectually to white people. Noting Jefferson's commitment to the biblical statement that God had created "us all of one flesh," and Jefferson's words in the Declaration of Independence, Banneker called the great man to account concerning slavery.

Referring to the Declaration, Banneker wrote, "You were then impressed with proper ideas of the great valuation of liberty, and the free possession of those blessings, to which you were entitled by nature; but, Sir, how pitiable is it to reflect, that altho you were so fully convinced of the benevolence of the Father of Mankind, and of his equal and impartial distribution of these rights and privileges . . . that you should at the Same time counteract his mercies, in detaining by fraud and violence so numerous a part of my brethren, under groaning captivity and cruel oppression."

African Americans in the War for Independence

When it came to fighting between Patriots on one side and the British and their Loyalist American allies on the other, African Americans joined the side that offered freedom. In the South, where the British held out the promise of freedom in exchange for military service, black men eagerly fought on the British side as Loyalists.

The war began in earnest in August 1776 when the British landed a large army at Brooklyn, New York, and drove Washington's Continental Army across New Jersey into Pennsylvania. The military and diplomatic turning point in the war came the following year at Saratoga, New York, when a poorly executed British strategy to take control of the Hudson River led British general John Burgoyne to surrender his entire army to Patriot forces. This victory led France and other European powers to enter the war against Britain. Significant fighting ended in October 1781 when Washington forced Lord Cornwallis to surrender another British army at Yorktown, Virginia.

When Washington had organized the Continental Army in July 1775, he forbade the enlistment of new black troops and the reenlistment of black men who had served at Lexington and Concord, Bunker Hill, and other early battles. Shortly thereafter, all thirteen states followed Washington's example. Several reasons account for Washington's decision and its ratification by the Continental Congress. Although several black men had served during the French and Indian War, the colonies had traditionally excluded African Americans from militia service. Like others before them, Patriot leaders feared that if they enlisted African-American soldiers, it would encourage slaves to leave their masters without permission. White people—especially in the South—also feared that armed black men would endanger the social order. Paradoxically, white people simultaneously believed black men were too cowardly to be effective soldiers. Although apparently contradictory, these last two beliefs persisted into the twentieth century.

Black Loyalists

Because so many Patriot leaders resisted employing black troops, by mid-1775 the British had taken the initiative in recruiting African Americans. From Maryland southward, during the spring of that year, rumors circulated that the British would instigate slave revolt. However, no such uprisings occurred. Instead, many slaves escaped and sought British protection as Loyalists. The British employed most black men who escaped to their lines as laborers and foragers.

Black Loyalists were most numerous in the low country of South Carolina and Georgia. At the end of the war in 1783, approximately twenty thousand African Americans left with the British forces as they evacuated Savannah and Charleston. A few who remained carried out guerrilla warfare there until 1786.

The most famous British appeal to African Americans to fight for the empire in return for freedom came in Virginia. On November 7, 1775, Lord Dunmore, the last royal governor of the Old Dominion, issued a proclamation offering to liberate slaves who joined "His Majesty's Troops . . . for the more speedily reducing this Colony to a proper sense of their duty to His Majesty's crown and dignity." Among those who responded to Dunmore's offer was Ralph Henry, a twenty-six-year-old slave of Patrick Henry. Perhaps Ralph Henry recalled his famous master's "Give me liberty or give me death" speech.

Dunmore recruited black soldiers out of desperation, although he became the strongest advocate—on either the British or American side—of their fighting ability. When he issued his appeal, Dunmore had only three hundred British troops and had been driven from Williamsburg, the colonial capital. Mainly because Dunmore had to seek refuge on British warships, only about eight hundred African Americans managed to reach his forces. Defeat by the Patriots at the Battle of Great Bridge in December 1775 curtailed his efforts.

But Dunmore's proclamation and the black response to it struck a tremendous psychological blow against his enemies. Of Dunmore's six hundred troops at Great Bridge, half were African Americans whose uniforms bore the motto "Liberty to Slaves." As more and more Virginia slaves escaped, masters blamed Dunmore. Throughout the war, other British and Loyalist commanders followed his example, recruiting thousands of black men who worked and sometimes fought in exchange for their freedom. In all, more African Americans became active Loyalists than Patriots during the war.

Five hundred of Dunmore's black troops died of typhus or smallpox. When he had to abandon Virginia, the remainder sailed with his fleet to New York City (which had become British headquarters in America). One of them, the notorious Colonel Tye, conducted guerrilla raids in Monmouth County, New Jersey, for several years. Until he was killed in 1780, Tye and his interracial band of about twenty-five Loyalists plundered villages, spiked cannons, and kidnapped Patriot officers.

AFRICAN AMERICANS AND THE WAR FOR INDEPENDENCE	
April 18, 1775	Black Minutemen participate in Battle of Lexington and Concord.
May 10, 1775	The Second Continental Congress convenes in Philadelphia.
June 15, 1775	Congress appoints George Washington commander in chief of the new Continental Army.
June 17, 1775	Black men fight with the Patriots at Bunker Hill.
November 7, 1775	Lord Dunmore, the royal governor of Virginia, offers freedom to slaves who will fight for the British.
July 9, 1775	George Washington bans African-American enlistment in the Continental Army.
December 30, 1775	Washington allows black reenlistments in the Continental Army.

Black Patriots

Washington's July 1775 policy to the contrary, black men fought on the Patriot side from the very beginning of the Revolutionary War to its conclusion (see Map 4–1). Prior to Washington's arrival in Massachusetts, there were black Minutemen at Lexington and Concord; and some of the same men distinguished themselves at the bloody Battle of Bunker Hill in June 1775.

It was Dunmore's use of African-American soldiers that prompted Washington to reconsider his ban on black enlistment. "If that man, Dunmore," he wrote in late 1775, "is not crushed before the Spring he will become the most dangerous man in America. His strength will increase like a snowball running down hill. Success will depend on which side can arm the Negro faster." After having received encouragement from black veterans, Washington, on December 30, 1775, allowed African-American reenlistment in the Continental Army. Congress, fearful of alienating slaveholders, initially would not allow him to go further. By the end of 1776, however, troop shortages forced Congress and the state governments to recruit black soldiers in earnest for the Continental Army and state militias. Even then, South Carolina and Georgia refused to permit black men to serve in regiments raised within their boundaries, although black men from these states joined other Patriot units.

The Patriot recruitment policy changed most quickly in New England. In early 1777 Massachusetts opened its militia to black men, and Rhode Island formed a black regiment. Connecticut enabled masters to free their slaves to serve as substitutes for the masters or their sons in the militia or Continental Army. New York and New Jersey adopted similar statutes.

Also in 1777, when Congress set state enlistment quotas for the Continental Army, state recruitment officers began to fill those quotas with black men so white men might serve closer to home in the militia. With considerable reluctance, the southern states of Delaware, Maryland, Virginia, and North Carolina began enlisting free black men. Of these states, only Maryland allowed slaves to serve in return for freedom, but the others sometimes allowed slaves to enlist as substitutes for their masters, and this usually led to freedom.

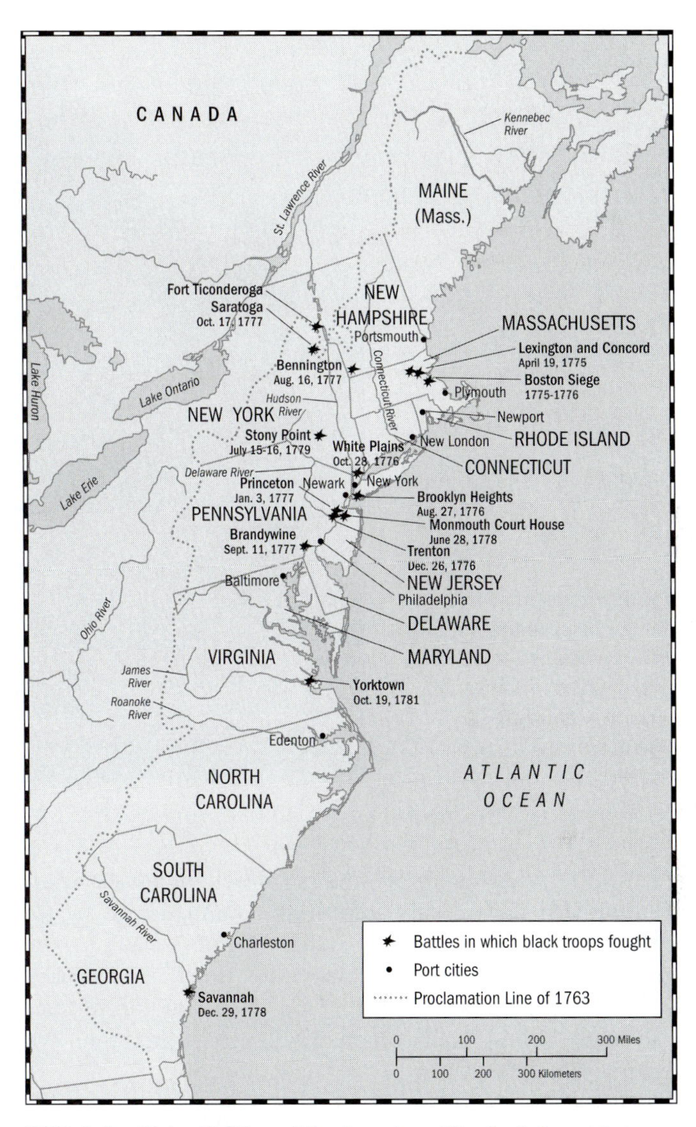

MAP 4–1 Major Battles of the American War for Independence, Indicating Those in Which Black Troops Participated. Black troops fought on both sides during the American War for Independence and participated in most of the major battles.

Adapted from *The Atlas of African-American History and Politics*, 1/e, by A. Smallwood and J. Elliot, © 1998, The McGraw-Hill Companies. Reproduced with permission of The McGraw-Hill Companies.

Except for Rhode Island's black regiment and some companies in Massachusetts, black Patriots served in integrated military units. Enrollment officers often did not specify a man's race when he enlisted, so it is difficult to know how many black men actually served in Patriot armies. The figure usually given is 5,000 black soldiers out of a total of 300,000. A few black men, such as Salem Poor, became junior officers. Others

The black soldier in this detail from John Trumbull's contemporary oil painting *The Battle of Bunker Hill* is presumed to be Peter Salem. The battle took place in June 1775. The "Peter Salem Gun" is on display at the Bunker Hill Monument.
The Granger Collection, New York

were drummers and fifers, sailors on privateers (merchant vessels armed and authorized by a government to raid enemy shipping) commissioned by the Continental Congress, and informants and spies.

There were also black women who supported the Patriot cause. As did white women, black women sometimes accompanied their soldier husbands into army camps, if not into battle. A few black women also demonstrated their sympathy for the Patriots in defiance of British authority.

The Revolution and Emancipation

The willingness of African Americans to risk their lives in the Patriot cause encouraged northern legislatures to emancipate slaves within their borders. By the late 1770s, most of these legislatures were debating abolition. Petitions and lawsuits initiated by black people in Massachusetts, Connecticut, New Hampshire, and elsewhere encouraged such consideration. But an emerging market economy, the Great Awakening, and the Enlightenment established the cultural context in which people who believed deeply in the sanctity of private property could consider such a momentous change. Economic, religious, and intellectual change had convinced many that slavery should be abolished.

In the North, where all these forces operated and the economic stake in slave labor was relatively small, emancipation made steady progress. In the Chesapeake, where some of these forces operated, emancipationist sentiment grew and many masters manumitted their slaves, but there was no serious threat to the slave system. In the low country of South Carolina and Georgia, where economic interest and white solidarity against large black populations outweighed intellectual and religious considerations, white commitment to black bondage remained absolute.

The movement among white people to abolish slavery began within the Society of Friends, or Quakers. Quakers had always emphasized conscience, human brotherhood, and nonviolence. Moreover, many leading Quaker families were engaged in international business ventures that required educated, efficient, moral workers. This predisposed them against a system that forced workers to be uneducated, recalcitrant, and often ignorant of Christian religion. Growing numbers of Quakers, therefore, concluded that slaveholding was sinful, although members of the Society of Friends had owned and traded slaves for generations. Under Quaker leadership, antislavery societies came into existence in both the North and the Chesapeake. By 1774 such societies had joined African Americans in petitioning northern legislatures and, in one instance, the Continental Congress to act against slavery or the slave trade.

The Revolutionary Impact

In calling for emancipation, the antislavery societies emphasized black service in the war against British rule and the religious and economic progress of northern African Americans. They also contended that emancipation would prevent black rebellions. As a result, by 1784 all the northern states except New Jersey and New York had undertaken either immediate or gradual abolition of slavery. Delaware, Maryland, and Virginia made manumission easier. Even the deep South saw efforts to mitigate the most brutal excesses that slavery encouraged among masters. Many observers believed the Revolution had profoundly changed the prospects for African Americans.

In fact, the War for Independence dealt a heavy, although not mortal, blow to slavery (see Figure 4–1). While northern states prepared to abolish involuntary servitude, an estimated 100,000 slaves escaped from their masters in the South. In South Carolina alone, approximately 25,000 escaped—about 30 percent of the state's black population. Twenty thousand black people left with the British at the end of the war (see Map 4–2). Meanwhile, numerous escapees found their way to southern cities or to the North, where they became part of a rapidly expanding free black class.

In the Chesapeake, as well as in the North, individual slaves gained freedom either in return for service in the war or because their masters had embraced Enlightenment principles. The Virginia legislature ordered masters to free slaves who had fought for American independence.

Those Chesapeake slaves who did not become free also made gains during the Revolution because the war hastened the decline of tobacco raising. As planters switched to wheat and corn, they required fewer year-round, full-time workers. This encouraged them to free their excess labor force or to negotiate contracts that let slaves serve for a term of years rather than for life. Another alternative was for masters to allow slaves—primarily males—to practice skilled trades instead of doing fieldwork.

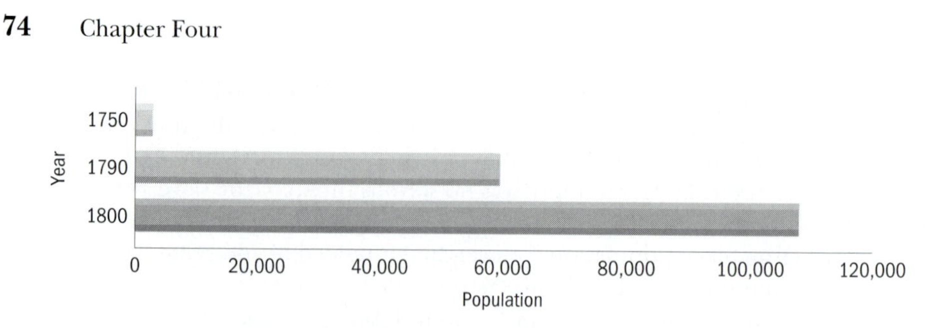

Figure 4–1 **The Free Black Population of the British North American Colonies in 1750 and of the United States in 1790 and 1800**
The impact of revolutionary ideology and a changing economy led to a great increase in the free black population during the 1780s and 1790s.
Source: *A Century of Population Growth in the United States, 1790–1900* (1909), p. 80. Data for 1750 estimated.

Such slaves were often hired out or "hired their own time" in return for giving their masters a large percentage of their wages.

Even those slaves who remained agricultural workers had more time to garden, hunt, and fish to supply themselves and their families with food and income. They gained more freedom to visit relatives who lived on other plantations, attend religious meetings, and interact with white people.

In South Carolina and Georgia, greater autonomy for slaves during the revolutionary era took a different form. The war increased absenteeism among masters and reduced contacts between the black and white populations. The black majorities in these regions grew larger, more isolated, and more African in culture as both South Carolina and Georgia imported more slaves from Africa. The constant arrival of Africans helped the region's African-American population retain a distinctive culture and the Gullah dialect. The increase in master absenteeism also permitted the task system of labor to expand.

The Revolutionary Promise

Most newly free African Americans lived in the Chesapeake. They gained their freedom by serving in the war or escaping or because of economic and ideological change. In 1782 Virginia had only 1,800 free people within a total black population of 220,582. By 1790 the state had 12,766 free people within a total black population of 306,193. By 1810 it was 30,570 within 423,088. Free black populations also grew in Delaware and Maryland, where—unlike Virginia—the number of slaves began a long decline.

But in South Carolina and Georgia, the free black class remained tiny. Most low-country free black people were the children of white slave owners. They tended to be less independent of their former masters than their Chesapeake counterparts and lighter complexioned because their freedom was often a result of a family relationship to their masters.

In the North and the Chesapeake, free African Americans frequently moved to cities. Boston, New York, Philadelphia, Baltimore, Richmond, and Norfolk gained substantial free black populations after the Revolution. Black women predominated in this migration because they could more easily find jobs as domestics in the cities than in rural areas. Cities also offered free black people opportunities for community development that did not exist in thinly settled farm country. Although African

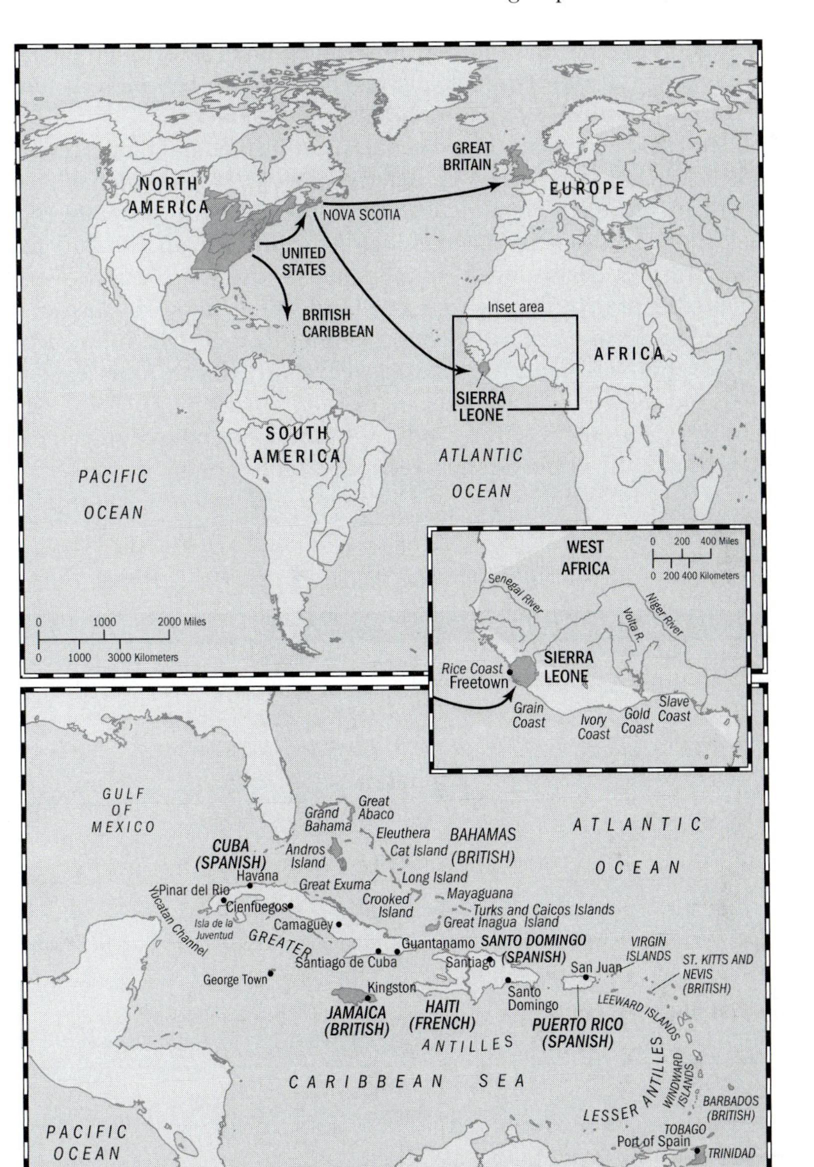

MAP 4–2 The Resettlement of Black Loyalists After the American War for Independence. Like their white Loyalist counterparts, many black Loyalists left with the British following the Patriot victory. Most of those who settled in Nova Scotia soon moved on to Great Britain or the British free black colony of Sierra Leone. Some black migrants to the British Caribbean were reenslaved.

Adapted from *The Atlas of African-American History and Politics*, 1/e, by A. Smallwood and J. Elliot, © 1998, The McGraw-Hill Companies. Reproduced with permission of The McGraw-Hill Companies.

Americans often used their new mobility to reunite families disrupted by slavery, relocating to a city could disrupt families that had survived enslavement. It took about a generation for stable, urban, two-parent households to emerge.

Newly freed black people also faced economic difficulty, and their occupational status often declined. Frequently they emerged from slavery without the economic resources needed to become independent farmers, shopkeepers, or tradespeople. In the North such economic restraints sometimes forced them to remain with their former masters long after formal emancipation. To make matters worse, white artisans used legal and extralegal means to protect themselves from black competition so African Americans who had learned trades as slaves had difficulty employing their skills in freedom.

Yet, in both the North and the Chesapeake, most African Americans refused to work for their old masters and left the site of their enslavement. Those who had escaped had to leave; for others, leaving indicated a desire to put the stigma of servitude behind and embrace the opportunities freedom offered despite the risks.

TIMELINE

AFRICAN-AMERICAN EVENTS	AMERICAN EVENTS
1750	
1750 Crippus Attucks escapes from slavery	**1754** French and Indian War begins
1755	
1760	
1760 Jupiter Hammon publishes a book of poetry **1761** Phillis Wheatley arrives in Boston	**1763** Expulsion of French power from North America **1764** Parliament passes Sugar Act
1765	
1765 African Americans in Boston join protests against Stamp Act **1766** Slaves in Charleston, South Carolina demand "liberty"	**1765** Stamp Act Congress
1770	
1770 Crispus Attucks is killed during Boston Massacre **1773** Phillis Wheatley publishes a book of poetry Black Bostonians petition for freedom	**1770** Boston Massacre **1773** Boston Tea Party

continued

AFRICAN-AMERICAN EVENTS	AMERICAN EVENTS
1775	
1775 Black Minutement fight at Lexington and Concord	**1775** Battles of Lexington and Concord
1776 Lord Dunmore recruits black soldiers in Virginia	**1776** Declaration of Independence
1777 Emancipation begins in the North	**1777** British general John Burgoyne surrenders at Saratoga
1780	
1781–1783 20,000 black Loyalists depart with the British troops	**1781** Cornwallis surrenders at Yorktown
	1783 Britain recognizes U.S. independence
1785	

CONCLUSION

In this chapter, we have sought to place the African-American experience during the struggle for independence in the broad context of revolutionary ideology derived from the Enlightenment. Black men and women, such as Benjamin Banneker and Phillis Wheatley, exemplified the intellectually liberating impact of eighteenth-century rationalism and recognized its application to black freedom.

Within the context of the war and with the assistance of white opponents of slavery, African Americans combined arguments for natural rights with action to gain freedom. The American Revolution seemed about to fulfill its promise of freedom to a minority of African Americans, and they were ready to embrace the opportunities it offered. By the end of the War for Independence in 1783, slavery was dying in the North and seemed to be on the wane in the Chesapeake. The first steps toward forming free black communities were under way. Black leaders and intellectuals had begun to emerge. Although most of their brothers and sisters remained in slavery, although the slave system began to expand again during the 1790s, and although free black people achieved *at best* second-class citizenship, they had made undeniable progress. Yet African Americans were also learning how difficult freedom could be despite the new republic's embrace of revolutionary ideals.

REVIEW QUESTIONS

1. How did the Enlightenment affect African Americans during the revolutionary era?
2. What was the relationship between the American Revolution and black freedom?

3. What was the role of African Americans in the War for Independence? How did their choices in this conflict affect how the war was fought?
4. How did the American Revolution encourage assimilation among African Americans? How did it discourage assimilation?
5. Why did a substantial class of free African Americans emerge from the revolutionary era?

Recommended Reading

Ira Berlin and Ronald Hoffman, eds. *Slavery and Freedom in the Age of the American Revolution.* Charlottesville: University Press of Virginia, 1983. The essays in this collection focus on black life in America during the revolutionary era.

David Brion Davis. *The Problem of Slavery in the Age of Revolution, 1770–1823.* Ithaca, NY: Cornell University Press, 1975. This magisterial study discusses the influence of the Enlightenment and the industrial revolution on slavery and opposition to slavery in the Atlantic world.

Sylvia R. Frey. Water *from the Rock: Black Resistance in a Revolutionary Age.* Princeton, NJ: Princeton University Press, 1991. This book portrays the War for Independence in the South as a three-way struggle among Patriots, British, and African Americans. It emphasizes the role of religion and community in black resistance to slavery.

Benjamin Quarles. *The Negro in the American Revolution,* 1961; reprint, New York: Norton, 1973. This classic study remains the most comprehensive account of black participation in the War for Independence. It also demonstrates the impact of the war on black life.

Ellen Gibson Wilson. *The Loyal Blacks.* New York: G. P. Putnam's Sons, 1976. This book discusses why many African Americans chose the British side in the War for Independence. It also focuses on the fate of those loyal blacks who departed Nova Scotia in Canada for Sierra Leone.

Arthur Zilversmit. *The First Emancipation: The Abolition of Slavery in the North.* Chicago: University of Chicago Press, 1967. Zilversmit discusses the rise of an antislavery movement in the North and the process of emancipation there during the revolutionary era.

• CHAPTER FIVE •

AFRICAN AMERICANS IN THE NEW NATION

1783–1820

Forces for Freedom

During the decades after the War for Independence ended in 1783, a strong trend in the North and the Chesapeake favored emancipation. It had roots in economic change, evangelical Christianity, and a revolutionary ethos based on the natural rights doctrines of the Enlightenment. African Americans took advantage of these forces to escape from slavery, purchase the freedom of their families and themselves, sue for freedom in the courts, and petition state legislatures to grant them equal rights.

In the postrevolutionary North, slavery, although widespread, was not economically essential. Farmers could more efficiently hire hands during the labor-intensive seasons of planting and harvesting than they could maintain a year-round slave labor force. Northern slaveholders, therefore, were a tiny class with limited political power. Moreover, transatlantic immigration brought to the North plenty of white laborers, who worked cheaply and resented slave competition. As the Great Awakening initiated a new religious morality, as natural rights doctrines flourished, and as a market economy based on wage labor emerged, northern slaveholders had difficulty defending perpetual black slavery.

The Abolition of Slavery in the North	
1777	Vermont constitutional convention prohibits slavery within what becomes the fourteenth state
1780	Pennsylvania begins gradually abolishing slavery within its borders
1783	Massachusetts's supreme court abolishes slavery there
1784	Connecticut and Rhode Island adopt gradual abolition plans
1785	New Jersey and New York legislatures defeat gradual abolition plans
1799	The New York legislature provides for gradual abolition within its jurisdiction
1804	New Jersey becomes the last northern state to initiate gradual abolition

In Chapter 4, we saw that emancipation in the North was a direct result of the War for Independence. But the *process* of doing away with slavery unfolded in these states only after the war. Meanwhile the national Congress set an important precedent in discouraging the expansion of slavery, and antislavery societies proliferated in the North and upper South.

Northern Emancipation

Slavery collapsed in the New England states because African Americans who lived there refused to remain in servitude and because most white residents acquiesced. The struggle against slavery in the middle states was longer and harder because more white people there had a vested interest in maintaining it (see Map 5–1). Vermont and

MAP 5–1 Emancipation and Slavery in the Early Republic. This map indicates the abolition policies adopted by the states of the Northeast between 1777 and 1804, the antislavery impact of the Northwest Ordinance of 1787, and extent of slavery in the South during the early republic.

Massachusetts, certainly, and New Hampshire, probably, abolished slavery immediately during the 1770s and 1780s. Vermont, where there had never been more than a few slaves, prohibited slavery in the constitution it adopted in 1777. Massachusetts, in its constitution of 1780, declared "that all men are born free and equal; and that every subject is entitled to liberty." Although this constitution did not specifically ban slavery, within a year Elizabeth Freeman and other slaves in Massachusetts sued under it for their freedom. In 1783 the Massachusetts Supreme Court ruling that "slavery is . . . as effectively abolished as it can be by the granting of rights and privileges wholly incompatible and repugnant to its existence." These decisions encouraged other Massachusetts slaves to sue for their freedom or to leave their masters.

As a result, the first U.S. census in 1790 found no slaves in Massachusetts. Even before then, black men in the state had gained the right to vote. In 1780 Paul and John Cuffe, free black brothers who lived in the town of Dartmouth, protested with five other free black men to the state legislature that they were being taxed without representation. After several setbacks, the courts finally decided in 1783 that African-American men who paid taxes in Massachusetts could vote there.

New Hampshire's record on emancipation is less clear than that of Vermont and Massachusetts. In 1779 black residents petitioned the New Hampshire legislature for freedom. Evidence also indicates that court rulings based on New Hampshire's 1783 constitution, which was similar to Massachusetts's constitution, refused to recognize human property. Nevertheless, New Hampshire still had about 150 slaves in 1792, and slavery may have simply withered away there rather than having been abolished by the courts.

In Connecticut and Rhode Island, the state legislatures, rather than individual African Americans, took the initiative against slavery. In 1784 these states adopted gradual abolition plans, which left adult slaves in bondage but proposed to free their children over a period of years. In Connecticut all children born to enslaved mothers after March 1, 1784, were to become free at age twenty-five. Rhode Island's plan was less gradual. Beginning that same March 1, it freed the children of enslaved women at birth. By 1790 only 3,763 slaves remained in New England out of a total black population there of 16,882. By 1800 only 1,339 slaves remained in the region, and by 1810 only 418 were left (108 in Rhode Island and 310 in Connecticut).

In New Jersey, New York, and Pennsylvania, the investment in slaves was much greater than in New England. After considerable debate, the Pennsylvania legislature in 1780 voted that the children of enslaved mothers would become free at age twenty-eight. Under this scheme, Pennsylvania still had 403 slaves in 1830 (see Table 5–1). But

Table 5–1
Slave Populations in the Mid-Atlantic States, 1790–1860

	1790	1800	1810	1820	1830	1840	1850	1860
New York	21,324	20,343	15,017	10,888	75	4		
New Jersey	11,432	12,343	19,851	7,557	2,243	674	236	18
Pennsylvania	3,737	1,706	795	211	403	64		

Source: Philip S. Foner, *History of Black Americans, from Africa to the Emergence of the Cotton Kingdom*, vol. 1 (Westport, CT: Greenwood, 1975), 374.

many African Americans in the state gained their freedom much earlier by lawsuits or by simply leaving their masters. Emancipation came even more slowly in New York and New Jersey. In 1785 their legislatures *defeated* proposals for gradual abolition. White revolutionary leaders, such as Alexander Hamilton and John Jay, worked for abolition in New York, and Quakers had long advocated it in New Jersey. But these states had relatively large slave populations, powerful slaveholders, and white workforces fearful of free black competition.

In 1799 the New York legislature finally agreed that male slaves born after July 4 of that year were to become free at age twenty-eight and females at age twenty-five. In 1804 New Jersey adopted a similar law that freed male slaves born after July 4 of that year when they reached age twenty-five and females when they reached age twenty-one. Under this plan, New Jersey still had eighteen slaves in 1860.

The Northwest Ordinance of 1787

During the 1780s, Congress drew its authority from a constitution known as the Articles of Confederation. The Articles created a weak central government that lacked power to tax or to regulate commerce. Despite its weaknesses, this government acquired jurisdiction over the region west of the Appalachian Mountains and east of the Mississippi River, where several states previously had conflicting land claims.

During the War for Independence, increasing numbers of white Americans had migrated across the Appalachians into this huge region. Some of the migrants brought slaves with them. The migrants also provoked hostilities with Indian nations. Those migrants who moved into the Northwest faced British opposition, and those who moved into the Southwest contested with Spanish forces for control of that area. In response to these circumstances, Congress formulated policies to protect the migrants and provide for their effective government. The new nation's leaders were also concerned with the expansion of slavery, and Thomas Jefferson sought to deal with both issues. First, he suggested that the western region be divided into separate territories and prepared for statehood. Second, he proposed that after 1800 slavery be banned from the entire region stretching from the Appalachians to the Mississippi River and from Spanish Florida (Spain had regained Florida in 1783) to British Canada.

In 1784 Jefferson's antislavery proposal failed by a single vote to pass Congress. Three years later, Congress adopted the Northwest Ordinance. This legislation applied the essence of Jefferson's plan to the region north of the Ohio River—what historians call the Old Northwest. The ordinance provided for the orderly sale of land, support for public education, territorial government, and the eventual formation of new states. Unlike Jefferson's plan, the ordinance banned slavery immediately. But, because it applied only to the Northwest Territory, the ordinance left the huge region south of the Ohio River open to slavery expansion.

Yet, by preventing slaveholders from taking slaves legally into areas north of the Ohio River, the ordinance set a precedent for excluding slavery from U.S. territories. Whether Congress had the power to do this became a contentious issue after President Jefferson annexed the huge Louisiana Territory in 1803 (see p. 87). The issue continued to divide northern and southern politicians until the Civil War.

Antislavery Societies in the North and the Upper South

While African Americans participated in the destruction of slavery in the northeastern states and Congress blocked its advance into the Old Northwest, a few white people organized to spread antislavery sentiment. In 1775 Quaker abolitionist Anthony Benezet organized the first antislavery society in the world. It became the Pennsylvania Society for Promoting the Abolition of Slavery in 1787, and Benjamin Franklin became its president. Similar societies were founded in Delaware in 1788 and Maryland in 1789. By the end of the eighteenth century, there were societies in New Jersey, Connecticut, and Virginia. Organized antislavery sentiment also quickly rose in the new slave states of Kentucky and Tennessee. However, such societies never appeared in the deep South.

From 1794 to 1832, antislavery societies cooperated within the loose framework of the American Convention for Promoting the Abolition of Slavery and Improving the Condition of the African Race. Only white people participated in these Quaker-dominated organizations, although members often cooperated with black leaders. As the northern states adopted abolition plans, the societies focused their attention on Delaware, Maryland, and Virginia. They aimed at gradual, compensated emancipation, encouraged masters to free their slaves, attempted to protect free black people from reenslavement, and frequently advocated sending freed black people out of the country.

Experience with emancipation in the northern states encouraged the emphasis on gradual abolition. So did the reluctance of white abolitionists to challenge the property rights of masters. Abolitionists also feared that immediate emancipation might lead masters to abandon elderly slaves and assumed that African Americans would require long training before they could be free. Yet gradualism played into the hands of slaveholders who, like Thomas Jefferson, opposed slavery in the abstract but had no intention of freeing their own slaves.

The antislavery societies of the upper South tended to be small and short lived. A Wilmington, Delaware, society established in 1788 peaked at 50 members and ceased to exist in 1800. The Maryland society organized in 1781 with 6 members grew to 250 in 1797 but disbanded in 1798. African Americans and their white friends, nevertheless, hoped that antislavery sentiment was advancing southward.

Manumission and Self-Purchase

Another hopeful sign for African Americans was that after the Revolution most southern states liberalized their manumission laws. In general, masters could free individual slaves by deed or will. They no longer had to go to court or petition a state legislature to prove that an individual they desired to manumit had performed a "meritorious service." Virginia led the way in 1782 by repealing its long-standing ban on private manumissions. Delaware in 1787, Maryland in 1790, Kentucky in 1792, and the slave-holding territory of Missouri in 1804 followed.

As a result, hundreds of slaveholders in the upper South began freeing slaves. Religious sentiment and natural rights principles motivated many of these masters. Even though most of them opposed general emancipation, they considered the slave system immoral. Yet noble motives were not always the most important. Masters often

The title of this 1811 painting by German-American artist John Lewis Krimmel is *Pepper-Pot, a Scene in the Philadelphia Market.* Slavery still existed in Pennsylvania when Krimmel recorded this scene. It is likely, however, that the black woman who is selling pepper-pot (a type of stew) was free.
2001-196-1 Krimmel, John Lewis, "Pepper Pot, A Scene in the Philadelphia Market." Philadelphia Museum of Art: Gift of Mr. and Mrs. Edward B. Leisenring, Jr. in honor of the 125th Anniversary of the Museum, 2001. Sumpter Priddy III, Inc.

negotiated self-purchase agreements with slaves that, although ending in manumission, gave masters a profit. To purchase their freedom, or that of loved ones, slaves raised money over a number of years by marketing farm produce or through outside employment. This allowed masters to enjoy income in addition to the slave's labor over the period of time the slave needed to raise the entire purchase price.

Masters also sometimes manumitted slaves who were no longer profitable investments. A master might be switching from tobacco to wheat or corn—crops that did not need a year-round workforce. Or a master might manumit older slaves whose best years as workers were behind them. Frequently, however, slaves, usually young men, presented masters with the alternative of manumitting them after a term of years or seeing them escape immediately.

Self-purchase often left African Americans in precarious financial condition. Sometimes they used up their savings to buy their freedom. In other instances, they went into debt to their former masters, to white lawyers who acted as their agents, or to other white people who had loaned them money to cover their purchase price. On occasion, masters reneged on their agreement to manumit after receiving money from a slave. Many of the freedom suits that became common in the upper South during this period resulted from such unethical behavior.

The Emergence of a Free Black Class in the South

As a result of manumission, self-purchase, and freedom suits, the free black population of the upper South blossomed. Maryland and Virginia had the largest such populations. Between 1790 and 1820, the number of free African Americans in Maryland climbed from 8,043 to 39,730 and in Virginia from 12,766 to 36,889. By 1820 the upper South (Delaware, Maryland, Virginia, District of Columbia, Kentucky, Missouri, North Carolina, and Tennessee) had a free black population of 114,070, compared with a northern free black population of 99,281. However, most of the upper South's black population remained in slavery while the North's was on the way to general emancipation. In the North, 83.9 percent of African Americans were free in 1820, compared with 10.6 percent of those in the upper South.

In the deep South (South Carolina, Georgia, Florida, Louisiana, and Mississippi), both the percentage and the absolute numbers of free black people remained much smaller. During the eighteenth century, neither South Carolina nor Georgia restricted the right of masters to manumit their slaves, but far fewer masters in these states exercised this right after the Revolution than was the case in the Chesapeake. Manumission declined in Louisiana following its annexation to the United States. Generally, masters in the deep South freed only their illegitimate slave children, other favorites, or those unable to work. Only 20,153 free black people lived in the deep South in 1820. In North Carolina, a transitional area between the upper and deep South, the state legislature made manumission more difficult after 1777. But many masters—especially those who were Quakers—freed their slaves anyway or let them live in quasi freedom.

The emergence of a free black class in the South, especially in the deep South, produced social strata more similar to that in Latin America than was the case in the North. As in the Caribbean, South America, and portions of Mexico, there were dominant white people, free people of color, and slaves. In southern cities, such as Charleston, Savannah, and New Orleans, some free African Americans not only identified economically and culturally with their former masters, they also acquired slaves.

Forces for Slavery

The forces for black freedom in the new republic rested on widespread African-American dissatisfaction with slavery, economic change, Christian morality, and revolutionary precepts. Most black northerners had achieved freedom by 1800, three-quarters were free by 1810, and by 1840 only 0.7 percent remained in slavery. Yet for the nation as a whole and for the mass of African Americans, the forces favoring slavery proved to be stronger.

The U.S. Constitution

The U.S. Constitution, which went into effect in 1789, became a major force in favor of the continued enslavement of African Americans. Earlier, during the War for Independence, the Continental Congress had been the weak central government of the United States, and each of the thirteen states had retained control over its own internal affairs. This system of divided sovereignty was formalized under the Articles of Confederation, which served as the American constitution from 1781 to 1789.

In 1787 the Constitutional Convention in Philadelphia produced the Constitution under which the United States is still governed. The new constitution gave the central government power to regulate commerce, to tax, and to have its laws enforced in the states. But the convention could not create a more powerful central government without first making important concessions to southern slaveholders.

The delegates to the convention omitted the words *slave* and *slavery* from the Constitution. But they included clauses designed to maintain the enslavement of African Americans in the southern states. These clauses provided for continuing the Atlantic slave trade for twenty years, for national military aid in suppressing slave revolts, and for returning to their masters slaves who escaped to other states. The Constitution also enhanced representation for slaveholders in Congress and in the electoral college that elected the president.

Humanitarian opposition to the Atlantic slave trade had mounted during the revolutionary era. Under pressure from black activists, such as Prince Hall of Boston, and Quakers, northern state legislatures during the 1780s forbade their citizens to engage in the slave trade. Rhode Island led the way in 1787. Massachusetts, Connecticut, and Pennsylvania followed in 1788. Economic change in the upper South also prompted opposition to the trade. Virginia, for example, banned the importation of slaves from abroad nearly a decade before Rhode Island.

Yet convention delegates from South Carolina and Georgia maintained that their states had an acute labor shortage. They threatened that citizens of these states would not tolerate a central government that could stop them from importing slaves—at least not in the near future. Torn between these conflicting perspectives, the convention compromised by including a provision in the Constitution that prohibited Congress from abolishing the trade until 1808. During the twenty years prior to 1808, when Congress banned the trade, thousands of Africans were brought into the southern states. Between 1804 and 1808, for example, forty thousand entered through Charleston. Overall, more slaves entered the United States between 1787 and 1808 than during any other twenty years in American history. Such huge numbers helped fuel the westward expansion of the slave system.

Other proslavery clauses of the U.S. Constitution aimed to counteract slave rebellion and escape. The Constitution gave Congress power to put down "insurrections" and "domestic violence." It also provided that persons "held to service or labour in one State, escaping into another . . . shall be delivered up on claim of the party to whom such service or labour may be due." This clause was the basis for the Fugitive Slave Act of 1793, which allowed masters or their agents to pursue slaves across state lines, capture them, and take them before a magistrate. There, on presentation of satisfactory evidence, masters could regain legal custody of the person they claimed. This act did not stop slaves from escaping from Virginia and Maryland to Pennsylvania. But it did extend the power of masters into the North, force the federal and northern state governments to uphold slavery, create personal tragedies for those who were recaptured, and encourage the kidnapping of free black northerners falsely claimed as escapees.

Finally, the Constitution strengthened the political power of slaveholders through the Three-Fifths Clause. The Three-Fifths Clause provided that a slave be counted as three-fifths of a free person in determining a state's representation in the House of Representatives and in the electoral college. Slaves would be counted similarly if and when Congress instituted a per capita tax. This gave southern slaveholders increased representation on the basis of the number of slaves they owned—slaves who, of course, had no vote or representation. The South gained enormous political advantage from it.

Four other factors, however, were more important than constitutional provisions in fostering the continued enslavement of African Americans in the new republic: increased cultivation of cotton, the Louisiana Purchase, declining revolutionary fervor, and intensified white racism.

Cotton

By the late eighteenth century, Britain was the world's leading textile producer. As mechanization made the spinning of cotton cloth more economical, Britain's demand for raw cotton increased dramatically. The United States took the lead in filling that demand as a result of Eli Whitney's invention of the cotton gin in 1793. This simple machine provided an easy and quick way to remove the seeds from the type of cotton most commonly grown in the South.

British demand combined with the cotton gin encouraged cotton production in the United States to rise from 3,000 to 178,000 bales between 1790 and 1810. Cotton became by far the most lucrative U.S. export. Southern cotton production also encouraged the development of textile mills in New England, thereby creating a proslavery alliance between the "lords of the lash and the lords of the loom."

Cotton reinvigorated the slave-labor system, which spread rapidly across Georgia and later into Alabama, Mississippi, Louisiana, and Texas. Cotton was also cultivated in South Carolina, North Carolina, and parts of Virginia and Tennessee. To make matters worse for African Americans, the westward expansion of cotton production encouraged an internal slave trade. Masters in the old tobacco-growing regions of Maryland, Virginia, and other states began to support themselves by selling their slaves to the new cotton-growing regions.

The Louisiana Purchase and African Americans in the Lower Mississippi Valley

The Jefferson administration's purchase of Louisiana from France in 1803 accelerated the westward expansion of slavery and the domestic slave trade. The purchase nearly doubled the area of the United States. That slavery might extend over this entire vast region was an issue of great importance to African Americans. The purchase also brought under American sovereignty those black people, both free and slave, who lived in the portion of the territory that centered on the city of New Orleans. As Chapter 3 indicates, black life in this region had developed a distinctive pattern under French rule from 1699 to 1763, under Spanish rule from 1763 to 1801, and briefly under French rule again between 1801 and 1803. Although people of African descent constituted a majority of the region's population, they were divided into two groups. First were the free people of color who referred to themselves as Creoles. They were craftsmen and shopkeepers in New Orleans and other port cities. They spoke French, belonged to the Roman Catholic Church, and aspired to equal rights with other free inhabitants. Some of them bought and sold slaves. Their numbers had increased under Spanish rule as urban slaves purchased their freedom. This route to freedom became more difficult under American sovereignty, but, as a group, Louisiana's free people of color remained optimistically integrationist in outlook.

It was, nevertheless, the second black group that was growing more rapidly. It consisted of plantation slaves, most of whom had come directly from Africa and worked on the region's plantations. Spain had encouraged white Americans to settle in the lower Mississippi Valley. The Americans, in turn, demanded more strictly enforced slave codes and the expansion of the external slave trade. At first the slaves continued to produce tobacco and indigo, but by the 1790s sugar and cotton had emerged as the crops of the future. As demand for these crops grew, conditions for slaves in Louisiana became increasingly harsh, especially after the region became part of the United States. The slaves' rural location, their predominantly African culture, and, eventually, their Protestant religion cut them off from free people of color. In 1770 Louisiana's slave population was 5,600. By 1810 it was 34,660. By 1820 it was 149,654. This tremendous growth, involving an extremely harsh form of slavery in a huge region, constituted a warning to all opponents of that institution. With the termination of the external slave trade, the notorious slave markets of New Orleans became the dreaded destination of thousands of African Americans "sold south" by their masters in the domestic slave trade.

Conservatism and Racism

The waning of revolutionary humanitarianism and the rise of a more intense racism among white people were less tangible forces than cotton production and the Louisiana Purchase, but they were just as important in strengthening slavery. They also made life more difficult for free African Americans.

By the 1790s white Americans had begun a long retreat from the egalitarianism of the revolutionary era. In the North and Chesapeake, most white people became less willing to challenge the prerogatives of slaveholders and more willing to accept slavery as suitable for African Americans. Most Marylanders and Virginians came to think of emancipation as best left to the distant future. This outlook strengthened the slaveholders and their nonslaveholding white supporters in the deep South who had never embraced the humanitarian precepts of the Enlightenment and Great Awakening.

Increasing proslavery sentiment among white Americans stemmed, in part, from revulsion against the radicalism of the French Revolution that had begun in 1789. Reports of bloody class warfare, disruption of the social order, and redistribution of property in France led most Americans to value property rights—including rights to human property—and order above equal rights. In addition, as cotton production spread westward and the value of slaves soared, rationalist and evangelical criticism of human bondage withered. Antislavery sentiment in the upper South that had flourished among slaveholders, nonslaveholders, Deists, Methodists, and Baptists became increasingly confined to African Americans and Quakers. By the early 1800s, manumissions began a long decline.

Using race to justify slavery was an important component of this conservative trend. Unlike white people, the argument went, black people were unsuited for freedom or citizenship. The doctrines embodied in the Declaration of Independence were, therefore, not applicable to them. A new scientific racism supported this outlook.

As early as the 1770s, some American intellectuals challenged the Enlightenment's explanation that perceived racial differences were not essential or inherent but the results of different environments in which Africans and Europeans lived. Scholars began to propose that God had created a great chain of being from lesser creatures to higher creatures. In this chain, they contended, black people constituted a separate species as close to the great apes as to white people. During the 1780s Thomas Jefferson reflected this view when he argued that "scientific observation" supported the conclusion that black people were inherently "inferior to whites in the endowments of both body and mind."

Such views were common among white northerners and white southerners and had practical results. During the 1790s Congress expressed its determination to exclude African Americans from the benefits of citizenship in "a white man's country." A 1790 law limited the granting of naturalized citizenship to "any alien, being a white person." Two years later, Congress limited enrollment in state militias to "each and every free, able-bodied white male citizen." These laws implied that African Americans had no place in the United States except as slaves. In other words, the free black class was an anomaly and, in the opinion of most white people, a dangerous anomaly.

The Emergence of Free Black Communities

The competing forces of slavery and racism, on one hand, and freedom and opportunity, on the other, shaped the growth of African-American communities in the early American republic. A distinctive black culture had existed since the early colonial period. But enslavement had limited black community life. The advent of large free black populations in the North and upper South after the Revolution allowed African Americans to establish autonomous and dynamic communities. They appeared in Philadelphia, Baltimore, Newport (Rhode Island), Richmond, Norfolk, New York, and Boston. Although smaller and less autonomous, there were also free black communities in such deep South cities as Charleston, Savannah, and New Orleans. As free black people in these cities acquired a modicum of wealth and education, they established institutions that have shaped African-American life ever since.

A combination of factors encouraged African Americans to form these distinctive institutions. First, as they emerged from slavery, they realized they would have inferior status in white-dominated organizations or not be allowed to participate in them at all. Second, black people valued the African heritage they had preserved over generations in slavery. They wanted institutions that would perpetuate their heritage.

The earliest black community institutions were mutual aid societies. Patterned on similar white organizations, these societies were like modern insurance companies and benevolent organizations. They provided for their members' medical and burial expenses and helped support widows and children. African Americans in Newport, Rhode Island, organized the first such black mutual aid society in 1780. Seven years later, Richard Allen and Absalom Jones established the more famous Free African Society in Philadelphia.

Most early free black societies admitted only men, but similar organizations for women appeared during the 1790s. For example, in 1793 Philadelphia's Female Benevolent Society of St. Thomas took over the welfare functions of the city's Free

African Society. Other black women's organizations in Philadelphia during the early republic included the Benevolent Daughters—established in 1796 by Richard Allen's wife Sarah—Daughters of Africa established in 1812, the American Female Bond Benevolent Society formed in 1817, and the Female Benezet begun in 1818.

These ostensibly secular societies maintained a decidedly Christian moral character. They insisted that their members meet standards of middle-class propriety and, in effect, became self-improvement as well as mutual aid societies. Members had to pledge to refrain from fornication, adultery, drunkenness, and other "disreputable behavior." By the early 1800s, such societies also organized resistance to kidnappers who sought to recapture fugitive slaves or enslave free African Americans.

Because such societies provided real benefits and reflected black middle-class aspirations, they spread to every black urban community. More than one hundred such organizations existed in Philadelphia alone by 1830. Although these societies were more common in the North than in the South, Baltimore had about thirty of them by that same year, and Charleston, South Carolina, had at least two. One of them was the Brown Fellowship, founded in 1790, which admitted only black men with light complexions. The other was open to all free black men in Charleston.

Of particular importance were the black freemasons because, unlike other free black organizations, the masons united black men from several northern cities. Combining rationalism with secrecy and obscure ritual, freemasonry was a major movement among European and American men during the late eighteenth and early nineteenth centuries. Opportunities for male bonding, wearing fancy regalia, and achieving prestige in a supposedly ancient hierarchy attracted both black and white men. As historians James Oliver Horton and Lois E. Horton suggest, black people drew special satisfaction from the European-based order's claims to have originated in ancient Egypt, which black people associated with their own African heritage.

The most famous black mason of his time was Prince Hall, the Revolutionary War veteran and abolitionist. During the 1770s he founded what became known as the African Grand Lodge of North America, or, more colloquially, the Prince Hall Masons. In several respects, Hall's relationship to masonry epitomizes the free black predicament in America.

In 1775 the local white masonic lodge in Boston rejected Hall's application for membership because of his black ancestry. Instead, Hall, who was a Patriot, got a limited license for what was called African Lodge No. 1 from a British lodge associated with the British Army that then occupied Boston. The irony of this situation was compounded when, after the War for Independence, American masonry refused to grant the African Lodge a full charter. Hall again had to turn to the British masons who approved his application in 1787. It was under this British charter that Hall in 1791 became provincial grand master of North America and began authorizing black lodges in other cities, notably Philadelphia, Pennsylvania, and Providence, Rhode Island.

The Origins of Independent Black Churches

Although black churches emerged at least a decade later than black benevolent associations, the churches quickly became the core of African-American communities. Not only did these churches attend to the spiritual needs of free black people and—in some southern cities—slaves, their pastors also became the primary African-American leaders. Black church buildings housed schools, social organizations, and antislavery meetings.

During the late eighteenth century, as the egalitarian spirit of the Great Awakening waned among white Baptists, Methodists, and Episcopalians, separate, but not independent, black churches appeared in the South. The biracial churches spawned by the Awakening had never embraced African Americans on an equal basis with white people. Although there had initially been promising tendencies within biracial churches, as time passed white people denied black people significant influence in church governance and subjected them to segregated seating, communion services, Sunday schools, and cemeteries. Separate black congregations, usually headed by black ministers but subordinate to white church hierarchies, were the result of these policies. The first such congregations appeared during the 1770s in South Carolina and Georgia.

In contrast to these subordinate churches, a truly independent black church emerged gradually in Philadelphia between the 1780s and the early 1800s. The movement for such a church began within the city's white-controlled St. George's Methodist Church. The movement's leaders were Richard Allen and Absalom Jones, who could rely on the Free African Society they had established to help them.

These men were former slaves who had purchased their freedom: Allen in 1780 and Jones in 1783. Allen, a fervent Methodist since the 1770s, had received permission from St. George's white leadership to preach to black people in the evenings in what was then a simple church building. By the mid-1780s, Jones had joined Allen's congregation, and soon they and other black members of St. George's chafed under policies they considered unchristian and insulting. But Allen's and Jones's faith that Methodist egalitarianism would prevail over racial discrimination undermined their efforts during the 1780s to create a separate black Methodist church.

The break finally came in 1792 when St. George's white leaders grievously insulted the church's black members. An attempt by white trustees to prevent Jones from praying in what the trustees considered the white section of the church led black members to walk out. "We all went out of the church in a body," recalled Allen, "and they were no more plagued with us in the church."

St. George's white leaders fought hard and long to control the expanding and economically valuable black congregation. Yet other white Philadelphians, led by abolitionist Benjamin Rush, applauded the concept of an independent "African church." Rush and other sympathetic white people contributed to the new church's building fund. When construction began in 1793, Rush and at least one hundred other white people joined with African Americans at a banquet to celebrate the occasion.

However, the black congregation soon split. When the majority determined that the new church would be Episcopalian rather than Methodist, Allen and a few others refused to join. The result was *two* black churches in Philadelphia. St. Thomas's Episcopal Church, with Jones as priest, opened in July 1794 as an African-American congregation within the white-led national Episcopal Church. Then Allen's Mother Bethel congregation got under way as the first truly independent black church. The white leaders of St. George's tried to control Mother Bethel until 1816. That year Mother Bethel became the birthplace of the African Methodist Episcopal (AME)

This drawing portrays Philadelphia's Bethel African Methodist Episcopal Church as it appeared in 1829. It had been built in 1793 under the direction of Richard Allen, the first bishop of the AME denomination, and had been "rebuilt" in 1803.
The Library Company of Philadelphia

Church. Allen became the first bishop of this organization, which quickly spread to other cities in the North and the South.

The more significant among the other AME congregations were Daniel Coker's in Baltimore, the AME Zion in New York, and those in Wilmington, Delaware; Salem, New Jersey; and Attleboro, Pennsylvania. Additional independent black churches formed at this time out of similar conflicts with white-led congregations. Among them were the African Baptist Church established in Boston in 1805 and led by Thomas Paul from 1806 to 1808, the Presbyterian Evangelical Society founded in 1811 by John Gloucester, the Abyssinian Baptist Church organized in New York City in 1808 by Paul, and the African Presbyterian Church, established in Philadelphia by Samuel E. Cornish in 1822.

The First Black Schools

Schools for African-American children, slave and free, date to the early 1700s. In both North and South, white clergy, including Cotton Mather, ran the schools. So did Quakers, early abolition societies, and missionaries acting for the Anglican Society for the Propagation of the Gospel in Foreign Parts. But the first schools established by African Americans to instruct African-American children arose after the Revolution. The new black mutual aid societies and churches created and sustained them.

Schools for black people organized or taught by white people continued to flourish. But in other instances, black people founded their own schools because local white authorities regularly refused either to admit black children to public schools or to maintain adequate separate schools for them. For example, in 1796, when he failed to convince Boston's city council to provide a school for black students, Prince Hall had the children taught in his own home and that of his son Primus. By 1806 the school was meeting in the basement of the new African Meeting House, which housed Thomas Paul's African Baptist Church.

Hall was not the first to take such action. As early as 1790, Charleston's Brown Fellowship operated a school for its members' children. Free black people in Baltimore supported schools during the same decade, and during the early 1800s, similar schools opened in Washington, D.C. Such schools frequently employed white teachers. Not until Philadelphia's Mother Bethel Church established the Augustine School in 1818 did a school entirely administered and taught by African Americans for black children exist.

These schools faced great difficulties. Many black families could not afford the fees, but rather than turn children away, the schools strained their meager resources by taking charity cases. Some black parents also believed education was pointless when African Americans often could not get skilled jobs. White people feared competition from skilled black workers, believed black schools attracted undesirable populations, and, particularly in the South, feared that educated free African Americans would encourage slaves to revolt.

Threats of violence against black schools and efforts to suppress them were common. The case of Christopher McPherson exemplifies these dangers. McPherson, a free African American, established a night school for black men at Richmond, Virginia, in 1811 and hired a white teacher. All went well until McPherson advertised the school in a local newspaper. In response, white residents forced the teacher to leave the city, and local authorities had McPherson committed to the state lunatic asylum. Nevertheless, similar schools continued to operate in both the North and upper South, producing a growing class of literate African Americans.

Black Leaders and Choices

By the 1790s an educated black elite that was well able to provide leadership for African Americans in religion, economic advancement, and racial politics had come into existence in the North and Chesapeake. Experience had driven members of this elite to a contradictory perception of themselves and of America. They were acculturated, patriotic Americans who had achieved some personal well-being and security. But they were well aware that American society had not lived up to its revolutionary principles. They lamented the continued enslavement of the mass of African Americans, and they had misgivings about the future.

Prominent among these leaders were members of the clergy. Two of the most important of them were Richard Allen and Absalom Jones. Besides organizing his church, Allen opened a school in Philadelphia for black children, wrote against slavery and racial prejudice, and made his home a refuge for fugitive slaves. A year before his death in 1831, Allen presided over the first national black convention.

Jones, too, was an early abolitionist. In 1797 his concern for fugitives facing reenslavement led him to become the first African American to petition Congress. His petition anticipated later abolitionists in suggesting that slavery violated the spirit of the U.S. Constitution and that Congress could abolish it.

Vying with clergy for influence were African-American entrepreneurs. Prince Hall, for example, owned successful leather dressing and catering businesses in Boston, and Peter Williams, principal founder of New York's AME Zion church, was a prosperous tobacco merchant. Another prominent black entrepreneur was James Forten of Philadelphia, described as "probably the most noteworthy free African-American entrepreneur in the early nineteenth century." Born to free parents in 1766, Forten was a Patriot during the War for Independence, learned the craft of sail making, and became the owner of his own business in 1798. For the rest of his life, he advocated equal rights and abolition.

American patriotism, religious conviction, organizational skill, intellectual inquisitiveness, and antislavery activism delineate the lives of most free black leaders in this era. Yet these leaders often were torn in their perceptions of what was best for African Americans. Hammon and Chavis were accommodationist about slavery and racial oppression. They both condemned slavery and lauded human liberty, but they were not activists.

Allen, Jones, Hall, and Forten were more optimistic than Hammon and Chavis about the ability of African Americans to mold their own destiny in the United States. Although they each expressed misgivings, they believed that, despite setbacks, the egalitarian principles of the American Revolution would prevail if black people insisted on liberty. Forten never despaired that African Americans would be integrated into the larger American society on the basis of their individual talent and enterprise. Although he was often frustrated, Hall for four decades pursued a strategy based on the assumption that white authority would reward black protest and patriotism. Allen and Jones put more emphasis on separate black institutions than did Forten or Hall. Yet they were just as willing to organize, protest, and petition to establish the rights of black people as American citizens.

Migration

African Americans, however, had another alternative: migration from the United States to establish their own society free from white prejudices. In 1787 British philanthropists, including Olaudah Equiano, had established Freetown in Sierra Leone on the West African coast as a refuge for former slaves. As we mentioned in Chapter 4, some African Americans who had been Loyalists during the American Revolution settled there. Other black and white Americans proposed that free black people should settle western North America or in the Caribbean islands. There were great practical obstacles to mass black migration to each of these regions. Migration was extremely expensive, difficult to organize, and involved long, often fruitless, negotiations with foreign governments. But no black leader during the early national period was immune to the appeal of such proposals.

Aware of Freetown, Hall in 1787 petitioned the Massachusetts legislature to support efforts by black Bostonians to establish a colony in Africa. Although he recognized black progress in Massachusetts, Hall maintained that he and others found themselves "in many respects, in very disagreeable and disadvantageous circumstances; most of which must attend us so long as we and our children live in America." By the mid-1810s, a few influential white Americans had also decided there was no place in the United States for free African Americans. In 1816 they organized the American Colonization Society. Under its auspices, Coker in 1820 led the first party of eighty-six African Americans to the new colony of Liberia on the West African coast.

The major black advocate of migration to Africa during this period, however, was Paul Cuffe, the son of an Ashanti (in modern Ghana) father and Wampanoag Indian mother. He became a prosperous New England sea captain and, by the early 1800s, cooperated with British humanitarians and entrepreneurs to promote migration. He saw African-American colonization in West Africa as a way to end the Atlantic slave trade, spread Christianity, create a refuge for free black people, and make profits. Before his death in 1817, Cuffe had influenced not only Coker but also—at least temporarily—Forten, Allen, and Jones to consider colonization as a viable alternative for African Americans.

Slave Uprisings

While black northerners became increasingly aware of the limits to their freedom after the Revolution, black southerners saw the perpetuation of their enslavement. As cotton production expanded westward, as new slave states entered the Union, and as masters in such border slave states as Maryland and Virginia turned away from the revolutionary commitment to gradual emancipation, slaves faced several choices.

Some lowered their expectations and loyally served their masters. Most continued patterns of day-to-day resistance. Mounting numbers of men and women escaped. A few risked their lives to join revolutionary movements to destroy slavery violently. When just several hundred out of hundreds of thousands of slaves rallied behind Gabriel in 1800 near Richmond or Charles Deslondes in 1811 near New Orleans, they frightened white southerners and raised hopes for freedom among countless African Americans.

The egalitarian principles of the American and French revolutions influenced Gabriel and Deslondes. Unlike earlier slave rebels, they acted not to revenge personal grievances or to establish maroon communities but to destroy slavery because it denied natural human rights to its victims. The American Declaration of Independence and the legend of Haiti's Toussaint Louverture provided the intellectual foundations for their efforts. Louverture, against great odds, had led the enslaved black people of the French sugar colony of Saint Domingue—modern Haiti—to freedom and independence. This bitter and bloody struggle lasted from 1791 to 1804. Many white planters fled the island with their slaves to take refuge in Cuba, Jamaica, South Carolina, Virginia, and, somewhat later, Louisiana. The Haitian slaves carried the spirit of revolution with them to their new homes.

During the early 1790s, black unrest and rumors of pending revolt mounted in Virginia. The state militia arrested suspected plotters, who got off with whippings. In this revolutionary atmosphere, Gabriel, the human property of Thomas Prosser Sr., prepared to lead a massive slave insurrection. Gabriel was an acculturated and literate

Toussaint Louverture (1744–1803) led the black rebellion in the French colony of St. Domingue on the Caribbean island of Hispaniola that led to the creation of the independent black republic of Haiti in 1804. Louverture became an inspiration for black rebels in the United States.
Stock Montage, Inc./Historical Pictures Collection

blacksmith who was well aware of the rationalist and revolutionary currents of his time. He was also a large and powerful man with a violent temper. In the fall of 1799, for example, a local court convicted him of "'biting off a considerable part of [the] left Ear' of a white neighbor."

The ideology of the American Revolution shaped Gabriel's actions. He was also aware that white people were politically divided and distracted by an undeclared naval war with France. He enjoyed some secret white support and hoped that poor people generally would rally to his cause as he and his associates planned to kill those who supported slavery and take control of central Virginia.

But on August 30, 1800—the day the uprising was to occur—two slaves revealed the plan to white authorities while a tremendous thunderstorm prevented Gabriel's followers from assaulting Richmond. Then governor—and future U.S. president—James Monroe quickly had suspects arrested. Gabriel, who relied on white allies to get to Norfolk, was among the last captured. In October he and twenty-six others, convicted of "conspiracy and insurrection," were hanged. By demonstrating that slaves could organize for large-scale rebellion, they left a legacy of fear among slaveholders and hope for liberation among southern African Americans.

The far less famous Louisiana Rebellion took place under similar circumstances. By the early 1800s, refugees from Haiti had settled with their slaves in what was then known as Orleans Territory. As they arrived, rumors of slave insurrection spread across the territory. The rumors became reality on January 8, 1811, when Deslondes, a Haitian native and slave driver on a plantation north of New Orleans, initiated a massive revolt in cooperation with maroons.

Although no record of Deslondes's rhetoric survives and his goals may have been less ideologically coherent than Gabriel's, he organized a force of at least 180 men and women. They marched south along the Mississippi River toward New Orleans, with leaders on horseback, and with flags and drums, but few guns. The revolutionaries plundered and burned plantations but killed only two white people and one recalcitrant slave. They were overwhelmed on January 10 by a force of about seven hundred territorial militia, slaveholding vigilantes, and U.S. troops. The "battle" was a massacre. The well-armed white men slaughtered sixty-six of the rebels and captured twenty-one, including Deslondes. These captives were tried without benefit of counsel, found guilty of rebellion, and shot. The white authorities cut off each executed rebel's head and displayed it on a pike to warn other African Americans of the consequences of revolt.

The White Southern Reaction

Although Deslondes's uprising was one of the few major slave revolts in American history, Gabriel's conspiracy and events in Haiti left the more significant legacy. For generations, enslaved African Americans regarded Louverture as a black George Washington and recalled Gabriel's revolutionary message. The networks among slaves that Gabriel established continued to exist after his death. As the external slave trade carried black Virginians southwestward, they took his promise of liberation with them.

The fears that the Haitian revolution and Gabriel's conspiracy raised among white southerners deepened their reaction against the egalitarian values of the Enlightenment. Because they feared race war and believed emancipation would encourage African Americans to begin such a war, most white people in Virginia and throughout the South determined to make black bondage stronger, not weaker.

Beginning with South Carolina in December 1800, southern states outlawed assemblies of slaves, placed curfews on slaves and free black people, and made manumissions more difficult. The old colonial practice of white men on horseback patrolling slave quarters revived. Assuming that revolutionaries like Gabriel received encouragement from white abolitionists as well as free African Americans, white southerners became suspicious of such outsiders as Yankee peddlers, evangelicals, and foreigners. Forcing free black people out of southern states became more attractive to some white southerners and brought about the odd alliance between them and black advocates of emigration to Africa.

The War of 1812

Many of the themes developed in this chapter—African-American patriotism, opportunities for freedom, migration sentiment, and influences pushing slaves toward revolutionary action—are reflected in the black experience during the U.S. war with Great Britain that began in 1812. The roots of this conflict lay in a massive military and economic struggle between Britain and France for mastery over the Atlantic world. The struggle lasted from 1793, during the French Revolution, to the defeat of Napoleon Bonaparte by a British-led coalition in 1815.

British military support for American Indian resistance in the Old Northwest, an American desire to annex Canada, and especially Britain's interference with American ships trading with Europe drew the United States into the war, which lasted until early 1815. Although the United States won some important victories, it failed to achieve its major objective—the conquest of Canada—and the war ended in a draw. Yet many Americans regarded the war as a second struggle for independence and, as had been the case during the American Revolution, black military service and white fear of slave revolt played important roles.

When the war began, white prejudice and fear of black revolt had nearly nullified memories of the service of black Patriot soldiers during the Revolution. The Militia Act of 1792 had eliminated armed black participation in all state militias except that of North Carolina. The secretary of the navy ended black service on American warships in 1798. Because of the news from Haiti and because of Gabriel's conspiracy, white southerners joined John Randolph of Virginia in regarding African Americans as "an internal foe." When the war with Great Britain began, therefore, the southern states refused to enlist black men for fear they would use their guns to aid slave revolts. Meanwhile the lack of enthusiasm for the war among many northerners, combined with the absence of a British threat to their part of the country, kept northern states from mobilizing black troops during 1812 and 1813.

Southern fears of slave revolt mounted in the spring of 1813 when the British invaded the Chesapeake. As they had during the Revolution, British generals offered slaves freedom in Canada or the British West Indies in return for help. In response, African Americans joined the British army that burned Washington, D.C., in 1814 and attacked Baltimore.

The threat this British army posed to Philadelphia and New York led to the first active black involvement in the war on the American side. The New York state legislature authorized two black regiments, offered freedom to slaves who enlisted, and promised compensation to their masters. Meanwhile, African Americans in Philadelphia and New York City volunteered to help build fortifications. In Philadelphia, James Forten, Richard Allen, and Absalom Jones patriotically raised a "Black Brigade," which never saw action because the British halted when they failed to capture Baltimore.

African-American men did fight, however, at two of the war's most important battles. During the naval engagement at Put-in-Bay on Lake Erie in September 1813 that secured control of the Great Lakes for the United States, one-quarter of Commandant Oliver Hazard Perry's four hundred sailors were black. Although Perry had been staunchly prejudiced against using these men, after the battle he praised their valor. At the Battle of New Orleans—fought in January 1815, about a month after a peace treaty had been negotiated (news of peace had not yet reached the area)—African Americans also fought bravely. Yet white memories of Deslondes's recent uprising almost prevented them from being allowed to fight on the American side. Many white people feared that, if mobilized, the local free black militia, which dated back to the Spanish occupation of Louisiana from 1763 to 1801, would make common cause with slaves and the British rather than take the American side. In defiance of such fears, General Andrew Jackson included the black troops in his force defending New Orleans and offered them equal pay and benefits. At least six hundred free black men fought on the American side at the Battle of New Orleans, and Jackson lived up to his promise of equal treatment. It was a choice, he later informed President James Monroe, between having the free African Americans "in our ranks or . . . in the ranks of the enemy."

THE MISSOURI COMPROMISE

During the years following 1815, as the United States emerged from a difficult war, sectional issues between the North and South, which had been pushed into the background by constitutional compromises and the political climate, revived. The nation's first political parties—the Federalist and the Republican—had failed to confront slavery as a national issue. The northern wing of the modernizing Federalist Party had abolitionist tendencies. But during the 1790s when they controlled the national government, the Federalists did not raise the slavery issue. Then the victory of the state-rights-oriented Republican Party in the election of 1800 fatally weakened the Federalists as a national organization and brought a series of implicitly proslavery administrations to power in Washington.

It took innovations in transportation and production that began during the 1810s, as well as the continuing disappearance of slavery in the northern states, to transform the North into a region consciously at odds with the South's traditional culture and slave-labor economy. The first major expression of intensifying sectional differences over slavery and its expansion came in 1819 when the slaveholding Missouri Territory, which had been carved out of Louisiana Territory, applied for admission to the Union as a slave state. Northerners expressed deep reservations about the creation of a new slaveholding state, which threatened to destroy the political balance between the sections and the expansion of slavery in general. The aged Thomas Jefferson called this negative northern reaction a "fire bell in the night." It awakened slaveholders to an era in which slavery could no longer be avoided as an issue in national politics.

Concerned African Americans were also aware of the significance of the Missouri crisis. Black residents of Washington, D.C., crowded into the U.S. Senate gallery as that body debated the issue. Finally, Henry Clay of Kentucky, the slaveholding Speaker of the House of Representatives, directed an effort that produced in 1820 a compromise that temporarily quieted discord. This Missouri Compromise (see Map 5–2) permitted Missouri to become a slave state, maintained a sectional political balance by admitting Maine, which had been part of Massachusetts, as a free state, and banned slavery north of the 36° 30′ line of latitude in the old Louisiana Territory. Yet sectional relations would never be the same, and a new era of black and white antislavery militancy soon confronted the South.

MAP 5–2 The Missouri Compromise of 1820. Under the Missouri Compromise, Missouri entered the Union as a slave state, Maine entered as a free state, and Congress banned slavery in the huge unorganized portion of the old Louisiana Territory north of the 36° 30′ line of latitude.

TIMELINE

AFRICAN-AMERICAN EVENTS	NATIONAL EVENTS
1775	
1775 First antislavery society formed	**1776** Declaration of Independence
1777 Vermont bans slavery	**1777** Battle of Saratoga
1780	
1780 Pennsylvania begins gradual emancipation	**1781** Articles of Confederation ratified
1781 Elizabeth Freeman begins her legal suit for freedom	**1783** Great Britain recognizes independence of the United States

continued

AFRICAN-AMERICAN EVENTS	NATIONAL EVENTS
1782 Virginia repeals its ban on manumission **1783** Massachusetts bans slavery and black men gain the right to vote there **1784** Connecticut and Rhode Island begin gradual abolition	
1785	
1785 New Jersey and New York defeat gradual emancipation **1787** Northwest Ordinance bans slavery in the territory north of the Ohio River	**1786** Shays's Rebellion **1787** Constitutional Convention **1789** Constitution ratified; George Washington becomes president
1790	
1793 Congress passes Fugitive Slave Law **1794** Mother Bethel Church established in Philadelphia New York adopts gradual abolition plan	
1795	
	1796 John Adams elected president of United States **1799** Undeclared war against France
1800	
1800 Gabriel's revolt conspiracy	**1800** Thomas Jefferson elected president **1803** Louisiana Purchase
1805	
1808 Congress bans the external slave trade	**1808** James Madison elected president of United States
1810	
1811 Louisiana slave rebellion	**1812** War of 1812 begins

continued

AFRICAN-AMERICAN EVENTS	NATIONAL EVENTS
1815	
1815 AME Church formally established	**1815** War of 1812 ends **1819** Panic of 1819
1820	
1820 Daniel Coker leads first black settlers to Liberia	**1820** Missouri Compromise

Conclusion

The period between the War for Independence and the Missouri Compromise was a time of transition for African Americans. On one hand, the legacy of the American Revolution brought emancipation in the North and a promise of equal opportunity with white Americans. On the other hand, by the 1790s slavery and racism had begun to grow stronger. Through a combination of antiblack prejudice among white people and African Americans' desire to preserve their own cultural traditions, black urban communities arose in the North, upper South, and, occasionally—in Charleston and Savannah, for example—in the deep South.

Spreading freedom in the North and the emergence of black communities in both the North and South were heartening developments. There were new opportunities for education, spiritual expression, and economic growth. But the mass of African Americans remained in slavery. The forces for human bondage were growing stronger. Freedom for those who had gained it in the upper South and North was marginal and precarious.

Gabriel's conspiracy in Virginia and Deslondes's rebellion in Louisiana indicated that revolutionary principles persisted among black southerners. But these rebellions and British recruitment of slaves during the War of 1812 convinced most white southerners that black bondage had to be permanent. Therefore, African Americans looked to the future with mixed emotions. A few determined that the only hope for real freedom lay in migration from the United States.

Review Questions

1. Which were stronger in the era of the early American republic, the forces in favor of black freedom or those in favor of continued enslavement?
2. How were African Americans able to achieve emancipation in the North?
3. How was the U.S. Constitution, as it was drafted in 1787, proslavery? How was it antislavery?

4. How important were separate institutions in shaping the lives of free black people during the late eighteenth and early nineteenth centuries?
5. What led Gabriel to believe he and his followers could abolish slavery in Virginia through armed uprising?

Recommended Reading

Ira Berlin. *Slaves without Masters: The Free Negro in the Antebellum South.* New York: New Press, 1974. The early chapters of this classic study indicate the special difficulties the first large generation of free black southerners faced.

Douglas R. Egerton. *Gabriel's Rebellion: The Virginia Slave Conspiracies of 1800 and 1802.* Chapel Hill: University of North Carolina Press, 1993. This most recent account of Gabriel's conspiracy emphasizes both the revolutionary context within which he acted and his legacy.

Philip S. Foner. *History of Black Americans, from Africa to the Emergence of the Cotton Kingdom.* Westport, CT: Greenwood, 1975. This is the first volume of a comprehensive three-volume history of African Americans. It is detailed and informative about black life between 1783 and 1820.

James Oliver Horton and Lois E. Horton. *In Hope of Liberty: Culture, Community, and Protest among Northern Free Blacks, 1700–1860.* New York: Oxford University Press, 1997. This is a well-written interpretation of the northern free black community and its origins.

Sidney Kaplan and Emma Nogrady Kaplan. *The Black Presence in the Era of the American Revolution,* Rev. ed. Amherst: University of Massachusetts Press, 1989. This delightfully written book provides informative accounts of black leaders who lived during the early American republic.

Gary B. Nash. *Forging Freedom: The Formation of Philadelphia's Black Community, 1720–1840.* Cambridge, MA: Harvard University Press, 1988. This path-breaking study of a black community analyzes the origins of separate black institutions.

Donald R. Wright. *African Americans in the Early Republic, 1789–1831.* Arlington Heights, IL: Harlan Davidson, 1993. This is a brief but comprehensive account that reflects recent interpretations.

• CHAPTER SIX •

LIFE IN THE COTTON KINGDOM

THE EXPANSION OF SLAVERY

Eli Whitney's invention of the cotton gin in 1793 made the cultivation of cotton profitable on the North American mainland. It was the key to the rapid and extensive expansion of slavery from the Atlantic coast to Texas. By 1811 cotton cultivation had spread across South Carolina, Georgia, and parts of North Carolina and Virginia. By 1821 it had crossed Alabama and reached Mississippi, Louisiana, and parts of Tennessee. It then expanded again into Arkansas, Florida, and eastern Texas. Enslaved black labor cleared forests and drained swamps to make these lands fit for cultivation.

The expansion of the cotton culture led to the removal of the American Indians—some of them slaveholders—who inhabited this vast region. During the 1830s the U.S. Army forced the Cherokee, Chickasaw, Choctaw, Creek, and most Seminole to leave their ancestral lands for Indian Territory in what is now Oklahoma. Many Indians died during this forced migration, and the Cherokee remember it as "The Trail of Tears." Yet the Cherokees created in Oklahoma an economy dependent on black slave labor. By 1860 there were seven thousand slaves there, amounting to 14 percent of the population.

Slave Population Growth

In the huge region stretching from the Atlantic coast to Texas, however, a tremendous increase in the number of African Americans in bondage accompanied territorial expansion. Although slave populations in Latin American countries failed to reproduce themselves and declined drastically prior to general emancipation, the slave population of the United States grew almost sixfold between 1790 and 1860, from 697,897 to 3,953,760 (see Table 6–1). Agricultural laborers constituted 75 percent of the South's slave population. But slaves were not equally distributed across the region. In western North Carolina, eastern Tennessee, western Virginia, and most of Missouri, for example, there were never many slaves. The slave population grew fastest in the newer cotton-producing states, such as Alabama and Mississippi.

Virginia had the largest slave population throughout the period. But between 1820 and 1860, that population increased by only 15 percent, from 425,153 to 490,865. During the same forty years, the slave population of Louisiana increased by 209 percent, from 149,654 to 462,198, and that of Mississippi by 1,231 percent, from 32,814 to 436,631. By 1860 Mississippi had joined South Carolina as the only states that had more slave than free inhabitants.

Table 6–1
U.S. Slave Population, 1820 and 1860

	1820	1860
United States	1,538,125	3,953,760
North	19,108	64
South	1,519,017	3,953,696
Upper South	965,514	1,530,229
Delaware	4,509	1,798
Kentucky	127,732	225,483
Maryland	107,397	87,189
Missouri	10,222	114,931
North Carolina	205,017	331,059
Tennessee	80,107	275,719
Virginia	425,153	490,865
Washington, D.C.	6,377	3,185
Lower South	553,503	2,423,467
Alabama	41,879	435,080
Arkansas	1,617	111,115
Florida	*	61,745
Georgia	149,654	462,198
Louisiana	69,064	331,726
Mississippi	32,814	436,631
South Carolina	258,475	402,406
Texas	*	182,566

*Florida and Texas were not states in 1820.
Source: Ira Berlin, *Slaves without Masters: The Free Negro in the Antebellum South* (New York: New Press, 1974), 396–97.

Ownership of Slaves in the Old South

Slaveholders were as unevenly distributed as the slaves and, unlike slaves, were declining in number. In 1830, 1,314,272 white southerners (36 percent), out of a total white southern population of 3,650,758, owned slaves. In 1860 only 383,673 white southerners (4.7 percent), out of a total white southern population of 8,097,463, owned slaves. Even counting the immediate families of slaveholders, only 1,900,000 (or less than 25 percent of the South's white population) had a direct interest in slavery in 1860.

Almost half of the South's slaveholders owned fewer than 5 slaves, only 12 percent owned more than 20 slaves, and just 1 percent owned more than 50 slaves. Yet more than half the slaves belonged to masters who had 20 or more slaves. So although the typical slaveholder owned few slaves, the typical slave lived on a sizable plantation.

Since the time of Anthony Johnson in the mid-1600s, a few black people had been slaveholders, and this class continued to exist. In 1830 only 2 percent, or 3,775 free African Americans, owned slaves. Many of them became slaveholders to protect their families from sale and disruption. This was because, as the nineteenth century progressed, southern states made it more difficult for masters to manumit slaves and for slaves to purchase their freedom. The states also threatened to expel former slaves from their territory. In response to these circumstances black men and women sometimes purchased relatives who were in danger of sale to traders and who—if legally free—might be forced by white authorities to leave a state.

Some African Americans, however, purchased slaves for financial reasons and passed those slaves on to their heirs. Most black people who became masters for financial reasons owned five or fewer slaves. But William Johnson, a wealthy free black barber of Natchez, Louisiana, owned many slaves whom he employed on a plantation he purchased. Some black women, such as Margaret Mitchell Harris of South Carolina and Betsy Somayrac of Natchitoches, Louisiana, also became slaveholders for economic reasons. Harris was a successful rice planter who inherited twenty-one slaves from her white father. She prospered by carefully managing her resources in land and slaves. By 1849, when she sold out, she had more than forty slaves and nearly a thousand acres, which produced 240,000 pounds of rice per year.

Slave Labor in Agriculture

About 55 percent of the slaves in the South cultivated cotton; 10 percent grew tobacco; and 10 percent produced sugar, rice, or hemp. About 15 percent were domestic servants, and the remaining 10 percent worked in trades and industries.

Tobacco

Tobacco remained important in Virginia, Maryland, Kentucky, and parts of North Carolina and Missouri during the 1800s (see Map 6–1). A difficult crop to produce, tobacco required a long growing season and careful cultivation. In the spring slaves had to transfer seedlings from sterilized seed beds to well-worked and manured soil. Then they had to hoe weeds, pick off insects, and prune lower leaves so the topmost leaves grew to their full extent. Slaves also built scaffolds used to cure the tobacco leaves and made the barrels in which the tobacco was shipped to market.

Robert Ellett, a former slave, recalled that when he was just eight years old he worked in Virginia "a-worming tobacco." He "examined tobacco leaves, pull[ed] off the worms, if there were any, and killed them." He claimed that if an overseer discovered that slaves had overlooked worms on the tobacco plants, the slaves were whipped or forced to eat the worms. Nancy Williams, another Virginia slave, recalled that sometimes as a punishment slaves had to inhale burning tobacco until they became nauseated.

Rice

Unlike the cultivation of tobacco, which spread westward and southward from Maryland and Virginia, rice production remained confined to the coastal waterways of South Carolina and Georgia. As they had since colonial times, slaves in these regions

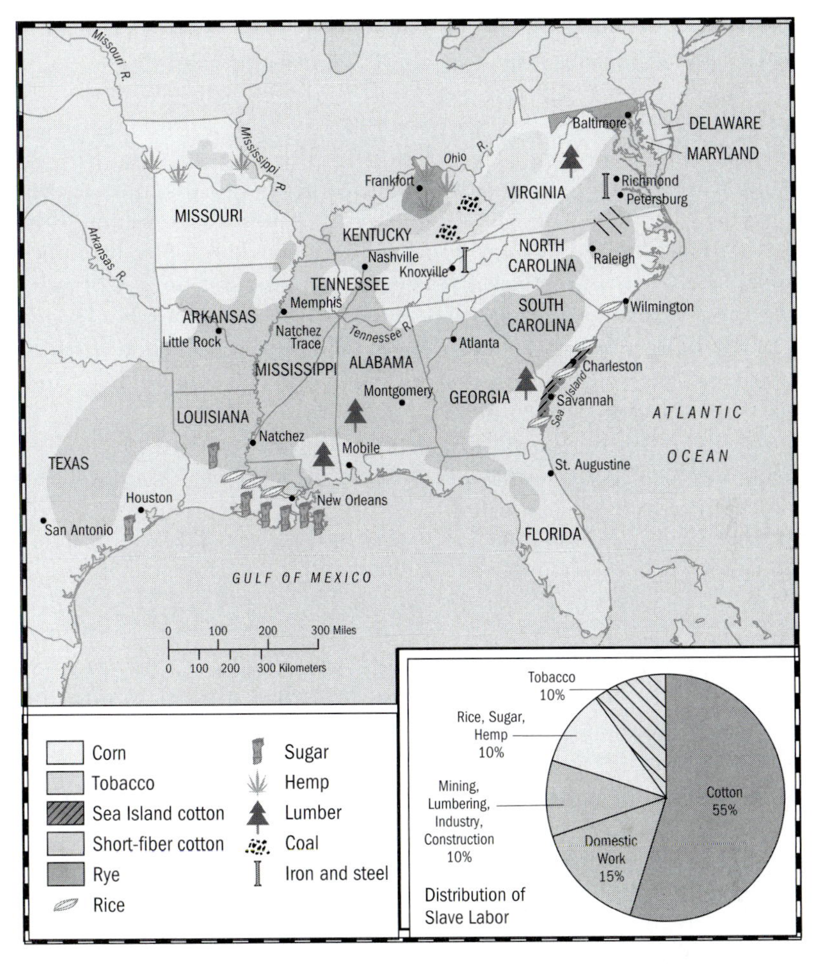

MAP 6–1 Agriculture, Industry, and Slavery in the Old South, 1850. The experience of African Americans in slavery varied according to their occupation and the region of the South in which they lived.

worked according to task systems that allowed them considerable autonomy. Because rice fields needed to be flooded for the seeds to germinate, slaves maintained elaborate systems of dikes and ditches. Influenced by West African methods, they sowed, weeded, and harvested the rice crop.

Rice cultivation was labor intensive, and rice plantations needed large labor forces to grow and harvest the crop and maintain the fields. By 1860 twenty rice plantations had 300 to 500 slaves, and eight others had between 500 and 1,000. The only American plantation employing more than 1,000 slaves was in the rice-producing region. These vast plantations represented sizable capital investments, and masters or overseers carefully monitored slave productivity. Although slaves enjoyed considerable leeway in how they performed their assigned duties, those who missed a day's work risked forfeiting their weekly allowance "of either bacon, sugar, molasses, or tobacco."

Sugar

Another important crop that grew in a restricted region was sugar, which slaves cultivated on plantations along the Mississippi River in southern Louisiana. Commercial production of sugarcane did not begin in Louisiana until the 1790s. It required a consistently warm climate, a long growing season, and at least sixty inches of rain per year.

Raising sugarcane and refining sugar also required constant labor. Together with the great profitability of the sugar crop, these demands encouraged masters to work their slaves hard. Slave life on sugar plantations was extremely harsh, and African Americans across the South feared being sent to labor on them.

Slaves did this work in hot and humid conditions, adding to the toll it took on their strength and health. Because cane could not be allowed to stand too long in the fields, harvesttime was hectic. As one former slave recalled, "On cane plantations in sugar time, there is no distinction as to the days of the week. They [the slaves] worked on the Sabbath as if it were Monday or Thursday."

Cotton

Although tobacco, rice, and sugar were economically significant, cotton was by far the South's and the country's most important staple crop. By 1860 cotton exports amounted to more than 50 percent annually of the dollar value of all U.S. exports. This was almost ten times the value of its nearest export competitors—wheat and wheat flour.

Cotton as a crop did not require cultivation as intensive as that needed for tobacco, rice, or sugar. But the cotton culture was so extensive that cotton planters as a group employed the most slave labor. By 1860 out of the 2,500,000 slaves employed in agriculture in the United States, 1,815,000 were producing cotton. Cotton drove the South's economy and its westward expansion. Even in rice-producing South Carolina and sugar-producing Louisiana, cotton was dominant, and cotton plantations employed the bulk of the slave populations.

Demand for cotton fiber in the textile mills of Britain and New England stimulated the westward spread of cotton cultivation. This demand increased by at least 5 percent per year between 1830 and 1860. In response—and with the essential aid of Whitney's cotton gin—American production of cotton rose from 10,000 bales in 1793 to 500,000 annually during the 1820s to 4,491,000 bales in 1860. The new states of Alabama, Louisiana, and Mississippi led this mounting production.

Potential profits drew white farmers to the rich Black Belt lands of Mississippi and Alabama during the early nineteenth century. Rapid population growth allowed Mississippi to gain statehood in 1817 and Alabama in 1819. White men with few slaves led the way into this southwestern cotton belt, and its frontier social structure allowed them to become plantation owners. Although their success was not certain and many of them failed, those who succeeded created large agricultural units because profits were directly related to the amount of cotton harvested. As a result, Mississippi and

Alabama—the leading producers of cotton—had by 1860 the greatest concentration of plantations with one hundred or more slaves. Twenty-four of Mississippi's slaveholders each owned between 308 and 899 slaves.

As these large agricultural units drew in labor, the price of slaves increased. During the 1830s, for example, a prime male field hand sold for $1,250 (about 21,000 current dollars) in the New Orleans slave market. Prices dipped during the hard times of the early 1840s. But by the 1850s, such slaves cost $1,800 (about 33,000 current dollars). Young women usually sold for up to $500 less than young men. Prices for elderly slaves dropped off sharply unless they were highly skilled.

The enslaved men and women who worked in the cotton fields rose before dawn when the master or overseer sounded the plantation bell or horn. They ate breakfast and then assembled in work gangs of twenty or twenty-five under the control of black slave drivers. They plowed and planted in the spring. They weeded with heavy hoes in the summer and harvested in the late fall. During harvest season, adult slaves picked about two hundred pounds of cotton per day. Regardless of the season, the work was hard, and white overseers frequently whipped those who seemed to be lagging. Slaves usually got a two-hour break at midday in the summer and an hour to an hour and a half in the winter. Then they returned to the fields until sunset, when they went back to their cabins for dinner and an early bedtime enforced by the master or overseer.

Other Crops

Besides cotton, sugar, tobacco, and rice, slaves in the Old South produced other crops, including hemp, corn, wheat, oats, rye, white potatoes, and sweet potatoes. They also raised cattle, hogs, sheep, and horses. The hogs, and corn and other grains, were mainly for consumption on the plantations themselves. But all the hemp, and much of the livestock and wheat, were raised for the market. In fact wheat replaced tobacco as the main cash crop in much of Maryland and Virginia. The transition to wheat encouraged many planters to substitute free labor for slave labor, but slaves grew wheat in the South until the Civil War.

Kentucky was the center of the hemp industry. Before the Civil War, Americans used hemp, which is closely related to marijuana, to make rope and bagging for cotton bales. As a result, hemp production tied Kentucky economically to the deep South. Hemp also led to a distinctive system of slavery in Kentucky because it required much less labor than rice, sugar, or cotton. Because three slaves could tend fifty acres of hemp, slave labor forces in Kentucky were much smaller than elsewhere. Robert Wickliffe, who was the largest slaveholder in the state during the 1840s, owned just two hundred slaves—a large number, but far fewer than his counterparts in the Cotton Belt.

House Servants and Skilled Slaves

About 75 percent of the slave workforce in the nineteenth century consisted of field hands. But because masters wanted to make their plantations as self-sufficient as possible, they employed some slaves as house servants and skilled craftsmen. Slaves who did not have to do field labor were an elite. Those who performed domestic duties, drove carriages, or learned a craft considered themselves privileged. However, they were also suspended between two different worlds.

House slaves worked as cooks, maids, butlers, nurses, and gardeners. Their work was less physically demanding than fieldwork, and they often received better food and clothing. Nevertheless, nineteenth-century kitchen work could be grueling, and maids and butlers were on call at all hours. House servants' jobs were also more stressful than field hands' jobs because the servants were under closer white supervision.

In addition, house servants were by necessity cut off from the slave community centered in the slave quarters. Nevertheless, as Olmsted pointed out during the 1850s, house servants rarely sought to become field hands. Conversely, field hands had little desire to be exposed to the constant surveillance house servants had to tolerate.

Skilled slaves tended to be even more of a slave elite than house slaves. As had been true earlier, black men had a decided advantage over black women—apart from those who became seamstresses—in becoming skilled. Slave carpenters, blacksmiths, and millwrights built and maintained plantation houses, slave quarters, and machinery. Because they might need to travel to get tools or spare parts, such skilled slaves gained a more cosmopolitan outlook than field hands or house servants. They got a taste of freedom, which from the masters' point of view was dangerous.

As plantation slavery declined in the Chesapeake, skilled slaves were able to leave their master's estate to "hire their time." Either they or their masters negotiated labor contracts with employers who needed their expertise. In effect, these slaves worked for money. Although masters often kept all or most of what they earned, some of these skilled slaves merely paid their master a set rate and lived as independent contractors.

Urban and Industrial Slavery

Most skilled slaves, who hired their time, lived in the South's towns and cities where they interacted with free black communities. Many of them resided in Baltimore and New Orleans, which were major ports and the Old South's largest cities. But there were others in such smaller southern urban centers as Richmond and Norfolk, Virginia; Atlanta and Augusta, Georgia; Washington, D.C.; Charleston, South Carolina; Louisville, Kentucky; and Memphis, Tennessee.

Slave populations in southern cities were often large, although they tended to decline between 1800 and 1860. In 1840 slaves were a majority of Charleston's population of 29,000. They nearly equaled white residents in Memphis and Augusta, which had total populations of 14,700 and 6,000, respectively. Slaves were almost one-quarter of New Orleans's population of 145,000.

Life in a city could be much more complicated for a slave than life on a plantation. When urban slaves were not working for their masters, they could earn money for themselves, and as a result, masters had a harder time controlling their lives. Those who contracted to provide their masters with a certain amount of money per year could live on their own, buying their own food and clothing. "You couldn't pay me," observed one slave woman, "to live at home if I could help myself."

Urban slaves served as domestics, washwomen, waiters, artisans, stevedores, drayers, hack drivers, and general laborers. In general, they did the urban work that foreign immigrants undertook in northern cities. If urban slaves purchased their freedom, they usually continued in the same line of work they had done as slaves. Particularly in border cities like Baltimore, Louisville, and Washington urban slaves increasingly relied on their free black neighbors—and sympathetic white people—to escape north. Urban masters often let slaves purchase their freedom over a term of years to keep them from leaving. In Baltimore, during the early nineteenth century, this sort of "term slavery" was gradually replacing slavery for life.

Industrial slavery overlapped with urban slavery, but southern industries that employed slaves were often in rural areas. By 1860 about 5 percent of southern slaves—approximately 200,000 people—worked in industry. Enslaved men, women, and children worked in textile mills in South Carolina and Georgia, sometimes beside white people. In Richmond and Petersburg, Virginia, during the 1850s, about six thousand slaves, most of whom were male, worked in factories producing chewing tobacco. Richmond's famous Tredegar Iron Works also employed a large slave workforce. So did earlier southern ironworks in Virginia, Maryland, northern Tennessee, and southern Kentucky.

The bulk of the sixteen thousand people who worked in the South's lumber industry in 1860 were slaves. Under the supervision of black drivers, they felled trees, operated sawmills, and delivered lumber. Slaves also did most of the work in the naval stores industry of North Carolina and Georgia, manufacturing tar, turpentine, and related products. In western Virginia, they labored in the salt works of the Great Kanawha River Valley, producing the salt used to preserve meat—especially the southern mainstay salt pork. During the 1820s the Maryland Chemical Works in Baltimore, which manufactured industrial chemicals, pigments, and medicines, included many slaves among its workers. Most southern industrialists hired slaves from their masters rather than buy them themselves, and the work slaves performed for them was often dangerous, as well as physically tiring. But, as historian John B. Boles points out, slaves came to prefer industrial jobs to plantation labor. Like urban slaves, industrial slaves had more opportunities to advance themselves, enjoyed more autonomy, and were often paid cash incentives. Industrial labor, like urban labor, was a path to freedom for some.

PUNISHMENT

Those who used slave labor, whether on plantations, small farms, in urban areas, or industry, frequently offered incentives to induce slaves to perform well. Yet slave labor by definition is forced labor based on the threat of physical punishment.

Southern whites also believed that African Americans would not work unless they were threatened with beatings. Fear of the lash drove slaves to do their work and to cooperate among themselves for mutual protection. Black parents and other older relatives taught slave children how to avoid punishment and still resist masters and overseers. They worked slowly—but not too slowly—and feigned illness to maintain their strength. They broke tools and injured mules, oxen, and horses to tacitly protest their condition. This pattern of covert resistance and physical punishment caused anxiety for both masters and slaves. Resistance often forced masters to reduce work hours and improve conditions. Yet few slaves escaped being whipped at least once during their lives in bondage.

The Domestic Slave Trade

The expansion of the Cotton Kingdom south and west combined with the decline of slavery in the Chesapeake to stimulate the domestic slave trade. As masters in Delaware, Maryland, Virginia, North Carolina, and Kentucky trimmed excess slaves from their workforces—or switched entirely from slave to wage labor—they sold men, women, and children to slave traders. The traders in turn shipped these unfortunate people to the slave markets of New Orleans and other cities for resale. Masters also sold slaves as punishment, and fear of being "sold down river" led many slaves in the Chesapeake to escape. A vicious circle resulted: masters sold slaves south to prevent their escape and slaves escaped to avoid being sold south.

The number of people traded was huge and, considering that many of them were ripped away from their families, tragic. Starting in the 1820s, about 150,000 slaves per decade moved toward the southwest either with their masters or traders. Between 1820 and 1860, an estimated 50 percent of the slaves of the upper South moved involuntarily into the Southwest.

Traders operated compounds called slave prisons or slave pens in Baltimore, Maryland; Washington, D.C.; Alexandria and Richmond, Virginia; Charleston, South Carolina; and in smaller cities as well. Most of the victims of the trade moved on foot in groups called "coffles," chained or roped together. From the 1810s onward, northern and European visitors to Washington noted the coffles passing before the U.S. Capitol. There was also a considerable coastal trade in slaves from Chesapeake ports to New Orleans and, by the 1840s, some slave traders were carrying their human cargoes in railroad cars.

The domestic slave trade demonstrated the falseness of slaveholders' claims that slavery was a benign institution. Driven by economic necessity, by profit, or by a desire to frustrate escape plans, masters in the upper South irrevocably separated husbands and wives, mothers and children, brothers and sisters. Traders sometimes tore babies from their mothers' arms. The journey from the Chesapeake to Mississippi, Alabama, or Louisiana could be long and hard, and some slaves died along the way. A few managed to keep in touch with those they had left behind through letters and travelers. But most could not, and after the abolition of slavery in 1865, many African Americans used their new freedom to travel across the South looking for relatives from whom they had been separated long before.

Slave Families

The families that enslaved African Americans sought to preserve had been developing in America since the seventeenth century. However, such families had no legal standing. Most enslaved men and women could choose their own mates, although masters sometimes arranged such things. Masters encouraged pairings among female and male slaves because they assumed correctly that black husbands and fathers would be less rebellious than single men. Masters were also aware that they would benefit if their human chattel reproduced. As Thomas Jefferson put it, "I consider a [slave] woman who brings [gives birth to] a child every two years as more profitable than the best man on the farm. What she produces is an addition to the capital, while his labors disappear in mere consumption."

Families were also the core of the African-American community in slavery. Even though no legal sanctions supported slave marriages and the domestic slave trade could sunder them, many such marriages endured. Before they wed, some couples engaged in courting rituals while others rejected "such foolishness." Similarly, slave weddings ranged from simply "taking up" to religious ceremonies replete with food and frolics.

"Jumping the broom" was often part of these ceremonies, although this custom was not African but European. During the 1930s former slave Tempie Herndon recalled her wedding ceremony conducted by "de nigger preacher dat preached at de plantation church." In particular, she remembered that after the religious ceremony, "Marse George got to have his little fun" by having the newlyweds jump backward over a broomstick. "You got to do dat to see which one gwine be boss of your household," she commented. "If both of dem jump over without touchin' it, dey won't gwine be no bossin', dey just gwine be congenial." In fact, more equality existed between husbands and wives in slave marriages than in those of the masters. Southern white concepts of patriarchy required male dominance. But because black men lacked power, their wives were more like partners than servants.

Slave couples usually lived together in cabins on their master's property. They had little privacy because nineteenth-century slave cabins were rude, small one-room dwellings that two families might have to share. But couples who shared cabins were generally better off than husbands and wives who were the property of different masters and lived on different plantations. In these cases, children lived with their mother, and their father visited when he could in the evenings. Work patterns that changed with the seasons or with the mood of a master could interfere with such visits. So could the requirement that slaves have passes to leave home.

Children

Despite these difficulties, slave parents were able to instruct their children in family history, religion, and the skills required to survive in slavery. They sang to their children and told them stories full of folk wisdom. In particular, they impressed on them the importance of extended family relationships. The ability to rely on grandparents, aunts and uncles, cousins, and honorary relatives was a hedge against the family disruption that the domestic slave trade might inflict. In this manner, too, the extended black family became the core of the black community that provided slaves with the independent resources they needed to avoid complete physical, intellectual, cultural, and moral subjugation to their masters.

During an age when infant mortality rates were much higher than they are today, those for black southerners were even higher than they were for white people. There were several reasons for this. Enslaved black women usually had to do field labor up to the time they delivered a child, and their diets lacked necessary nutrients. Consequently, they tended to have babies whose weights at birth were less than normal. In addition, black infants were more likely to be subject to such postpartum maladies as rickets, tetany, tetanus, high fevers, intestinal worms, and influenza than were other children. More than 50 percent of slave children died before the age of five.

This is an 1862 photograph of a multigenerational black family held in slavery on a plantation in Beaufort, South Carolina. The photograph provides information regarding the type of clothing slaves wore and the sort of living conditions they endured.
Courtesy of the Library of Congress

Slaveholders contributed to high infant mortality rates probably more from ignorance than malevolence. It was, after all, in the master's economic self-interest to have slave mothers produce healthy children. Masters often allowed mothers a month to recuperate after giving birth and time off from fieldwork to nurse their babies for several months thereafter. Although this reduced the mother's productivity, the losses would be made up by the children's labor when they entered the plantation workforce. Unfortunately, many infants needed more than a few months of breast-feeding to survive.

The care of slave children varied with the size of a slaveholder's estate, the region it was in, and the mother's work. House servants could carry their babies with them while they did their work. On small farms, slave women strapped their babies to their backs or left them at the edge of fields, so they could nurse them periodically, although the latter practice risked exposing an infant to ants, flies, or mosquitoes. On larger plantations, mothers could leave a child with an elderly or infirm adult. This encouraged a sense of community and a shared responsibility among the slaves for all black children on a plantation.

Slave childhood was short. Early on, parents and other elders taught children about the realities of plantation life. By witnessing whippings—sometimes of their parents—and through admonitions from their elders, slave children learned they had to be extremely careful about what they said to white people. Deceit and guile became survival skills. Slave childhood was also short because children as young as six had to do so-called light chores. Such work became physically more taxing as a child grew older, until the child began doing adult fieldwork between the ages of eight and twelve. That slave children were subject to sale away from their families, particularly in the upper South, also accelerated their progress to adulthood.

Sexual Exploitation

As with forced separations, masters' sexual exploitation of black women disrupted enslaved families. This abuse of black women began during the middle passage and continued after the abolition of slavery in the United States in 1865. Long-term relationships between masters and enslaved women were common in the nineteenth-century South. Such continuing relationships were based not on overt coercion but on masters' implicit power and authority. But even more common were masters, overseers, and their sons who, by one means or another, forced slave women to have sex against their will. This routine conduct caused great distress. Former slave Harriet Jacobs wrote in her autobiography, "I cannot tell how much I suffered in the presence of these wrongs, nor how I am still pained by the retrospect."

One of the more famous antebellum (pre–Civil War) cases of sexual exploitation occurred in Missouri during the 1850s. It involved sixty-year-old Robert Newsom and Celia, a fourteen-year-old girl he had purchased in 1850. Newsom repeatedly raped Celia until she killed him in 1855. Celia's attorneys put up a spirited defense at her trial. They argued that an 1845 Missouri law that made it a crime to "take any woman unlawfully against her will and by force, menace or duress, compel her to be defiled" gave Celia a right to defend her virtue. But the white male jury convicted her of murder anyway, and she was executed.

Throughout its existence, slavery in America encouraged white men to exploit black women for sexual purposes and to physically abuse black men and women. *Virginian Luxuries*, painted c. 1810, aims to expose and ridicule these practices.
Abby Aldrich Rockefeller Folk Art Museum, Williamsburg, VA. Colonial Williamsburg Foundation, Williamsburg, VA

White southerners justified sexual abuse of black women in several ways. They maintained that black women were naturally promiscuous and seduced white men. Some proslavery apologists argued that the sexual exploitation of black women by white men reduced prostitution and promoted purity among white women. These apologists ignored the devastating emotional impact of sexual exploitation on black women. They failed to note that the rape of black women by white men emphasized in the most degrading manner the inability of black men to protect their wives and daughters.

Diet

The typical plantation's weekly ration of one peck of cornmeal and three to four pounds of salt pork or bacon was enough to maintain an adult's body weight and, therefore, appeared to be adequate. But even when black men and women added vegetables and poultry that they raised or fish and small game that they caught, this diet was deficient in calcium, vitamin C, riboflavin, protein, and iron. Because these vitamins and nutrients were essential to the health of people who performed hard labor in a hot climate, slaves frequently suffered from chronic illnesses.

Yet masters and white southerners generally consumed the same sort of food that slaves ate and, in comparison to people in other parts of the Atlantic world, enslaved African Americans were not undernourished. Although adult slaves were on average an inch shorter than white northerners, they were three inches taller than new arrivals from Africa, two inches taller than slaves who lived in the West Indies, and one inch taller than British Royal Marines.

African-American cooks, primarily women, developed a distinctive cuisine based on African culinary traditions. They seasoned foods with salt, onions, pepper, and other spices and herbs. They fried meat and fish, served sauce over rice, and flavored vegetables with bits of smoked meat. The availability in the South of such African foods as okra, yams, benne seeds, and peanuts strengthened their culinary ties to that continent. Cooking also gave black women the ability to control part of their lives and to demonstrate their creativity.

Clothing

Slaves in general rarely had the time or skill to make their own clothes. They went barefoot during the warm months and wore cheap shoes, usually made by local cobblers, in the winter. Slaveholding women, with the help of trained female house servants, sewed the clothes slaves wore. This clothing was usually made of homespun cotton or wool.

Slaves usually received clothing allotments twice a year. At the fall distribution, slave men received two outfits for the cold weather along with a jacket and a wool cap. At the spring distribution, they received two cotton outfits. Slave drivers wore garments of finer cloth and greatcoats during the winter. Butlers and carriage drivers wore liveries appropriate to their public duties. Slave women received at each distribution two simply cut dresses of calico or homespun. In the winter they wore capes or cloaks and covered their heads with kerchiefs or bonnets.

Because masters gave priority to clothing adult workers, small children often went naked during the warm months. Depending on their ages and the season, children received garments called *shirts* if worn by boys and *shifts* if worn by girls.

Although they received standard-issue clothing, black women particularly sought to individualize what they wore. They changed the colors of clothes with dyes they extracted from roots, berries, walnut shells, oak leaves, and indigo. They wove threads of different color into their clothes to make "checkedy" and other patterns.

To further adorn themselves, young women wore hoops under their skirts fashioned from grapevines, stiffly starched petticoats, intricately arranged turbans, and colorful kerchiefs. On special occasions they braided or twisted their hair, used rouge made from berries, eye shadow made from soot, and perfume derived from honeysuckle. Urban slaves, of course, had access to commercial products, and even plantation slaves often bought clothes, shoes, ribbons, and kerchiefs at local stores or from peddlers.

Health

Low birth weight, diet, and clothing all affected the health of slaves. Before the 1830s various diseases were endemic among bond people, and death could come quickly. Much of this ill health resulted from overwork in the South's hot, humid summers, from exposure to cold during the winter, and from poor hygiene. Slave quarters, for example, rarely had privies; drinking water could become contaminated; and food was prepared under less than healthy conditions. Dysentery, typhus, food poisoning, diarrhea, hepatitis, typhoid fever, salmonella, and intestinal worms were common and sometimes fatal maladies.

The South's warm climate encouraged mosquito-borne diseases, the growth of bacteria, and the spread of viruses. Some diseases were passed from one race to another. Smallpox, measles, and gonorrhea were European diseases; malaria, hookworm, and yellow fever came from Africa. The sickle-cell blood trait protected people of African descent from malaria but could cause sickle-cell anemia, a painful, debilitating, and fatal disease. African Americans were also more susceptible to other afflictions than were persons of European descent.

They suffered from lactose intolerance, which greatly limited the amount of calcium they could absorb from dairy products, and from a limited ability to acquire enough vitamin D from the sunlight in temperate regions. Because many slaves also lost calcium through perspiration while working, these characteristics led to a high incidence of debilitating diseases. These included, according to historian Donald R. Wright, "blindness or inflamed and watery eyes; lameness or crooked limbs; loose, missing or rotten teeth; and skin sores. Also, they made African Americans much more apt than whites to suffer from a number of often fatal diseases—tetanus, intestinal worms, diphtheria, whooping cough, pica (or dirt eating), pneumonia, tuberculosis, and dysentery."

However, black southerners constituted the only New World slave population that grew by natural reproduction. Although the death rate among slaves was higher than among white southerners, it was similar to that of Europeans. Slave health also improved after 1830 when their rising economic value persuaded masters to improve slave quarters, provide warmer winter clothing, reduce overwork, and hire physicians to care for bond people. During the 1840s and 1850s, slaves were more likely than white southerners to be cared for by a physician.

Enslaved African Americans also used traditional remedies—derived from Africa and passed down by generations of women—to treat the sick. Wild cherry bark and herbs like pennyroyal or horehound went into teas to treat colds. Slaves used jimsonweed tea to counter rheumatism and chestnut leaf tea to relieve asthma. One former slave recalled that her grandmother dispensed syrup to treat colic and teas to cure fevers and stomachaches. Nineteenth-century medical knowledge was so limited that some of these folk remedies were more effective than those prescribed by white physicians. This was especially true of kaolin, a white clay also used in ceramics, which black women used to treat dysentery.

The Socialization of Slaves

African Americans had to acquire the skills needed to protect themselves and their loved ones from a brutal slave system. Folktales often derived from Africa, but on occasion from American Indians, helped pass such skills from generation to generation. Parents, other relatives, and elderly slaves generally told such tales to teach survival, mental agility, and self-confidence.

The heroes of the tales are animal tricksters with human personalities. Most famous is Brer Rabbit who in his weakness and cleverness represents African Americans in slavery. Although the tales portray Brer Rabbit as far from perfect, he uses his wits to overcome threats from strong and vicious antagonists, principally Brer Fox, who represents slaveholders. By hearing these stories and rooting for Brer Rabbit, slave children learned how to conduct themselves in a difficult environment.

They learned to watch what they said to white people, not to talk back, to withhold information about other African Americans, to dissemble. In particular, they refrained from making antislavery statements and camouflaged their awareness of how masters exploited them. As Henry Bibb, who escaped from slavery, put it, "The only weapon of self defense that I could use successfully was that of deception." Another former slave, Charshee Charlotte Lawrence-McIntyre, summed up the slave strategy in rhyme: "Got one mind for the boss to see; got another for what I know is me."

Masters tended to miss the subtlety of the divided consciousness of their bond people. When slaves refused to do simple tasks correctly, masters saw it as black stupidity rather than resistance.

Religion

Along with family and socialization, religion helped African Americans cope with slavery. Some masters denied their slaves access to Christianity, and some slaves ignored the religion. In New Orleans, Baltimore, and a few other locations there were Roman Catholic slaves, who were usually the human property of individual Roman Catholic masters. In Maryland during the 1830s the Jesuits, an order of Roman Catholic priests and brothers, collectively owned approximately three hundred slaves. But by the mid-nineteenth century, the overwhelming majority of American slaves practiced a Protestantism similar, but not identical, to that of most white southerners.

Biracial Baptist and Methodist congregations persisted in the South longer than they did in northern cities. The southern congregations usually had racially segregated seating, but blacks and whites joined in communion and church discipline, and they shared cemeteries. Many masters during the nineteenth century sponsored plantation churches for slaves, and white missionary organizations also supported such churches.

In the plantation churches, white ministers told their black congregations that Christian slaves must obey their earthly masters as they did God. This was not what slaves wanted to hear. Cornelius Garner, a former slave, recalled that "dat ole white preacher jest was telling us slaves to be good to our marsters. We ain't keer'd a bit 'bout dat stuff he was telling us' cause we wanted to sing, pray, and serve God in our own way." At times slaves walked out on ministers who preached obedience.

Instead of services sponsored by masters, slaves preferred a semisecret black church they conducted themselves. This was a church characterized by self-called, often illiterate black preachers. It emphasized Moses and deliverance from bondage rather than a consistent theology or Christian meekness. Services were quite emotional and involved singing, dancing, shouting, moaning, and clapping. Mixed in with this black Christianity were, according to historian Peter Kolchin, African "potions, concoctions, charms, and rituals [used] to ward off evil, cure sickness, harm enemies, and produce amorous behavior."

The Character of Slavery and Slaves

For over a century, historians have debated the character of the Old South's slave system and the people it held in bondage. During the 1910s southern historian Ulrich B. Phillips portrayed slavery as a benign, paternalistic institution in which Christian slaveholders cared for largely content slaves. Slavery, Phillips argued—as had the slaveholders themselves—rescued members of an inferior race from African barbarism and permitted them to rise as far as they possibly could toward civilization. With a much different emphasis, Marxist historian Eugene D. Genovese has, since the 1960s, seen paternalism at the heart of southern plantation slavery.

Other historians, however, have denied that paternalism had much to do with a system that rested on force. Since the 1950s historians have contended that slaveholders exploited their bond people in a selfish quest for profits. Although some slaveholders were concerned about the welfare of their slaves, this brutal portrait of slavery is persuasive at the dawn of the twenty-first century. Many masters never met their slaves face to face. Most slaves experienced whipping at some point in their lives, and over half the slaves caught up in the domestic slave trade were separated from their families.

The character of enslaved African Americans has also been debated. Historians such as Phillips, who were persuaded by the slaveholders' justifications of the "peculiar institution," argued that African Americans were genetically predisposed to being slaves and were therefore content in their status. In 1959 Stanley M. Elkins changed the debate by arguing that black people were not inherently inferior or submissive, but that concentration-camp-like conditions on plantations made them into childlike "Sambos" as dependent on their masters as inmates in Nazi extermination camps were on their guards.

Elkins's study stimulated the scholarship that shapes current understandings of the character of African Americans in slavery. Since the 1960s historians have argued that rather than dehumanize them, slavery led African Americans to create institutions that allowed them some control over their lives. According to these historians, African-American resistance forced masters to accept the slaves' own work patterns and their autonomy in the slave quarters. Slaves built families, churches, and communities. Although these studies may overidealize the strength of slave communities within the brutal context of plantation slavery, they have enriched our understanding of slave life.

TIMELINE

AFRICAN-AMERICAN EVENTS	NATIONAL EVENTS
1810	
	1812 Louisiana becomes a state
1815	
1816 William Ellison purchases his freedom **818** Suppression of Charleston's AME Church **1819** Frederick Douglass born in Maryland	**1817** Mississippi becomes a state **1819** Alabama becomes a state
1820	
1822 Denmark Vesey Conspiracy, Charleston, S.C.	**1820** Missouri Compromise **1821** Missouri becomes a state **1824** John Quincy Adams elected president of United States
1825	
	1828 Andrew Jackson elected president

continued

AFRICAN-AMERICAN EVENTS	NATIONAL EVENTS
1830	
1831 Nat Turner's Revolt **1832** Virginia Legislature defeats gradual abolition	
1835	
1838 Frederick Douglass apprenticed in Baltimore **1839** *Amistad* Slave revolt	**1836** Cherokee Trail of Tears
1840	
1841 Solomon Northup kidnapped	
1845	
1845 Betsy Somayrac's will	**1845** Texas annexed as a slave state **1846** War against Mexico begins **1848** Annexation of New Mexico and California
1850	
1852 Frederick Law Olmsted's first tour of southern states **1853** Solomon Northup publishes *Twelve Years a Slave*	**1850** Compromise of 1850 **1854** Kansas-Nebraska Act
1855	
1855 Celia's trial and execution for killing her master **1857** Supreme Court issues Dred Scott Decision	**1856** Republican Party's first presidential election
1860	
	1860 The secession movement begins

CONCLUSION

African-American life in slavery during the time of the Cotton Kingdom is a vast subject. As slavery expanded westward before 1860, it varied from region to region and according to the crops slaves cultivated. Although cotton became the South's most important product, many African-American slaves continued to produce tobacco, rice, sugar, and hemp. In the Chesapeake, slaves worked on wheat farms. Others tended livestock or worked in cities and industry. Meanwhile, enslaved African Americans continued to build the community institutions that allowed them to maintain their cultural autonomy and persevere within a brutal system.

The story of African Americans in southern slavery is one of labor, perseverance, and resistance. Black labor was responsible for the growth of a southern economy that helped produce prosperity throughout the United States. Black men and women preserved and expanded an African-American cultural heritage that included African, European, and American Indian roots. They resisted determined efforts to dehumanize them. They developed family relationships, communities, churches, and traditions that helped them preserve their character as a people.

Review Questions

1. How did the domestic slave trade and the exploitation of black women by white males affect slave families?
2. Were black slaveholders significant in the history of slavery?
3. How did urban and industrial slavery differ from plantation slavery in the Old South?
4. What impact did housing, nutrition, and disease have on the lives of slaves between 1820 and 1860?
5. How did black Christianity differ from white Christianity in the Old South? How did black Christianity in the South differ from black Christianity in the North?

Recommended Reading

Charles B. Dew. *Bonds of Iron: Masters and Slaves at Buffalo Forge.* New York: Norton, 1994. Dew offers an excellent account of one type of industrial slavery in the Old South.

Michael P. Johnson and James L. Roark. *Black Masters: A Free Family of Color in the Old South.* New York: Norton, 1984. This book provides a full account of William Ellison and his slaveholding black family.

Norrece T. Jones Jr. *Born a Child of Freedom, Yet a Slave: Mechanisms of Control and Strategies of Resistance in Antebellum South Carolina.* Middleton, CT: Wesleyan University Press, 1990. This book explores how masters controlled slaves and how slaves resisted.

Wilma King. *Stolen Childhood: Slave Youth in Nineteenth-Century America.* Bloomington: Indiana University Press, 1995. This is the most up-to-date account of enslaved black children. It is especially useful concerning the children's work.

Peter Kolchin. *American Slavery, 1619–1877.* New York: Hill and Wang, 1993. The bulk of this book deals with slavery during the antebellum period. It provides a brief but comprehensive introduction to the subject.

Melton A. McLaurin. *Celia, a Slave.* Athens: University of Georgia Press, 1991. This is the most complete study of an enslaved woman's response to sexual exploitation. MacLaurin establishes the social and political contexts for this famous case.

• CHAPTER SEVEN •

FREE BLACK PEOPLE IN ANTEBELLUM AMERICA

DEMOGRAPHICS OF FREEDOM

In 1820 there were 233,504 free African Americans living in the United States. In comparison there were 1,538,125 slaves and 7,861,931 white people. Of the free African Americans, 99,281 lived in the North, 114,070 in the upper South, and just 20,153 in the deep South. Free people of color accounted for 2.4 percent of the American population and 3 percent of the southern population. More black women than black men were free, and—particularly in urban areas—this remained true throughout the period. As the southern states made freedom suits and manumission more difficult, the northern free black population increased more rapidly than the free black populations in either the upper or deep South.

By 1860 the free African-American population had reached 488,070. Of these, 226,152 lived in the North, 224,963 in the upper South, and 36,955 in the deep South (see Figure 7–1). A few thousand free black people also lived in the west beyond Missouri, Arkansas, and Texas. Yet slaves had increased to just under four million, and massive immigration had tripled the white population to 26,957,471. The proportion of free African Americans had actually dropped to just 1.6 percent of the total American population and to 2.1 percent of the southern population when the Civil War in 1861 began the process of making all black people free.

However, 47.3 percent of the free black population lived in cities in 1860 compared with only 32.9 percent of white people—and of those urban African Americans, 62.5 percent lived in cities with populations over 100,000. As a result, free African Americans accounted for a significantly larger percentage of the population of large cities than they did of the total American population.

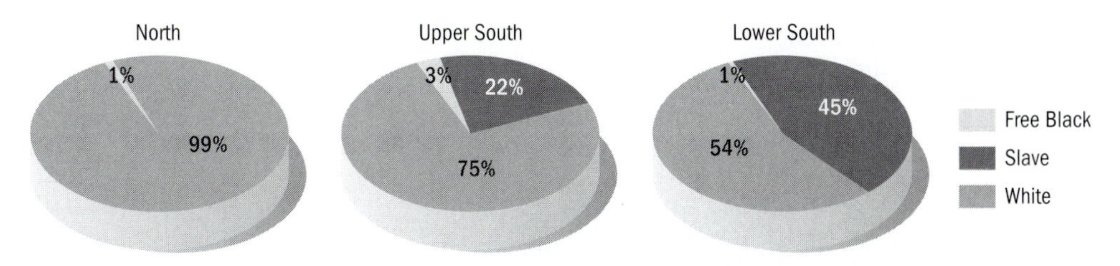

Figure 7–1 **The Free Black, Slave, and White Population by Region, 1860**
These pie charts compare the free black, slave, and white populations of the North, upper South, and lower South in 1860. Note the near balance of the races in the deep South.

The black populations of such important northern cities as New York, Boston, Providence, New Haven, and Cincinnati were considerably smaller than Philadelphia's, but they were still large enough to develop dynamic communities. In Baltimore, Richmond, Norfolk, and other cities of the upper South, free African Americans interacted with enslaved populations to create black communities embracing both groups.

The Jacksonian Era

After the War of 1812, free African Americans—like other Americans of the time—witnessed rapid economic, social, and political change. Between 1800 and 1860, a market revolution transformed the North into a modern industrial society. An economy based on subsistance farming, goods produced by skilled artisans, and local markets grew into one marked by commercial farming, factory production, and national markets. The industrial revolution that had begun in Britain a century earlier set the stage for these changes. But transportation had to improve enormously to allow for such a revolution in America. After Robert Fulton demonstrated the practicality of steam-powered river vessels in 1807, steamboats speeded travel on the country's inland waterways. By the 1820s a system of turnpikes and canals began to unite the North and parts of the South. Of particular importance were the National Road extending westward from Baltimore and the Erie Canal that in 1825 opened a water route from New York City to the Old Northwest. By the 1830s railroads began to link urban and agricultural regions.

As faster transportation revolutionized trade, as a factory system began to replace small shops run by artisans, and as cities expanded, northern society changed in profound ways. A large urban working class arose. Artisans and small farmers feared for their future. Entrepreneurs began to replace the traditional social elite. The North also became increasingly different from a still largely premodern South. By the 1820s the northern states were bristling with reform movements designed to deal with the social dislocations the market revolution had caused.

The market revolution also helped create mass political parties. By 1810 states across the country began dropping the traditional property qualifications that had limited citizens' right to vote. One by one, they moved toward universal white manhood suffrage. This trend doomed the openly elitist Federalist Party and disrupted its foe, the Republican Party. As the market revolution picked up during the 1820s, unleashing hopes and fears among Americans, politicians recognized the need for more broadly based political parties.

A turning point came in 1825 when Congress chose Secretary of State John Quincy Adams of Massachusetts to become president over war hero Andrew Jackson of Tennessee, after no candidate received a majority of the electoral votes. As president, Adams paradoxically represented both the old elitist style of politics and the entrepreneurial spirit of emerging northern capitalism. Adams, along with his secretary of state, Henry Clay, hoped to promote industrialization through a national program of federal government aid.

Jackson's supporters, led by Martin Van Buren of New York, organized a new Democratic Party to counter Adams and Clay's program by making Jackson president. By appealing to slaveholders, who feared that economic nationalism would favor the North over the South, and to "the common man" throughout the country, the Democrats elected Jackson in 1828.

Jackson was a strong but controversial president. During the Nullification Crisis of 1832–1833 he acted as a nationalist in facing down the attempt of South Carolina to nullify—to block—the collection of the U.S. tariff (tax) on imports within the state. Otherwise, Jackson, who owned many slaves, promoted states' rights, economic localism, and the territorial expansion of slavery. In opposition to Jackson, Henry Clay, a Kentucky slaveholder, and others formed the Whig Party during the early 1830s.

A national organization that fought the Democrats for power from 1834 to 1852, the Whig Party mixed traditional and modern politics. It was a mass political party, but many of its leaders questioned the legitimacy of mass parties. It favored a nationalist approach to economic policy, which made it more successful in the North than in the South, opposed territorial expansion, worried about the growing number of immigrants, and endorsed the moral values of evangelical Protestantism. In contrast to Democratic politicians who increasingly made racist appeals to antiblack prejudices among white voters, Whigs generally adopted a more conciliatory tone regarding race. By the late 1830s, a few northern Whigs believed their party actually opposed slavery and racial oppression. They were, however, exaggerating. The Whigs constantly nominated slaveholders for the presidency, and few Whig politicians defended the rights of African Americans.

LIMITED FREEDOM IN THE NORTH

Addressing an interracial audience in Boston, white abolitionist Joseph C. Lovejoy in 1846 described the North as a land "partially free." Lovejoy was especially concerned that the Fugitive Slave Law of 1793 extended into the northern states the power of southern slaveholders to enslave African Americans. But white northerners also limited black freedom by enacting black laws, by rarely allowing black men to vote, by advocating segregated housing, schools, and transportation, and by limiting African Americans' employment opportunities.

The Fugitive Slave Law endangered the freedom of northern black men, women, and children. Those who had escaped from slavery, of course, lived in fear that as long as they stayed in the United States they might be seized and returned to their erstwhile masters. In fact, any black northerner could be kidnapped, taken to a southern state, and enslaved under the aegis of this law.

Black Laws

Most white northerners wanted nothing to do with African Americans. Like white southerners, they considered black people inferior in every way. They paradoxically dismissed black people as incapable of honest work and feared black competition for jobs. Contact with African Americans, they believed, had degraded white southerners and would also corrupt white northerners if they permitted it. Therefore, as historian Leon Litwack puts it, "Nearly every northern state considered, and many adopted, measures to prohibit or restrict the further immigration of Negroes" into its jurisdiction.

Such measures were adopted more often in the Old Northwest than in the Northeast. In 1821 a bill to restrict black people from entering Massachusetts failed to reach a vote in the state legislature on the grounds that it was inconsistent with "love of humanity." In Pennsylvania, which had a much larger influx of southern African Americans than did Massachusetts, the legislature defeated attempts to limit their entry to the state. But Ohio, Illinois, Indiana, Michigan, Iowa, and Wisconsin all limited or banned black immigration and discriminated against black residents.

Between 1804 and 1849, Ohio's "black laws" required that African Americans entering the state produce legal evidence that they were free, register with a county clerk, and post a $500 bond "to pay for their support in case of want." State and local authorities rarely enforced these provisions, and when the Ohio Free Soil Party brought about their repeal in 1849, Ohio had about 25,000 African Americans. But these rules certainly made black people insecure. In 1829, for example, Cincinnati used them to force between 1,100 and 2,200 black residents to depart. Moreover, other provisions of Ohio's black laws were rigorously enforced, including those that prohibited black testimony against white people, black service on juries, and black enlistment in the state militia.

In 1813 the Illinois Territory threatened that African Americans who tried to settle within its borders would be repeatedly whipped until they left. In 1847, long after it had become a state, Illinois updated this provision by mandating that African Americans who sought to become permanent residents could be fined. Those who could not pay the fine could be sold at public auction into indentured servitude.

This lithograph, published in 1818 by antislavery author Jesse Torrey Jun, depicts a free black man still in handcuffs and leg irons after an attempt to kidnap him into slavery. He is relating details of his experience to a sympathetic white man. The sparsely furnished attic room reflects the living conditions of many free African Americans of the time.
Courtesy of the Library of Congress

Indiana citizens ratified a state constitution in 1851 that explicitly banned all African Americans from the state, and Michigan, Iowa, and Wisconsin followed Indiana's example. These laws testify to white prejudice and fear. They suggest how uncomfortable African Americans felt in the Old Northwest. Yet, as in Ohio, these states rarely enforced such restrictive laws. As long as they did not feel threatened, white people were usually willing to tolerate a few black people.

Disfranchisement

The disfranchisement of black voters was, excepting most of New England, common throughout the North during the antebellum decades. The same white antipathy to African Americans that led to exclusionary legislation supported the movement to deny the right to vote to black men (no women could vote anywhere in the United States during most of the nineteenth century). Because northern antiblack sentiment was strongest in the Old Northwest, prior to the Civil War no black men were allowed to vote in Ohio, Indiana, Illinois, Michigan, Wisconsin, and Iowa. But the older northern states had allowed black male suffrage, and efforts to curtail it were by-products of Jacksonian democracy.

During the eighteenth and early nineteenth centuries, the dominant elite in the northeastern states had used property qualifications to prevent both poor black and poor white men from voting. Because black people were generally poorer than white people, these property qualifications gave most white men the right to vote but denied it to most black men. Under such circumstances white people saw no danger in letting a few relatively well-to-do black men exercise the franchise. It was the egalitarian movement to remove property qualifications that led to the outright disfranchisement of most black voters in the Northeast.

Both advocates and opponents of universal white male suffrage argued it would be dangerous to extend the same privilege to black men. They alleged that in certain places black men would be elected to office, morally suspect African Americans would corrupt the political process, black people would be encouraged to try to mix socially with white people, and that justifiably angry white people would react violently. Therefore, the movement for universal white manhood suffrage transformed a class issue into a racial one, and although a few white politicians opposed disfranchisement of black voters, the outcome was predictable.

New Jersey stopped allowing black men to vote in 1807 and in 1844 adopted a white-only suffrage provision in its state constitution. In 1818 Connecticut determined that, although black men who had voted before that date could continue to vote, no new black voters would be allowed. At the other extreme, Maine, New Hampshire, Vermont, and Massachusetts—none of which had a significant African-American minority—made no effort to deprive black men of the vote. In the middle were Rhode Island, New York, and Pennsylvania, which had protracted struggles over the issue.

In 1822 Rhode Island denied that black men were eligible to vote in its elections, but in 1842 a popular uprising against the state's conservative government extended the franchise to all men, black as well as white. In New York an 1821 state constitutional convention defeated an attempt to disfranchise all black men. Instead, it raised the property qualification for black voters while eliminating it for white voters. To vote in New York, black men had to have property worth $250 (approximately 3,000 current dollars) and pay taxes, whereas white men simply had to pay taxes or serve in the state militia. This provision denied the right to vote to nearly all of the ten thousand black men who had previously voted in the state.

From 1780 to 1837, black men who met property qualifications could vote in some of this state's counties but not in others. Then, in 1838, a convention to draft a new state constitution enfranchised all white men and disfranchised all black men. As late as 1855, black Pennsylvanians, arguing that without the right to vote they faced mounting repression, petitioned Congress to help them gain equal access to the polls. But their efforts failed.

Segregation

Exclusionary legislation was confined to the Old Northwest, and not all northern states disfranchised black men. But no black northerner could avoid being victimized by a pervasive determination among white people to segregate society.

Northern hotels, taverns, and resorts turned black people away unless they were the servants of white guests. African Americans were either banned from public lecture halls, art exhibits, and religious revivals or could attend only at certain times. When they were allowed in churches and theaters, they had to sit in segregated sections. Ohio excluded African Americans from state-supported poorhouses and insane asylums. In relatively enlightened Massachusetts, prominent black abolitionist and orator Frederick Douglass was "within the space of a few days . . . turned away from a menagerie on Boston Common, a lyceum and revival meeting in New Bedford, [and] an eating house."

African Americans faced special difficulty trying to use public transportation. They could ride in stagecoaches only if there were no white passengers. As rail travel became more common during the late 1830s, companies set aside special cars for African Americans. In Massachusetts in 1841, a railroad first used the term *Jim Crow,* which derived from a blackface minstrel act, to describe these cars. Later the term came to define other forms of racial segregation as well. In cities, many omnibus and streetcar companies barred African Americans entirely, even though urban black people had little choice but to try to use them anyway. Steamboats accepted black passengers but refused to rent them cabins. African Americans had to remain on deck at night and during storms.

All African Americans, regardless of their wealth or social standing, were treated this way. Frederick Douglass, who made a point of challenging segregation, refused to ride in Jim Crow train cars unless physically forced to do so. In 1854, in New York City, a black public school teacher named Elizabeth Jenkins was beaten by a white streetcar conductor who tried to expel her from his vehicle.

African Americans moving to northern cities, therefore, were not surprised to find segregated black neighborhoods. There were "Nigger Hill" in Boston, "Little Africa" in Cincinnati, "Hayti" in Pittsburgh, and Philadelphia's Southside. Conditions in these ghettoes were often dreadful, but they provided a refuge from constant insult and places where black institutions could develop.

Because African Americans representing all social and economic classes lived in these segregated neighborhoods, the quality of housing in them varied. But, at its worst,

Art and Culture Gallery I

Colonial Williamsburg Foundation, Abby Aldrich Rockefeller Folk Art Center, Williamsburg, VA

Continuities between the culture of West Africa and the emerging culture of African Americans appear clearly in this eighteenth-century painting of slaves on a South Carolina plantation. The religious dance, the instruments (including drums and a banjo), and elements of the participants' clothing are all West African in origin.

Colonial Williamsburg Foundation, Abby Aldrich Rockefeller Folk Art Center, Williamsburg, VA

This woodcarving testifies to the persistence of African artistic traditions in America. The form of the work, produced about 1850 by a black man living in Fayetteville, New York, closely resembles that of Yoruba ceremonial offering bowls.

African Americans in South Carolina and Georgia created many ceramic face jugs like these during the period from the 1850s through the 1870s. They are similar in style to wood carvings produced by artisans living in the Kingdom of Kongo. The glazing on the jugs is distinctively African American.

Harriet Powers was born a slave in 1837. Although she never learned to read or write, she expressed herself eloquently in her quilts. The eleven panels in this Bible Quilt, finished in 1886, illustrate stories from the Old and New Testaments that Powers absorbed from church sermons. Included are Adam and Eve, Cain and Abel, Jacob, the Birth of Christ, Betrayal of Judas, the Last Supper, and the Crucifixion.

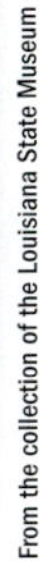

From the collection of the Louisiana State Museum

Julien Hudson of New Orleans painted this self-portrait in 1839. Hudson shows himself to be of mixed racial ancestry and a well-to-do member of New Orlean's well-established free black community.

Bannister Health and Rehabilitation Center, Providence, RI

Edward Mitchell Bannister (1828-1901) began painting portraits in Boston during the 1850s and later established himself as a landscape painter in Providence, Rhode Island. This portrait of his wife, Christiana Carteaux Bannister, hangs in the Bannister Nursing Care Center in Providence, which she established in 1890.

Edmonia Lewis, *Hagar in the Wilderness* 1875. Carved marble. 52 5/8 x 15 1/4 x 17 inches (133.6 x 43.4 cm). The National Museum of American Art, Washington DC/Art Resource, NY. Gift of Delta Sigma Theta Sorority, Inc.1983.95.178.

Edmonia Lewis, the daughter of a Chippewa mother and an African-American father, was a leading black sculptor of the late nineteenth century. She produced this sculpture, *Hagar in the Wilderness,* in Rome in 1869. Hagar was the Egyptian servant of the biblical patriarch Abraham, whom he expelled with her son after the birth of Isaac. Many nineteenth-century American artists saw her as a symbol of slavery.

Henry Ossawa Tanner, *The Banjo Lesson* 1893. Oil on canvas. 49" x 35 1/2". Hampton University Museum, Hampton, Virginia.

Henry Ossawa Tanner, the son of a bishop of the AME church, was raised in Philadelphia and studied there with the artist Thomas Eakins. In *The Banjo Lesson* (1893), one of his best known paintings, he sought to counter the prevalent racism of his times with evocations of the humanity, decency, and quiet dignity of black people.

housing was bleak and dangerous. People lived in unheated shacks and shanties, in dirt-floored basements, or in houses without doors and windows. These conditions nurtured disease, infant mortality, alcoholism, and crime. Southern visitors to northern cities blamed the victims, insisting that the plight of many urban black northerners proved that African Americans were better off in slavery.

BLACK COMMUNITIES IN THE URBAN NORTH

Northern African Americans lived in both rural and urban areas during the antebellum decades, but it was urban neighborhoods with their more concentrated black populations that nurtured black community life. African-American urban communities of the antebellum period developed from the free black communities that had emerged from slavery in the North during the late eighteenth century. The communities varied from city to city and from region to region, yet they had much in common and interacted with each other. They were characterized by resilient families, poverty, class divisions, active church congregations, the continued development of voluntary organizations, and concern for education. Particularly in the Northeast, urban black communities attracted people of American Indian descent who often married African Americans.

The Black Family

As they became free, northern African Americans left their masters and established their own households. By the 1820s the average black family in northern cities had two parents and between two and four children. However, in both the Northeast and Northwest, single-parent black families, usually headed by women, became increasingly common during the antebellum period. This trend may have been influenced by the difficulty black men had gaining employment. It certainly was a function of a high mortality rate among black men, which made many black women widows during their forties.

Both financial need and African-American culture encouraged black northerners to take in boarders and create extended families. By 1850 approximately one-third of black adults in such cities as Boston, Buffalo, Chicago, Detroit, and Cincinnati boarded. Economic considerations were implicit in such arrangements, but friendship and family relationships also played a part. Sometimes entire nuclear families boarded, but most boarders were young, single, and male. As historians James Oliver Horton and Lois E. Horton put it, "The opportunity to rely on friends and family for shelter enhanced the mobility of poor people who were often forced to move to find employment. It provided financial assistance when people were unemployed; it provided social supports for people who faced discrimination; and it saved those who had left home or run away from slavery from social isolation."

The Struggle for Employment

The rising tide of immigration from Europe hurt northern African Americans economically. Before 1820 black craftsmen had been in demand but, given the choice, white people preferred to employ other white people, and black people suffered. To make matters worse for African Americans, white workers excluded young black men from apprenticeships, refused to work with black people, and used violence to prevent employers from hiring black workers when white workers were unemployed. By the 1830s these practices had driven African Americans from the skilled trades. For the rest of the antebellum period, most northern black men performed menial day labor, although a few worked as coachmen, teamsters, waiters, barbers, carpenters, masons, and plasterers.

By 1847 in Philadelphia, for example, 80 percent of employed black men did unskilled labor. Barbers and shoemakers predominated among those black workers with skills. Only one-half of 1 percent held factory jobs. Among employed black women, 80 percent either washed clothes or worked as domestic servants. Three-quarters of the remaining 20 percent were seamstresses. By the 1850s black women, too, were losing work to Irish immigrants. A few became prostitutes. About 5 percent of black men and women were self-employed, selling food or secondhand clothing.

Unskilled black men were often unable to find work. When they did work, they received low wages. To escape such conditions in Philadelphia and other port cities, they became sailors. By 1850 about 50 percent of the crewmen on American merchant and whaling vessels were black. Not only did these sailors have to leave their families for months at a time and endure brutal conditions at sea, but they also risked imprisonment if their ship anchored at southern ports.

The Northern Black Elite

Despite the poor prospects of most northern African Americans, a northern black elite emerged during the first six decades of the nineteenth century. Membership in this elite could be achieved through talent, wealth, occupation, family connections, complexion, and education. The elite led in the development of black institutions and culture, in the antislavery movement, and in the struggle for racial justice. It was also the bridge between the black community and sympathetic white people.

Although few African Americans achieved financial security during the antebellum decades, black people could become rich in many ways. Segregated neighborhoods gave rise to a black professional class of physicians, lawyers, ministers, and undertakers who served an exclusively black clientele. Black merchants could gain wealth selling to black communities. Other relatively well-off African Americans included skilled tradesmen, such as carpenters, barbers, waiters, and coachmen, who generally found employment among white people.

Although less so than among African Americans in the South, complexion influenced social standing among African Americans in the North, especially in cities like Cincinnati that were close to the South. White people often preferred to hire people of mixed race, successful black men often chose light-complexioned brides, and African Americans generally accepted white notions of human beauty.

By the 1820s the black elite was becoming better educated and more socially polished than its less wealthy black neighbors, yet it could never disassociate itself from them. Segregation and discriminatory legislation in the North applied to all African Americans regardless of class and complexion, and all African Americans shared a common culture and history.

Conspicuous among the black elite were entrepreneurs who, against considerable odds, gained wealth and influence in the antebellum North. Perhaps most successful was Stephen Smith, who owned a lumber and coal business in Lancaster County, Pennsylvania, and speculated in real estate. In 1849 Smith and his partner William Whipper owned, in addition to a huge inventory of coal and lumber, twenty-two railroad cars and bank stock worth $9,000 (about 175,000 current dollars). They grossed $100,000 (nearly 2,000,000 current dollars) per year, and by 1860 Smith owned real estate in Lancaster and Philadelphia worth $23,000 (about 420,000 current dollars).

Black Professionals

The northern black elite also included physicians and lawyers. Among the physicians, some, such as James McCune Smith and John S. Rock, received medical degrees. Smith, the first African American to earn a medical degree, graduated from the University of Glasgow in Scotland in 1837 and practiced in New York City until his death in 1874. Rock, who had been a dentist in Philadelphia, graduated from the American Medical College in 1852 and practiced medicine in Boston until 1860 when he undertook the study of law. In 1865 he became the first African American to argue a case before the U.S. Supreme Court.

Either because they had been forced out of medical school or they chose not to go, other prominent black physicians practiced medicine without having earned a degree. (This was legal in the nineteenth century.) James Still of Medford, New Jersey, had meager formal education but used natural remedies to develop a successful practice among both black and white people. The multitalented Martin R. Delany, who had been born free in Charles Town, Virginia, in 1812, practiced medicine in Pittsburgh after having been expelled from Harvard Medical School at the insistence of two white classmates.

Prominent black attorneys included Macon B. Allen, who was admitted to the Maine bar in 1844, and Robert Morris, who qualified to practice law in Massachusetts in 1847. Both Allen and Morris apprenticed with white attorneys, and Morris had a particularly successful and lucrative practice. Yet white residents thwarted his attempt to purchase a mansion in a Boston suburb.

Artists and Musicians

Although they rarely achieved great wealth and have not become famous, black artists and musicians were also part of the northern African-American elite. Among the best-known artists were Robert S. Duncanson, Robert Douglass, Patrick Reason, and Edmonia Lewis. Several of them supported the antislavery movement through their artistic work.

Douglass, a painter who studied in England before establishing himself in Philadelphia, and Reason, an engraver, created portraits of abolitionists during the 1830s. Reason also etched illustrations of the sufferings of slaves. Duncanson, who was born in Cincinnati and worked in Europe between 1843 and 1854, painted landscapes and portraits. Lewis, the daughter of a black man and a Chippewa woman, was admitted with abolitionist help to Oberlin College in Ohio and studied sculpture in Rome. Her works, which emphasized African-American themes, came into wide demand after the Civil War.

The reputations of black professional musicians of the antebellum period have suffered in comparison with the great tradition of black folk music epitomized by spirituals. But in Philadelphia a circle of black musicians wrote and performed a wide variety of music for orchestra, voice, and solo instruments. Similar circles existed in New Orleans, Boston, Cleveland, New York, Baltimore, and St. Louis. The best-known professional black singer of the period was Elizabeth Taylor Greenfield, who was born a slave in Mississippi and raised by Quakers in Philadelphia. Known as the "Black Swan," Taylor gained renown for her vocal range.

Black Authors

In some respects, the antebellum era was a golden age of African-American literature. Driven by suffering in slavery and limited freedom in the North, black authors portrayed an America that had not lived up to its revolutionary ideals. Black autobiography recounted life in bondage and dramatic escapes. Although the antislavery movement promoted the publication of scores of such narratives, the best known is Frederick Douglass's classic *Narrative of the Life of Frederick Douglass, an American Slave* published in 1845.

African Americans also published history, novels, and poetry. In 1855 William C. Nell published *The Colored Patriots of the American Revolution,* which reminded its readers that black men had fought for freedom. William Wells Brown, who had escaped

Educated at Oberlin College, Edmonia Lewis (1843–1911?) studied sculpture in Rome and emerged as one of the more prolific American artists of the late nineteenth century.

Photographs and Prints Division, Schomburg Center for Research in Black Culture/Art Resource. The New York Public Library. Astor, Lenox and Tilden Foundations. Photo by H. Rocher from slavery in Kentucky, became the first African-American novelist. His *Clotel, or the President's Daughter*, published in 1853, used the affair between Thomas Jefferson and Sally Hemings to explore in fiction the moral ramifications of slaveholders who fathered children with their bondwomen. Another black novelist of the antebellum years was Martin R. Delany. His *Blake, or the Huts of America*, a story of emerging revolutionary consciousness among southern slaves, ran as a serial in the *Weekly Anglo-African* during 1859. Black poets included George M. Horton, a slave living in North Carolina, who in 1829 published *The Hope of Liberty*, and James W. Whitfield of Buffalo who in 1853 lampooned the song "My Country 'tis of Thee" when he wrote the following:

> *America, it is to thee*
> *Thou boasted land of liberty,—*
> *Thou land of blood, and crime, and wrong.*

African-American women who published fiction during the period included Frances Ellen Watkins Harper and Harriet E. Wilson. Harper was born free in Baltimore in 1825. Associated with the antislavery cause in Pennsylvania and Maine, she published poems that depicted the sufferings of slaves. Her first collection, *Poems on Various Subjects*, appeared in 1854. Wilson published *Our Nig: Or, Sketches from the Life of a Free Black, in a Two-Story White House, North* in 1859. This was the first novel published by a black woman in the United States. It was autobiographical fiction and compared the lives of black domestic workers in the North with those of southern slaves. Wilson's book, however, received little attention during her lifetime, and until the 1980s critics believed a white author had written it.

At about the same time that Wilson wrote *Our Nig*, Hanna Crafts, who had recently escaped from slavery in North Carolina, wrote *The Bondwoman's Narrative.* Unpublished until 2002, this melodramatic autobiographical novel tells the story of a house slave and her escape.

African-American Institutions

In the antebellum decades, the black institutions that had appeared during the revolutionary era in urban areas of the North, upper South, and—to a lesser extent—the deep South became stronger, more numerous, and more varied. This was the result of growing black populations, the exertions of the African-American elite, and the persistence of racial exclusion and segregation. Black institutions of the time included schools, mutual aid organizations, benevolent and fraternal societies, self-improvement and temperance associations, literary groups, newspapers and journals, and theaters. But, aside from families, the most important black community institution remained the church.

Black Churches

Black church buildings were community centers. They housed schools and were meeting places for a variety of organizations. Antislavery societies often met in churches, and the churches harbored fugitive slaves. This went hand in hand with the community leadership black ministers provided. They began schools and various voluntary associations. They spoke against slavery, racial oppression, and what they considered weaknesses among African Americans. However, black ministers never spoke with one voice. Throughout the antebellum decades, many followed Jupiter Hammon in admonishing their congregations that preparing one's soul for heaven was more important than gaining equal rights on earth.

By 1846 the independent African Methodist Episcopal (AME) Church had 296 congregations in the United States and Canada with 17,375 members. In 1848 Frederick Douglass maintained that the AME Mother Bethel Church in Philadelphia was "the largest church in this Union," with between two and three thousand worshippers each Sunday. The AME Zion Church of New York City was probably the second largest black congregation with about two thousand members.

Most black Baptist, Presbyterian, Congregationalist, Episcopal, and Roman Catholic congregations remained affiliated with white denominations, although they were rarely represented in regional and national church councils. For example, the Episcopal Diocese of New York in 1819 excluded black ministers from its annual conventions,

This lithograph depicts the bishops of the AME church and suggests both the church's humble origins and its remarkable growth during the antebellum years. Founder Richard Allen is portrayed at the center.

Courtesy of the Library of Congress

maintaining that African Americans "*are* socially degraded, and are not regarded as proper associates for the class of persons who attend our convention." Not until 1853 was white abolitionist William Jay able to convince New York Episcopalians to admit black representatives.

Many northern African Americans continued to attend white churches. To do so, they had to submit to the same second-class status that had driven Richard Allen and Absalom Jones to establish separate black churches in Philadelphia during the 1790s. Throughout the antebellum years, northern white churches required their black members to sit in special sections during services, provided separate Sunday schools for black children, and insisted that black people take communion after white people. Even Quakers, who spearheaded white opposition to slavery in the North and South, often provided separate seating for black people at their meetings.

By the 1830s and 1840s, some black leaders had begun to criticize the existence of separate black congregations and denominations. Frederick Douglass called them "negro pews, on a higher and larger scale." Such churches, Douglass and others maintained, were part and parcel of a segregationist spirit that divided America according to complexion. Douglass also denounced what he considered the illiteracy and anti-intellectual bias of most black ministers. Growing numbers of African Americans, nevertheless, regarded such churches as sources of spiritual integrity and legitimate alternatives to second-class status among white Christians.

Schools

Education, like religion, was racially segregated in the North between 1820 and 1860. Tax-supported compulsory public education for children in the United States began in Massachusetts in 1827 and spread throughout the Northeast and Old Northwest during the 1830s. Some public schools, such as those in Cleveland, Ohio, during the 1850s, were racially integrated. But usually, as soon as twenty or more African-American children appeared in a school district, white parents demanded that black children attend separate schools. White people claimed that black children lacked mental capacity and lowered the quality of education. White people also feared that opening schools to black children would encourage more black people to live in the school district.

How to educate African-American children who were not allowed to attend school with white children became a persistent issue in the North. Until 1848 Ohio and the other states of the Old Northwest simply excluded black children from public schools and refused to allocate tax revenues to support separate facilities. The northeastern states were more willing to undertake such expenditures. But across the North, white people were reluctant to use tax dollars to fund education for African Americans. As a result, appropriations for black public schools lagged far behind those for public schools white children attended.

This tendency extended to cities where African-American leaders and white abolitionists had created private schools for black children. In 1812 the African School established by Prince Hall in 1798 became part of Boston's public school system. As a result, like newly created black public schools in the city, it began to suffer from inadequate funding and a limited curriculum. The African Free Schools, begun in New York City in 1787 by the New York Society for Promoting the Manumission of Slaves, had a similar fate. In 1834, when these schools became part of New York's public school system, funding and attendance declined. By the 1850s public support for the city's black schools had become negligible.

Woefully inadequate public funding resulted in poor education or none at all for most black children across the North. The few black schools were dilapidated and overcrowded. White teachers who taught in them received lower pay than those who taught in white schools, and black teachers received even less, so teaching was generally poor. Black parents, however, were often unaware that their children received an inadequate education. Even black and white abolitionists tended to expect less from black students than from white students.

Some black leaders defended segregated schools as better for black children than integrated ones. They probably feared that the real choice was between separate black schools or none at all. But, by the 1830s, most northern African Americans favored racially integrated public education, and during the 1840s Frederick Douglass became a leading advocate for such a policy. Douglass, other black leaders, and their white abolitionist allies made the most progress in Massachusetts, where by 1845 all public schools, except for those in Boston, had been integrated. After a ten-year struggle, the Massachusetts legislature finally ended segregated schools in that city too. This victory encouraged the opponents of segregated public schools across the North. By 1860 integration had advanced among the region's smaller school districts. But, except for those in Boston, urban schools remained segregated on the eve of the Civil War.

In fact, the black elite had more success gaining admission to northern colleges during the antebellum period than most African-American children had in gaining an adequate primary education. Some colleges were exclusively for African Americans. Ashmum Institute in Oxford, Pennsylvania, was founded in 1854 to prepare black missionaries who would go to Africa. Ashmum, later renamed Lincoln University, was the first black institution of higher learning in the United States. Another exclusively black college was Wilberforce University, founded by the AME church in 1855 near Columbus, Ohio. Earlier some northern colleges had begun to admit a few black students. They included Bowdoin in Maine, Dartmouth in New Hampshire, Harvard and Mount Pleasant in Massachusetts, Oneida Institute in New York, and Western Reserve in Ohio. Because of its association with the antislavery movement, Oberlin College in Ohio became the most famous biracial institution of higher learning during the era. By 1860 many northern colleges, law schools, medical schools, and seminaries admitted black applicants, although not on an equal basis with white applicants.

Voluntary Associations

The African-American mutual aid, benevolent, self-improvement, and fraternal organizations that originated during the late eighteenth century proliferated during the antebellum decades. So did black literary and temperance associations. Mutual aid societies became especially attractive to black women. For example, in 1830 black women in Philadelphia had 27 such organizations compared with 16 for black men. By 1855 Philadelphia had 108 black mutual aid societies, enrolling 9,762 members, with a combined annual income of $29,600 (approximately 550,000 current dollars).

Among black benevolent societies, African Dorcas Associations were especially prevalent. Originally organized in 1828 in New York City by black women, these societies distributed used clothing to the poor, especially poor schoolchildren. During the early 1830s, black women also began New York City's Association for the Benefit of Colored Orphans, which operated an orphanage that by 1851 had helped 524 children. Other black benevolent organizations in New York maintained the Colored Seaman's Home and a home for the elderly.

Meanwhile, the Prince Hall Masons created new lodges in the cities of the Northeast and the Chesapeake. Black Odd Fellows lodges also became common from the 1840s on. But more prevalent were self-improvement, library, literary, and temperance organizations. These were manifestations of the reform spirit that swept the North and much of the upper South during the antebellum decades. Closely linked to evangelical Protestantism, reformers maintained that the moral regeneration of individuals was essential to perfecting society. African Americans shared this belief and formed myriad organizations to put it into practice.

Black temperance societies were even more widespread than literary and benevolent organizations, although they also tended to be more short lived. Like their white counterparts, black temperance advocates were members of the middle class who sought to stop the abuse of alcoholic beverages by those lower on the social ladder. The temperance societies organized lecture series and handed out literature that portrayed the negative physical, economic, and moral consequences of liquor. Whether such societies were effective is debatable, but they helped unite black communities.

Free African Americans in the Upper South

The free black people of the upper South had much in common with their northern counterparts. In particular, African Americans in the Chesapeake cities of Baltimore, Washington, Richmond, and Norfolk had many ties to black northerners, ranging from family and church affiliations to business connections and membership in fraternal organizations. But significant differences, which resulted from the South's agricultural economy and slavery, set free people of color in the upper South apart from those in the North. Although nearly half of the free black population in the North lived in cities, only one-third did so in the upper South, hampering the development of black communities there.

A more important difference was the impact of slavery on the lives of free African Americans in the upper South. Unlike black northerners, free black people in the upper South lived alongside slaves. Many had family ties to slaves and were more directly involved than black northerners in the suffering of the enslaved. Free black people of the upper South often tried to prevent the sale south of relatives or friends. They paid for manumissions and freedom suits and earned a reputation among white southerners as inveterate harborers of escaped slaves. Southern white politicians and journalists used this close connection between free black southerners and slaves to justify limiting the freedom of the former group.

Free black people of the upper South were also more at risk of *being* enslaved than were black northerners. Except for Louisiana, with its French and Spanish heritage, all southern states assumed African Americans were slaves unless they could prove otherwise. Free black people had to carry free papers, which they had to renew periodically. They could be enslaved if their papers were lost or stolen, and sheriffs in the upper South routinely arrested free black people on the grounds they might be fugitive slaves. Even when those arrested proved they were free, they were sometimes sold as slaves to pay the cost of imprisoning them. Free African Americans who got into debt in the South risked being sold into slavery to pay off their creditors.

As the antebellum period progressed, the distinction between free and enslaved African Americans narrowed in the upper South. Although a few northern states allowed black men to vote, no southern state did after 1835 when North Carolina followed Tennessee—the only other southern state to allow black suffrage—in revoking the franchise of property-owning black men. Free black people of the upper South also had more problems in traveling, owning firearms, congregating in groups, and being out after dark than did black northerners. Although residential segregation was less pronounced in southern cities than in the North, African Americans of the upper South were more thoroughly excluded from hotels, taverns, trains and coaches, parks, theaters, and hospitals.

Free black people in the upper South also experienced difficulties in earning a living, although, during the nineteenth century, their employment expanded as slavery declined in Maryland and northern Virginia. Free persons of color in rural areas were generally tenant farmers. Some of them had to sign labor contracts that reduced them to semislavery. But others owned land and a few owned slaves. Free African Americans also worked in rural areas as miners, lumberjacks, and teamsters. In upper South urban areas, most free black men were unskilled day laborers, waiters, whitewashers, and stevedores; free black women worked as laundresses and domestic servants. As in the North, the most successful African Americans were barbers, butchers, tailors, caterers, merchants, and those teamsters and hack drivers who owned their own horses and vehicles. Before 1850 free black people in the upper South faced less competition from European immigrants for jobs than those did who lived in northern cities. Therefore, although the upper South had fewer factories than the North, more free black men worked in them. This changed during the 1850s when Irish and German immigrants competed against free black people in the upper South just as they did in the North for all types of employment. As was the case in the North, immigrants often used violence to drive African Americans out of skilled trades.

These circumstances made it more difficult for free black people in the upper South to maintain community institutions. In addition, the measures white people adopted out of fear of slave revolt greatly limited free black autonomy, and such measures grew more pervasive after the revolt Nat Turner led in southern Virginia in 1831. Throughout the South, white authorities forced black churches and schools to close. The Baltimore Conference of the AME Church, which had been expanding during the 1820s, declined during the early 1830s. Some states required that black churches have white ministers, and some black ministers left for the North. Yet free black southerners persevered. During the late 1830s, black churches organized in Louisville and Lexington, Kentucky, and in St. Louis, Missouri. Between 1836 and 1856, the Baltimore AME Conference rebounded and more than doubled its membership. By 1860 Baltimore had fifteen black churches. Louisville had nine, and Nashville, St. Louis, and Norfolk had four each. Most of these churches ministered to both enslaved and free members.

Black schools and voluntary associations also survived white efforts to suppress them, although the schools faced great difficulties. Racially integrated schools and public funding for segregated black schools were out of the question in the South. Most black children received no formal education. Black churches, a few white churches, and a scattering of black and white individuals maintained what educational facilities the upper South had for black children. The schools met—often sporadically—in rooms furnished by churches or in private homes and generally lacked books, chalkboards, and student desks. Particularly noteworthy were the efforts of the Oblate Sisters of Providence, who constituted the first black Roman Catholic religious order in the United States, and John F. Cook, who for twenty years conducted a black school in Washington, D.C.

Elizabeth Clovis Lange, who was of Haitian descent, established the Oblate Sisters of Providence, an order of Roman Catholic nuns, in Baltimore in 1829 to provide a free education to the children of French-speaking black refugees from the Haitian Revolution. The sisters taught English, math, composition, and religion. Cook, who was an AME and Presbyterian minister, taught similar subjects at his Union Seminary from 1834 until his death in 1854. Both the sisters and Cook faced persecution from local whites and inadequate funding. Cook had to flee Washington temporarily in 1835 to avoid being killed. Nevertheless, Cook was able to pass his school on to his son, who kept it going through the Civil War years. Meanwhile, the Oblate Sisters had become a widely influential part of the black community. They built a chapel in 1836 that became the first black Catholic church in the United States.

Black voluntary associations, particularly in urban areas of the upper South, fared better than black schools. By 1838 Baltimore had at least forty such organizations, including chapters of the Prince Hall Masons, Black Odd Fellows, literary societies, and temperance groups. In Norfolk, the Masons enrolled slaves as well as freemen. As in the North, black women also organized voluntary associations. Washington's Colored Female Roman Catholic Beneficial Society, for example, provided death benefits for its members. Black benevolent organiza-tions in the upper South also sought to apprentice orphans to black tradesmen; sponsored fairs, picnics, and parades; and provided protection against kidnappers.

Free African Americans in the Deep South

Neither the natural rights ideology of the revolutionary era nor changing economic circumstances led to many manumissions in the deep South. Free black people there were not only far fewer than in either the upper South or the North, they were also "largely the product of illicit sexual relations between black slave women and white men." Slaveholder fathers either manumitted their mixed-race children or let them buy their freedom. However, some free black people of the deep South traced their ancestry to free mixed-race refugees from Haiti, who sought during the 1790s to avoid that island nation's bloody revolutionary struggle by fleeing to such deep South cities as Charleston, Savannah, and New Orleans.

A three-caste system similar to that in Latin America developed in the deep South during the antebellum period. It was composed of white people, free black people, and slaves. Most free African Americans in the region identified more closely with their former masters than with slaves. To ensure the loyalty of such free people of color, powerful white people provided them with employment, loans, protection, and such special privileges as the ability to vote and to testify against white people. Some states and municipalities formalized this relationship by requiring free African Americans to have white guardians—often their blood relatives. Some people of mixed descent were able to cross the racial boundary and pass as white.

The relationship between free African Americans of the deep South and their former masters was also evident in religion. An AME church existed in Charleston until 1818, when the city authorities suppressed it, fearing it would become a center of sedition. African Baptist churches existed in Savannah during the 1850s. In 1842 New Orleans's Sisters of the Holy Family became the second Roman Catholic religious order for women in the United States. But free black people in the region were more likely than those farther north to remain in white churches largely because they identified with the white elite.

In the deep South, free African Americans—over half of whom lived in cities—were also more concentrated in urban areas than in either the North or the upper South. Although deep South cities restricted their employment opportunities, free black people in Charleston, Savannah, Mobile, and New Orleans maintained stronger positions in the skilled trades than free black people in the upper South or the North. By 1860 in Charleston three-quarters of the free black men were employed in skilled trades. Free African Americans made up only 15 percent of Charleston's male population. Yet they were 25 percent of its carpenters, 40 percent of its tailors, and 75 percent of its millwrights. In New Orleans, free black men predominated as carpenters, masons, bricklayers, barbers, tailors, cigar makers, and shoemakers. In both cities, free African Americans compared favorably to white people in their ratio of skilled to unskilled workers. The close ties between free black people and upper class white people who did business with them explain much of this success.

Despite such ties, free black communities comparable to those in the upper South and North arose in the cities of the deep South. Although they usually lacked separate black churches as community centers, free African Americans in the region created other institutions. In Charleston, for example, the Brown Fellowship Society survived throughout the antebellum period. Charleston also had a chapter of the Prince Hall Masons, and other fraternal and benevolent associations were maintained by free black men and women. In addition to these sorts of organizations, the free black elite in New Orleans published literary journals and supported an opera house. Savannah—where black churches did exist—during the 1850s also had at least three black volunteer fire companies, a porters' association, and several benevolent societies.

Because black churches were rare, wealthy African Americans and fraternal organizations organized private schools for black children in the cities of the deep

South. In Charleston the Brown Fellowship Society organized an academy. New Orleans had several schools, most of which were conducted in French—the first or second language for many free black people in the city. Some of the more wealthy free black families in these cities sent their children abroad for an education, and the literacy rate among free black people in both Charleston and New Orleans was markedly high for the antebellum period.

In all, free people of color in the deep South differed substantially from those in the upper South and the North. Their ties to the white slaveholding class gave them tangible advantages. However, they were not without sympathy for those who remained in slavery, and white authorities were never certain of their loyalty to the slave regime. In particular, white people feared contact between free African Americans in the port cities of the deep South and black northerners—especially black sailors. As a new round of slave unrest began in the South and a more militant northern antislavery movement got under way during the 1820s, free black people in the deep South faced difficult circumstances.

Free African Americans in the Trans-Mississippi West

In the huge region stretching from the Mississippi River to the Pacific coast, which had become part of the United States by the late 1840s, free black people were rare. Black communities there were just emerging in a few isolated localities. As historian Quintard Taylor notes, the four thousand "nominally free" African Americans who lived in California in 1860 constituted "75 percent of the free black population of the West." The prevalence of discriminatory "black laws" in the region's states and territories partially explains the small number of free black westerners. Like similar laws in the states of the Old Northwest, these laws either banned African Americans entirely or restricted the activities of those who were allowed to settle. Nevertheless, a few black families sought economic opportunities in the West. During the 1840s they joined white Americans in settling Oregon. The California gold rush of 1849 had by 1852 attracted about two thousand African Americans, the great majority of whom were men, among hundreds of thousands of white Americans.

Usually black Californians lived and worked in multicultural communities that also included people of Chinese, Jamaican, Latin American, and white American descent. But in a few localities African Americans predominated. Some black Californians were prosperous gold prospectors. Others worked as steamship stewards, cooks, barbers, laundresses, mechanics, saloonkeepers, whitewashers, porters, and domestics. By the early 1850s, there were black communities centered on churches in San Francisco, Sacramento, and Los Angeles. In 1851 Bernard Fletcher established an AME church in Sacramento, and the following year, John Jamison Moore established an AME Zion church in San Francisco. As was the case in the East, these black communities organized a variety of benevolent and self-help societies.

Although most African Americans who went west were men, a black woman named Mary Ellen Pleasant—later known as "Mammy Pleasant"—arrived in San Francisco around 1849. Already wealthy, she amassed another fortune as a cook, laundress, real estate investor, and perhaps as a madam of a house of prostitution.

TIMELINE

AFRICAN-AMERICAN EVENTS	NATIONAL EVENTS
1800	
1804 Ohio enacts black laws	**1803** Louisiana Purchase
1805	
1807 New Jersey disfranchises black men	**1807** Robert Fulton's steamboat is launched in New York harbor
1810	
1812 African School becomes part of Boston public school system	**1812** War of 1812 begins **1814** War of 1812 ends
1815	
1818 Connecticut bars new black voters	**1819** Panic of 1819 begins
1820	
1821 New York retains property qualification for black voters **1822** Rhode Island disfranchises black voters **1824** Massachusetts defeats attempt to ban black migration to that state	
1825	
1827 Freedom's Journal begins publication **1828** African Dorcas Association is established **1829** Cincinnati expels black residents	**1825** John Quincy Adams becomes president of the United States Erie Canal opens **1827** Massachusetts pioneers compulsory public education **1828** Andrew Jackson is elected president

continued

AFRICAN-AMERICAN EVENTS	NATIONAL EVENTS
1830	
1831 Maria W. Stewart criticizes treatment of black workers **1834** African Free Schools become part of New York City public school system	**1832** Surge in European immigration begins **1832–33** Nullification Crisis occurs
1835	
1838 Pennsylvania disfranchises black voters Gold discovered in California	**1837** Panic of 1837 begins
1840	
1842 Rhode Island revives black male voting **1843** Edmonia Lewis born	
1845	
1845 *Narrative of the Life of Frederick Douglass* is published **1849** Ohio black laws are repealed	**1846–48** War is fought against Mexico
1850	
	1850 Compromise of 1850 passed

Conclusion

During the antebellum period, free African-American communities that had emerged during the revolutionary era grew and fostered black institutions. Particularly in the urban North, life in these segregated communities foreshadowed the pattern of black life from the end of the Civil War into the twentieth century. Although the black elite could gain education, professional expertise, and wealth despite white prejudices, most northern people of color were poor. Extended families, churches, segregation, political marginality, and limited educational opportunities still influence African-American life today.

Life for the free black populations of the upper South and deep South was even more difficult than in the North. Presumed to be slaves if they could not prove otherwise, free black people in the South were in greater danger of enslavement and were subjected to more restrictive legislation than in the North. But energetic black communities existed in the upper South throughout the antebellum period. In the deep

South, the small free black population was better off economically than were free black people in other regions, but it depended on the region's white slaveholders, who were unreliable allies as sectional controversy mounted. The antislavery movement, secession, and the Civil War would have a more profound impact on the free black communities in the South than in the North. Although it is not wise to generalize about free black people in the Trans-Mississippi West, their presence on the Pacific coast in particular demonstrates their involvement in the westward expansion that characterized the United States during the antebellum years. Their West Coast communities indicate the adaptability of black institutions to new circumstances.

Review Questions

1. How was black freedom in the North limited in the antebellum decades?
2. How did northern African Americans deal with these limits?
3. What was the relationship of the African-American elite to urban black communities?
4. How did African-American institutions fare between 1820 and 1861?
5. Compare black life in the North to free black life in the upper South, deep South, and California.

Recommended Reading

Ira Berlin. *Slaves without Masters: The Free Negro in the Antebellum South.* New York: New Press, 1971. This classic study is still the most comprehensive treatment of free African Americans in the antebellum South.

W. Jeffrey Bolster. *Black Jacks: African American Seamen in the Age of Sail.* Cambridge, MA: Harvard University Press, 1997. Black Jacks explores the lives of black seamen between 1740 and 1865.

Leonard Curry. *The Free Black in Urban America, 1800–1850: The Shadow of the Dream.* Chicago: University of Chicago Press, 1981. Curry provides a comprehensive account of urban African-American life in the antebellum period.

Philip S. Foner. *History of Black America: From the Emergence of the Cotton Kingdom to the Eve of the Compromise of 1850.* Westport, CT: Greenwood Press, 1983. This second volume of Foner's three-volume series presents a wealth of information about African-American life between 1820 and 1861, especially about the northern black community.

James Oliver Horton and Lois E. Horton. *In Hope of Liberty: Culture, Community, and Protest among Northern Free Blacks, 1700–1860.* New York: Oxford University Press, 1997. The authors focus on how the black community responded to difficult circumstances, especially during the antebellum decades.

Leon F. *Litwack. North of Slavery: The Negro in the Free States, 1790–1860.* Chicago: University of Chicago Press, 1961. This book emphasizes how northern white people treated African Americans. It is an essential guide to the status of African Americans in the antebellum North.

Quintard Taylor. *In Search of the Racial Frontier: African Americans in the American West, 1528–1990.* New York: Norton, 1998. This is the first book-length study of black westerners.

•CHAPTER EIGHT•

OPPOSITION TO SLAVERY

1800–1833

A Country in Turmoil

When Walker wrote his *Appeal*, the United States was in economic, political, and social turmoil. As we have shown in earlier chapters, the invention of the cotton gin in 1793 led to a vast westward expansion of cotton cultivation. Where cotton went, so did slavery. By the late 1820s, southern slaveholders and their slaves had pushed into what was then the Mexican province of Texas. Meanwhile, the states of the Old Northwest were passing from frontier conditions to commercial farming.

Particularly in the North, the transportation and market revolutions changed how people lived and worked. As steamboats became common and as networks of macadam turnpikes (paved with crushed stone and tar), canals, and railroads spread, travel time diminished. As Americans began to move from one region to another, families became more scattered, and ties to local communities became less permanent. For African Americans, subject to the domestic slave trade, mobility came with a high price.

Life in America changed further when the factory system arose in urban areas of the Northeast and spread to parts of the Old Northwest and upper South. Industrialization encouraged immigration from Europe, and native black and white people had to compete with growing numbers of foreign-born workers for urban employment. Although most northerners remained farmers, they became dependent on urban markets for their crops. A money economy grew more pervasive, the banking industry became essential, and vast private fortunes began to influence public policy. Many Americans believed forces beyond their control were threatening their way of life and the nation's republican values. They began to distrust change and wanted someone to blame for the uncertainties they faced. This outlook encouraged American politics to become paranoid—dominated by fear of hostile conspiracies.

Political Paranoia

The Jacksonian Era began with charges leveled by Andrew Jackson's supporters that John Quincy Adams and Henry Clay had conspired to cheat Jackson out of the presidency in 1824. Jackson had won a plurality of the popular vote but failed to get a majority in the electoral college, and Congress chose Adams to be president. These charges and the belief that Adams and his political allies represented the interests of rich businessmen and intellectuals, rather than those of the common people, led to the organization of the Democratic Party to contest the national election of 1828. The Democrats claimed to stand for the natural rights and economic well-being of American workers and farmers against what they called the "money power," a conspiratorial alliance of bankers and businessmen.

Yet, from its start, the Democratic Party also represented the interests of the South's slaveholding elite. Democratic politicians from both the North and South favored a states' rights doctrine that protected slavery from interference by the national government. They sought through legislation, judicial decisions, and diplomacy to make the right to hold human property inviolate. They became the most ardent supporters of expanding slavery into new regions, leading their opponents to claim they were part of a "slave power" conspiracy. Most Democratic politicians also openly advocated white supremacy. Although their rhetoric demanded equal rights for all and special privileges for none, they were really concerned only with the rights of white men.

This was clear in their outlook toward American Indians, women, and African Americans. Democratic politicians were in the forefront of those who demanded the removal of Indians to the area west of the Mississippi River, which culminated in the Cherokee "Trail of Tears" in 1838. Generally, Democrats were also traditionalists concerning the role of women in society. They supported patriarchy and a subservient role for women in both the family and the church. Finally, almost all Democratic leaders in both the North and the South believed God and nature had designed African Americans to be slaves.

By the mid-1830s, those Americans who favored a more enlightened social policy than the Democrats offered turned—often reluctantly—to the Whig Party, which opposed Jackson and the Democrats.

From the late 1820s onward, politicians such as Henry Clay, Daniel Webster, William H. Seward, and John Quincy Adams, who identified with the Whig Party, placed much more emphasis on Christian morality and an active national government than the Democrats did. They regarded themselves as conservatives, did not seek to end slavery in the southern states, and included many wealthy slaveholders within their ranks. But in the North, the party's moral orientation and its opposition to territorial expansion by the United States made it attractive to slavery's opponents.

The Whig Party also served as the channel through which evangelical Christianity influenced politics. In the North, Whig politicians appealed to evangelical voters. Distrustful of slaveholders and expansionism, some northern Whig politicians and journalists defended the human rights of African Americans and American Indians. They criticized the inhumanity of slaveholders and tried to limit the federal government's support for the peculiar institution. When and where they could, black men voted for Whig candidates.

The Second Great Awakening

Evangelicals were motivated to carry their Christian morality into politics by a new era of revivalism in America. Known as the Second Great Awakening, it lasted into the 1830s. The new evangelicalism led ordinary black and white Americans to try to take control of religion from the established clergy and to impose moral order on an increasingly turbulent American society.

The Second Great Awakening influenced Richard Allen and Absalom Jones's efforts to establish separate black churches in Philadelphia during the 1790s. It helped shape the character of other black churches that emerged during the 1800s and 1810s. These black churches became an essential part of the antislavery movement. However, the Second Great Awakening did not reach its peak until the 1820s. With particular force in the North and Northwest, Charles G. Finney, a white Presbyterian, and other revivalists helped democratize religion in America. At camp meetings that lasted for days, Finney and other revivalists preached that all men and women—not just a few—could become faithful Christians and save their souls. Just as Jacksonian democracy revolutionized politics in America, the Second Great Awakening revolutionized the nation's spiritual life and led many Americans to join reform movements.

Evangelicals—both black and white—emphasized "practical Christianity." Those who were saved, they maintained, would not be content with their own salvation. Instead, they would help save others. Black evangelicals, in particular, called for "a *liberating* faith" that would advance material and spiritual well-being. An emphasis on action led to what became known during the 1810s and 1820s as the Benevolent Empire, a network of church-related voluntary organizations designed to fight sin and save souls. The Benevolent Empire launched what is now known as antebellum or Jacksonian reform.

This social movement flourished from the 1810s through the 1850s. It consisted of voluntary associations dedicated to a host of causes: public education, self-improvement, limiting or abolishing alcohol consumption (the temperance movement), prison reform, and aid to the mentally and physically handicapped. The self-improvement, temperance, and missionary associations that free black people—and sometimes slaves—formed in conjunction with their churches in urban areas were part of this movement.

This 1844 lithograph by Peter S. Duval, derived from a painting by Alfred Hoffy, portrays Julianne Jane Tillman. Tillman was an AME preacher and one of the few women of her time to be employed in such a capacity.
Courtesy of the Library of Congress

The most important of these societies, however, were those dedicated to the problem of African-American bondage in the United States. Their members were *abolitionists,* people who favored doing away with or abolishing slavery in their respective states and throughout the country. To understand American abolitionism in the 1820s, we must return to the first abolitionist organizations that arose during the revolutionary era.

Abolitionism Begins in America

The Age of Revolution forged *two* antislavery movements that continued to exist until the end of the Civil War. The first of these movements existed in the South among slaves with the help of free African Americans and a few sympathetic white people. As we mentioned in earlier chapters, from the seventeenth century onward, enslaved African Americans individually and in groups sought their freedom through both violent and nonviolent means. Before the revolutionary era, however, these slaves only wanted to free themselves and did not seek to destroy slavery as a social system.

The second antislavery movement consisted of black and white abolitionists in the North, with outposts in the upper South. Far more white people were in this movement than in the one southern slaves conducted. In the North, white people controlled the larger antislavery organizations, although African Americans led in direct action against slavery and its influences in the North. In the upper South, African Americans could not openly establish or participate in antislavery organizations, but they cooperated covertly and informally with white abolitionists.

This second and essentially northern movement took root during the 1730s when white Quakers in New Jersey and Pennsylvania became convinced that slaveholding contradicted their belief in spiritual equality. For the rest of the eighteenth century, they advocated the abolition of slavery—at least among their fellow Quakers—in their home states and in the Chesapeake. Quakers always remained prominent in the northern antislavery movement. As members of a denomination that emphasized nonviolence, they generally expected slavery to be abolished peacefully and gradually.

The American Revolution, together with the French Revolution that began in 1789 and the Haitian struggle for independence between 1791 and 1804, revitalized both the northern and southern antislavery movements and changed their nature. The revolutionary doctrine that all men had a natural right to life, liberty, and property led other northerners besides Quakers and African Americans to endorse the antislavery cause.

Philadelphia Quakers in 1775 organized what became the first antislavery society. But when it was reorganized in 1784 as the Society for the Promotion of the Abolition of Slavery, it attracted non-Quakers. Among the first of these were Benjamin Rush and Benjamin Franklin, both of whom were influenced by natural rights doctrines. Revolutionary principles also influenced Alexander Hamilton and John Jay, who helped organize New York's first antislavery society. Prince Hall, the most prominent black abolitionist of his time, also based his effort to abolish slavery in Massachusetts on universal natural rights. He contended that African Americans "have in common with all other men a natural right to our freedom."

The efforts of northern black and white abolitionists were instrumental in abolishing slavery in the North. However, the early northern antislavery movement had several limiting features. First, black and white abolitionists had similar goals but worked in separate organizations. Even white Quaker abolitionists were reluctant to mix socially with African Americans or welcome them to their meetings. Second, except in parts of New England, abolition in the North proceeded *gradually* to protect the economic interests of slaveholders. Third, white abolitionists did not advocate equal rights for black people. In most northern states, laws kept black people from enjoying full freedom after their emancipation. Fourth, early northern abolitionists did little to bring about abolition in the South where most slaves lived.

All this indicates that neither Quaker piety nor natural rights principles created a truly egalitarian or sectionally aggressive northern abolitionism. It took the moralistic emotionalism of the Second Great Awakening combined with the activism of the Benevolent Empire to establish the framework for a more biracial and wide-ranging antislavery movement. Even more important in providing a prod were southern slaves and their free black allies, who had their own plans for emancipation.

From Gabriel to Denmark Vesey

Gabriel's abortive slave revolt of 1800 owed as much to revolutionary ideology as did the northern antislavery movement. The arrival of Haitian refugees in Virginia had led to slave unrest throughout the 1790s. Gabriel himself hoped to attract French revolutionary support. His conspiracy, though, was betrayed, and he and twenty-six of his followers were executed. But the revolutionary spirit and insurrectionary network Gabriel established lived on. Virginia authorities had to suppress another slave conspiracy in 1802, and sporadic minor revolts erupted for years.

Gabriel's conspiracy had two unintended consequences. First, the Quaker-led antislavery societies of the Chesapeake declined rapidly. The chance all but vanished that Maryland, Virginia, and North Carolina would follow the northern example by gradually abolishing slavery.

Second, white southerners and many white northerners became convinced that, as long as black people lived among them, a race war like the one in Haiti could erupt in the United States. Slaveholders and their defenders argued that this threat did not result from the oppressiveness of slavery. On the contrary, they maintained, the slaves were naturally suited for and content in bondage. It was the growing class of free black people, they asserted, who instigated otherwise passive bondpeople to revolt.

Free African Americans were, slavery's defenders contended, a dangerous, criminal, and potentially revolutionary class that had to be regulated, subdued, and ultimately expelled from the country. No system of emancipation that would increase the number of free black people in the United States could be tolerated. Slaveholders who had never shown a willingness to free their slaves began to claim they would favor emancipation if it were not for fear of enlarging such a dangerous group. As an elderly Thomas Jefferson put it, white southerners had a wolf by the ears: once they had enslaved black people, it was impossible to free them safely.

Events in and about Charleston, South Carolina, in 1822 appeared to confirm the threat. In that year black informants revealed a conspiracy for a massive slave revolt.

A free black man named Denmark Vesey had carefully organized it. Like Gabriel before him, Vesey could read and was well aware of the revolutions that had shaken the Atlantic world. Born most likely on the Caribbean island of St. Thomas, a carpenter by trade, and a former sailor who had been to Haiti, Vesey hoped for Haitian aid for an antislavery revolution in the South Carolina low country. He understood the significance of the storming of the Bastille on July 14, 1789, that marked the start of the French Revolution and planned to start his revolution on July 14, 1822. Vesey was also familiar with the antislavery speeches of northern members of Congress during the 1820 debates over the admission of Missouri to the Union and may have hoped for northern aid.

However, as befitted an evangelical and romantic era, religious influence was more prominent in Vesey's plot than in Gabriel's. Vesey was a Bible-quoting Methodist who conducted religious classes. Like other free black people and slaves in Charleston, he deeply resented attempts by the white authorities to suppress the city's AME church in 1818. He believed passages in the Bible about the enslavement and deliverance of the Hebrews in Egypt promised freedom for African Americans as well.

Vesey also used aspects of African religion that had survived among low-country slaves to promote his revolutionary efforts. To reach slaves whose Christian convictions were blended with West African spiritualism, he relied on his closest collaborator, Jack Pritchard, who was known as Gullah Jack. A "conjure-man" who had been born in East Africa, Pritchard distributed charms and cast spells that he claimed would make revolutionaries invincible.

Vesey and his associates planned to capture arms and ammunition and seize control of Charleston. But Gullah Jack's charms were ineffective against white vigilance and black informers. About a month before the revolt was to begin, the arrest of one of Vesey's lieutenants put local authorities on guard. Vesey moved the date of the uprising to June 16. But on June 14 a house servant revealed the conspiracy to his master, the local government called in the state militia, and arrests ensued. Over several weeks, the authorities rounded up 131 suspects. The accused received public trials, and juries convicted seventy-one. Thirty-five, including Vesey and Gullah Jack, were hanged. Thirty-seven were banished. Four white men—three of them foreigners—were convicted of inciting slaves to revolt. They were imprisoned and fined.

After the executions, Charleston's city government destroyed what remained of the local AME church, and white churches assumed responsibility for supervising other black congregations. Meanwhile, white South Carolinians sought to make slave patrols more efficient. The state legislature outlawed assemblages of slaves and banned teaching slaves to read. Local authorities jailed black seamen whose ships docked in Charleston until the ships were ready to leave port. Assuming that free black and white abolitionists inspired slave unrest, white South Carolinians became increasingly suspicious of local free African Americans, as well as of white Yankees who visited their state.

The American Colonization Society

Fear of free African Americans as a subversive class shaped the program of the most significant white antislavery organization of the 1810s and 1820s—but whether its aim was actually abolition is debatable. In late 1816 concerned white leaders met in

Washington, D.C., to form the American Society for Colonizing Free People of Colour of the United States, usually known as the American Colonization Society (ACS). Among its founders were such prominent slaveholders as Bushrod Washington—a nephew of George Washington—and Henry Clay. In 1821 the ACS, with the support of the U.S. government, established the colony of Liberia in West Africa as a prospective home for African Americans.

The ACS had a twofold program. First, it proposed to abolish slavery gradually in the United States, perhaps giving slaveholders financial compensation for their human property. Second, it proposed to send emancipated slaves and free black people to Liberia. The founders of the ACS believed that masters would never emancipate their slaves if they thought emancipation would increase the free black population in the United States. Moral and practical objections to this program were not immediately clear to either black or white abolitionists. In fact, the ACS became an integral part of the Benevolent Empire and commanded widespread support among many who regarded themselves friends of humanity.

Although the ACS was always strongest in the upper South and enjoyed the support of slaveholders, including Francis Scott Key, Andrew Jackson, John Tyler, and John Randolph, by the 1820s it had branches in every northern state. Such northern white abolitionists as Arthur and Lewis Tappan, Gerrit Smith, and William Lloyd Garrison initially supported colonization. They tended to emphasize the abolitionist aspects of the ACS and clung to a belief that free and soon-to-be-emancipated African Americans could choose whether to stay in the United States or go to Liberia. In either case, they hoped, black people would be free.

Black Nationalism and Colonization

Prominent black abolitionists initially shared this positive assessment of the ACS. They were part of a black nationalist tradition dating back at least to Prince Hall that—disappointed with repeated rebuffs from white people—endorsed black American migration to Africa. During the early 1800s, the most prominent advocate of this point of view was Paul Cuffe of Massachusetts. In 1811, six years before the ACS organized, Cuffe, a Quaker of African and American Indian ancestry, addressed Congress on the subject of African-American Christian colonies in Africa.

The ACS argument that appealed to Cuffe and many other African Americans was that white prejudice would never allow black people to enjoy full citizenship, equal protection under the law, and economic success in the United States. Black people born in America, went the argument for African colonization, could enjoy equal rights only in the continent of their ancestors. In the spirit of American evangelicalism, African Americans were also attracted by the prospect of bringing Christianity to African nations. Like white people, many African Americans considered Africa a pagan, barbaric place that could benefit from their knowledge of Christianity and republican government. Other black leaders who favored colonization objected to this view of Africa. They considered African cultures superior to those of America and Europe. They were often Africans themselves, the children of African parents, or individuals who had been influenced by Africans.

In 1815 Cuffe, who was the captain of his own ship, took thirty-four African-American settlers to the British free black colony of Sierra Leone, located just to the north of present-day Liberia. Cuffe himself would probably have later settled in Liberia if his American Indian wife had not refused to leave her native land. So it was the AME bishop Daniel Coker who led the first eighty-six African-American colonists to Liberia in 1820–1821. Pro-ACS sentiment was especially strong among African Americans in Coker's home city of Baltimore and other Chesapeake urban areas. By 1838 approximately 2,500 colonists had made the journey and were living less than harmoniously with Liberia's 28,000 indigenous inhabitants (see Map 8–1).

In 1847 Liberia became an independent republic. But despite the efforts of such Black Nationalist advocates as Henry Highland Garnet and Alexander Crummell, only about ten thousand African-American immigrants had gone there by 1860. This amounted to just .3 percent of the increase of the black population in the United States since 1816. Well before 1860 it was clear African colonization would never fulfill the dreams of its black or white advocates.

Other African Americans saw Haiti as a potential refuge from the oppression they suffered in the United States. By the end of the 1820s, between eight and thirteen thousand African Americans had arrived there, but African Americans found Haitian culture to be more alien than they had anticipated. They had difficulty learning French and distrusted the Roman Catholic Church. By 1826 about one-third of the emigrants had returned to the United States.

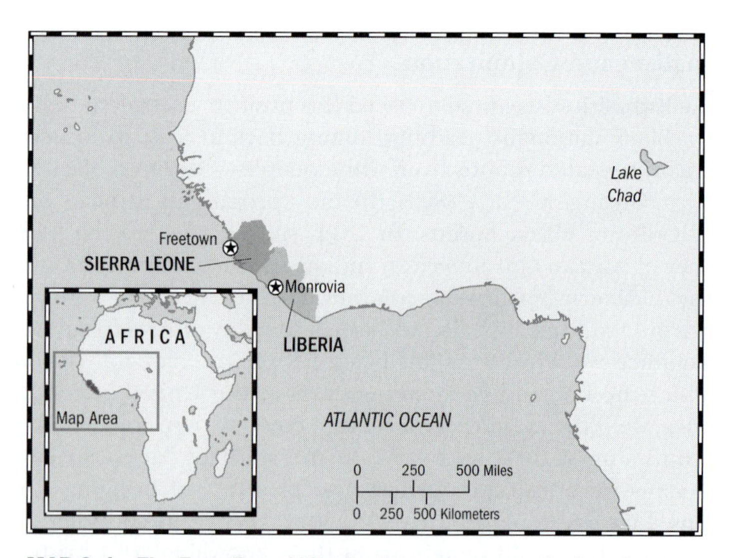

MAP 8–1 The Founding of Liberia. This map shows the location of Sierra Leone and Liberia in West Africa. British abolitionists established Sierra Leone as a colony for former slaves in 1800. The American Colonization Society established Liberia for the same purpose in 1821.

Black Opposition to Colonization

Some African Americans had always opposed overseas colonization. As early as 1817, such influential black leaders as James Forten were wavering in their support of the ACS. Although Forten continued to support colonization in private, he led a meeting that year of three thousand black Philadelphians to denounce it. By the mid-1820s, many black abolitionists in East Coast cities from Richmond to Boston were criticizing colonization in general and the ACS in particular.

Among them was Samuel Cornish, who with John Russwurm began publication of *Freedom's Journal* in New York City in 1827 as the first African-American newspaper. Cornish, a young Presbyterian minister and a fierce opponent of the ACS, called for independent black action against slavery. The *Journal*—reflecting the values of antebellum reform—encouraged self-improvement, education, black civil rights in the North, and sympathy among black northerners for slaves in the South. Russwurm, however, was less opposed to the ACS than was Cornish. This disagreement helped lead to the suspension of the newspaper in 1829. That same year Russwurm, who was one of the first African Americans to earn a college degree, moved to Liberia.

People like Cornish regarded themselves as Americans, not Africans, and wanted to improve their condition in this country. They considered Liberia foreign and unhealthy. They had no desire to go there themselves or send other African Americans there. They feared that ACS talk about *voluntary* colonization was misleading. They knew that nearly every southern state required the expulsion of slaves individually freed by their masters. They were also aware of efforts in the Maryland and Virginia legislatures to require *all* free black people to leave or be enslaved. These efforts had little practical impact, but they made African Americans fear that colonization would be forced on them. In 1858 Arkansas actually required the reenslavement of free black people who did not leave that state. But, rather than migrate to Africa, most of its small free black population fled to the North, Canada, Louisiana, or the Indian territory.

By the mid-1820s most black abolitionists had concluded that the ACS was part of a proslavery effort to drive free African Americans from the United States. The ACS, they maintained in public meetings, was not an abolitionist organization at all but a proslavery scheme to force free black people to choose between reenslavement or banishment. America, they argued, was their native land. They knew nothing of Africa. Any effort to force them to go there was based on the racist assumption that they were not entitled to and were incapable of living in freedom in the land of their birth. "Do they think to drive us from our country and homes, after having enriched it with our blood and tears?" asked David Walker.

Black Abolitionist Women

Black women, of course, joined black men in opposing slavery. When considering their role, we need to remember that the United States in the early nineteenth century was a society with a rigid gender hierarchy. Law and custom proscribed women from all political, professional, and most business activities. Those women deemed by black and white Americans to be respectable—the women of wealthy families—were expected to devote themselves exclusively to domestic concerns and to remain socially aloof. Church and benevolent activities were one of their few opportunities for public action. Even in these arenas, custom relegated them to work as auxiliaries of men's organizations.

This was certainly true of the first *formal* abolitionist groups of black women. Among the leaders were Charlotte Forten, the wife of James Forten, and Maria W. Stewart, the widow of a well-to-do Boston ship outfitter. Charlotte and her daughters Sarah, Margaretta, and Harriet joined with other black and white women to found the Philadelphia Female Anti-Slavery Society in 1833. A year earlier, in 1832, other black women had established in Salem, Massachusetts the first women's antislavery society. Women of the black elite were also active in the education of black children, which they hoped would overcome the white prejudices that supported slavery.

Many African-American women (as well as many white women), however, did not fit the early nineteenth-century criteria for respectability that applied to the Fortens, Stewart, and others in the African-American elite. Most black women were poor. They lacked education. They had to work outside their homes. Particularly in the upper South, these women were *practical* abolitionists.

From the revolutionary era onward, countless anonymous black women, both slave and free, living in such southern border cities as Baltimore, Louisville, and Washington risked everything to harbor fugitive slaves. Other heroic women saved their meager earnings to purchase freedom for themselves and their loved ones. Among them was Alethia Tanner of Washington, who purchased her own freedom in 1810 for $1,400 (about 16,000 current dollars). During the 1820s she also purchased the freedom of her sister, her sister's ten children, and her sister's five grandchildren. During the 1830s Tanner purchased the freedom of seven more slaves. Meanwhile, according to an account written in the 1860s, "Mrs. Tanner was alive to every wise scheme for the education and elevation of her race."

The Baltimore Alliance

Among the stronger black abolitionist opponents of the ACS were William Watkins, Jacob Greener, and Hezekiah Grice, associates in Baltimore of Benjamin Lundy, a white Quaker abolitionist who published an antislavery newspaper named the *Genius of Universal Emancipation*. By the mid-1820s, Watkins, a schoolteacher, had emerged, in a series of letters he published in *Freedom's Journal* and in Lundy's paper, as one of the more articulate opponents of colonization. Greener, a whitewasher and schoolteacher, helped Lundy publish the *Genius* and promoted its circulation. Grice, who later changed his mind and supported colonization, became the principal founder of the National Black Convention Movement, which during the 1830s, 1840s, and 1850s became a forum for black abolitionists.

In 1829 in Baltimore, Watkins, Greener, and Grice profoundly influenced a young white abolitionist and temperance advocate named William Lloyd Garrison, who later became the most influential of all the American antislavery leaders. Lundy had convinced Garrison to leave his native Massachusetts to come to Baltimore as the associate editor of the *Genius*. Garrison, a deeply religious product of the Second Great Awakening and a well-schooled journalist, had already decided before he came to Baltimore that *gradual* abolition was neither practical nor moral. Gradualism was impractical, he said, because it continually put off the date of general emancipation. It was immoral because it encouraged slaveholders to go on sinfully and criminally oppressing African Americans.

Garrison, however, tolerated the ACS until he came under the influence of Watkins, Greener, and Grice. They set Garrison on a course that transformed the abolitionist movement in the United States during the early 1830s. They also initiated a bond between African Americans and Garrison that—although strained at times—shaped the rest of his antislavery career. That bond intensified in 1830 when Garrison was imprisoned in Baltimore jail for forty-nine days on charges he had libeled a slave trader. While in jail, Garrison met imprisoned fugitive slaves and denounced—to their faces—masters who came to retrieve them.

In 1831 when he began publishing his own abolitionist newspaper, The *Liberator*, in Boston, Garrison led the antislavery movement in a new, more radical direction. Although Garrison had called for the *immediate*, rather than the *gradual*, abolition of slavery before he arrived in Baltimore, he was not the first to make that demand or to oppose compensating masters who liberated their slaves. What made Garrison's brand of abolitionism revolutionary was the insight he gained from his association with African Americans in Baltimore: that immediate emancipation must be combined with a commitment to racial justice in the United States.

DAVID WALKER'S *APPEAL*

Two other black abolitionists shaped Garrison's brand of abolitionism. They were David Walker and Nat Turner. This chapter begins with a quote from David Walker's *Appeal . . . to the Colored Citizens of the World*, which Walker published in 1829. As historian Clement Eaton commented in 1936, this *Appeal* was "a dangerous pamphlet in the Old South." In aggressive language, Walker furiously attacked slavery and white racism. He suggested that slaves use violence to secure their liberty. "I do declare," he wrote, "that one good black can put to death six white men." This especially frightened white southerners because Walker's *Appeal* circulated among slaves in southern ports.

The *Appeal* shaped the struggle over slavery in three ways. First, although Garrison was committed to peaceful means, Walker's aggressive writing style influenced the tone of Garrison and other advocates of immediate abolition. Second, Walker's desperate effort to instill hope and pride in an oppressed people inspired an increasingly militant black abolitionism. Third, Walker's pamphlet and its circulation in the South made white southerners fearful of encirclement from without and subversion from within. This fear encouraged southern leaders to make demands on the North that helped bring on the Civil War.

NAT TURNER

In this last respect, Nat Turner's contribution was even more important than Walker's. Slave conspiracies had not ended with Denmark Vesey's execution in 1822. But in 1831 Turner, a privileged slave from eastern Virginia, became the first African American actually to initiate a large-scale slave uprising since Charles Deslondes had done so in Louisiana in 1811. As a result Turner inspired far greater fear among white southerners than Walker had.

During the late 1820s and early 1830s, unrest among slaves in Virginia had increased. Walker's *Appeal,* which was circulating among some southern free black people by late 1829, may have contributed to this increase. Meanwhile divisions among white Virginians encouraged slaves to seek advantages for themselves. In anticipation of a state constitutional convention in 1829, white people in western Virginia, where there were few slaveholders, called for emancipation. Poorer white men demanded an end to the property qualifications that denied them the vote. As the convention approached, a "spirit of dissatisfaction and insubordination" became manifest among slaves. Some armed themselves and escaped northward. As proslavery white Virginians grew fearful, they demanded further restrictions on the ability of local free black people and northern abolitionists to influence slaves.

Yet no evidence indicates that Nat Turner or any of his associates had read Walker's *Appeal,* had contact with northern abolitionists, or were aware of divisions among white Virginians. Although Turner knew about the successful slave revolt in Haiti, he was more of a religious visionary than a political revolutionary. Born in 1800 he learned to read as a child, and as a young man, he spent much of his time studying and memorizing the Bible. He became a lay preacher and a leader among local slaves. By the late 1820s, he had begun to have visions that convinced him God intended him to lead his people to freedom through violence.

After considerable planning, Turner began his uprising on the evening of August 21, 1831. His band, which numbered between sixty and seventy, killed fifty-seven white men, women, and children—the largest number of white Americans ever killed by slave rebels—before militia put down the revolt the following morning. In November, Turner and seventeen others were found guilty of insurrection and treason and were hanged. Meanwhile panicked white people in nearby parts of Virginia and North Carolina killed more than one hundred African Americans whom they—almost always wrongly—suspected of being in league with the rebels.

This contemporary drawing depicts the capture of Nat Turner in October 1831. Turner had avoided apprehension for nearly two months following the suppression of his revolt. The artist indicates Turner's personal dignity.
Courtesy of the Library of Congress

Turner, like Walker and Garrison, shaped a new era in American abolitionism. The bloodshed in Virginia inspired general revulsion. White southerners—and some northerners—accused Garrison and other abolitionists of inspiring the revolt. In response, northern abolitionists of both races asserted their commitment to a peaceful struggle against slavery. Yet both black and white abolitionists respected Turner. Black abolitionists accorded him the same heroic stature they gave Toussaint Louverture and Gabriel. Garrison and other white abolitionists compared Turner to George Washington and other leaders of national liberation movements. This tension between lip service to peaceful means and admiration for violence against slavery characterized the antislavery movement for the next thirty years.

Conclusion

This chapter has focused on the two principal antislavery movements in the United States before the 1830s. One movement existed in the South among slaves. The other was centered in the North and the Chesapeake among free African Americans and white abolitionists. Both movements had roots in the age of revolution and gained vitality from evangelical Christianity. The Second Great Awakening and the reforming spirit of the Benevolent Empire shaped the northern antislavery effort. The black church, the Bible, and elements of African religion helped inspire slave revolutionaries.

Gabriel, Denmark Vesey, and Nat Turner had to rely on violence to fight slavery; northern abolitionists used newspapers, books, petitions, and speeches to spread their views. But the two movements had similarities and influenced each other. David Walker's life in Charleston at the time of Denmark Vesey's conspiracy influenced his beliefs. In turn, his *Appeal* may have influenced the enslaved. Turner's revolt helped determine the course of northern abolitionism after 1831. During the subsequent decades, the efforts of slaves to resist their masters, to rebel, and to escape influenced radical black and white abolitionists in the North.

In fact the antislavery movement that existed in the North and portions of the upper South was always biracial. During the 1810s and for much of the 1820s, most black abolitionists embraced a form of nationalism that encouraged them to cooperate with the conservative white people who led the ACS. As the racist and proslavery nature of that organization became clear, northern black and white abolitionists called for immediate, uncompensated general emancipation that would not force former slaves to leave the United States.

Slavery, the explicit legal disabilities imposed on free African Americans, and the widespread religious revivalism of the early nineteenth century created conditions that were very different from those that exist today. But some similarities between then and now are striking. As it was in the 1810s and 1820s, the United States today is in turmoil. Technological innovation and corporate restructuring have created a volatile job market, which has helped to increase interracial tension. As they did in the early nineteenth century, African-American leaders today advocate various strategies to improve black life.

Samuel Cornish, William Watkins, and others who opposed the ACS sought through peaceful means to abolish slavery and gain recognition of African Americans as American citizens. David Walker advocated a more forceful strategy to achieve the same ends. Cornish, Watkins, and Walker all cooperated with white abolitionists. Paul

Cuffe and others took a position closer to black nationalism by linking the abolition of slavery to an independent black destiny in Africa.

As is true today, African Americans of the early nineteenth century, who sought to deal with the problems of their time, faced difficult choices. The strategies they followed each had virtues, weaknesses, and dangers.

TIMELINE

AFRICAN-AMERICAN EVENTS	NATIONAL AND WORLD EVENTS
1790	
	1791 Haitian Revolution begins
1795	
1796 or 1797 David Walker born	**1796** John Adams elected U.S. president **1798** Undeclared Franco-American war
1800	
1800 Gabriel's conspiracy is exposed **1803** Maria W. Stewart born	**1800** Thomas Jefferson elected U.S. president **1803–1806** Lewis and Clark Expedition
1805	
1805 William Lloyd Garrison born	**1807** Britain bans Atlantic slave trade **1808** United States bans Atlantic slave trade
1810	
1811 Louisiana Slave Revolt	**1812** War of 1812 begins
1815	
1815 Paul Cuffe leads African Americans to Sierra Leone **1816** American Colonization Society is formed	**1815** War of 1812 ends **1816** James Madison elected U.S. president
1820	
1822 Denmark Vesey's conspiracy is exposed **1824** Benjamin Lundy comes to Baltimore	**1820** Missouri Compromise passed **1824** John Quincy Adams is elected U.S. president

continued

AFRICAN-AMERICAN EVENTS	NATIONAL AND WORLD EVENTS
1825	
1827	**1828**
Freedom's Journal begins publication	Andrew Jackson is elected U.S. president
1829	
William Lloyd Garrison comes to Baltimore; David Walker's *Appeal*	
1830	
1831	**1830**
Nat Turner's Revolt is suppressed	Indian Removal Act passed by Congress
1832	
Great increase in migration to U.S. begins	
1835	

Review Questions

1. What did the program of the ACS mean for African Americans? How did they respond to this program?
2. Analyze the role in abolitionism played (1) by Christianity and (2) by the revolutionary tradition in the Atlantic world. Which was more important in shaping the views of black and white abolitionists?
3. Evaluate the interaction of black and white abolitionists during the early nineteenth century. How did their motives for becoming abolitionists differ?
4. How did Gabriel, Denmark Vesey, and Nat Turner influence the northern abolitionist movement?
5. What risks did Maria W. Stewart take when she called publicly for antislavery action?

Recommended Reading

Merton L. Dillon. *Slavery Attacked: Southern Slaves and Their Allies, 1619–1865*. Baton Rouge: Louisiana State University Press, 1990. Integrates slave resistance and revolt with the northern abolitionist movement.

Eugene D. Genovese. *From Rebellion to Revolution: Afro-American Slave Revolts in the Making of the Modern World*. Baton Rouge: Louisiana State University Press, 1979. Places the major American slave revolts and conspiracies in an Atlantic context.

Peter P. Hinks. *To Awaken My Afflicted Brethren: David Walker and the Problem of Antebellum Slave Resistance*. University Park: Pennsylvania State University Press, 1997. The most recent biography of Walker, which places him within the black abolitionist movement and attempts to clarify what little we know about his life.

Benjamin Quarles. *Black Abolitionists.* New York: Oxford University Press, 1969. A classic study that emphasizes cooperation between black and white abolitionists.

Harry Reed. *Platform for Change: The Foundations of the Northern Free Black Community, 1775–1865.* East Lansing: Michigan State University Press, 1994. An excellent study of the relationship between free black culture in the North and antislavery action.

P. J. Staudenraus. *The American Colonization Movement, 1816–1865.* New York: Columbia University Press, 1961. Although published in the 1960s, the most recent account of the American Colonization Society.

Shirley J. Yee. *Black Women Abolitionists: A Study in Activism, 1828–1860.* Knoxville: University of Tennessee Press, 1992. Concentrates on the period after 1833, but it is the best place to start reading about black abolitionist women.

• CHAPTER NINE •

LET YOUR MOTTO BE RESISTANCE

1833–1850

A Rising Tide of Racism and Violence

The growing militancy among abolitionists occurred within a context of increasing racism and violence in the United States, lasting from the 1830s through the Civil War. By the 1840s white Americans had embraced an exuberant nationalism called *Manifest Destiny* that defined political and economic progress in racial terms and legitimized war to expand the boundaries of the United States.

During this same period, American ethnologists—scientists who studied racial diversity—rejected the eighteenth-century idea that the physical and mental characteristics of the world's peoples are the product of environment. Instead, they argued that what they perceived to be racial differences are intrinsic and permanent. White people—particularly white Americans—they maintained, were a superior race culturally, physically, economically, politically, and intellectually.

This theory provided white Americans with an apparently scientific justification for the continued enslavement of African Americans and extermination of American Indians, because both these groups were deemed inferior. Prejudice against European immigrants to the United States also increased. By the late 1840s, a movement known as *nativism* pitted native-born Protestants against foreign-born Roman Catholics, whom the natives saw as competitors for jobs and as culturally subversive.

Accompanying these broad intellectual and cultural developments was a wave of racially motivated violence committed by the federal and state governments, as well as by white vigilantes. From 1829 until the Civil War, white mobs led by "gentlemen of property and standing" attacked abolitionist newspaper presses and wreaked havoc in African-American neighborhoods.

Antiblack and Anti-Abolitionist Riots

Antiblack urban riots predated the start of immediate abolitionism during the late 1820s. But such riots became more common as abolitionism gained strength during the 1830s and 1840s (see Figure 9–1 and Map 9–1). Although few northern cities escaped racist mob attacks on African Americans and their property, riots in Cincinnati, Providence, New York City, and Philadelphia were infamous.

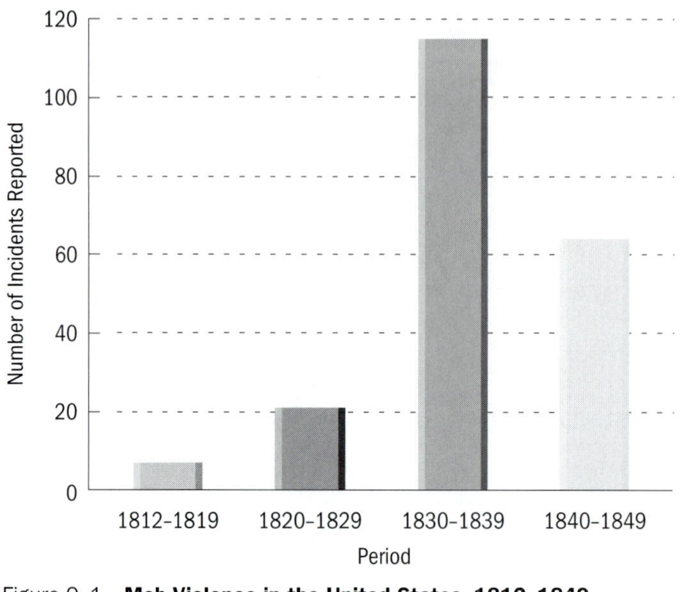

Figure 9–1 **Mob Violence in the United States, 1812–1849**
This graph illustrates the rise of mob violence in the North in reaction to abolitionist activity. Attacks on abolitionists peaked during the 1830s and then declined as antislavery sentiment spread in the North.

In 1829 a three-day riot instigated by local politicians led many black people in Cincinnati to flee to Canada. In 1836 and 1841 mob attacks on the *Philanthropist*, Cincinnati's white-run abolitionist newspaper, expanded into attacks on African-American homes and businesses. Both times, black residents defended their property with guns. In 1831 white sailors led a mob in Providence that literally tore that city's black neighborhood to pieces.

In New York City in 1834, a mob destroyed twelve houses owned by black residents, a black church, a black school, and the home of white abolitionist Lewis Tappan. But no city had worse race riots than Philadelphia. The ugliest riot came in 1842 when Irish immigrants led a mob that assaulted members of a black temperance society, who were commemorating the abolition of slavery in the British colony of Jamaica. When African Americans defended themselves with muskets, the mob looted and burned Philadelphia's principal black neighborhood.

Texas and the War Against Mexico

Violence was not confined to northern cities. Under President James K. Polk, the United States adopted a belligerent foreign policy that culminated in a war against Mexico that lasted from 1846 to 1848. During the 1820s slaveholding Americans had begun to settle in Texas, which was then part of the Republic of Mexico. In 1822 Mexico had gained its independence from Spain and in 1829 had abolished slavery within its borders. At the time, Mexico also included the gigantic region that now comprises the

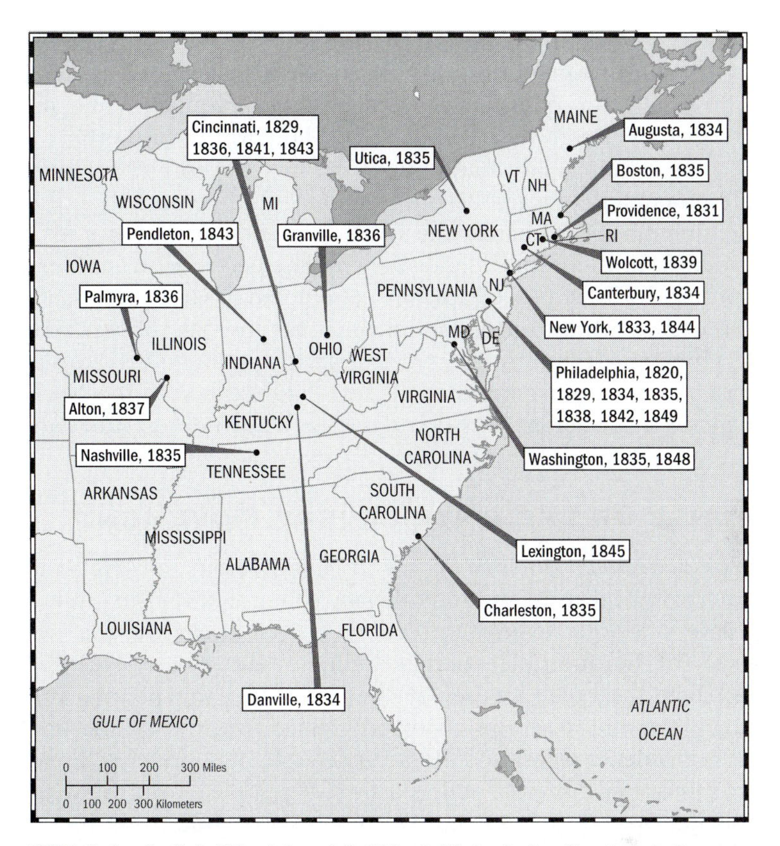

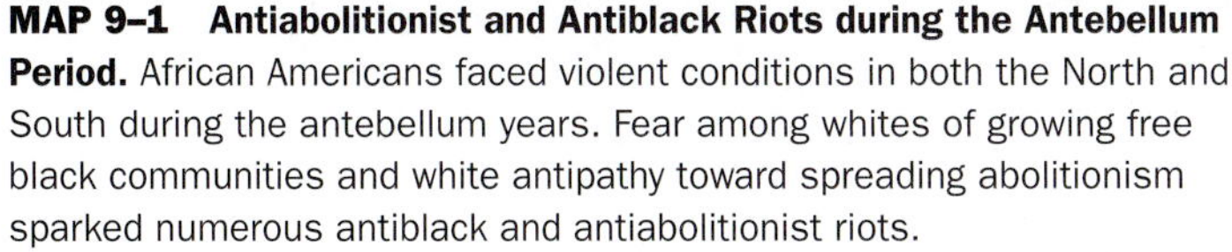

MAP 9–1 Antiabolitionist and Antiblack Riots during the Antebellum Period. African Americans faced violent conditions in both the North and South during the antebellum years. Fear among whites of growing free black communities and white antipathy toward spreading abolitionism sparked numerous antiblack and antiabolitionist riots.

states of California, Arizona, New Mexico, Utah, and part of Colorado. In 1836 the Americans in Texas won independence from Mexico. Once Texas had become an independent slaveholding republic, its leaders immediately applied for annexation to the United States. They were rebuffed for nine years because Democratic and Whig Party leaders recognized that adding a large new slave state to the Union would divide the country along North-South sectional lines. But the desire for new territory encouraged by Manifest Destiny and an expanding slave-labor economy could not be denied. In 1844 Polk, the Democratic presidential candidate, called for the annexation of Texas and Oregon, a huge territory in the Pacific Northwest that the United States and Great Britain had been jointly administering. When Polk defeated the Whig candidate Henry Clay, who favored delaying annexation, Congress in early 1845 annexed Texas by joint resolution. This vastly expanded the area within the United States that was open to slavery.

In early 1846 Polk backed away from a confrontation with Great Britain over Oregon. A few months later, however, he provoked a war with Mexico that by 1848 had forced that country to recognize American sovereignty over Texas and to cede what were then the Mexican provinces of New Mexico and California (see Map 10–1 on page 187). Immediately, the question of whether slavery would expand into these southwestern territories became a burning issue. Many white northerners assumed that slaveholders, by creating slave states out of the new territories, would dominate the federal government and enact policies detrimental to white workers and farmers.

As these sentiments spread across the North, slaveholders became fearful they would be excluded from the western lands they had helped wrest from Mexico. The resulting Compromise of 1850 (see Chapter 10) attempted to satisfy both sections. But it subjected African Americans to additional violence because part of the Compromise met slaveholders' demands for a stronger fugitive slave law. Not only did this law make it easier for masters to recapture bondpeople who had escaped to the North, but it also caused an increase in attempts to kidnap free black northerners into slavery.

The Response of the Antislavery Movement

This rising tide of race-related violence caused difficulties for an antislavery movement that suffered internal racial strife and was officially committed to using only peaceful means against slavery. African Americans found their most loyal white allies within the antislavery movement. But interracial understanding was rarely easy. White abolitionists assumed they should set policy for their black collaborators, who became increasingly resentful of this presumption as the 1840s progressed. Meanwhile the abolitionist commitment to nonviolence weakened. It had arisen as both a principled rejection of the violence that pervaded America and as a shrewd response to proslavery charges that abolitionists were responsible for unrest among slaves. But, from the start, nonviolence seemed to limit abolitionist options in an increasingly violent environment. Whether to adopt violent means and greater autonomy for black abolitionists had become contentious issues within the antislavery movement by the 1840s.

The American Anti-Slavery Society

Well before the era of Manifest Destiny, the American Anti-Slavery Society (AASS)—the most significant abolitionist organization—emerged from a major turning point in the abolitionist cause. This was William Lloyd Garrison's decision in 1831 to create a movement dedicated to immediate, uncompensated emancipation and to equal rights for African Americans in the United States. To reach these goals, abolitionists led by Garrison organized the AASS in December 1833 at Philadelphia's Adelphi Hall. Well aware of the fears raised by Nat Turner's revolt, those assembled declared, "The society will never, in any way, countenance the oppressed in vindicating their rights by resorting to physical force."

No white American worked harder than Garrison to bridge racial differences. He spoke to black groups, stayed in the homes of African Americans when he traveled, and welcomed them to his home. Black abolitionists responded with affection and loyalty. But Garrison, like most other white abolitionists, remained stiff and condescending in conversation with his black colleagues, and the black experience in the AASS reflected this.

On one hand, it is remarkable that the AASS allowed black men to participate in its meetings without formal restrictions. At the time, no other American organization did so. On the other hand, that black participation was paltry. Three African Americans—James McCrummell, Robert Purvis, and James G. Barbadoes—helped found the AASS, and McCrummell presided at its first meeting. But, among sixty white people attending that meeting, they were the only African Americans. Although three white women participated in the meeting, no black women did so. Throughout the history of the AASS, black people rarely held positions of authority.

With some exceptions, black and white women could observe, but not participate, in the proceedings of these organizations. It took a three-year struggle between 1837 and 1840 over "the woman question" before an AASS annual meeting elected a woman to a leadership position, and that victory helped split the organization.

Black and Women's Antislavery Societies

The black organizations arose both because of racial discord in the predominantly white organizations and because of a black desire for racial solidarity. But historian Benjamin Quarles makes an essential point when he writes that during the 1830s "the founders of Negro societies did not envision their efforts as distinctive or self-contained; rather they viewed their role as that of a true auxiliary—supportive, supplemental, and subsidiary." Despite their differences, black and white abolitionists were still members of a single movement.

Although racially integrated female antislavery societies did not entirely overcome the racism of their time, they elevated more African Americans to prominent positions than their male counterparts did. Black abolitionist Susan Paul became a member of the board of the Boston Female Anti-Slavery Society when it was established in 1833. Later that year, Margaretta Forten became recording secretary of the Female Anti-Slavery Society of Philadelphia, founded by white Quaker abolitionist Lucretia Mott. Black Quaker Sarah M. Douglass of Philadelphia and Sarah Forten—Margaretta's sister—were delegates to the First Anti-Slavery Convention of American Women in New York City in May 1837. At the second convention, Susan Paul became a vice president, and Douglass became treasurer.

The main task of all the women's antislavery societies was fund-raising. They held bake sales, organized antislavery fairs and bazaars, and sold antislavery memorabilia with the proceeds going to the AASS or to antislavery newspapers. But the separate women's societies also inspired the birth of feminism by creating an awareness that women had rights and interests that a male-dominated society had to recognize. By writing essays and poems on political subjects and making public speeches, black and white female abolitionists challenged a culture that relegated *respectable* women to domestic duties. By the 1850s the famous African-American speaker Sojourner Truth was emphasizing that all black women through their physical labor and the pain they suffered in slavery had earned equal standing with both men and their more favored white sisters.

Black men and women also formed auxiliaries during the early 1830s to the Quaker-initiated Free Produce Association, which tried to put economic pressure on slaveholders by boycotting agricultural products produced by slaves. James Cornish led the Colored Free Produce Society of Pennsylvania, which marketed meat, vegetables, cotton, and sugar produced by free labor. Judith James and Laetitia Rowley organized the Colored Female Free Produce Society of Pennsylvania with a similar aim. Other black affiliates to the Free Produce Association existed in New York and Ohio, and black abolitionist William Whipper operated a free produce store in Philadelphia in 1834. During the 1850s Frances Ellen Watkins Harper, one of the few prominent black female speakers of the time, always included the free produce movement in her abolitionist lectures and wrote newspaper articles on its behalf.

The Black Convention Movement

The dozens of local, state, and national black conventions held in the North between 1830 and 1864 were further removed from the AASS. They were a black manifestation of the antebellum American reform impulse, and the antislavery cause was not their only agenda. They did, nevertheless, provide an independent forum for the more prominent black male abolitionists, such as Henry Highland Garnet, Frederick Douglass, and, later, Martin R. Delany. They also provided a setting in which abolitionism could grow and change its tactics to meet the demands of the sectionally polarized and violent 1840s.

Hezekiah Grice, a young black man who had worked with Benjamin Lundy and William Lloyd Garrison in Baltimore during the 1820s, organized the first Black National Convention. It met on September 24, 1830, at the Bethel Church in Philadelphia with the venerable churchman Richard Allen presiding. The national convention became an annual event for the next five years and then met irregularly in such cities as Philadelphia, New York, Buffalo, Rochester, Syracuse, and Cleveland into the Civil War years. Meanwhile, many state and local black conventions also met across the North. By current standards, these conventions were small and informal—particularly those at the local level—and had no strict guidelines for choosing delegates. These characteristics, however, did not prevent the conventions from becoming effective forums for black concerns. They invariably called for the abolition of slavery and for improving the conditions of northern African Americans. Among other reforms, the conventions called for integrated public schools and the right of black men to vote, serve on juries, and testify against white people in court.

During the 1830s the conventions also stressed black self-help through temperance, sexual morality, education, and thrift. These causes remained important parts of the conventions' agenda throughout the antebellum years. But by the early 1840s, politics and the active resistance to oppression that Garnet called for in the speech quoted at the start of this chapter received more emphasis. By the late 1840s, assertions of black nationalism and endorsements of black migration to Africa or Latin America had become common.

Black Community Institutions

Although the persistence of slavery and oppression helped shape the agenda of the Black Convention Movement, the movement itself was a product of a maturing African-American community. Free black people in the United States grew from 59,000 in 1790 to 319,000 in 1830. Gradual emancipation in the northern states, acts of individual manumission in the upper South, and escapes accounted for this fivefold increase. The growing free black population was concentrated in such large cities as New York, Philadelphia, Baltimore, Boston, and Cincinnati. These cities had enough free African Americans to provide the resources that built the churches, schools, benevolent organizations, and printing presses that created a self-conscious black community. Between 1790 and 1830, this community provided the foundations for the black antislavery institutions of the decades that followed.

Black Churches in the Antislavery Cause

Black churches were especially significant for the antislavery movement. With a few major exceptions, the leading black abolitionists were ministers. Among them were Garnet, Jehiel C. Beman, Samuel E. Cornish, Theodore S. Wright, Charles B. Ray, James W. C. Pennington, Nathaniel Paul, Alexander Crummell, Daniel A. Payne, and Samuel Ringgold Ward. Some of these men led congregations affiliated with separate African-American churches, such as the African Baptist Church or the African Methodist Episcopal (AME) Church. Others preached to black congregations affiliated with predominantly white churches. A few black ministers, such as Amos N. Freeman of Brooklyn, New York, served white antislavery congregations. These clergy used their pulpits to attack slavery, racial discrimination, proslavery white churches, and the American Colonization Society (ACS). Black churches also provided forums for abolitionist speakers, such as Frederick Douglass and Garrison, and meeting places for predominantly white antislavery organizations, which were frequently denied space in white churches.

Black Newspapers

Less influential than black churches in the antislavery movement, black newspapers still played an important role, particularly by the 1840s. Abolitionist newspapers, whether owned by black or white people, almost always faced financial difficulties. Few survived for more than a few years because *reform,* as opposed to *commercial,* newspapers were a luxury that many subscribers both black and white could not afford. Black newspapers faced added difficulties finding readers because most African Americans were poor, and many were illiterate. Moreover, white abolitionist newspapers, such as the *Liberator,* served a black clientele. They published speeches by black abolitionists and reported black convention proceedings. Some black abolitionists argued, therefore, that a separate black press was unnecessary. An additional, self-imposed, burden was that publishers eager to get their message out almost never required subscribers to pay in advance, thereby compounding their papers' financial instability.

Nevertheless several influential black abolitionist newspapers were in existence between the late 1820s and the Civil War. The first black newspaper, *Freedom's Journal,* owned and edited by Samuel Cornish and John B. Russwurm, lasted only from 1827 to 1829. It showed, nevertheless, that African Americans could produce interesting and competent journalism and attract both black and white subscribers. The *Journal* also established a framework for black journalism during the antebellum period by emphasizing antislavery, racial justice, and Christian and democratic values.

The most ubiquitous black journalist of the period was Philip A. Bell. Bell was either publisher or co-publisher of the *New York Weekly Advocate* in 1837, the *Colored American* from 1837 to 1842, and two San Francisco newspapers, the *Pacific Appeal* and the *Elevator*, during the 1860s. But the black clergyman Charles B. Ray of New York City was the real spirit behind the *Colored American*. Well aware of the need for financial success, Ray declared in 1838, "If among the few hundred thousand free colored people in the country—to say nothing of the white population from whom it ought to receive a strong support—a living patronage for the paper cannot be obtained, it will be greatly to their reproach."

However, Frederick Douglass's *North Star* and its successor *Frederick Douglass' Paper* were the most influential black antislavery newspapers of the late 1840s and the 1850s. Heavily subsidized by Gerrit Smith, a wealthy white abolitionist, and attracting more white than black subscribers, Douglass's weeklies were supported by many black abolitionist organizations. The papers were extremely well edited and attractively printed. They also employed able assistant editors, including Martin R. Delany during the late 1840s, and insightful correspondents, such as William J. Wilson of Brooklyn and James McCune Smith of New York City.

Moral Suasion

During the 1830s the AASS adopted a reform strategy based on moral suasion—what we would call moral *persuasion* today. This was an appeal to Americans to support abolition and racial justice on the basis of their Christian consciences and concern for their immortal souls. Slaveholding, the AASS argued, was a sin and a crime that deprived African Americans of the freedom of conscience they needed to save their souls. Slaveholding, according to the AASS, also led white masters to eternal damnation through indolence, sexual exploitation of black women, and unrestrained brutality. In addition, abolitionists argued slavery was an inefficient labor system that enriched a few masters but impoverished most black and white southerners and hurt the economy of the United States as a whole.

Abolitionists, however, did not restrict themselves to criticizing white southerners. They noted that northern industries thrived by manufacturing cloth from cotton produced by slave labor. The U.S. government protected the interests of slaveholders in the District of Columbia, in the territories, in the interstate slave trade, and through the Fugitive Slave Act of 1793. Northerners who profited from slave labor and supported the national government with their votes and taxes, therefore, bore their share of guilt for slavery and faced divine punishment.

The AASS sought to use these arguments to convince masters to free their slaves and to persuade northerners and nonslaveholding white southerners to put moral pressure on slaveholders. To reach a southern audience, the AASS in 1835 launched the Great Postal Campaign, designed to send antislavery literature to southern post offices and individual slaveholders. At about the same time, the AASS organized a massive petitioning campaign aimed to introduce the slavery issue into Congress. Antislavery women led in circulating and signing the petitions. In 1836 over thirty thousand of the petitions reached Washington.

In the North, AASS agents gave public lectures against slavery and distributed antislavery literature. Often a pair of agents—one black and one white—traveled together on speaking tours. Ideally, the black agent would be a former slave, so he could attack the brutality and immorality of slavery from personal experience. During the early 1840s, the AASS paired fugitive slave Frederick Douglass with William A. White, a young white Harvard graduate, in a tour through Ohio and Indiana. In 1843 the Eastern New York Anti-Slavery Society paired white Baptist preacher Abel Brown with "the noble colored man," Lewis Washington. At first, all the agents were men. Later, the abolitionist organizations also employed women as agents.

The reaction to these efforts in both the North and the South was not what the leaders of the AASS anticipated. By speaking of racial justice and exemplifying interracial cooperation, the abolitionists were treading new ground. In doing so, they created awkward situations that are—in retrospect—humorous. But their audiences often reacted violently. Southern postmasters burned antislavery literature when it arrived at their offices, and southern states censored the mail. Vigilantes drove off white southerners who openly advocated abolition. Black abolitionists, of course, did not even attempt openly to denounce slavery while in the South.

In Congress, southern representatives and their northern allies passed the Gag Rule in 1836. It required that no petition related to slavery could be introduced in the House of Representatives. In response, the AASS sent 415,000 petitions in 1838, and Congressman John Quincy Adams (a former president) launched his long struggle against the Gag. Technically not an abolitionist, but a defender of the First Amendment right to petition Congress, Adams succeeded in having the Gag Rule repealed in 1844.

Meanwhile, in the North, mobs attacked abolitionist agents, disrupted their meetings, destroyed their newspaper presses, and burned black neighborhoods. In 1837 a proslavery mob killed Elijah P. Lovejoy, a white abolitionist newspaper editor, when he tried to defend his printing press in Alton, Illinois. On another occasion, Douglass, White, and an older white abolitionist named George Bradburn were conducting antislavery meetings in the small town of Pendleton, Indiana, when an enraged mob attempted to kill Douglass.

The American and Foreign Anti-Slavery Society and the Liberty Party

In 1840 the AASS splintered. Most of its members left to establish the American and Foreign Anti-Slavery Society (AFASS) and the Liberty Party, the first antislavery political party. On the surface, the AASS broke apart over long-standing disagreements about the role of women in abolitionism and William Lloyd Garrison's broadening radicalism. By denouncing most organized religion, by becoming a feminist, and by embracing a form of Christian anarchy that precluded formal involvement in politics, Garrison seemed to many to be losing sight of the AASS's main concern. But the failure of moral suasion to make progress against slavery—particularly in the South—and the question of how abolitionists should respond to the increasing signs of slave unrest also helped fracture the AASS.

Garrison and a minority of abolitionists, who agreed with his radical critique of American society and were centered in New England, retained control of what became known as the "Old Organization." By 1842 they had deemphasized moral suasion and had begun calling for disunion—the separation of the North from the South—as the only means of ending northern support for slavery. The U.S. Constitution, Garrison declared, was a thoroughly proslavery document that had to be destroyed before African Americans could gain their freedom.

Those who withdrew from the AASS took a more traditional stand on the role of women, believed the country's churches could be converted to abolitionism, and asserted the Constitution could be used in behalf of abolitionism. Under the leadership of Lewis Tappan, a wealthy white New York City abolitionist, some of them formed the church-oriented AFASS. Others created the Liberty Party and nominated James G. Birney, a slaveholder-turned-abolitionist, as their candidate in the 1840 presidential election. Birney received only 7,069 votes out of a total cast of 2,411,187, and William Henry Harrison, the Whig candidate, became president. But the Liberty Party constituted the beginning of an increasingly powerful political crusade against slavery.

Black abolitionists joined in the disruption of the Old Organization. Only in New England did most black abolitionists remain loyal to the AASS. Frederick Douglass, William Wells Brown, Robert Purvis, Charles L. Remond, Susan Paul, and Sarah Douglass were notable Garrison loyalists. As might have been expected, most black clerical abolitionists joined the AFASS.

The Liberty Party also attracted black support, although few black men could vote. Particularly appealing to black abolitionists was the platform of the radical New York wing of the party led by Gerrit Smith. Philip A. Bell, Charles B. Ray, Samuel E. Cornish, Henry Highland Garnet, and Jermain Wesley Loguen endorsed the New York Liberty Party because, of all the antislavery organizations, it advocated the most aggressive action against slavery in the South and was most directly involved in helping slaves escape.

A More Aggressive Abolitionism

The New York Liberty Party maintained that the U.S. Constitution, interpreted in the light of the Bible and natural law, outlawed slavery throughout the country—not only in the District of Columbia and in the territories, which were governed by the federal government, but in the states as well. This, the party's leaders asserted, meant Congress could abolish slavery in the southern states. More practically it meant that for slaves to escape and for others to help them escape were perfectly legal actions. Some argued that neither northern state militia nor the U.S. Army should help suppress slave revolts.

This body of thought, which dated to the late 1830s, supported growing northern abolitionist empathy with the slaves as they struggled for freedom against their masters. While the AASS disintegrated, escapes and minor rebellions proliferated in the border slave states of Maryland, Virginia, Kentucky, and Missouri as enslaved black people reacted to worsening conditions there. Throughout this region black families were being torn apart by the domestic slave trade, which was funneling black workers into the newly opened cotton-producing areas of the Southwest. In response, the radical wing of the Liberty Party cited the Constitution in support of slave resistance to this brutal traffic. It also encouraged black and white northerners to go south to help slaves escape.

The *Amistad* and the *Creole*

Two maritime slave revolts were crucial in encouraging rising militancy among northern abolitionists. The first of these revolts, however, did not involve enslaved Americans. In June 1839 fifty-four African captives aboard the Spanish schooner *Amistad,* meaning "friendship," successfully rebelled under the leadership of Joseph Cinque and attempted to sail to Africa. When a U.S. warship recaptured the *Amistad* off the coast of Long Island, New York, the Africans attracted the support of Lewis Tappan and other abolitionists. As a result of the abolitionists' efforts and arguments presented by Congressman Adams, the U.S. Supreme Court ruled in November 1841 that Cinque and the others were free.

Later that same month, Madison Washington led a revolt aboard the brig *Creole,* which was transporting 135 American slaves from Richmond, Virginia, to the slave markets of New Orleans. Washington and about a dozen other black men seized control of the vessel and sailed it to the British colony of the Bahamas. There local black fishermen surrounded the *Creole* with their boats to protect it, and most of the people on board immediately gained their freedom under British law.

Cinque and Washington inspired others to risk their lives and freedom to help African Americans escape bondage. The New York Liberty Party reinforced this commitment by maintaining that what they did was both divinely ordained and strictly legal.

The Underground Railroad

The famous underground railroad must be placed within the context of increasing southern white violence against black families, slave resistance, and aggressive northern abolitionism. Because the underground railroad had to be secret, few details of how it operated are known. We do not even know the origin of the term *underground railroad.* Slaves had always escaped from their masters, and free black people and some white people had always assisted them. But the organized escape of slaves from the Chesapeake, Kentucky, and Missouri along predetermined routes to Canada became much more common after the mid-1830s. A united national underground railroad with a president or unified command never existed. Instead there were different organizations separated in both time and space from one another (see Map 9–2). Even during the 1840s and 1850s, most of the slaves who escaped did so on their own.

The best documented underground railroad organizations were centered in Washington, D.C., and Ripley, Ohio. In Washington Charles T. Torrey, a white Liberty Party abolitionist from Albany, New York, and Thomas Smallwood, a free black resident of Washington, began in 1842 to help slaves escape along a predetermined northward route. Between March and November of that year, they sent at least 150 enslaved men, women, and children to Philadelphia. From there, a local black vigilance committee provided the fugitives with transportation to Albany, New York, where a local, predominantly white, vigilance group smuggled them to Canada. In southern Ohio, some residents, black and white, had for years helped fugitive slaves as they headed north from the slaveholding state of Kentucky. From the late 1840s into the Civil War years, former slave John P. Parker made the Ripley-based underground railroad more aggressive.

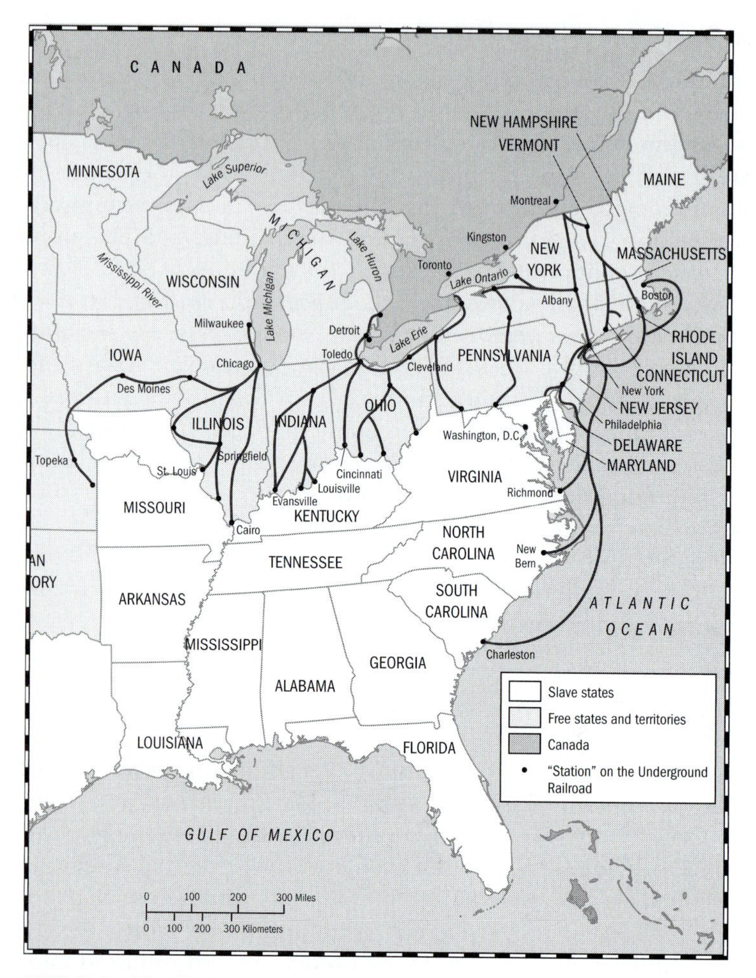

MAP 9–2 The Underground Railroad. This map illustrates *approximate* routes traveled by escaping slaves through the North to Canada. Although some slaves escaped from the deep South, most who utilized the underground railroad network came from the border slave states.

By the early 1850s, Harriet Tubman, a fugitive slave herself, had become the most active worker on the eastern branch of the underground railroad. She was born in 1820 on a Maryland plantation. Her master abused her, but she did not escape until he threatened to sell her and her family south. After her escape in 1849, Tubman returned about thirteen times to Maryland to help others flee. She had the help of Thomas Garrett, a white Quaker abolitionist who lived in Wilmington, Delaware, and William Still, the black leader of the Philadelphia Vigilance Association. Still, who as a child had been a fugitive slave himself, for years coordinated the work of many black and white underground agents between Washington and Canada.

Canada West

The ultimate destination for many African Americans on the underground railroad was Canada West—present-day Ontario—between Buffalo and Detroit on the northern shore of Lake Erie. Black Americans had begun to settle in Canada West as early as the 1820s and, because slavery was illegal in the British Empire after 1833, fugitive slaves were safe there.

The chief advocate of black migration to Canada West—and the only advocate of migration who also supported racial integration—was Mary Ann Shadd Cary. She edited the *Provincial Freeman*, an abolitionist paper in Toronto, between 1854 and 1858, and lectured in northern cities promoting emigration to Canada. Yet, although African Americans enjoyed security in Canada, by the 1850s they also faced the same sort of segregation and discrimination there that existed in the northern United States.

Black Militancy

During the 1840s growing numbers of black abolitionists were willing to consider forceful action against slavery. This resolve accompanied a trend to create their separate black antislavery organizations. The black convention movement revived during the 1840s, and there were well-attended meetings in Buffalo in 1843, in Troy, New York, in 1844, and in Cleveland in 1848. More newspapers owned and edited by black abolitionists appeared.

The rise in black militancy had several causes. The breakup of the AASS had weakened abolitionist loyalty to the national antislavery organizations. All abolitionists, black and white, were exploring new types of antislavery action. Many black abolitionists had become convinced that most white abolitionists enjoyed debate and theory more than action against slavery.

Influenced by the examples of Cinque, Madison Washington, and other rebellious slaves, many black abolitionists in the 1840s and 1850s wanted to do more to encourage slaves to resist and escape. This militancy inspired Garnet's "Address to the Slaves." A willingness to act rather than just talk helped make the Liberty Party—especially its radical New York wing—attractive to African Americans. However, black abolitionists, like white abolitionists, approached violence and slave rebellion with caution. As late as 1857, Garnet and Frederick Douglass described slave revolt as "inexpedient."

The black abolitionist desire to go beyond rhetoric found its best outlet in the local vigilance organizations. The most famous of these is William Still's Philadelphia Vigilance Association, which was active during the late 1840s and 1850s. But such associations were first organized during the late 1830s and often had white as well as black members. As the 1840s progressed, African Americans formed more such associations and began to lead those that already existed. In this they were reacting to a facet of the growing violence in the United States—the use of force by "slave catchers" in northern cities to recapture fugitive slaves.

Another aspect of black militancy during the 1840s was a willingness to charge publicly that white abolitionists were not living up to their own advocacy of racial justice. Economic slights rankled African Americans the most. At the annual meeting of

Harriet Tubman, standing at the left, is shown in this undated photograph with a group of people she helped escape from slavery. Because she worked in secret during the 1850s, she was known only to others engaged in the underground railroad, the people she helped, and a few other abolitionists.
Sophia Smith Collection, Smith College

the AFASS in 1852, a black delegate demanded to know why Lewis Tappan did not employ a black clerk in his business. In 1855 Samuel Ringgold Ward denounced Garrison and his associates for failing to have an African American "as clerk in an anti-slavery office, or editor, or lecturer to the same extent . . . as white men of the same calibre." These charges reflected factional struggles between the AASS and the AFASS. But they also represented real grievances among black abolitionists and real inconsistencies among their white counterparts.

Frederick Douglass

The career of Frederick Douglass illustrates the impact of the failure of white abolitionists to live up to their egalitarian ideals. Douglass was born a slave in Maryland in 1818. Intelligent, ambitious, and charming, he resisted brutalization, learned to read, and acquired a trade before escaping to New England in 1838. By 1841 he had, with Garrison's encouragement, become an antislavery lecturer, which led to the travels with William White discussed earlier.

But as time passed, Douglass, who had remained loyal to Garrison during the 1840s when most other black abolitionists had left the AASS, suspected his white colleagues wanted him to continue in the role of a fugitive slave when, in fact, he was becoming one of the premier American orators of his time. "People won't believe you ever was a slave, Frederick, if you keep on this way," a white colleague advised him.

Finally, Douglass decided he had to free himself from the AASS. In 1847 he asserted his independence by leaving Massachusetts for Rochester, New York, where he began publishing the *North Star*. This decision angered Garrison and his associates but permitted Douglass to chart his own course as a black leader. Although Douglass continued to work closely with white abolitionists, especially Gerrit Smith, he could now do it on his own terms and be more active in the black convention movement, which he considered essential to gaining general emancipation and racial justice. In 1851 he completed his break with the AASS by endorsing the constitutional arguments and tactics of the New York Liberty Party as better designed to achieve emancipation than Garrison's disunionism.

Black Nationalism

Douglass always believed black people were part of a larger American nation and their best prospects for political and economic success lay in the United States. He was, despite his differences with some white abolitionists, an ardent integrationist. He opposed separate black churches and predicted that African Americans would eventually disappear into a greater American identity. Most black abolitionists did not go that far, but they agreed racial oppression in all its forms could be defeated in the United States.

During the 1840s and 1850s, however, an influential minority of black leaders disagreed with this point of view. Prominent among them were Garnet and Douglass's sometime colleague on the *North Star* Martin R. Delany. Although they differed between themselves over important details, Delany and Garnet both endorsed African-American migration and nationalism as the best means to realize black aspirations.

Since the postrevolutionary days of Prince Hall, some black leaders had believed African Americans could thrive only as a separate nation. They suggested sites in Africa, Latin America, and the American West as possible places to pursue this goal. But it took the rising tide of racism and violence emphasized in this chapter to induce a respectable minority of black abolitionists to consider migration. Almost all of them staunchly opposed the African migration scheme of the ACS, which they continued to characterize as proslavery and racist. Nevertheless, Garnet conceded in 1849 that he would "rather see a man free in Liberia [the ACS colony], than a slave in the United States."

Douglass and most black abolitionists rejected this outlook, insisting the aim must be freedom in the United States. Nevertheless, emigration plans developed by Garnet and Delany during the 1850s were a significant part of African-American reform culture. Delany, a physician and novelist, was born free in western Virginia in 1812. He grew up in Pennsylvania and by the late 1840s was a champion of black self-reliance. To further this cause, he promoted mass black migration to Latin America or Africa. "We must MAKE an ISSUE, CREATE an EVENT, and ESTABLISH a NATIONAL POSITION for OURSELVES," he declared in 1852.

In contrast, Garnet welcomed white assistance for his plan to foster Christianity and economic development in Africa by encouraging *some*—not all—African Americans to migrate there under the patronage of his African Civilization Society. In 1858 he wrote, "Let those who wished to stay, stay here—and those who had enterprise and wished to go, go and found a nation, if possible, of which the colored Americans could be proud."

Little came of these nationalist visions, largely because of the successes of the antislavery movement. Black and white abolitionists, although not perfect allies, awoke many in the North to the brutalities of slavery. They helped convince most white northerners

This c. 1844 oil portrait of Frederick Douglass is attributed to E. Hammond. Douglass escaped from slavery in 1838. By the mid-1840s, he had emerged as one of the more powerful speakers of his time. He began publishing his influential newspaper, the *North Star*, in 1847.

Frederick Douglass (1817?–95). Oil on canvas, c. 1844, attr. to E. Hammond. The Granger Collection, New York

that the slave-labor system and slaveholder control of the national government threatened their economic and political interests. At the same time, abolitionist aid to escaping slaves and their defense of fugitive slaves from recapture pushed southern leaders to adopt policies that led to secession and the Civil War. The northern victory in the war, general emancipation, and constitutional protection for black rights made most African Americans—for a time—optimistic about their future in the United States.

TIMELINE

AFRICAN-AMERICAN EVENTS	NATIONAL EVENTS
1830	
1831 Publication of *Liberator* begun by William Lloyd Garrison **1833** Formation of AASS	**1832** Andrew Jackson reelected president **1833** End of Nullification Controversy
1835	
1835 Abolitionist Postal Campaign **1839** *Amistad* mutiny	**1836** Martin Van Buren elected president; Texas independence

continued

AFRICAN-AMERICAN EVENTS	NATIONAL EVENTS
1840	
1840 Breakup of AASS **1841** *Creole* revolt **1843** Henry Highland Garnet's "Address to the Slaves"	**1840** William H. Harrison elected president **1844** James K. Polk elected president
1845	
1847 Publication of the *North Star* begun by Frederick Douglass **1849** Harriet Tubman's career begins	**1845** Annexation of Texas **1846** War against Mexico begins **1848** Annexation of Mexico's California and New Mexico Provinces
1850	
1851 Start of resistance to the Fugitive Slave Act of 1850 Black migration advocated by Martin Delany	**1850** Compromise of 1850
1855	

Conclusion

In this chapter, we have focused on the radical movement for the immediate abolition of slavery. The movement flourished in the United States from 1831, when William Lloyd Garrison began publishing the *Liberator*, through the Civil War. Garrison hoped slavery could be abolished peacefully. But during the 1840s abolitionists had to adjust their antislavery tactics to deal with increasing racism and antiblack violence, both of which were related to the existence of slavery. Many black and white abolitionists concluded that the tactic of moral suasion, which they had emphasized during the 1830s, would not by itself achieve their goals or prevent violence against free and enslaved black people. Slave resistance also inspired a more confrontational brand of abolitionism. Most black abolitionists came to believe a combination of moral suasion, political involvement, and direct action against slavery was required to end slavery and improve the lives of African Americans in the United States. By the late 1840s, however, a minority of black abolitionists contended they had to establish an independent nation beyond the borders of the United States to promote their rights, interests, and identity.

Although much has changed since the abolitionist era, these two perspectives remain characteristic of the African-American community today. Most African Americans prefer integration with a larger American nation. But black nationalism still has a powerful appeal. Individuals often embrace parts of both views, just as Frederick Douglass embraced some black nationalism and Henry Highland Garnet some integrationism. Similarly, reformers are still debating whether peaceful persuasion is more effective than confrontation.

Review Questions

1. What was the historical significance of Henry Highland Garnet's "Address to the Slaves"? How did Garnet's attitude toward slavery differ from that of William Lloyd Garrison?
2. Evaluate Frederick Douglass's career as an abolitionist. How was he consistent? How was he inconsistent?
3. Discuss the contribution of black women to the antislavery movement. How did participation in this movement alter their lives?
4. Compare and contrast the integrationist views of Frederick Douglass with the nationalist views of Martin Delany and Henry Highland Garnet.
5. Why did black abolitionists leave the AASS in 1840?

Recommended Reading

Stanley Harrold. *The Abolitionists and the South, 1831–1861.* Lexington: University Press of Kentucky, 1995. Emphasizes the formative impact of slave resistance on northern abolitionism and the aggressiveness of that movement toward the South.

Jane H. Pease and William H. Pease. *They Who Would Be Free: Blacks' Search for Freedom, 1830–1861.* New York: Athenaeum, 1974. Deals with cooperation and conflict between black and white abolitionists. The book emphasizes conflict.

Benjamin Quarles. *Black Abolitionists.* New York: Oxford University Press, 1969. A classic study that emphasizes cooperation between black and white abolitionists.

Harry Reed. *Platforms for Change: The Foundations of the Northern Free Black Community, 1776–1865.* East Lansing: Michigan State University Press, 1994. Places black abolitionism and black nationalism within the context of community development.

Shirley J. Yee. *Black Women Abolitionists: A Study of Activism.* Knoxville: University of Tennessee Press, 1992. Discusses the activities of black women abolitionists in both white and black organizations.

R. J. Young. *Antebellum Black Activists: Race, Gender, Self.* New York: Garland, 1996. A sophisticated study of the motivation of black abolitionists.

• CHAPTER TEN •

AND BLACK PEOPLE WERE AT THE HEART OF IT

THE UNITED STATES DISUNITES OVER SLAVERY

The Lure of the West

Even before the war with Mexico, hundreds of Americans made the long journey west, drawn by the opportunity to settle the fertile valleys of California and the Oregon territory, which included what is today the states of Oregon and Washington. African Americans were not exempt from these hopes and dreams.

Free Labor Versus Slave Labor

Westward expansion revived the issue of slavery's future in the territories. Should slavery be legal in western lands, or should it be outlawed? Most white Americans held thoroughly ingrained racist beliefs that people of African descent were not and could never be their intellectual, political, or social equals. Yet those same white Americans disagreed vehemently on where those unfree African Americans should be permitted to labor and reside.

By the mid-nineteenth century, northern black and white people embraced the system of free labor, that is, free men and women working to earn a living and improve their lives. If southern slave owners managed to gain a foothold for their unfree labor on the western plains, in the Rocky Mountains, or on the Pacific coast, then the future for free white laborers would be severely restricted, if not destroyed.

The Wilmot Proviso

In 1846, during the Mexican War, a Democratic congressman from Pennsylvania, David Wilmot, introduced a measure in Congress to prohibit slavery in any lands acquired from Mexico. Wilmot later explained that he wanted neither slavery nor black people to taint territory that should be reserved exclusively for whites. Wilmot's Proviso failed to become law, but white Southerners, who saw the measure as a blatant attempt to prevent them from moving west and enjoying the prosperity and way of life that an expanding slave-labor system would create, were enraged. They considered any attempt to limit the growth of slavery to be the first step toward eliminating it.

White Southerners had convinced themselves that black people were a childlike and irresponsible race wholly incapable of surviving as a free people if they were emancipated and compelled to compete with white Americans. Thus southern white people considered slavery "a positive good" that benefited both races and resulted in a society vastly superior to that of the North.

To prevent slavery's expansion, the Free-Soil Party was formed in 1848. It was composed mainly of white people who vigorously opposed slavery's expansion and the supposed desecration that the presence of black men and women might bring to the new western lands. But some black and white abolitionists also supported the Free-Soilers as a way to oppose slavery. Frederick Douglass felt comfortable enough with the Free-Soil Party to attend its convention in 1848. Ten Free-Soil congressmen were elected, and the party provided a growing forum to oppose slavery's advance.

California and The Compromise of 1850

The discovery of gold in California in 1848 sent thousands of Americans hurrying west in search of wealth in 1849. As California's population quickly soared to more than 100,000, its new residents applied for admission to the Union as a free state. Southern whites were aghast at the prospect of California prohibiting slavery. Most Northerners would not accept this.

Into the dispute stepped Whig senator Henry Clay, who had assisted with the Missouri Compromise thirty years earlier. In 1850 the aging Clay put together an elaborate compromise designed not only to settle the controversy over California, but also to resolve the issue of slavery's expansion once and for all. Clay attempted to satisfy both sides. To placate Northerners, he proposed admitting California as a free state and eliminating the slave trade (but not slavery) in the District of Columbia. To satisfy white Southerners, he offered a stronger fugitive slave law to make it easier for slave owners to apprehend runaway slaves and return them to slavery. New Mexico and Utah would also be organized as territories with no mention of slavery.

Clay's measures were hammered into a single bill and produced one of the most remarkable debates in the history of the Senate, but it did not pass. Northern opponents like Senator William Seward of New York could not tolerate a tougher fugitive slave law. President Zachary Taylor shocked his fellow Southerners and insisted California should be admitted as a free state, and that Clay's compromise was unnecessary. Taylor promised to veto the compromise if the House and Senate passed it.

Clay's effort had failed—or so it seemed. But in the summer of 1850, Taylor died unexpectedly and was succeeded by Millard Fillmore, who was willing to accept the compromise. Senator Stephen Douglas, an ambitious Democrat from Illinois, guided Clay's compromise through Congress by breaking it into separate bills. California entered the Union as a free state, and a stronger fugitive slave law entered the federal legal code.

Fugitive Slave Laws

Those who may have hoped the compromise would resolve the dispute over slavery forever were mistaken. The Fugitive Slave Law of 1850 created bitter resentment among black and white abolitionists and made slavery a more emotional and personal issue for many white people who had previously considered slavery a remote southern institution.

Had runaway slaves not been an increasingly frustrating problem for slave owners—particularly those in the upper South states of Maryland, Virginia, and Kentucky—the federal fugitive slave law would not have needed to be strengthened in 1850. The U.S. Constitution and the fugitive slave law passed in 1793 would seem to have provided ample authority for slave owners to recover runaway slaves.

The Constitution in Article IV, Section 2, stipulates that "any person held to service or labor in one State" who ran away to another state "shall be delivered up on claim of the party to whom such service or labor may be due." The fugitive slave law of 1793 permitted slave owners to recover slaves who escaped to other states. The escaped slave had no rights—no right to a trial, no right to testify, and no guarantee of habeas corpus (the legal requirement that a person be brought before a court and not imprisoned illegally).

But by the 1830s and 1840s, as hundreds if not thousands of slaves escaped to freedom by way of the underground railroad, white Southerners increasingly found the 1793 law too weak to overcome the resistance of northern communities to the return of escapees. For example, in January 1847 four Kentuckians and a local law officer attempted to capture Adam Crosswhite, his wife, and four children after the family had escaped from slavery in Kentucky and settled on a farm near Marshall, Michigan. When the would-be abductors arrived, an old black man mounted a horse and galloped through town ringing a bell warning that the Crosswhites were in danger. Having been aroused by this "Black Paul Revere," about one hundred people helped rescue the family and put them on a railroad train to Canada. The local citizens who had aided the Crosswhites were later sued successfully by the slave owner and fined an amount equal to the estimated value of the Crosswhites had the family been sold as slaves.

Several northern states had enacted personal liberty laws that made it illegal for state law enforcement officials to help capture runaways. (Michigan passed such a law in 1855 after the Crosswhites escaped to Canada.) Not only did many Northerners refuse to cooperate in returning fugitives to slavery under the 1793 law, but they also encouraged and assisted the escaped slaves. The local black vigilance committees that were created in many northern communities and discussed in Chapter 9—among them the League of Freedom in Boston and the Liberty Association in Chicago—were especially effective in these efforts. These actions infuriated white Southerners and prompted their demand for a stricter fugitive slave law.

The Fugitive Slave Law of 1850 was one of the toughest and harshest measures the U.S. Congress ever passed. Anyone apprehended under the law was almost certain to be sent back to slavery. The law required U.S. marshals, their deputies, and even ordinary citizens to help seize suspected runaways. Those who refused to help apprehend fugitives or who helped the runaway could be fined or imprisoned. The law made it nearly impossible for black people to prove they were free. Slave owners and their agents only had to provide legal documentation from their home state or the testimony of white witnesses before a federal commissioner that the captive was a runaway slave. The federal commissioners were paid $10 for captives returned to bondage but only $5 for those declared free. Supporters of the law claimed the extra paperwork involved in returning a fugitive to slavery necessitated the $10 fee. Opponents of the law saw the $10 as a bribe to encourage federal authorities to return men and women to bondage. During the time the law was in effect, 332 captives were returned to the South and slavery, and only 11 were released as free people.

The new fugitive slave law outraged many black and white Northerners. An angry Frederick Douglass insisted in October 1850 that "the only way to make the Fugitive

Slave Law a dead letter is to make a half dozen or more dead kidnappers." White abolitionist Wendell Phillips exhorted his listeners to disobey the law. "We must trample this law under our feet."

FUGITIVE SLAVES

The fugitive slave law did more than anger black and white Northerners. It exposed them to cruel and heart-wrenching scenes as southern slave owners and slave catchers took advantage of the new law and—with the vigorous assistance of federal authorities—relentlessly pursued runaway slaves. Many white people and virtually all black people felt genuine revulsion over this crackdown on those who had fled from slavery to freedom.

In September 1850 in New York City, federal authorities captured a black porter and returned him to slavery in Baltimore, even though he insisted that because his mother was a free woman he had not been a slave. (In each of the slave states, the law stipulated the status of the mother determined a child's legal status—free or slave.) In Poughkeepsie, New York, slave catchers captured a well-to-do black tailor and returned him to slavery in South Carolina. In Indiana, a black man was apprehended while his wife and children looked on, and he was sent to Kentucky where his owner claimed he had escaped nineteen years earlier.

Not all fugitives were forced back into bondage. A Maryland slave owner attempted to recover a black woman in Philadelphia who, he asserted, had escaped twenty-two years earlier. Since then, she had had six children, and the slave owner insisted they were also his property. In this instance, the federal commissioner ruled the woman and her children were free.

Even California was not immune to the furor over fugitive slaves. Although slavery was prohibited in the new state, several hundred black people were held illegally there as slaves in the 1850s. Nevertheless there were some slaves who ran away to the west rather than the north. Black abolitionist Mary Ellen Pleasant hid fugitive Archy Lee in San Francisco in 1858; other members of the black community provided security for runaways from as far east as Maryland.

William and Ellen Craft

Black and white abolitionists organized vigilance committees to resist the fugitive slave law and to prevent—by force if necessary—the return of fugitives to slavery. In October 1850 slave catchers arrived in Boston fully prepared to return William and Ellen Craft to slavery in Georgia. In 1848 the Crafts had devised an ingenious escape. Ellen's fair complexion enabled her to disguise herself as a sickly young white man who, accompanied by "his" slave, was traveling north for medical treatment. They journeyed to Boston by railroad and ship and thus escaped from slavery—or so they thought.

Slave catchers vowed to return the Crafts to servitude no matter how long it took. While white abolitionists protected Ellen and black abolitionists hid William, the vigilance committee plastered posters around Boston describing the slave catchers, calling them "man-stealers," and threatening their safety. Within days (which must have seemed slightly less than eternity), the Southerners left without the Crafts. Soon thereafter, the Crafts sailed to security in England.

Leaflets like this reflect the outrage many Northerners felt in response to the capture and reenslavement of African Americans that resulted from the passage of a tougher Fugitive Slave Law as part of the Compromise of 1850.
Courtesy of the Library of Congress

Shadrach

Black and white abolitionists were fully prepared to use force against the U.S. government and the slave owners and their agents. Sometimes the abolitionists succeeded; sometimes they did not. In early 1851, a few months after the Crafts left Boston, federal marshals apprehended a black waiter there who had escaped from slavery and given himself the name Shadrach. But a well-organized band of black men led by Lewis Hayden invaded the courthouse and escaped with Shadrach. They spirited him to safety in Canada on the Underground Railroad. (Shadrach later became the owner of a restaurant in Montreal.) Federal authorities brought charges against four black men and four white men who were then indicted by a grand jury for helping Shadrach, but local juries refused to convict them.

The Battle at Christiana

In September 1851 a battle erupted in the little town of Christiana, in southern Pennsylvania, when a Maryland slave owner, Edward Gorsuch, arrived to recover two runaway slaves. Accompanied by several family members and three deputy U.S. marshals, they confronted a hostile and well-armed crowd of at least twenty-five black men and several white men. Black leader William Parker bluntly told Gorsuch to give up any plans to take the runaway slaves. Gorsuch refused, and a battle ensued. Gorsuch was killed, one of his sons was wounded, and several black and white men were hurt. The runaway slaves escaped to Canada.

Again the federal government made a determined effort to prosecute those who violated the fugitive slave law. President Fillmore sent U.S. Marines to Pennsylvania, and they helped round up the alleged perpetrators of the violence. Thirty-six black men and five white men were arrested and indicted for treason by a federal grand jury. But the government's case was weak, and after the first trial ended in acquittal, the remaining cases were dropped.

Anthony Burns

Of all the fugitive slave cases, none elicited more support or sorrow than that of Anthony Burns. In 1854 Burns escaped from slavery in Virginia by stowing away on a ship to Boston. After gaining work in a clothing store, he unwisely sent a letter to his brother who was still a slave. The letter was confiscated, and Burns's former owner set out to capture him. Burns was arrested by a deputy marshal who, recalling Shadrach's escape, placed him under guard in chains in the federal courthouse. Efforts by black and white abolitionists to break into the courthouse with axes, guns, and a battering ram failed, although a deputy U.S. marshal was killed during the assault.

President Franklin Pierce, a northern Democrat who had been elected with southern support in 1852, sent U.S. troops to Boston, including Marines, cavalry, and artillery, to uphold the law and return Burns to Virginia. Black minister Leonard A. Grimes and the vigilance committee tried to purchase Burns's freedom, but the U.S.

The "trial" and subsequent return of Anthony Burns to slavery in 1854 resulted in the publication of a popular pamphlet in Boston. Documents like this generated increased support—and funds—for the abolitionist cause.
Getty Images, Inc.—Liaison

attorney refused. In June 1854, with church bells tolling and buildings draped in black, thousands of Bostonians watched silently—many in tears—as Anthony Burns was marched through the streets to a ship in the harbor that would take him to Virginia.

People who had shown no particular interest in nor sympathy for fugitives or slaves were moved by the spectacle of a lone black man, escorted by hundreds of armed troops, trudging from freedom to slavery. Yet the government was unrelenting. A federal grand jury indicted seven black men and white men for riot and inciting a riot in their attempt to free Burns. One indictment was set aside on a technicality, and the other charges were then dropped because no Boston jury would convict the accused. Several months later, black Bostonians led by the Reverend Grimes, purchased Burns for $1,300. He settled in St. Catherine's, Ontario, in Canada where he died in 1862.

Margaret Garner

If the Burns case was the most moving, then Margaret Garner's was one of the most tragic examples of the lengths to which slaves might go to gain freedom for themselves and their children. In the winter of 1856, Margaret Garner and seven other slaves escaped from Kentucky across the Ohio River to freedom in Cincinnati. But their owner, Archibald Grimes, pursued them. Grimes, accompanied by a U.S. deputy marshal and several other people, attempted to arrest the eight fugitives at a small house where they had hidden. Refusing to surrender, the slaves fought back, but they were finally overpowered and subdued.

Before the fugitives were captured, Garner slit the throat of her daughter with a butcher knife rather than see the child returned to slavery. Before she could kill her two sons, she was disarmed. Ohio authorities charged her with murder, but by that time she had been returned to Kentucky and then sent with her surviving three children to Arkansas to be sold. On the trip down the river, her youngest child and twenty-four other people drowned in a shipwreck, thereby cruelly fulfilling her wish that the child not grow up to be a slave. Margaret Garner was later sold at a slave market in New Orleans. (Her story was the basis of Toni Morrison's novel *Beloved*, which won the 1988 Pulitzer Prize for fiction and was transformed into a film by Oprah Winfrey in 1998.)

The Rochester Convention, 1853

In 1853, while northern communities grappled with the consequences of the fugitive slave law, African-American leaders gathered for a national convention in Rochester, New York. The convention warned that black Americans were not prepared to submit quietly to a government more concerned about the interests of slave owners than people seeking to free themselves from bondage. The delegates looked past the grim conditions of the times to call for greater unity among black people and to find ways to improve their economic prospects. They asserted their claims to the rights of citizenship and equal protection before the law, and they worried that the wave of European immigrants entering the country would deprive poor black Northerners of the menial and unskilled jobs on which they depended. Frederick Douglass spoke of the need for a school to provide training in skilled trades and manual arts. There was even talk of establishing a Negro museum and library.

Nativism and the Know-Nothings

Not only did many white Americans look with disfavor and often outright disgust at African Americans, they were also distressed by and opposed to the increasing numbers of white immigrants coming to the United States. Hundreds of thousands of Europeans—mostly Germans and Irish—arrived in the 1840s and 1850s. In one year—1854—430,000 people arrived on American shores.

The stark reality of mass starvation that accompanied the potato famine of the 1840s in Ireland drove thousands of Irish people to the United States where they often encountered intense hostility. Native-born, Protestant, white Americans despised the Catholic Irish whom they considered crude, ignorant, and all too likely to drink to excess. Irish immigrants also competed with Americans for low-paying unskilled jobs. Ugly anti-Catholic propaganda raised fears that the influence of the Vatican and the papacy would weaken American institutions. Some even charged there was a Roman Catholic conspiracy to take over the United States. Mobs viciously attacked Catholic churches and convents.

These anti-immigrant, anti-Catholic, anti-alcohol sentiments helped foster in 1854 the rise of a nativist third political party, the American Party—better known as the "Know-Nothing Party." (Its members were supposed to reply "I know nothing" if someone inquired about their connection to the party.) For a brief time, the Know-Nothings attracted considerable support. Feeding on resentment and prejudice, the party grew to one million strong. Most Know-Nothings were in New England, and they even for a short time took political control of Massachusetts where many of the Irish had settled. But the party was also strong in Kentucky, Texas, and elsewhere.

Although Know-Nothings were in agreement about opposing immigrants and Catholics, they disagreed among themselves over slavery and its expansion. As a result this third party soon split into northern and southern factions and collapsed.

Uncle Tom's Cabin

No one contributed more to the growing opposition to slavery among white Northerners than Harriet Beecher Stowe. Raised in a deeply religious environment—her father, brothers, and husband were ministers—Stowe developed a hatred of slavery that she converted into a melodramatic, but moving, novel about slaves and their lives.

Uncle Tom's Cabin, or Life among the Lowly, was first published in installments in the antislavery newspaper *The National Era.* When it appeared as a book in 1852, it sold an astonishing 300,000 copies in a year. In the novel, Stowe depicted slavery's cruelty, inhumanity, and destructive impact on families through characters and a plot that appealed to the sentimentality of nineteenth-century readers. There was Little Eliza, with a babe in arms, barely escaping across the icy Ohio River from a slave owner in hot pursuit. There was Uncle Tom, the noble and devout Christian. Financial necessity forces Tom's decent master to sell the kindly slave to Simon Legree, a vicious brute and a Northerner who has embraced slavery. Legree takes perverse delight in beating Tom until the gentle old man dies.

Uncle Tom's Cabin moved Northerners to tears and made slavery more personal to readers who had previously considered it only a distant system of labor that exploited black people. In stage versions of the book that were later produced across the North, Uncle Tom was transformed from a dignified man into a pitiful and fawning figure eager to please white people—hence the derogatory term *Uncle Tom.*

Uncle Tom's Cabin infuriated white Southerners. They condemned it as a grossly false depiction of slavery and their way of life. They pointed out correctly that Stowe had little firsthand knowledge of slavery and had never even visited the deep South. But she had lived in Cincinnati for eighteen years and witnessed with anguish the desperate attempts of slaves to escape across the Ohio River. In response to her southern critics, Stowe wrote *A Key to Uncle Tom's Cabin*, citing the sources for her novel. Many of those sources were southern newspapers.

THE KANSAS-NEBRASKA ACT

In the wake of the Compromise of 1850, the disagreement over slavery's expansion intensified and became violent. In 1854 Stephen Douglas introduced a bill in Congress to organize the Kansas and Nebraska Territories that soon provoked white settlers in Kansas to kill each other over slavery. Douglas's primary concern was to secure the Kansas and Nebraska region, which until 1853 had been part of the Indian Territory the federal government had promised to protect from white settlement for the construction of a transcontinental railroad. To win the support of southern Democrats, who wanted slavery in at least one of the two new territories, he included a provision in the bill permitting residents of the Kansas Territory to decide for themselves whether to allow slavery (see Map 10–1).

MAP 10–1 The Kansas–Nebraska Act. This measure guided through Congress by Democratic Senator Steven A. Douglas opened up the Great Plains to settlement and to railroad development. It also deeply divided the nation by repealing the 1820 Missouri Compromise Line of 36° 30′ and permitting—through popular sovereignty—the people in Kansas to determine slavery's fate in that territory. Eastern Kansas became a bloody battleground between proslavery and antislavery forces.

This proposal—known as "popular sovereignty"—angered many Northerners because it created the possibility that slavery might expand to areas where it had been prohibited. The Missouri Compromise banned slavery north of the 36° 30′ N latitude. Douglas's Kansas-Nebraska Act would repeal that limitation and allow settlers in Kansas, which was north of that line, to vote on slavery there. Thus, if enough proslavery people moved to Kansas and voted for slavery, slaves and their slave owners would be legally permitted to dwell on land that had been closed to them for more than thirty years.

Douglas managed to muster enough Democratic votes in Congress to pass the bill, but its enactment destroyed an already divided Whig Party and drove a wedge between the North and South. The Whig Party disintegrated. Northern Whigs joined supporters of the Free-Soil Party to form the Republican Party, which was organized expressly to oppose the expansion of slavery. Southern Whigs drifted, often without much enthusiasm, to the Democrats or Know-Nothings.

Violence soon erupted in Kansas between proslavery and antislavery forces. "Border Ruffians" from Missouri invaded Kansas to attack antislavery settlers and vote illegally in Kansas elections. The New England Emigrant Aid Society dispatched people to the territory and the Reverend Henry Ward Beecher encouraged them to pack "Beecher's Bibles," which were firearms and not the Word of the Lord. By 1856 two territorial governments existed in Kansas, and a virtual civil war—causing the press to label the territory "Bleeding Kansas"—was under way among its 8,500 settlers, including 245 slaves.

More than two hundred people died in the escalating violence. Some five hundred "Border Ruffians" attacked the antislavery town of Lawrence, damaging businesses and killing one person. Abolitionist John Brown and four of his sons sought revenge by hacking five proslavery men (none of whom actually owned slaves) to death with swords in Pottowattamie. A proslavery firing squad executed nine Free-Soilers. John Brown reappeared in Missouri, killed a slave owner, and freed eleven slaves. Then he fled, to begin planning an even larger and more dramatic attack on slavery.

Preston Brooks Attacks Charles Sumner

In 1856 the violence in Kansas spread to Congress. In May of that year, Massachusetts Senator Charles Sumner delivered a tirade in the Senate denouncing the proslavery settlers in Kansas and the Southerners who supported them. Speaking of "The Crime against Kansas," Sumner accused South Carolina Senator Andrew P. Butler of keeping slavery as his lover. Butler "has chosen a mistress to whom he has made his vows, and who . . . though polluted in the sight of the world, is chaste in his sight—I mean the harlot slavery." Butler was not present for the speech, but his nephew, South Carolina Congressman Preston Brooks, was in the chamber, and Brooks did not take kindly to Sumner's attack.

Two days later, Brooks exacted his revenge. Waiting until the Senate adjourned, Brooks strode to the desk where Sumner was seated and attacked him with a rattan cane. The blows rained down until the cane shattered and Sumner tumbled to the floor, bloody and semiconscious. Brooks proudly recalled, "I gave him about thirty first rate stripes." Sumner suffered lingering physical and emotional effects from the beating and did not return to the Senate for almost four years. Brooks resigned from the House of Representatives, paid a $300 fine, and went home to South Carolina a hero. He was easily reelected to his seat.

In the 1856 presidential election, the Democrats—although divided over the debacle in Kansas—nominated James Buchanan of Pennsylvania, another northern Democrat who was acceptable to the South. The Republicans supported a handsome military officer, John C. Fremont. Their slogan was "Free Soil, Free Speech, Free Men, and Fremont." But the Republicans were exclusively a northern party, and with the demise of the Whigs the South had become largely a one-party region. Almost no white Southerners would support the Republicans, a party whose very existence was based on its opposition to slavery's expansion. Buchanan won the presidency with nearly solid southern support and enough northern votes to carry him to victory, but the Republicans gained enough support and confidence to give them hope for the 1860 election. Before then, however, the U.S. Supreme Court intervened in the controversy over slavery.

The Dred Scott Decision

Like most slaves, Dred Scott did not know his exact age. But when the U.S. Supreme Court accepted his case in 1856, Scott was in his fifties and had been entangled in the judicial system for more than a decade. Scott was born in Virginia, but by the 1830s he belonged to John Emerson, an army doctor in Missouri. Emerson took Scott to military posts in Illinois and Fort Snelling in what is now Minnesota. While at Fort Snelling, Scott married Harriet, a slave woman, and they had a daughter Eliza before Emerson returned with the three of them to St. Louis. (Another daughter, Lizzie, was born later.) In 1846, after Emerson's death, and with the support of white friends, Scott and his wife filed separate suits for their freedom. By agreement, her suit was set aside pending the

Dred Scott (1800–1858). *Dred Scott v. Sanford* was one of the most important Supreme Court cases in U.S. history. It further divided a nation already split over the issue of slavery. Though Scott lost the case, he was freed by his owner in May 1857. He died in September 1858, having lived a year and a half as a free man.
The Granger Collection, New York

outcome of her husband's litigation. Scott and his lawyers contended that because Scott had been taken to territory where slavery was illegal, he had become a free man.

Scott lost his first suit, won his second, but lost again on appeal to the Missouri Supreme Court. Scott's lawyers then appealed to the U.S. Circuit Court where they lost again. The final appeal in *Dred Scott v. Sanford* was to the U.S. Supreme Court. Although seventy-nine-year-old chief justice Roger Taney of Maryland had freed his own slaves, he was an unabashed advocate of the southern way of life. Moreover, Taney, a majority of the other justices, and President Buchanan were convinced that the prestige of the Court would enable it to render a decision about slavery that might be controversial but would still be accepted as the law of the land.

Questions for the Court

Taney framed two questions for the Court to decide in the Scott case. One, could Scott, a black man, sue in a federal court? Two, was Scott free because he had been taken to a state and a territory where slavery was prohibited? In response to the first question, the Court, led by Taney, ruled that Scott—and every other black American—could not sue in a federal court because black people were not citizens. Speaking for the majority (two of the nine justices dissented), Taney emphatically stated that black people had no rights: "They had for more than a century before been regarded as beings of an inferior order; and altogether unfit to associate with the white race, either in social or political relations; and so far inferior that they had no rights which the white man was bound to respect; and that the negro might justly and lawfully be reduced to slavery for his benefit."

Taney was wrong. Although not treated as equals, free black people in many states had enjoyed rights associated with citizenship since the ratification of the Constitution in 1788. Black men had entered into contracts, held title to property, sued in the courts, and voted at one time in five of the original thirteen states.

A majority of the Court also answered no to the second question. Scott was not a free man, although he had lived in places where slavery was illegal. Scott, Taney maintained, again speaking for the Court, was slave property—and the slave owner's property rights took precedence. To the astonishment of those who opposed slavery's expansion,

Table 10–1
Deepening Crisis over Slavery

1846	The Wilmot Proviso
1850	The Compromise of 1850
1854	The Kansas-Nebraska Act
1855-1856	Bleeding Kansas
1857	The Dred Scott Decision
1859	John Brown's Raid
1860	The Election of Lincoln as President
1860	South Carolina Secedes from the Union
1861	Formation of the Confederacy, Fort Sumter, Beginning of the Civil War

the Court also ruled that Congress could not pass measures—including the Missouri Compromise or the Kansas-Nebraska Act—that might prevent slave owners from taking their property into any territory. To do so, Taney implied, would violate the Fifth Amendment of the Constitution, which protected people from the loss of their life, liberty, or property without due process of law.

Following the decision, a new owner freed Dred and Harriet Scott. They settled in St. Louis, where he worked as a porter at Barnum's Hotel until he died of tuberculosis in 1858.

Reaction to the Dred Scott Decision

The Court had spoken. Would the nation listen? White Southerners were delighted with Taney's decision. Republicans were horrified. But instead of earning the acceptance—let alone the approval—of most Americans, the case further inflamed the controversy over slavery. But if white Americans were divided in their reaction to the Dred Scott decision, black Americans were discouraged, disgusted, and defiant. Taney's decision delivered another setback to a people—already held in forced labor—who believed their toil, sweat, and contributions over the previous two-and-a-half centuries to what had become the United States gave them a legitimate role in American society. Now the Supreme Court said they had no rights. They knew better.

At meetings and rallies across the North, black people condemned the decision. Black writer, abolitionist, and women's rights advocate Frances Ellen Watkins Harper heaped scorn on the U.S. government as "the arch traitor to liberty, as shown by the Fugitive Slave Law and the Dred Scott decision."

Only Frederick Douglass could find a glimmer of hope. He believed—and events were to prove him right—that the decision was so wrong that it would help destroy slavery.

> The Supreme Court . . . [was] not the only power in the world. We, the abolitionists and the colored people, should meet this decision, unlooked for and monstrous as it appears, in a cheerful spirit. The very attempts to blot out forever the hopes of an enslaved people may be one necessary link in the chain of events preparatory to the complete overthrow of the whole slave system.

White Northerners and Black Americans

Unquestionably, many white Northerners were genuinely concerned by the struggles of fugitive slaves, moved by *Uncle Tom's Cabin,* and disturbed by the Dred Scott decision. Yet as sensitive and sympathetic as some of them were to the plight of black people, most white Americans—including Northerners—remained decidedly indifferent to, fearful of, or bitterly hostile to people of color. By the 1850s, 200,000 black people lived in the northern states, and many white people there were not pleased with their presence. Many white Northerners, especially those living in southern Ohio, Indiana, and Illinois, supported the fugitive slave law and were eager to help return runaway slaves to bondage.

The same white Northerners who opposed the expansion of slavery to California or to Kansas also opposed the migration of free black people to northern states and communities. In 1851 Indiana and Iowa outlawed the emigration to their territory of black people, slave or free. Illinois did likewise in 1853. White male voters in Michigan in 1850 voted overwhelmingly—32,000 to 12,000—against permitting black men to vote. Only Ohio was an exception. In 1849 it repealed legislation excluding black people from the state.

These restrictive measures were not new. Most northern states had begun to restrict or deny the rights of black Americans in the early 1800s (see Chapter 6). Although only loosely enforced, the laws reflected the prevailing racial sentiments among many white Northerners, as did the widespread antiblack rioting of the 1830s and 1840s. During the debate over excluding black people from Indiana, a state senator explained that the Bible revealed God had condemned black people to inferiority. "The same power that has given him a black skin, with less weight or volume of brain, has given us a white skin, with greater volume of brain and intellect; and that we can never live together upon an equality is as certain as that no two antagonistic principles can exist together at the same time."

Foreign observers were struck by the depth of racism in the North. Alexis de Tocqueville, a French aristocrat, toured America in 1831 and wrote a perceptive analysis of American society. He considered Northerners more antagonistic toward black people than Southerners. "The prejudice of race appears to be stronger in the states that have abolished slavery than in those where it still exists; and nowhere is it so intolerant as in those states where servitude has never been known."

Abraham Lincoln and Black People

In 1858 Senator Stephen Douglas of Illinois, a Democrat, ran for reelection to the Senate against Republican Abraham Lincoln. The main issues in the campaign were slavery and race, which the two candidates addressed in a series of debates around the state. In carefully reasoned speeches and responses, these experienced and articulate lawyers focused almost exclusively on slavery's expansion and its future in the Union. At Freeport, Illinois, Lincoln, a former Whig congressman, attempted to trap Douglas, the incumbent, by asking him if slavery could expand now that the Dred Scott decision had ruled slaves were property whom their owners could take into any federal territory. In reply, Douglas, who wanted to be president and had no desire to offend either northern or southern voters, cleverly defended "popular sovereignty" and the Dred Scott decision. He insisted that slave owners could indeed take their slaves where they pleased. But, he contended, if the people of a territory failed to enact slave codes to protect and control slave property, a slave owner was not likely to settle there with his or her slaves.

But the Lincoln-Douglas debates did not always turn on the fine points of constitutional law or on the fate of slavery in the territories. Thanks mainly to Douglas, who accused Lincoln and the Republicans of promoting the interests of black people over those of white people, the debates sometimes degenerated into crude and savage exchanges about which candidate favored white people more and black people less. Douglas proudly advocated white supremacy. "The signers of the Declaration [of Independence] had no reference to the negro . . . or any other inferior or degraded race when they spoke of the equality of men." He later charged that Lincoln and the Republicans wanted black and white equality. "If you, Black Republicans, think the negro ought to be on social equality with your wives and daughters, . . . you have a perfect right to do so. . . . Those of you who believe the negro is your equal . . . of course will vote for Mr. Lincoln."

Lincoln did not believe in racial equality, and he made that plain. In exasperation, he explained that merely because he opposed slavery did not mean he believed in equality. "I do not understand that because I do not want a negro woman for a slave I must necessarily have her for a wife." He bluntly added,

> I am not, nor ever have been in favor of bringing about in any way the social and political equality of the white and black races—that I am not nor ever have been in favor of making voters or jurors of negroes, nor of qualifying them to hold office, nor to intermarry with white people; and I will say in addition to this that there is a physical difference between the races which I believe will forever forbid the two races living together on terms of social and political equality.

But without repudiating these views, Lincoln later tried to transcend this blatant racism. "Let us discard all this quibbling about this man and the other man—this race and that race and the other race being inferior." Instead, he added, let us "unite as one people throughout this land, until we shall once more stand up declaring that all men are created equal." Lincoln stated unequivocally that race had nothing to do with whether a man had the right to be paid for his labor. He pointed out that the black man, "in the right to eat the bread, without leave of anybody else, which his own hand earns, he is my equal and the equal of Judge Douglas, and the equal of every living man."

Lincoln may have won the debate in the minds of many, but Douglas won the Senate election. Lincoln, however, made a name for himself that would work to his political advantage in the near future, and Douglas, despite his best efforts, had thoroughly offended many Southerners by opposing the proslavery Kansas Lecompton constitution that Douglas and many others believed had been fraudulently adopted. In two years, this would contribute to a deep split in the Democratic Party.

John Brown and the Raid on Harpers Ferry

While Lincoln and Douglas were debating, John Brown was plotting. Following his attack on Pottowattamie in Kansas, Brown began to plan the violent overthrow of slavery in the South itself. In May 1858, accompanied by eleven white followers, he met thirty-four black people led by Martin Delany at Chatham in Canada West (now the province of Ontario) and appealed for their support. Brown was determined to invade the South and end slavery. He hoped to attract legions of slaves as he and his "army" moved down the Appalachian Mountains into the heart of the plantation system.

Only one man at the Chatham gathering agreed to join the raid. Brown returned to the United States and garnered financial support from prosperous white abolitionists. Contributing money rather than risking their lives seemed more realistic to these men, who preferred to keep their identities confidential and thus came to be known as the Secret Six: Gerrit Smith, Thomas Wentworth Higginson, Samuel Gridley Howe, George L. Stearns, Theodore Parker, and Franklin Sanborn.

Brown also asked Frederick Douglass and Harriet Tubman to join him. They declined. By the summer of 1859, at a farm in rural Maryland, Brown had assembled an "army" consisting of seventeen white men (including three of his sons) and five black men. The black men who enlisted were Osborne Anderson, one of the Chatham participants; Sheridan Leary, an escaped slave who had become a saddle and harness maker in Oberlin, Ohio; Leary's nephew John A. Copeland, an Oberlin College student; and two escaped slaves, Shields Green and Dangerfield Newby.

Newby was determined to rescue his wife, Harriet, and their seven children who were about to be sold from Virginia down the river to Louisiana. Harriet sent her husband a plaintive letter begging for him. "Oh Dear Dangerfield, com this fall . . . without fail . . . I want to see you so much that is one bright hope I have before me."

The Raid

Brown's invasion began on Sunday night October 16, 1859, with a raid on Harpers Ferry, Virginia, and the federal arsenal there. Brown hoped to secure weapons and then advance south, but the operation went awry from the start. The dedication and devotion of Brown and his men were not matched by their strategy or his leadership. The first man Brown's band killed was ironically a free black man, Heyward Shepard, who was a baggage handler at the train station. The alarm then went out, and opposition gathered.

Even though they had lost the initiative, Brown and his men neither advanced nor retreated, but instead they remained in Harpers Ferry while Virginia and Maryland militia converged on them. Fighting began, and two townspeople, the mayor, and eight of Brown's men, including Sheridan Leary, Dangerfield Newby, and two of Brown's sons, were killed. Newby died carrying his wife's letter. But Brown managed to seize several hostages, among them Lewis W. Washington, the great grandnephew of George Washington.

By Tuesday morning, Brown, with his hostages and what remained of his "army," was holed up in an engine house. A detachment of U.S. Marines under the command of Robert E. Lee arrived, surrounded the building, and demanded Brown's surrender. He refused. The Marines broke in. Brown was wounded and captured.

The raid was an utter failure. No slaves were freed. Shields Green and John A. Copeland fled but were caught. Osborne Anderson eluded capture and later fought in the Civil War. Virginia quickly tried Brown, Green, and Copeland for treason. They were found guilty and sentenced to hang.

The Reaction

The raid failed, but Brown and his men succeeded brilliantly in intensifying the deeply felt emotions of those who supported and those who opposed slavery. At first regarded as crazed zealots and insane fanatics, they showed they were willing—even eager—to die for the antislavery cause. The dignity and assurance that Brown, Green, and Copeland displayed as they awaited the gallows impressed many black and white Northerners.

Black teacher and abolitionist Frances Ellen Watkins Harper wrote to John Brown's wife two weeks before Brown was executed to express compassion and admiration for both husband and wife:

> Belonging to the race your dear husband reached forth his hand to assist, I need not tell you that my sympathies are with you. I thank you for the brave words you have spoken. A republic that produces such a wife and mother may hope for better days. Our heart may grow more hopeful for humanity when it sees the sublime sacrifice it is about to receive from his hands. Not in vain had your dear husband periled all, if the martyrdom of one hero is worth more than the life of a million cowards.

James A. Copeland wrote home to his family that he was proud to die:

> I am not terrified by the gallows, which I see staring me in the face, and upon which I am soon to stand and suffer death for doing what George Washington was made a hero for doing. . . . Could I die in a manner and for a cause which would induce true and honest men more to honor me, and the angels more ready to receive me to their happy home of everlasting joy above? . . . I imagine that I hear you, and all of you, mother, father, sisters and brothers, say—"No, there is not a cause for which we, with less sorrow, could see you die."

Brown also eloquently and calmly announced his willingness to die as so many had died before him. "Now, if it is deemed necessary that I should forfeit my life for the furtherance of the ends of justice, and mingle my blood further with the blood of my children and with the blood of millions in this slave country whose rights are disregarded by wicked, cruel, and unjust enactments, I say, let it be done."

For many Northerners, the day Brown was executed, December 2, 1859, was a day of mourning. Church bells tolled, and people bowed their heads in prayer. White Southerners were terrified and traumatized by the raid, and outraged that Northerners made Brown a hero and a martyr. A wave of hysteria and paranoia swept the South as incredulous white people wondered how Northerners could admire a man who sought to kill slave owners and free their slaves.

Brown's raid and the reaction to it propelled the South toward secession from the Union, and thereby moved the nation closer to destroying slavery.

The Election of Abraham Lincoln

With the country fracturing over slavery, four candidates ran for president in the election of 1860. The Democrats split into a northern faction, which nominated Stephen Douglas, and a southern faction, which nominated John C. Breckenridge of Kentucky. The Constitutional Union Party, a new party formed by former Whigs, nominated John Bell of Tennessee. The breakup of the Democratic Party assured victory for the Republican candidate, Abraham Lincoln (see Map 10–2).

Lincoln's name was not even on the ballot in most southern states, because his candidacy was based on the Republican Party's adamant opposition to the expansion of slavery into any western territory. Although Lincoln took pains to reassure white

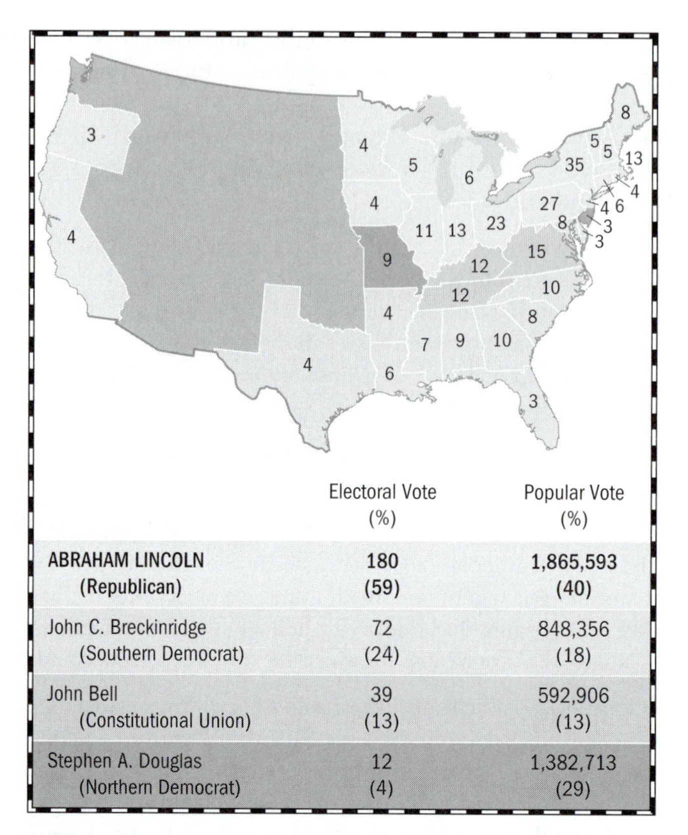

	Electoral Vote (%)	Popular Vote (%)
ABRAHAM LINCOLN (Republican)	**180 (59)**	**1,865,593 (40)**
John C. Breckinridge (Southern Democrat)	72 (24)	848,356 (18)
John Bell (Constitutional Union)	39 (13)	592,906 (13)
Stephen A. Douglas (Northern Democrat)	12 (4)	1,382,713 (29)

MAP 10–2 The Election of 1860. The results reflect the sectional schism over slavery. Lincoln carried the election although he won only in northern states. His name did not even appear on the ballot in most southern states.

Southerners that slavery would continue in states where it already existed, they were not in the least persuaded. A South Carolina newspaper was convinced Lincoln would abolish slavery. "[Lincoln] has openly proclaimed a war of extermination against the leading institutions of the Southern States. He says that there can be no peace so long as slavery has a foot hold in America."

A Georgia newspaper preferred a bloody civil war to a Lincoln presidency. "Let the consequences be what they may—whether the Potomac is crimsoned in human gore, and Pennsylvania Avenue is paved ten fathoms deep with mangled bodies . . . the South will never submit to such humiliation and degradation as the inauguration of Abraham Lincoln."

Black People Respond to Lincoln's Election

Although they were less opposed to Lincoln than white Southerners, black Northerners and white abolitionists were not eager to see Abraham Lincoln become president. Dismayed by his contradictions and racism—he opposed slavery, but he tolerated it; he was against slavery's expansion, but he condemned black Americans as inferiors—many black people refused to support him or did so reluctantly. The New York *Anglo-African* opposed both Republicans and Democrats in the 1860 election, telling its readers to depend on each other. "We have no hope from either [of the] political parties. We must rely on ourselves, the righteousness of our cause, and the advance of just sentiments among the great masses of the . . . people."

Abolitionists such as William Lloyd Garrison and Wendell Phillips believed Lincoln was too willing to tolerate slave-holding interests. But Frederick Douglass wrote, "Lincoln's election will indicate growth in the right direction" and his presidency "must and will be hailed as an anti-slavery triumph."

After Lincoln's election, black leaders almost welcomed the secession of southern states. H. Ford Douglas urged the southern states to leave the Union. "Stand not upon the order of your going, but go at once. . . . There is no union of ideas and interests in this country, and there can be no union between freedom and slavery." Frederick Douglass was convinced that there were men prepared to follow in the footsteps of John Brown's "army" to destroy slavery. "I am for dissolution of the Union—decidedly for a dissolution of the Union! . . . In case of such a dissolution, I believe that men could be found . . . who would venture into those states and raise the standard of liberty there."

DISUNION

When South Carolina seceded on December 20, 1860, it began a procession of southern states out of the Union. By February 1861 seven states—South Carolina, Mississippi, Alabama, Florida, Louisiana, Georgia, and Texas—had seceded and formed the Confederate States of America in Montgomery, Alabama. Before there could be the kind of undertaking against slavery that Douglass had proposed, Abraham Lincoln tried to persuade the seceding states to reconsider. In his inaugural address of March 4, 1861, Lincoln attempted to calm the fears of white Southerners but informed them he would not tolerate their withdrawal from the Union. Lincoln repeated his assurance he would not tamper with slavery in the states where it was already legal. "I have no purpose, directly or indirectly, to interfere with the institution of slavery in the States where it exists. I believe I have no lawful right to do so, and I have no inclination to do so."

Lincoln added that the "only" dispute between the North and South was over the expansion of slavery. He emphatically warned, however, that he would enforce the Constitution and not permit secession. "Plainly, the central idea of secession is the essence of anarchy." He pleaded with white Southerners to contemplate their actions patiently and thoughtfully, actions that might provoke a civil conflict. "In your hands, my dissatisfied fellow-countrymen, and not in mine, is the monumental issue of civil war."

Southern whites did not heed him. Slavery was too essential to give up merely to preserve the Union. Arthur P. Hayne of South Carolina had succinctly summed up its importance in an 1860 letter to President James Buchanan. "Slavery with us is no abstraction—but a great and vital fact. Without it our every comfort would be taken from us. Our wives, our children, made unhappy—education, the light of knowledge—all lost and our people ruined forever. Nothing short of separation from the Union can save us."

Barely a month after Lincoln's inauguration, Confederate leaders demanded that U.S. Army major Robert Anderson surrender Fort Sumter, located in the harbor of Charleston, South Carolina. Anderson refused, and on April 12, 1861, Confederate artillery fired on the fort. In the aftermath, four additional states—Virginia, North Carolina, Tennessee, and Arkansas—joined the Confederacy. The Civil War had begun.

TIMELINE

AFRICAN-AMERICAN EVENTS	NATIONAL EVENTS
1820	
	1820 Missouri Compromise **1823** Missouri Compromise
1825	
1829 David Walker publishes his *Appeal to the Colored Citizens of the World*	
1830	
1831 William Lloyd Garrison begins publication of *Liberator* **1823** American Anti-Slavery Society founded	
1835	
1840	
1845	
1847 Crosswhite family eludes capture in Michigan **1848** William and Ellen Craft escape from slavery in Georgia	**1846–1847** Mexican War **1846** Wilmot Proviso **1847** Mormons begin settlement of Utah **1848** Formation of the Free-Soil Party Election of Zachary Taylor Women's rights convention at Seneca Falls, NY

continued

AFRICAN-AMERICAN EVENTS	NATIONAL EVENTS
1850	
1850 Fugitive Slave Act **1850–1860** Fugitive slaves captured **1851** Shadrach eludes capture in Boston; Thomas Sims returned to slavery; "Battle" at Christiana **1853** Black convention at Rochester, New York **1854** Anthony Burns returned to slavery in Boston	**1850** Compromise of 1850 and the Fugitive Slave Act **1852** Publication of Uncle Tom's Cabin Election of Franklin Pierce **1854** Kansas-Nebraska Act
1855	
1856 Margaret Garner kills her daughter in unsuccessful escape **1857** The Dred Scott decision **1859** John Brown's raid on Harpers Ferry	**1855–1856** "Bleeding" Kansas **1856** Congressman Preston Brooks assaults Senator Charles Sumner **1858** The Lincoln-Douglas debates
1860	
1861 Free black men in Charleston offer their support to South Carolina	**1860** Abraham Lincoln elected president South Carolina secedes from the union **1861** Six more southern states secede and form the Confederacy; Civil War begins after firing on Fort Sumter in April; four more southern states join the Confederacy

CONCLUSION

Virtually every event and episode of major or minor consequence in the United States between 1849 and 1861 involved black people and the expansion of slavery. From the Wilmot Proviso and the Compromise of 1850 to the Dred Scott decision and John Brown's raid, white Americans were increasingly perplexed about how the nation could remain half slave and half free. They were unable to resolve the problem of slavery's expansion.

Without the presence of black people in America, neither secession nor civil war would have occurred. Yet the Civil War began because white Americans had developed contradictory visions of the future. White Southerners contemplated a future that inextricably linked their security and prosperity to slavery. The South, they believed, could neither advance nor endure without slavery.

Northern white people believed their future rested on the opportunities for white men and their families to flourish as independent, self-sufficient farmers, shopkeepers, and skilled artisans. For their future to prevail, they insisted the new lands in the American West should exclude the slave system that white Southerners considered so vital. Neither northern nor southern white people—except for some abolitionists—ever believed people of color should fully participate as free people in American society or in the future of the American nation.

REVIEW QUESTIONS

1. How and why did southern and northern white people differ over slavery? On what did white people of both regions agree and disagree about race and slavery?
2. If you were an African American living in the North in the 1850s, how would you have responded to the policies of the U.S. government?
3. If you were a white Southerner in the 1850s, would you have been encouraged or discouraged by those policies?
4. Why did seven southern states secede from the Union within three months after Abraham Lincoln was elected president in 1860?
5. If you were a black person—either a slave or free—would you have welcomed the secession of the southern states? How might secession affect the future of your people?

RECOMMENDED READING

Eric Foner. *Free Soil, Free Labor and Free Men: The Ideology of the Republican Party before the Civil War.* New York: Oxford University Press, 1970. An excellent overview of attitudes on free soil, slavery, and race.

Vincent Harding. *There Is a River: The Black Struggle for Freedom in America.* New York: Harcourt, Brace, Jovanovich, 1981. A tribute to and a masterful narrative about the black people who challenged the white majority in nineteenth-century America.

Leon Litwack. *North of Slavery: The Negro in the Free States, 1790–1860.* Chicago: University of Chicago Press, 1961. A story of black Northerners and the discrimination they encountered.

James McPherson. *Battle Cry of Freedom: The Civil War Era.* New York: Oxford University Press, 1988. A superb account of the crisis leading up to the Civil War and of the war itself.

David Potter. *The Impending Crisis, 1848–1861.* New York: Harper & Row, 1976. Another fine account of the events leading up to the Civil War.

• C H A P T E R E L E V E N •

LIBERATION

AFRICAN AMERICANS AND THE CIVIL WAR

Lincoln's Aims

When the war began, as it was fought, and when it ended, President Abraham Lincoln's unwavering objective was to preserve the Union. Any policies that helped or hindered black people were subordinate to that goal. Following the attack on Fort Sumter in April 1861 and Lincoln's call for state militias to help suppress the rebellion, four more slave states—North Carolina, Virginia, Tennessee, and Arkansas—seceded from the Union and joined the Confederacy. For most of 1861, Lincoln was determined to do nothing that would drive the four remaining slave states—Delaware, Maryland, Kentucky, and Missouri—into the Confederacy. Lincoln feared that if he did or said anything that could be interpreted as interfering with slavery, those four border states would leave the Union too.

Meanwhile, Lincoln issued a call for 75,000 men to enlist in the military for ninety days of service to the national government. Thousands of black and white men, far more than 75,000, responded to the call. White men were accepted; black men were rejected. Spurned by federal and state authorities, black men remained determined to aid the cause.

Black Men Volunteer and Are Rejected

Black people recognized long before most white Northerners that the fate of the Union was inextricably tied to the issue of slavery and the future of slavery was tied to the outcome of the war. "Talk as we may," insisted the *Anglo-African*, a black New York newspaper,

> we are concerned in this fight and our fate hangs upon its issues. The South must be subjugated, or we shall be enslaved. In aiding the Federal government in whatever way we can, we are aiding to secure our own liberty; for this war can end only in the subjugation of the North or the South.

Black men in New York formed their own military companies and began to drill. In Boston, they drew up a resolution modeled on the Declaration of Independence and appealed for permission to go to war:

> Our feelings urge us to say to our countrymen that we are ready to stand by and defend our Government as equals of its white defenders; to do so with "our lives, our fortunes, and our sacred honor," for the sake of freedom, and as good citizens; and we ask you to

> modify your laws, that we may enlist—that full scope may be given to patriotic feelings burning in the colored man's breast.

Black men in Philadelphia volunteered to infiltrate the South to incite slave revolts but were turned down. In Washington, Jacob Dodson, a black employee of the U.S. Senate, wrote a letter to Secretary of War Simon Cameron shortly after the fall of Fort Sumter volunteering the services of local black men. "I desire to inform you that I know of some 300 reliable colored free citizens of this city who desire to enter the service for the defense of the city." Cameron curtly replied, "This Department has no intention at the present to call into the service of the government any colored soldiers."

Union Policies toward Confederate Slaves

Slaves started to liberate themselves as soon as the war began, but Union political and military leaders had no coherent policy for dealing with them. To the deep disappointment of black Northerners and white abolitionists, Union military commanders showed more concern for the interests of Confederate slave owners than for the people in bondage. In May 1861 General George B. McClellan reassured Virginia slave owners: "Not only will we abstain from all interferences with your slaves, but we will, with an iron hand, crush any attempt at insurrection on their part."

General Henry Halleck ordered slaves who escaped in the Ohio Valley returned to their owners, and General Winfield Scott, the army's chief of staff, asked that Confederate slave owners be permitted to recover slaves who crossed the Potomac River to what they believed was the freedom of Union lines. In Tennessee in early 1862, General Ulysses S. Grant returned runaway slaves to their owners if the owners supported the Union cause, but Grant put black people to work on fortifications if their owners favored secession.

"Contraband"

Not all Union commanders were as callous as these generals. A month after the war began, three bondmen working on Confederate fortifications in Virginia escaped to the Union's Fortress Monroe on the coast. Their owner, a Confederate colonel, appeared at the fortress the next day under a flag of truce and demanded the return of his slaves under the 1850 Fugitive Slave Act. The incredulous Union commander, General Benjamin Butler, informed him that because Virginia had seceded from the Union, the fugitive slave law was no longer in force. Butler did not free the three slaves, but he did not reenslave them either. He declared them "contraband"—enemy property—and put them to work for the Union. Soon, over a thousand slaves fled to Fortress Monroe. The white authorities may have thought of them as contraband, but it is not likely that is how they viewed themselves.

On August 6, 1861, Congress clarified the status of runaway slaves when it passed the First Confiscation Act. Any property that belonged to Confederates used in the war effort could be seized by federal forces. Any slaves used by their masters to benefit the Confederacy—and only those slaves—would be freed. Almost immediately, Union general John C. Fremont (the 1856 Republican presidential candidate) exceeded the strict limits of the act by freeing all the slaves belonging to Confederates in Missouri.

President Lincoln quickly countermanded the order and told Fremont that only slaves actively used to aid the Confederate war effort were to be freed. Lincoln worried that Fremont would drive Missouri or Kentucky into the Confederacy.

Black leaders were—to put it mildly—displeased with Lincoln and with federal policies that both prohibited the enlistment of black troops and ignored the plight of the enslaved. To fight a war against the South without fighting against slavery, the institution on which the South was so thoroughly dependent, seemed absurd. Frederick Douglass stated the argument cogently: "To fight against slaveholders, without fighting against slavery, is but a half-hearted business, and paralyzes the hands engaged in it. . . . Fire must be met with water. . . . War for the destruction of liberty must be met with war for the destruction of slavery."

Others were less charitable. Joseph R. Hawley, a white Connecticut Republican, thought Lincoln was foolish to worry about whether the border states might leave the Union. "Permit me to say damn the border states. . . . A thousand Lincolns cannot stop the people from fighting slavery." Lincoln did not budge. Union military forces occupied an enclave on South Carolina's southern coast and the Sea Islands in late 1861, and on May 9, 1862, General David Hunter ordered slavery abolished in South Carolina, Georgia, and Florida. Lincoln quickly revoked Hunter's order and reprimanded him. Nevertheless, thousands of slaves along the South Carolina and Georgia coast threw off their shackles and welcomed Union troops as plantation owners fled to the interior.

Lincoln's Initial Position

For more than a year, Lincoln remained reluctant to strike decisively against slavery. He believed the long-term solution to slavery and the race problem in the United States was the compensated emancipation of slaves followed by their colonization outside the country. That is, slave owners would be paid for their slaves; the slaves would be freed but forced to settle in the Caribbean, Latin America, or West Africa.

As a Whig congressman in 1849, Lincoln voted for a bill that would have emancipated slaves and compensated their owners in the District of Columbia if it had passed. In 1861 he tried—but failed—to persuade the Delaware legislature to support compensated emancipation. Then in April 1862, at Lincoln's urging, Republicans in Congress (against almost unanimous Democratic opposition) voted to provide funds to "any state which may adopt gradual abolishment of slavery." Lincoln wanted to eliminate slavery from the border states with the approval of slave owners there and thus diminish the likelihood that those states would join the Confederacy.

But leaders in the border states rejected the proposal. Lincoln brought it up again in July. This time he warned congressmen and senators from the border states that if their states opposed compensated emancipation they might have to accept uncompensated emancipation. They ignored his advice and denounced compensated emancipation as a "radical change in our social system" and an intrusion by the federal government into a state issue.

To many white Americans, Lincoln's support for compensated emancipation and colonization was a misguided attempt to link the war to the issue of slavery. But to black Americans, abolitionists, and an increasing number of Republicans, Lincoln's refusal to abolish slavery immediately was tragic. Antislavery advocates regarded Lincoln's willingness to purchase the freedom of slaves as an admission that he considered those human beings to be property. They deplored his seeming inability to realize the Union would not win the war unless slaves were liberated.

Lincoln Moves Toward Emancipation

However, by the summer of 1862, after the border states rejected compensated emancipation, Lincoln concluded that victory and the future of the Union were tied directly to the issue of slavery. Slavery became the instrument Lincoln would use to hasten the end of the war and restore the Union.

In cabinet meetings on July 21 and 22, 1862, Lincoln discussed abolishing slavery. Except for Postmaster General Montgomery Blair, the cabinet supported emancipation. Blair feared that eliminating slavery would cost the Republicans control of Congress in the fall elections. Secretary of State William H. Seward supported abolition but advised Lincoln not to issue a proclamation until the Union Army won a major victory. Otherwise emancipation might look like the desperate gesture of the leader of a losing cause. Lincoln accepted Seward's advice and postponed emancipation.

Lincoln Delays Emancipation

Nevertheless, word circulated that Lincoln intended to abolish slavery. But weeks passed, and slavery did not end. Frustrated abolitionists and Republicans attacked Lincoln. Frederick Douglass was exasperated with a president who had shown inexcusable deference to white Southerners who had rebelled against the Union:

> Abraham Lincoln is no more fit for the place he holds than was [previous president] James Buchanan. . . . The country is destined to become sick of both [General George B.] McClellan and Lincoln, and the sooner the better. The one plays lawyer for the benefit of the rebels, and the other handles the army for the benefit of traitors. We should not be surprised if both should be hurled from their places before the rebellion is ended.

In his *Prayer of Twenty Millions*, Horace Greeley, editor of the New York *Tribune*, expressed his disappointment that the president had not moved promptly against slavery, the issue that had led the southern states to leave the Union and go to war: "We ask you to consider that Slavery [is the] inciting cause and sustaining base of treason. . . . We think timid counsels in such a crisis [are] calculated to prove perilous, probably disastrous."

On August 22, 1862, Lincoln replied to Greeley and offered a masterful explanation of his priorities. Placing the preservation of the Union before freedom for the enslaved, Lincoln declared, "My paramount object in this struggle is to save the Union, and is not either to save or destroy slavery. If I could save the Union without freeing any slave I would do it; and if I could save it by freeing all the slaves, I would do it; and if I could do it by freeing some and leaving others alone, I would also do that." Lincoln concluded, "I have here stated my purpose according to my view of *official* duty, and I intend no modification of my oft-expressed *personal* wish that all men, everywhere, could be free."

Black People Reject Colonization

Lincoln's policy on emancipation had shifted dramatically, but he remained committed to colonization. On August 14, 1862, Lincoln invited black leaders to the White House and appealed for their support for colonization. After condemning slavery as "the greatest wrong inflicted on any people," he explained that white racism made it unwise for black people to remain in the United States. "Your race suffer very greatly, many of them, by living among us, while ours suffer from your presence. There is an unwillingness on the part of our people, harsh as it may be, for you free colored people to remain among us. . . . I do not mean to discuss this, but to propose it as a fact with which we have to deal. I cannot alter it if I would." Lincoln asked the black leaders to begin enlisting volunteers for a colonization project in Central America.

Most black people were unimpressed by Lincoln's words and unmoved by his advice. A black leader from Philadelphia condemned the president. "This is our country as much as it is yours, and we will not leave it." Frederick Douglass accused Lincoln of hypocrisy and claimed that support for colonization would lead white men "to commit all kinds of violence and outrage upon the colored people."

Lincoln would not retreat from his support for colonization. Attempts were already under way to put compensated emancipation and colonization into effect. In April 1862 Congress enacted a bill to pay District of Columbia slave owners up to $300 for each slave they freed and to provide $100,000 to support the voluntary colonization of the freed people in Haiti or Liberia. In 1863 the government tried to settle 453 black American colonists at Ile à Vache, an island near Haiti. The settlers suffered terribly from disease and starvation. This sorry attempt at government-sponsored colonization ended in 1864 when the U.S. Navy returned 368 survivors to the United States.

The Preliminary Emancipation Proclamation

Finally on September 22, 1862, the president issued the Preliminary Emancipation Proclamation. It came five days after General George B. McClellan's Army of the Potomac turned back an invasion of Maryland at Antietam by General Robert E. Lee's Army of Northern Virginia. This bloody but less-than-conclusive victory allowed Lincoln to justify emancipation. But this first proclamation freed no people that September—or during the rest of 1862. Instead, it stipulated that anyone in bondage in states or parts of states still in rebellion on January 1, 1863, would be "thenceforward, and forever free." Lincoln's announcement gave the Confederate states one hundred days to return to the Union. If any or all of those states did rejoin the Union, the slaves there would remain in bondage. The Union would be preserved, and slavery would be maintained.

What were Lincoln's intentions? Lincoln knew there was virtually no chance that white Southerners would return to the Union just because he had threatened to free their slaves. Most Confederates expected to win the war, thereby confirming secession and safeguarding slavery. White Southerners ridiculed the preliminary proclamation.

Northern Reaction to Emancipation

In the Union, the Preliminary Emancipation Proclamation was greeted with little enthusiasm. Most black people and abolitionists, of course, were gratified that Lincoln, after weeks of procrastination, had finally issued the proclamation. Frederick Douglass was ecstatic. "We shout for joy that we live to record this righteous decree." In *The Liberator*, William Lloyd Garrison wrote that it was "an act of immense historical consequence." But they also worried that—however remote the possibility might be—some slave states would return to the Union by January 1, denying freedom to those enslaved.

Many white Northerners resented emancipation. A northern newspaper editor vilified Lincoln as a "half-witted usurper" and the Proclamation as "monstrous, impudent, and heinous . . . insulting to God as to man, for it declares those 'equal' whom God created unequal."

Even before the announcement of emancipation, antiblack riots flared in the North. In Cincinnati in the summer of 1862, Irish dock workers invaded black neighborhoods after black men had replaced the striking wharf hands along the city's river front. In Brooklyn, New York, Irish Americans set fire to a tobacco factory that employed black women and children.

Political Opposition to Emancipation

Northern Democrats almost unanimously opposed emancipation. They accused Lincoln and the Republicans of "fanaticism" and regretted that emancipation would liberate "two or three million semi savages" who would "overrun the North" and compete with white working people. The Democratic-controlled lower houses of the legislatures in Indiana and Illinois condemned the Proclamation as "wicked, inhuman, and unholy." Republicans recognized the intense hostility among many white Northerners to black people. Senator Lyman Trumball of Illinois conceded that "there is a very great aversion in the West—I know it to be so in my state—against having free negroes come among us. Our people want nothing to do with the negro."

And as some Republicans had predicted and feared, the Democrats capitalized on dissatisfaction with the war's progress and with Republican support for emancipation to make significant gains in the fall elections. Democratic governors were elected in New York and New Jersey, and Democrats won thirty-four more seats in the U.S. House of Representatives, although the Republicans retained a majority. Overjoyed Democrats proclaimed, "Abolition Slaughtered." Republicans took solace that their losses were not greater.

The Emancipation Proclamation

On January 1, 1863, Abraham Lincoln issued the Emancipation Proclamation. It was not the first step toward freedom. Since 1861 several thousand slaves had already freed themselves, but it was the first significant effort by Union authorities to assure freedom to nearly four million people of African descent who, with their ancestors, had been enslaved for 250 years in North America. The Civil War was now a war to make people free.

Black communities and many white people across the North celebrated. Church bells pealed. Poems were written, and prayers of thanksgiving were offered. Many considered it the most momentous day in American history since July 4, 1776. Frederick Douglass had difficulty describing the emotions of people in Boston when word reached the city late on the night of December 31 that Lincoln would issue the Proclamation the next day. "The effect of this announcement was startling beyond description, and the scene was wild and grand. Joy and gladness exhausted all forms of expression, from shouts of praise to sobs and tears. . . . A Negro preacher, a man of wonderful vocal power, expressed the heartfelt emotion of the hour, when he led all voices in the anthem, 'Sound the loud timbrel o'er Egypt's dark sea, Jehovah hath triumphed, his people were free.'"

Limits of the Proclamation

Despite this excitement, the language of the Emancipation Proclamation was uninspired and unmoving. It lacked the eloquence of the Declaration of Independence or the address Lincoln would deliver after the Union victory at Gettysburg in July 1863. Lincoln dryly wrote that "as a fit and necessary measure for suppressing said rebellion. . . I do order and declare that all persons held as slaves within said designated States, and parts of States, are, and henceforth shall be free."

Moreover, by limiting emancipation to those states and areas still in rebellion, Lincoln did not include enslaved people in the four border states still in the Union or in areas of Confederate states that Union forces had already occupied (see Map 11–1). Thus hundreds of thousands of people would remain in bondage despite the proclamation. The immediate practical effect of the Proclamation was negligible in the areas it was intended to affect. After all, slave owners in the Confederacy did not recognize Lincoln's authority, and they certainly did not free their slaves on January 1 or anytime soon thereafter. Yet the Emancipation Proclamation remains one of the most important documents in American history. It made the Civil War a war to free people, as well as to preserve the Union, and it gave moral authority to the Union cause. And as many black people had freed themselves before the Proclamation, now many more would liberate themselves after.

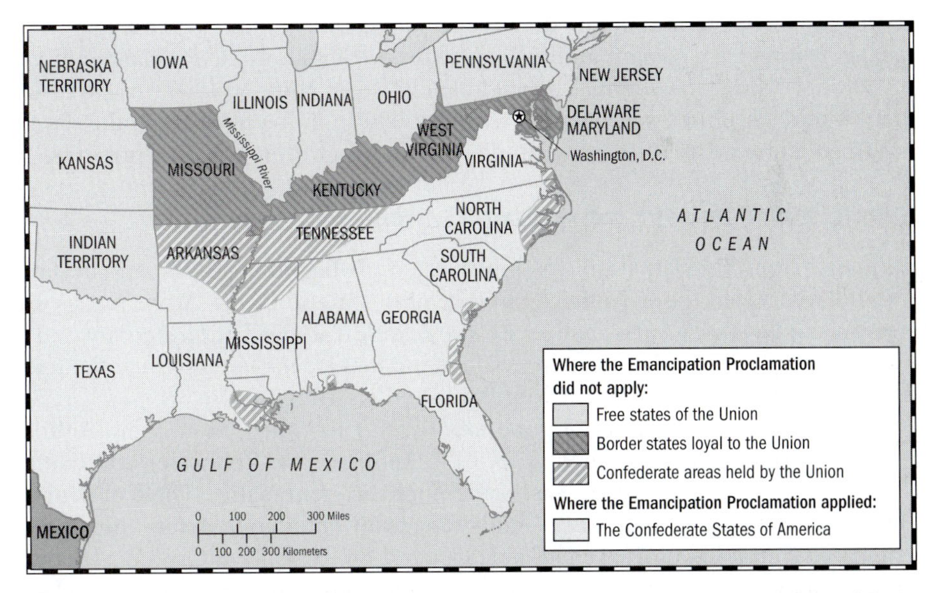

MAP 11–1 Effects of the Emancipation Proclamation. When Abraham Lincoln issued the Emancipation Proclamation on January 1, 1863, it applied only to slaves in those portions of the Confederacy not under Union authority. No southern slave owners freed their slaves at Lincoln's command. But many black people already had freed themselves, and many more would liberate themselves as well as family and friends in the aftermath of Lincoln's order. The Emancipation Proclamation was of extreme importance. It helped the Union to win the war. It meant that at long last the United States government had joined the abolitionist movement.

Effects of the Proclamation on the South

The Emancipation Proclamation destroyed any chance that Great Britain or France would offer diplomatic recognition to the Confederate government. Diplomatic recognition would have meant accepting the Confederacy as a legitimate state equal in international law to the Union, and it would almost surely have led to financial and military assistance for the South. British leaders, who had considered recognizing the Confederacy, now declined to support a "nation" that relied on slavery while its opponent moved to abolish it. In this sense, the Proclamation weakened the Confederacy's ability to prosecute the war.

Even more important, it undermined slavery in the South and contributed directly to the Confederacy's defeat. While the Proclamation may not have freed any of those in bondage on January 1, 1863, word of freedom spread rapidly across the South. Black people—aware a Union victory in the war meant freedom—were far less likely to labor for their owners or for the Confederacy. More slaves ran away, especially as Union troops approached. Slave resistance became more likely, although Lincoln cautioned against insurrection in the Proclamation: "And I hereby enjoin upon the people so declared to be free to abstain from all violence, unless in necessary self-defence." The institution of slavery cracked, crumbled, and collapsed after January 1, 1863.

Without emancipation, the United States would not have survived as a unified nation. Abraham Lincoln, after first failing to make the connection between eliminating slavery and preserving the Union, came to understand it fully and also grasped what freedom meant to both black and white people. In his annual message to Congress in December 1862, one month before the Proclamation, Lincoln described the importance of emancipation with a passion and feelings that were absent in the Proclamation itself. "We know how to save the Union. The world knows we do know how to save it. We—even we here—hold the power, and bear the responsibility. In giving freedom to the slave, we assure freedom to the free—honorable alike in what we give, and what we preserve."

Black Men Fight for the Union

The Emancipation Proclamation not only marked the beginning of the end of slavery, but it also authorized the enlistment of black troops in the Union Army. Just as white leaders in the North came to realize the preservation of the Union necessitated the abolition of slavery, they also began to understand that black men were needed for the military effort if the Union was to triumph in the Civil War.

By early 1863 the war had not gone well for the all-white Union Army. Although they had won significant battlefield victories in Kentucky and Tennessee and had captured New Orleans, the war in the east was a much different matter. The Union's Army of the Potomac faced a smaller but highly effective Confederate Army—the Army of Northern Virginia—led by the remarkable General Robert E. Lee. Confederate troops forced a Union retreat from Richmond during the 1862 Peninsular campaign. Union forces lost at the first and second battles of Bull Run. Their only victory over Lee at Antietam provided Lincoln with the opportunity to issue the Preliminary Emancipation Proclamation. But that was followed by a crushing Union loss at Fredericksburg.

Much like the decision to free the slaves, the decision to employ black troops proceeded neither smoothly nor logically. The commitment to the Civil War as a white man's war was deeply entrenched, and the initial attempts to raise black troops were strongly opposed by many white Northerners. As with emancipation, Lincoln moved slowly from outright opposition to cautious acceptance to enthusiastic support for enlisting black men in the Union Army.

The First South Carolina Volunteers

Some Union officers recruited black men long before emancipation was proclaimed and before most white Northerners were prepared to accept, much less welcome, black troops. In May 1862 General David Hunter began recruiting former slaves along the South Carolina coast and the Sea Islands, an area Union forces had captured in late 1861. But some black men did not want to enlist, and Hunter used white troops to force black men to "volunteer" for military service. He managed to organize a five-hundred-man regiment—the First South Carolina Volunteers.

The former slaves were outfitted in bright red pants, with blue coats and broad-brimmed hats. Through the summer of 1862, Hunter trained and drilled the regiment while awaiting official authorization and funds to pay them. When Congress balked, Hunter reluctantly disbanded all but one company of the regiment that August. The troops were dispersed, unpaid and disappointed. The surviving company was sent to St. Simon's Island off the Georgia coast to protect a community of former slaves.

Although Congress failed to support Hunter, it did pass the Second Confiscation Act and the Militia Act of 1862, which authorized President Lincoln to enlist black men. In Louisiana that fall, two regiments of free black men, the Native Guards, were accepted for federal service, and General Benjamin Butler organized them into the Corps d'Afrique. General Rufus Saxton gained the approval of Secretary of War Edwin Stanton to revive Hunter's dispersed regiment and to recall the company that had been sent to St. Simon's Island.

As commander, Saxton appointed Thomas Wentworth Higginson. Higginson was an ardent white abolitionist, one of the Secret Six who had provided financial support for John Brown's raid on Harpers Ferry. Higginson was determined not merely to end slavery but to prove that black people were equal to white people, a proposition most white people regarded as preposterous. Disposing of the unit's gaudy red trousers, Higginson set out to mold this regiment of mostly former slaves into an effective fighting force. On Emancipation Day, January 1, 1863, near Beaufort, South Carolina, the First South Carolina Volunteer Regiment was inducted into the U.S. Army.

The Second South Carolina Volunteers

A month later, the Second South Carolina Volunteers began enrolling ex-slaves, many from Georgia and Florida. James Montgomery, another former financial supporter of John Brown, commanded them. Montgomery was determined that the regiment would wipe out all vestiges of slavery, especially the homes, plantations, and personal possessions of families who owned slaves. But like Hunter, Montgomery found that many former slaves were reluctant to volunteer for military service, so he also used force to recruit them. He concluded that black men responded to the call to arms much the way white men did, except black men were less likely to desert once they joined the army:

> Finding it somewhat difficult to induce Negroes to enlist, we resolved to the draft. The negroes reindicate their claim to humanity by shirking the draft in every possible way; acting

> exactly like white men under similar circumstances. . . . The only difference that I notice is, the negro, after being drafted does not desert; but once dressed in the uniform with arms in his hands he feels himself a man; and acts like one.

The 54th Massachusetts Regiment

While ex-slaves joined the Union ranks in South Carolina, free black men in the North enlisted in what would become the most famous black unit, the 54th Massachusetts Regiment. In January 1863 governor of Massachusetts John A. Andrew received permission from Secretary of War Stanton to raise a black regiment, but because few black men lived in Massachusetts, Andrew asked prominent black men across the North for help. The Black Committee—as it became known—included Frederick Douglass, Martin Delany, Charles Remond, and Henry Highland Garnet.

These black leaders were convinced that by serving in the military, black men would prove they deserved to be treated as equals and had earned the right to be citizens. Frederick Douglass put it succinctly: "Once let the black man get upon his person the brass letters, U.S.; let him get an eagle on his button, and a musket on his shoulder and bullets in his pocket, and there is no power on earth which can deny that he has earned the right to citizenship." Two of Douglass's sons, Charles and Lewis, joined the 54th.

Lincoln, who had opposed emancipation and resisted enlisting black troops, became an enthusiastic supporter of black men in the Union Army. Writing to Andrew Johnson, who was the Union military governor of Tennessee, Lincoln perhaps overoptimistically predicted that "The bare sight of fifty thousand armed, and drilled black soldiers on the banks of the Mississippi, would end the rebellion at once. And who doubts that we can present that sight, if we but take hold in earnest."

Governor Andrew selected twenty-five-year-old Robert Gould Shaw to command the 54th Massachusetts Regiment. Shaw was a Harvard graduate from a prominent Massachusetts family, and he had already been wounded at the battle at Antietam. Although not an active abolitionist, he opposed slavery and was determined to prove that black men would fight well. The men the Black Committee recruited came from most of the northern states. Their average age was around twenty-five and virtually all of them were literate. They were farmers, seamen, butchers, blacksmiths, and teamsters. Only one of them had grown up in a slave state. As the ranks of the 54th filled, the 55th Massachusetts Regiment and the all-black 5th Massachusetts Cavalry Regiment were also formed.

Black Soldiers Confront Discrimination

Many white Northerners were willing to accept neither the presence of black troops nor the idea that black men could endure combat.

That black troops would serve in separate, all-black units was accepted as a matter of course. No one seriously proposed to integrate black men into previously all-white regiments. In 1863 the War Department created the Bureau of Colored Troops, and the Union Army remained segregated throughout the war. The only exception was the officers of the black regiments.

Almost all black troops had white officers. Yet many white officers, convinced their military record would be tainted by such service, refused to command black troops.

Others believed black men simply could not be trained for combat. Even those white officers who were willing to command black troops sometimes regarded their men as "niggers" suited only for work or fatigue duty. When the 110th U.S. Colored Infantry joined General William Tecumseh Sherman's army on its march through Georgia and South Carolina in 1864 and 1865, Sherman kept the black men out of combat.

Black soldiers were paid less than white soldiers. Based on the assumption that black troops would be used almost exclusively for construction, transportation, cooking, and burial details, and not for fighting, the War Department authorized a lower pay scale for them. A white private earned $13 per month; a black private earned $10 per month. This demoralized black soldiers, particularly after they had shown they were more than capable of fighting.

The 54th Massachusetts Regiment refused to accept their pay until they received equal pay. To take no compensation was an enormous sacrifice for men who had wives, children, and families to support. For some, it was more than a monetary loss. Sergeant William Walker insisted—despite orders—that the men in his company take no pay until they received equal pay. He was charged with mutiny, convicted, and shot.

The pay issue festered in Congress for nearly two years. Finally, near the end of the war, Congress enacted a compromise, but many black soldiers remained dissatisfied. The law equalized pay between black and white troops, but made it retroactive only to January 1, 1864—except for black men who had never been slaves. But the thousands of black men who had been slaves and had joined the military before January 1, 1864, would not be entitled to equal pay for the entire period of their service.

Black Men in Combat

Once black men put on the Union uniform, they took part in almost every battle that was fought during the rest of the Civil War. Black troops not only faced an enemy dedicated to the belief that the proper place of black people was in slavery, but they also confronted doubts about their fighting abilities among white Northerners. Yet by war's end, black units had suffered disproportionately more casualties than white units.

In October 1862 the first black unit went into combat in Missouri. James H. Lane, a white Free-Soiler, recruited five hundred black men in Kansas. Most were runaway slaves from Missouri and Arkansas. After some hasty training, they advanced against a Confederate position at Island Mountain. The black troops held off an attack until reinforcements arrived, and the Confederates were repulsed. Soon thereafter, the black unit became the First Kansas Colored Infantry.

On July 17, 1863, at Honey Springs in Indian territory (now Oklahoma), the Kansas soldiers attacked a Confederate force composed of white Texans and Cherokee Indians. After an intense twenty-minute battle, the black troops broke through the southern line and won a victory, capturing the colors of a Texas regiment.

In January 1863 Thomas Wentworth Higginson led the First South Carolina Volunteers on raids on the Georgia and Florida coasts. At one point, they were surrounded at night by Confederate cavalry but managed to fight their way out and escape.

On June 3, 1863, the 54th Massachusetts Regiment arrived in South Carolina and joined the raids in Georgia. Other raids in the Carolina low country devastated rice plantations and liberated hundreds of slaves.

On the evening of July 18, 1863, more than six hundred black men led by their white commander, Colonel Robert Gould Shaw, attacked heavily fortified Battery Wagner on Morris Island near the southern approach to Charleston harbor. They made a frontal assault through withering fire and managed to breach the battery before Confederate forces threw them back. Shaw was killed and the 54th suffered heavy losses. It was a defining moment of the Civil War, demonstrating to skeptical white people the valor and determination of black troops.
Courtesy of the Library of Congress

The Assault on Battery Wagner

Since 1861 and the Confederate capture of Fort Sumter in Charleston harbor that began the Civil War, Union leaders had been determined to retake the fort and occupy nearby Charleston—the heart of secession. In 1863 Union commanders began a combined land and sea offensive to seize the fort. But Battery Wagner, a heavily fortified installation on the northern tip of Morris Island, guarded the entrance to the harbor.

Frustrated in their initial efforts to enter the harbor, Major General Quincy A. Gilmore and Rear Admiral John Dahlgren decided on a full-scale assault on Wagner. After an unsuccessful attack by white troops, Colonel Shaw volunteered to lead the 54th in a second attack on the battery.

To improve the Union's chances, artillery fired more than nine thousand shells on Wagner on July 18, 1863. Everyone but the fort's Confederate defenders was convinced that no one could survive the bombardment. In fact, only 8 of the 1,620 defenders had been killed.

At sunset, 650 men of the first brigade of the 54th prepared to lead more than 5,000 Union troops in storming the battery. The regiment was tired and hungry but eager for the assault. Colonel Shaw offered brief words of encouragement to his troops: "Now I want you to prove yourselves men."

At 7:45 P.M., the 54th charged and was met by heavy rifle and artillery fire. Within minutes, the sand was littered with injured and dying men. Sergeant Major Lewis Douglass (the son of Frederick Douglass) was among those who took part. The 54th reached the walls only to be thrown back in hand-to-hand combat. Shaw was killed.

Although white troops fought to support the 54th, the attack could not be sustained, and the battle was over by 1 A.M. But within days, the courage of the 54th was known across the North, putting to rest—for a time—the myth that black men lacked the nerve to fight.

Altogether 246 black and white men were killed, 890 were wounded, and 391 were taken prisoner. Forty-two percent of the men of the 54th were killed or injured, and 80 men were taken prisoner.

Union forces never took Wagner. The Confederates abandoned Charleston as the war was ending in February 1865. Black Union troops—the 21st U.S. Colored Infantry and the 55th Massachusetts Regiment—occupied the city.

Olustee

On February 20, 1864, the 54th fought again and was joined by two black regiments—the First North Carolina and the Eighth U.S. of Pennsylvania—and six white regiments at the battle at Olustee in northern Florida. After almost five hours of bloody combat, Confederate forces prevailed and forced a Union retreat. The 54th had marched 110 miles in 100 hours prior to entering the engagement.

The Crater

In 1864, after Union troops laid siege to Petersburg, Virginia, white soldiers of the 48th Pennsylvania, who had been coal miners before the war, offered to dig a tunnel and set off an explosion under Confederate lines. General Ambrose Burnside agreed to the plan and assigned black troops to be prepared to lead the attack after the blast.

Four tons of powder were placed in the tunnel, but only hours before the blast was set to go off, Burnside's superior, General George Meade, replaced the black troops with inadequately trained white soldiers commanded by an alcoholic. Meade either lacked confidence in the black unit or was worried he would be blamed for using black men as shields for white soldiers if the attack failed.

On July 30, 1864, at 4:45 A.M., what was perhaps the largest man-made explosion in history up to that time buried a Confederate regiment and an artillery battery and created a crater 170 feet long, 60 feet wide, and 30 feet deep. But the white Union troops rushed down into the crater instead of fanning out around it in pursuit of the stunned enemy. While the Union soldiers marveled at the destruction, the Confederates launched a counterattack that threw back the Union troops, including the black troops that were finally brought forward. Some of the black men were murdered after they surrendered. More than four thousand Union troops, many of them black, were killed or wounded.

THE CONFEDERATE REACTION TO BLACK SOLDIERS

Confederate leaders and troops refused to recognize black men as legitimate soldiers. Captured black soldiers were persistently abused and even murdered, rather than treated as prisoners of war. Confederate Secretary of War James A. Seddon ordered that captured black soldiers be executed. "We ought never to be inconvenienced with such prisoners . . . summary execution must therefore be inflicted on those taken."

Protests erupted across the North after Confederate authorities decided to treat eighty men of the 54th Massachusetts Regiment who had been captured in the attack on Battery Wagner not as prisoners of war, but as rebellious slaves. Frederick Douglass refused to recruit any more black men and held Abraham Lincoln personally responsible for tolerating the mistreatment of black prisoners. "How many 54ths must be cut to pieces, its mutilated prisoners killed, and its living sold into slavery, to be tortured to death by inches, before Mr. Lincoln shall say, 'Hold, enough!'"

Lincoln issued General Order 11, threatening to execute southern troops or confine them to hard labor. "For every soldier of the United States killed in violation of the laws of war a rebel soldier shall be executed, and for every one enslaved by the enemy or sold into slavery a rebel soldier shall be placed at hard labor on the public works, and continued at such labor until the other shall be released and receive the treatment due to a prisoner of war."

Lincoln's order did not prevent the Confederates from sending the men of the 54th to trial by the state of South Carolina. The state regarded the black soldiers as either rebellious slaves or free black men inciting rebellion. Four black soldiers went on trial in Charleston police court, but the court declared it lacked jurisdiction. The black prisoners were eventually sent to prisoner of war camps.

The Fort Pillow Massacre

The Civil War's worst atrocity against black troops occurred at Fort Pillow in Tennessee on April 12, 1864. Confederates under the command of Nathan Bedford Forrest slaughtered black troops and their white commander, William F. Bradford, after they had surrendered. (After the Civil War, Forrest gained notoriety as a founder of the Ku Klux Klan. Before the war he had been a slave trader.) The Fort Pillow Massacre became the subject of an intense debate in Lincoln's cabinet. But rather than retaliate indiscriminately—as required by General Order 11—the cabinet decided only to punish those responsible for the killings, if and when they were apprehended, but no one was punished during or after the war. Instead, black troops exacted revenge themselves. In fighting around Petersburg, Virginia, later that year, black soldiers shouting, "Remember Fort Pillow!" reportedly murdered several Confederate prisoners. Captain Charles Francis Adams Jr. reported, "The darkies fought ferociously. . . . If they murdered prisoners, as I hear they did . . . they can hardly be blamed."

On their own, Union commanders in the field also retaliated for the Confederate treatment of captured black troops. When captured black men were virtually enslaved and forced to work at Richmond and Charleston on Confederate fortifications that were under Union attack, Union officers put Confederate prisoners to work on Union installations that were under fire. Aware they were not likely to be treated as well as white soldiers if they were captured, black men often fought desperately.

Black Men in the Union Navy

Black men had a tradition of serving at sea and had been in the U.S. Navy almost continuously since its creation in the 1790s. In the early nineteenth century, there were so many black sailors that some white people tried to ban black men from the navy. Nor did black sailors serve in segregated units. Naval crews were integrated.

Nonetheless, black sailors encountered rampant discrimination and exploitation during the Civil War. They were paid less than white sailors. They were assigned the hardest and filthiest tasks, such as loading coal and tending the boilers, on the navy's new steam-powered vessels. Many were stewards who waited on white officers. White officers and sailors often treated black sailors with contempt.

But some white men respected and admired the black sailors. One observed, "We never were betrayed when we trusted one of them, they were always our friends and were ready, if necessary, to lay down their lives for us." (He did not say whether white men were willing to lay down their lives for black men.) About 30,000 of the 120,000 men who served in the Union Navy were black sailors.

Liberators, Spies, and Guides

Besides serving as soldiers and sailors, black men and women aided themselves and the Union cause as liberators, spies, guides, and messengers. At about 3 A.M. on May 13, 1862, Robert Smalls, a twenty-three-year-old slave, fired the boiler on *The Planter*, a Confederate supply ship moored in Charleston harbor. With the aid of seven black crewmen, Smalls sailed *The Planter* past Confederate fortifications, including Fort Sumter, to the Union fleet outside the harbor and to freedom. Smalls liberated himself and fifteen other slaves, including the families of several crewmen and his own wife, daughter, and son.

In 1863 Harriet Tubman organized a spy ring in the South Carolina low country, and in cooperation with the all-black Second South Carolina Volunteer Regiment, she helped organize an expedition that destroyed plantations and freed nearly eight hundred slaves, many of whom joined the Union Army.

In Richmond in 1864, slaves helped more than one hundred escaped Union prisoners of war. Other slaves drew sketches and maps of Confederate fortifications and warned Union forces about troop movements. A black couple near Fredricksburg, Virginia, cleverly transmitted military intelligence to Union general Joseph Hooker. The woman washed laundry for a Confederate officer and hung shirts and blankets in patterns that conveyed information to her husband, who was a cook and groom for Union troops and relayed the information to Union officers.

Mary Elizabeth Bowser was a former slave who worked as a servant at the Confederate White House in Richmond. She overheard conversations by President Jefferson Davis and his subordinates, and—because she was literate—she covertly examined Confederate correspondence. She relayed the information to Union agents until the Confederates became suspicious. Bowser and slave Jim Pemberton managed to flee after unsuccessfully trying to burn down the mansion to distract their pursuers.

In Virginia's Shenandoah Valley, slave John Henry Woodson was a guide for Union general Philip H. Sheridan's cavalry in 1864 and 1865. Woodson was the father of Carter G. Woodson, who would become the "father" of black history in the twentieth century.

Violent Opposition to Black People

No matter how well black men fought, no matter how much individual black women contributed, and no matter how many people—black and white—died "to make men free," many white Northerners, both civilian and military, remained bitter and often violently hostile to black people. They used intimidation, threats, and terror to injure and kill people of color.

The New York City Draft Riot

Irish Catholic Americans, themselves held in contempt by prosperous white Protestants, indulged in an orgy of violence in New York City in July 1863. The New York draft riot arose from racial, religious, and class antagonisms. Poor, unskilled Irish workers and other white Northerners were convinced by leading Democrats, including New York governor Horatio Seymour, that the war had become a crusade to benefit black people.

The violence began when federal officials prepared to select the first men to be drafted by the Union for military service. An enraged mob made up mostly of Irish

During the draft riot in New York City in July 1863, black people were attacked, beaten, and killed. A mob lynched this black man near Clarkson Street. *Illustrated London News*, August 8, 1863.
Culver Pictures, Inc.

men attacked the draft offices and any unfortunate black people who were in the vicinity. Many of the Irish men were angry because black men had replaced striking Irish stevedores on the city's wharves the month before and because rich white Northerners could purchase an exemption from the draft.

The riot went on for four days. The poorly trained city police could not control it. Black people were beaten and lynched. The Colored Orphan Asylum was burned to the ground, although the children had already fled. The mob attacked businesses that employed black people. Protestant churches were burned. Rioters set fire to Horace Greeley's New York *Tribune.* The houses of Republicans and abolitionists were attacked and destroyed. The violence and destruction did not end until the U.S. Army arrived. Soldiers who had been fighting Confederates at Gettysburg two weeks earlier found themselves firing on New York rioters.

Refugees

Throughout the war, black people took advantage of the hostilities to free themselves. It was not easy. Confederate authorities did not hesitate to reenslave or even execute black people who sought freedom. Six black people were hanged near Georgetown, South Carolina, in 1862 when they were captured as they attempted to reach Union forces.

As Union armies plunged deep into the Confederacy in 1863 and 1864, thousands of black people liberated themselves and became refugees. When General William Tecumseh Sherman's army of 60,000 troops laid waste to Georgia in 1864, an estimated 10,000 former slaves followed his troops to Savannah, although they lacked adequate food, clothing, and housing. Sherman did not like black people, and his troops tried with little success to discourage the refugees. As one elderly black couple prepared to leave a plantation, Union soldiers as well as their master urged them to remain. They declined in no uncertain terms. "We must go, freedom is as sweet to us as it is to you."

Black People and the Confederacy

The Confederacy was based on the defense of slavery, and it benefited from the usually coerced, but sometimes willing, labor of black people. Slaves toiled in southern fields and factories during the Civil War. The greater the burden of work the slaves took on, the more white men there were who could become soldiers. When the war began, southern whites believed their disadvantage in manpower—the twenty-two northern states had 22,339,989 people and the eleven Confederate states had 9,103,332 (5,449,462 white people, 3,521,110 slaves, and 132,760 free black people)—would be partly offset by the slaves whose presence would free a disproportionately large number of white Southerners to go to war. While slaves would tend cotton, corn, and cattle, white southern men would fight.

The Impressment of Black People

As the war went on, the demand for more troops and laborers in the Confederacy increased. Slave owners were first asked and then compelled to contribute their slave laborers to the war effort. In July 1861 the Confederate Congress required the registration and enrollment of free black people for military labor. In the summer of 1862 the Virginia legislature authorized the impressment of 10,000 slaves between the ages of eighteen and forty-five for up to sixty days. The owners would receive $16 per month per slave.

The most important factory in the South was the Tredegar Iron Works in Richmond. During the war, more than twelve hundred slaves and free black men worked there in every capacity—from unskilled laborers to engineers—manufacturing artillery, locomotives, nails, and much more. Other black men across the South loaded and unloaded ships, worked for railroads, and labored in salt works.

In South Carolina in 1863, Confederate officials appealed to slave owners to provide 2,500 slaves to help fortify Charleston. The owners offered fewer than 1,000. During the Union bombardment of Fort Sumter, 500 slaves were employed in the difficult, dirty, and dangerous work of building and rebuilding the fort. Slaves were even forced into combat. Two Virginia slaves who were compelled to load and fire Confederate cannons near Yorktown were shot and killed.

Although many slave owners resisted the impressment of their bondmen, many white Southerners who did not own slaves were infuriated when the Confederate conscription law in 1862 exempted men who owned twenty or more slaves from military service. This "twenty nigger law" (later reduced to fifteen) meant that poor white men were drafted while wealthier planters remained home, presumably to supervise and discipline their slaves. One Mississippi soldier deserted the Confederate Army, claiming he "did not propose to fight for the rich men while they were home having a good time." Although the law was widely criticized, planters—always a small percentage of the white southern population—dominated the Confederate government and would not permit the repeal of the exemption.

Confederates Enslave Free Black People

After Lincoln's Emancipation Proclamation, Confederate president Jefferson Davis issued a counterproclamation in February 1863 declaring that free people would be enslaved, "all free negroes within the limits of the Southern Confederacy shall be placed on the slave status, and be deemed to be chattels . . . forever." This directive was not widely enforced. Davis, however, went on to order Confederate armies that invaded Union states to capture free black people in the North and enslave them. "All negroes who shall be taken in any of the States in which slavery does not now exist, in the progress of our arms, shall be adjudged, immediately after their capture, to occupy slave status."

This was done. Several hundred northern black people were taken south after Confederate forces invaded Pennsylvania in 1863 and fought at Gettysburg. Robert E. Lee's Army of Northern Virginia at Greensburg, Pennsylvania, captured at least fifty black people. A southern victory in the Civil War could conceivably have led to the enslavement of more than 300,000 free black residents of the Confederate States.

Black Confederates

Most of the labor black people did for the Confederacy was involuntary, but there were a few free black men and women who offered their services to the southern cause. In Lynchburg, Virginia, in the spring of 1861, seventy free black people volunteered "to act in whatever capacity may be assigned them." In Memphis in the fall, several hundred black residents cheered for Jefferson Davis and sang patriotic songs. These demonstrations of black support were made early in the conflict when the outcome was still much in doubt and long before the war became a crusade against slavery.

The status of many free black Southerners remained precarious. In Virginia in 1861, impressment laws, like those applying to slaves, compelled free black men to work on Confederate defenses around Richmond and Petersburg. Months before the war, South Carolina considered forcing its free black population to choose between enslavement and exile. The legislature rejected the proposal, but it terrified the state's free black people. Many people of color there had been free for generations. Fair in complexion, they had education, skills, homes, and businesses. Some even owned slaves. When the war came, many were willing to demonstrate their devotion to the South in a desperate attempt to gain white acceptance before they lost their freedom and property.

In early 1861, before the formation of the Confederacy, but after the secession of South Carolina, eighty-two free black men in Charleston petitioned Governor Francis W. Pickens "to be assigned any service where we can be useful." Pickens rejected the petition, but white South Carolinians were pleased at this show of loyalty.

White southern leaders generally ignored offers of free black support unless it was for menial labor. But in Charleston, when the city was under siege between 1863 and 1865, black and white residents were grateful that volunteer fire brigades composed of free black men turned out repeatedly to fight fires caused by Union artillery.

Personal Servants

Other black men contributed in different ways to the Confederate military effort. Black musicians in Virginia played for Confederate regiments and received the same pay as white musicians. Well-to-do white men often took their slaves—personal servants—with them when they went off to war. The servants cooked, cleaned uniforms, cared for weapons, maintained horses, and even provided entertainment. Some were loyal and devoted. They cared for owners who were wounded or fell sick. They accompanied the bodies of dead masters home.

Being the personal servant for a soldier was hard and sometimes dangerous work. Those close to combat could be killed or injured. One father warned his son not to take Sam, a valuable slave, into battle. "I hear you are likely to have a big battle soon, and I write to tell you not to let Sam go into the fight with you. Keep him in the rear, for that nigger is worth a thousand dollars." The father evidently placed a higher value on the slave than on his son.

Black Men Fighting for the South

Approximately 144,000 black men from the southern states fought with the Union Army. Most had been slaves. Although it was technically not legal until almost the end of the war, a much, much smaller number of black men did fight for the Confederacy.

White New York troops claimed to have encountered about seven hundred armed black men in late 1861 near Newport News, Virginia. In 1862 a black Confederate sharpshooter positioned himself in a chimney and shot several Union soldiers before he was finally killed. Fifty black men served as pickets for the Confederates along the Rappahannock River in Virginia in 1863.

Some black civilians supported the war effort and stood to profit if the South won. Buckner's uncles grew corn, sweet potatoes, peas, sorghum, and beans to feed Confederate troops on the Ellison family plantation. By hiring out horses, mules, and slaves they owned, the Ellisons had earned nearly $1,000 by 1863. By 1865 they had paid almost $5,000 in taxes to the Confederacy, nearly one-fifth of their total income. They also patriotically invested almost $7,000 in Confederate bonds and notes. Like prosperous white families, the Ellisons lost most of this investment with the defeat of the Confederacy. At war's end, the bonds were as worthless as Confederate cash, and the eighty slaves the Ellisons owned—worth approximately $100,000—were free people (see Chapter 6).

Other black Southerners also suffered economically from the Confederate defeat. Richard Mack, a South Carolina slave, went off to war as a personal servant. After his master died, he became an orderly for another Confederate officer. He worked hard and accumulated a large sum in Confederate currency. He later joked, "If we had won, I would be rich."

White Southerners effusively praised the few black people who actively supported the South. Several states awarded pensions to black men who served in the war and survived. Henry Clay Lightfoot was a slave in Culpeper, Virginia, who went to war as a body servant of Captain William Holcomb. After the war, he bought a house, raised a family, and was elected to the Culpeper town council. He collected a pension from Virginia, and when he died in 1931, the United Daughters of the Confederacy draped his coffin in a Confederate flag.

The Confederate Debate on Black Troops

By late 1863 and 1864, prospects for the Confederacy had become grim. The Union naval blockade of southern ports had become increasingly effective, and the likelihood of British aid had all but vanished. Confederate armies suffered crushing defeats at Vicksburg and Gettysburg in 1863 and absorbed terrible losses in Tennessee, Georgia, and Virginia in 1864.

As defeat loomed, some white Southerners began to discuss the possibility of arming black men. Several southern newspapers advocated it. In September 1863 the Montgomery (Alabama) *Weekly Mail* admitted it would have been preposterous to contemplate the need for black troops earlier in the war, but it had now become necessary to save the white South:

> We are forced by the necessity of our condition—by the insolence and barbarity of the enemy, by his revengeful and demoniacal spirit—to take a step which is revolting to every sentiment of pride, and to every principle that governed our institutions before the war. But the war has made great changes, and we must meet those changes, for the sake of preserving our very existence. It is a matter of necessity, therefore, that we should use

> every means within our reach to defeat the enemy. One of these, and the only one which will checkmate him, is the employment of negroes in the military service of the Confederacy.

In early 1864 Confederate general Patrick Cleburne recommended enlisting slaves and promising them their freedom if they remained loyal to the Confederacy. Cleburne argued that this policy would gain recognition and aid from Great Britain and would disrupt Union military efforts to recruit black Southerners. Yet most white Southerners considered arming slaves and free black men an appalling prospect. Jefferson Davis ordered military officers, including Cleburne, to cease discussing the issue.

Most white Southerners were convinced that to arm slaves and put black men in gray uniforms defied the assumptions on which southern society was based. Black people were inferior, and their proper status was to be slaves. The Richmond *Whig* declared in 1864 that "servitude is a divinely appointed condition for the highest good of the slave." It was absurd to contemplate black people as soldiers and as free people. Georgia politician Howell Cobb explained that slaves could not be armed. "If slaves will make good soldiers our whole theory of slavery is wrong."

The Civil War for white Southerners was a war to prevent the abolition of slavery. Now white southern voices were proposing abolition to preserve the southern nation. North Carolina senator Robert M. T. Hunter opposed any attempt to enlist slaves and free them. "If we are right in passing this measure we were wrong in denying to the old government the right to interfere with the institution of slavery and to emancipate slaves. Besides, if we offer slaves their freedom . . . we confess that we were insincere, were hypocritical, in asserting that slavery was the best state for the negroes themselves."

Nevertheless, as the military situation deteriorated, the South moved toward employing black troops. In November 1864 Virginia governor William Smith enthusiastically supported the idea. "There is not a man that would not cheerfully put the negro in the Army rather than become a slave himself. . . . Standing before God and my country, I do not hesitate to say that I would arm such portion of our able-bodied slaves population as may be necessary." In February 1865 Jefferson Davis and the Confederate cabinet conceded, "We are reduced to choosing whether the negroes shall fight for us or against us."

The opinion of General Robert E. Lee was critical to determining whether the Confederacy would decide to arm black men. No Southerner was more revered and respected. Lee announced in February 1865 that he favored both enrolling and emancipating black troops. "My own opinion is that we should employ them without delay." He believed their service as slaves would make them capable soldiers.

Less than a month later in March 1865, although many white Southerners still opposed it, the Confederate Congress voted to enlist 300,000 black men between the ages of eighteen and forty-five. They would receive the same pay, equipment, and supplies as white soldiers. But those who were slaves would not be freed unless their owner consented and the state where they served agreed to their emancipation. It was a desperate measure by a nearly defeated government and did not affect the outcome of the conflict. In April 1865 Lee surrendered to Grant at Appomattox Court House, and the Civil War ended.

TIMELINE

AFRICAN-AMERICAN EVENTS	NATIONAL EVENTS
1860	
	November 1860 Abraham Lincoln wins the presidential election **December 1860** South Carolina secedes from the Union
1861	
April–May 1861 Black men volunteer for military service and are rejected **August 1861** First Confiscation Act	**February 1861** The Confederate States of America is formed **March 1861** Lincoln inaugurated **April 1861** The firing on Fort Sumter begins the Civil War **November 1861** Union military forces capture the Sea Islands and coastal areas of South Carolina and Georgia
1862	
May 1862 Robert Smalls escapes with *The Planter* and sixteen slaves **May–August 1862** The First South Carolina Volunteers, an all-black regiment, forms **September 1862** Lincoln announces the Preliminary Emancipation Proclamation **October 1862** Black troops see combat for the first time in Missouri	**September 1862** Battle of Antietam is fought
1863	
January 1, 1863 Lincoln issues the Emancipation Proclamation **January–March 1863** Troops recruited for the 54th and the 55th Massachusetts Regiments **June 1863** Battle of Milliken's Bend **July 1863** Assault on Battery Wagner; New York City draft riots; Battle at Honey Springs	**March 1863** The U.S. government enacts a Conscription Act **July 1863** Battles of Vicksburg and Gettysburg

continued

AFRICAN-AMERICAN EVENTS	NATIONAL EVENTS
1864	
February 1864	**November 1864**
Battle at Olustee	Lincoln is reelected
April 1864	**November-December 1864**
Fort Pillow Massacre	Sherman makes his march to the sea
1865	
February 1865	**February 1865**
Black troops lead the occupation of Charleston	Charleston falls
March 1865	**March 1865**
Confederate Congress approves the enlistment of black men	Richmond falls
December 1865	**April 1865**
Thirteenth Amendment ratified	Lee surrenders at Appomatox; Lincoln is assassinated

CONCLUSION

The Civil War ended with the decisive defeat of the Confederacy. The Union was preserved. The long ordeal of slavery for millions of people of African descent was over. Slavery—having thrived in America for nearly 250 years—was finally abolished by an amendment to the U.S. Constitution. Congress passed the Thirteenth Amendment on January 31, 1865. It was ratified by twenty-seven states and declared in effect on December 18, 1865.

Were it not for the presence and labors of more than four million black people, there would have been no Civil War. Had it not been for the presence and contributions of more than 185,000 black soldiers and sailors, the Union would not have won. Almost forty thousand of those black men died in combat and of disease during the war. Twenty-one black men were awarded the Congressional Medal of Honor for heroism during the conflict.

No one better represents the dramatic shift in attitudes and policies toward African Americans during the Civil War than Abraham Lincoln. When the war began, Lincoln insisted it was a white man's conflict to suppress an insurrection of rebellious white Southerners. Black people, Lincoln remained convinced, would be better off outside the United States. But the war went on, and thousands of white men died. Lincoln issued the Emancipation Proclamation and welcomed the enlistment of black troops. The president came to appreciate the achievements and devotion of black troops and condemned the mean-spiritedness of white Northerners who opposed the war. Lincoln wrote in 1863, "And then there will be some black men who can remember that, with silent tongue, and clenched teeth, and steady eye, and well-poised bayonet, they have helped mankind on to this great consummation; while, I fear, there will be some white ones, unable to forget that, with malignant heart, and deceitful speech, they have strove to hinder it."

Review Questions

1. How did the Union's purposes in the Civil War change between 1861 and 1865? What accounts for those changes?
2. How did policies of the Confederate government toward slaves change during the Civil War? What were those changes, and when and why did they occur?
3. When the Civil War began, why did northern black men volunteer to serve in the Union army if the war had not yet become a war to end slavery?
4. To what extend did Abraham Lincoln's policies and attitudes toward black people change during the Civil War? Does Lincoln deserve credit as "the Great Emancipator"? Why or why not?
5. What was the purpose of the Emancipation Proclamation? Why was it issued? Exactly what did it accomplish?
6. What did black men and women contribute to the Union war effort? Was it in their interests to participate in the Civil War? Why or why not?
7. Why did at least some black people support the southern states and the Confederacy during the Civil War?
8. Was the result of the Civil War worth the loss of 620,000 lives?

Recommended Reading

Lerone Bennett. *Abraham Lincoln's White Dream.* Chicago: Johnson, 2000. Bennett is critical of Lincoln's attitudes and actions in the popular account.

Dudley Taylor Cornish. *The Sable Arm: Negro Troops in the Union Army, 1861–1865.* New York: Norton, 1956. The best single study of black men in the military during the war.

John Hope Franklin. *The Emancipation Proclamation.* Garden City, NY: Doubleday, 1963. A work written to commemorate the centennial of the Proclamation.

Michael P. Johnson and James L. Roark. *Black Masters: A Free Family of Color in the Old South.* New York: Norton, 1984. A depiction of life among prosperous free black people before and during the Civil War.

Ervin Jordon. *Black Confederates and Afro Yankees in Civil War Virginia.* Charlottesville: University of Virginia Press, 1995. A rich study of life and society among African Americans in Virginia during the war.

James McPherson. *Battle Cry of Freedom: The Civil War Era.* New York: Oxford University Press, 1988. A superb one-volume account of the Civil War.

George W. Williams. *History of the Negro Troops in the War of the Rebellion.* New York: Harper & Row, 1888. An account of black soldiers in the war by America's first African-American historian.

• CHAPTER TWELVE •

THE MEANING OF FREEDOM

THE PROMISE OF RECONSTRUCTION, 1865–1868

THE END OF SLAVERY

With the collapse of slavery, many black people were quick to inform white people that whatever loyalty, devotion, and cooperation they might have shown as slaves had never been a reflection of their inner feelings and attitudes. Near Opelousas, Louisiana, a Union officer asked a young black man why he did not love his master, and the youth responded sharply, "When my master begins to lub me, den it'll be time enough for me to lub him. What I wants is to get away. I want to take me off from dis plantation, where I can be free."

In North Carolina, planter Robert P. Howell was deeply disappointed that a loyal slave named Lovet fled at the first opportunity. "He was about my age and I had always treated him more as a companion than a slave. When I left I put everything in his charge, told him that he was free, but to remain on the place and take care of things. He promised me faithfully that he would, but he was the first one to leave . . . and I did not see him for several years."

Emancipation was a traumatic experience for many former masters. A Virginia freedman remembered that "Miss Polly died right after the surrender, she was so hurt that all the negroes was going to be free." Another former slave, Robert Falls, recalled that his master assembled the slaves to inform them they were free. "I hates to do it, but I must. You all ain't my niggers no more. You is free. Just as free as I am. Here I have raised you all to work for me, and now you are going to leave me. I am an old man, and I can't get along without you. I don't know what I am going to do." In less than a year, he was dead. Falls attributed his master's death to the end of slavery. "It killed him."

Differing Reactions of Former Slaves

Other slaves bluntly displayed their reaction to years of bondage. Aunt Delia, a cook with a North Carolina family, revealed that for a long time she had secretly gained retribution for the indignity of servitude. "How many times I spit in the biscuits and peed in the coffee just to get back at them mean white folks." In Goodman, Mississippi, a slave named Caddy learned she was free and rushed from the field to find her owner. "Caddy threw down that hoe, she marched herself up to the big house, then, she looked around and found the mistress. She went over to the mistress, she flipped up her dress and told the white woman to do something. She said it mean and ugly. This is what she said: 'Kiss my ass!'"

In contrast, some slaves, especially elderly ones, were fearful and apprehensive about freedom. On a South Carolina plantation, an older black woman refused to accept emancipation. "I ain' no free nigger! I is got a marster and mistiss! Dee right dar in de great house. Ef you don' b'lieve me, you go dar an' see."

Reuniting Black Families

As slavery ended, the most urgent need for many freed people was finding family members who had been sold away from them. Slavery had not destroyed the black family. Husbands, wives, and children went to great lengths to reassemble their families after the Civil War. For years and even decades after the end of slavery, advertisements appeared in black newspapers appealing for information about missing kinfolk. The following notice was published in the *Colored Tennessean* on August 5, 1865:

> Saml. Dove wishes to know of the whereabouts of his mother, Areno, his sisters Maria, Neziah and Peggy, and his brother Edmond, who were owned by Geo. Dove of Rockingham County, Shenandoah Valley, Va. Sold in Richmond, after which Saml. and Edmond were taken to Nashville, Tenn., by Joe Mick; Areno was left at the Eagle Tavern, Richmond. Respectfully yours, Saml. Dove, Utica, New York.

In North Carolina a northern journalist met a middle-age black man "plodding along, staff in hand, and apparently very footsore and tired." The nearly exhausted freedman explained that he had walked almost six hundred miles looking for his wife and children who had been sold four years earlier.

There were emotional reunions as family members found each other after years of separation. Ben and Betty Dodson had been apart for twenty years when Ben found her in a refugee camp after the war. "Glory! glory! hallelujah," he shouted as he hugged his wife. "Dis is my Betty, shuah. I foun' you at las'. I's hunted and hunted till I track you up here. I's boun' to hunt till I fin' you if you's alive."

Other searches had more heart-wrenching results. Husbands and wives sometimes learned that their spouses had remarried during the separation. Believing his wife had died, the husband of Laura Spicer remarried—only to learn after the war that Laura was still alive. Sadly, he wrote to her but refused to meet with her. "I would come and see you but I know I could not bear it. I want to see you and I don't want to see you. I love you just as well as I did the last day I saw you, and it will not do for you and I to meet."

Tormented, he wrote again pledging his love. "Laura I do not think that I have change any at all since I saw you last—I thinks of you and my children every day of my life. Laura I do love you the same. My love to you never have failed. Laura, truly, I have got another wife, and I am very sorry that I am. You feels and seems to me as much like my dear loving wife, as you ever did Laura."

One freedman testified to the close ties that bound many slave families when he replied bitterly to the claim that he had had a kind master who had fed him and never used the whip. "Kind! yes, he gib men corn enough, and he gib me pork enough, and he neber gib me one lick wid de whip, but whar's my wife?—whar's my chill'en? Take away de pork, I say; take away de corn, I can work and raise dese for myself, but gib me back de wife of my bosom, and gib me back my poor chill'en as was sold away."

Land

As freed people embraced freedom and left their masters, they wanted land. Nineteenth-century Americans of virtually every background associated economic security with owning land. Families wanted to work land and prosper as self-sufficient yeomen. Former slaves believed their future as a free people was tied to the possession of land. But just as it had been impossible to abolish slavery without the intervention of the U.S. government, it would not be possible to procure land without federal assistance. At first, federal authorities seemed determined to make land available to freedmen.

Special Field Order #15

Shortly after his army arrived in Savannah—after having devastated Georgia—Union general William T. Sherman announced that freedmen would receive land. On January 16, 1865, he issued Special Field Order #15. This military directive set aside a 30-mile-wide tract of land along the Atlantic coast from Charleston, South Carolina, 245 miles south to Jacksonville, Florida. White owners had abandoned the land, and Sherman reserved it for black families. The head of each family would receive "possessory title" to forty acres of land. Sherman also gave the freedmen the use of army mules, thus giving rise to the slogan, "Forty acres and a mule."

Former slaves assembled in a village near Washington, D.C. Black people welcomed emancipation, but without land, education, or employment, they faced an uncertain future.
Courtesy of the Library of Congress

Within six months, forty thousand freed people were working 400,000 acres in the South Carolina and Georgia low country and on the Sea Islands. Former slaves generally avoided the slave crops of cotton and rice and instead planted sweet potatoes and corn. They also worked together as families and kinfolk. They avoided the gang labor associated with slavery. Most husbands and fathers preferred that their wives and daughters not work in the fields as slave women had had to do.

The Port Royal Experiment

Meanwhile, hundreds of former slaves had been cultivating land for three years. In late 1861 Union military forces carved out an enclave around Beaufort and Port Royal, South Carolina, that remained under federal authority for the rest of the war. White planters fled to the interior, leaving their slaves behind. Under the supervision of U.S. Treasury officials and northern reformers and missionaries who hurried south in 1862, ex-slaves began to work the land in what came to be known as the "Port Royal Experiment." When Treasury agents auctioned off portions of the land for nonpayment of taxes, freedmen purchased some of it. But northern businessmen bought most of the real estate and then hired black people to raise cotton.

White owners sometimes returned to their former lands only to find that black families had taken charge. A group of black farmers told one former owner, "We own this land now, put it out of your head that it will ever be yours again." And on one South Carolina Sea Island, white men were turned back by armed black men.

The Freedmen's Bureau

As the war ended in early 1865, Congress created the Bureau of Refugees, Freedmen, and Abandoned Lands—commonly called the Freedmen's Bureau. Created as a temporary agency to assist freedmen to make the transition to freedom, the bureau was placed under the control of the U.S. Army and General Oliver O. Howard was put in command. Howard, a devout Christian who had lost an arm in the war, was eager to aid the freedmen.

The bureau was given enormous responsibilities. It was to help freedmen obtain land, gain an education, negotiate labor contracts with white planters, settle legal and criminal disputes involving black and white people, and provide food, medical care, and transportation for black and white people left destitute by the war. However, Congress never provided sufficient funds or personnel to carry out these tasks.

The Freedmen's Bureau never had more than nine hundred agents spread across the South from Virginia to Texas. Mississippi, for example, had twelve agents in 1866. One agent often served a county with a population of ten thousand to twenty thousand freedmen. Few of the agents were black because few military officers were black. John Mercer Langston of Virginia was an inspector of schools assigned to the bureau's main office in Washington, D.C.; Major Martin R. Delany worked with freedmen on the South Carolina Sea Islands.

The need for assistance was desperate as thousands of black and white Southerners endured extreme privation in the months after the war ended. The bureau established camps for the homeless, fed the hungry, and cared for orphans and the sick as best it could. It distributed more than thirteen million rations—consisting of flour, corn meal, and sugar—by 1866. The bureau provided medical care to a half million freedmen and thousands of white people who were suffering from smallpox, yellow fever, cholera, and pneumonia. Many more remained untreated.

In July 1865 the bureau took a first step toward distributing land when General Howard issued Circular 13 ordering agents to "set aside" forty-acre plots for freedmen. But the allocation had hardly begun when the order was revoked, and it was announced that land already distributed under General Sherman's Special Field Order #15 was to be returned to its previous white owners.

The reason for this reversal in policy was that President Andrew Johnson, who had become president after Lincoln's assassination in April 1865, began to pardon hundreds and then thousands of former Confederates and restore their lands to them. General Howard was forced to tell black people that they had to relinquish the land they thought they had acquired. In a speech before some two thousand freedmen on South Carolina's Edisto Island in October 1865, Howard pleaded with his audience to "lay aside their bitter feelings, and to become reconciled to their old masters." A black

Freedmen's Bureau agents often found themselves in the middle of angry disputes over land and labor that erupted between black and white Southerners. Too often the Bureau officers sided with the white landowners in these disagreements with former slaves.
Harper's Weekly, June 2, 1866.

man shouted a response, "Why, General Howard, why do you take away our lands? You take them from us who are true, always true to the Government! You give them to our all-time enemies. This is not right!"

A committee rejected Howard's appeal for reconciliation and forgiveness and they insisted the government provide land:

> You ask us to forgive the landowners of our island. You only lost your right arm in war and might forgive them. The man who tied me to a tree and gave me 39 lashes and who stripped and flogged my mother and my sister and who will not let me stay in his empty hut except I will do his planting and be satisfied with his price and who combines with others to keep away land from me well knowing I would not have anything to do with him if I had land of my own—that man I cannot well forgive.

Howard was moved by these appeals. He returned to Washington and attempted to persuade Congress to make land available. Congress refused, and President Johnson was determined that white people would get their lands back. It seemed so sensible to most white people. Property that had belonged to white families for generations simply could not be given to freedmen. Freedmen saw matters differently. They deserved land that they and their families had worked without compensation for generations. Freedmen believed it was the only way to make freedom meaningful and to gain independence from white people. As it turned out, most freedmen were forced off land they thought should belong to them.

Southern Homestead Act

In early 1866 Congress attempted to provide land for freedmen with the passage of the Southern Homestead Act. More than three million acres of public land were set aside for black people and southern white people who had remained loyal to the Union. Much of this land, however, was unsuitable for farming and consisted of swampy wetlands or unfertile pinewoods. More than four thousand black families—three-quarters of them in Florida—did claim some of this land, but many of them lacked the financial resources to cultivate it. Eventually southern timber companies acquired much of it, and the Southern Homestead Act largely failed.

Sharecropping

To make matters worse, by 1866 bureau officials tried to force freedmen to sign labor contracts with white landowners—putting black people once again under white authority. Black men who refused to sign contracts could be arrested. Theoretically, these contracts were legal agreements between two equals: landowner and laborer. But they were seldom freely concluded. Bureau agents usually sided with the landowner and pressured freedmen to accept unequal terms.

Occasionally, the landowner would pay wages to the laborer. But because most landowners lacked cash to pay wages, they agreed to provide the laborer with part of the crop. The laborer, often grudgingly, agreed to work under the supervision of the landowner. The contracts required labor for a full year; the laborer could neither quit nor strike. Landowners demanded that the laborers work the fields in gangs. Freedmen resisted this system. They sometimes insisted on making decisions involving planting, fertilizing, and harvesting as they sought to exercise independence.

Thus it took time for a new form of agricultural labor to develop. But by the 1870s, the system of sharecropping had emerged and dominated most of the South. There were no wages. Freedmen worked land as families—not in gangs—and not under direct white supervision. When the landowner provided seed, tools, fertilizer, and work animals (mules, horses, oxen), the black family received one-third of the crop. There were many variations on these arrangements, and frequently black families were cheated out of their fair share of the crop.

THE BLACK CHURCH

In the years after slavery, the church became the most important institution among African Americans other than the family. Not only did it fill deep spiritual and inspirational needs, it offered enriching music, provided charity and compassion to those in need, developed community and political leaders, and was free of white supervision. Before slavery's demise, free black people and slaves often attended white churches where they were encouraged to participate in religious services conducted by white clergymen and where they were treated as second-class Christians.

Once liberated, black men and women organized their own churches with their own ministers. Most black people considered white ministers incapable of delivering a meaningful message. Nancy Williams recalled, "Ole white preachers used to talk wid dey tongues widdout sayin' nothin', but Jesus told us slaves to talk wid our hearts."

Northern white missionaries were sometimes appalled by the unlettered and ungrammatical black preachers who nevertheless communicated effectively and emotionally with their parishioners. A visiting white clergyman was genuinely impressed and humbled on hearing a black preacher who lacked education, but more than made up for it with devout faith. "He talked about Christ and his salvation as one who understood what he said. . . . Here was an unlearned man, one who could not read, telling of the love of Christ, of Christian faith and duty in a way which I have not learned."

Other black and white religious leaders anguished over what they considered moral laxity and displaced values among the freed people. They preached about honesty, thrift, temperance, and elimination of sexual promiscuity. They demanded an end to "rum-suckers, bar-room loafers, whiskey dealers and card players among the men, and to those women who dressed finely on ill gotten gain."

Church members struggled, scrimped, and saved to buy land and to build churches. Most former slaves founded Baptist and Methodist churches. These denominations tended to be more autonomous and less subject to outside control. Their doctrine was usually simple and direct without complex theology. Of the Methodist churches, the African Methodist Episcopal (AME) church made giant strides in the South after the Civil War.

In Charleston, South Carolina, the AME church was resurrected after an absence of more than forty years. In 1822, during the turmoil over the Denmark Vesey plot, the AME church was forced to disband and its leader had to flee (see Chapter 8). But by the 1870s, three AME congregations were thriving in Charleston. In Wilmington,

North Carolina, the sixteen hundred members of the Front Street Methodist Church decided to join the AME church soon after the Civil War ended. They replaced the longtime white minister, the Reverend L. S. Burkhead, with a black man.

White Methodists initially encouraged cooperation with black Methodists and helped establish the Colored (now Christian) Methodist Episcopal church (CME). But the white Methodists lost some of their fervor after they tried but failed to persuade the black Methodists to keep political issues out of the CME church and to dwell solely on spiritual concerns.

The Presbyterian, Congregational, and Episcopal churches appealed to the more prosperous members of the black community. Their services tended to be more formal and solemn. Black people who had been free before the Civil War were usually affiliated with these congregations and remained so after the conflict. Well-to-do free black people in Charleston organized St. Mark's Protestant Episcopal Church when they separated from the white Episcopal church. But they retained their white minister Joseph Seabrook as rector. Poorer black people of darker complexion found churches like St. Mark's decidedly unappealing. Ed Barber visited, but only one time.

> When I was trampin' 'round Charleston, dere was a church dere called St. Mark, dat all de society folks of my color went to. No black nigger welcome dere, they told me. Thinkin' as how I was bright 'nough to git in, I up and goes dere one Sunday, Ah, how they did carry on, bow and scrape and ape de white folks. . . . I was uncomfortable all de time though, 'cause they were too "hifalootin" in de ways, in de singin', and all sorts of carryin' ons.

The Roman Catholic Church made modest in-roads among black Southerners. There were all-black parishes in St. Augustine, Savannah, Charleston, and Louisville after the Civil War. For generations prior to the conflict, large numbers of well-to-do free people of color in New Orleans had been practicing Catholics, and their descendants remained faithful to the church. On Georgia's Skidaway Island, Benedictine monks established a school for black youngsters in 1878 that survived for nearly a decade.

This unidentified photograph depicts the quality of housing that most former slaves inhabited in the decades after the Civil War. The black family shown here is attired in their best clothes as they pose for the photograph.

Courtesy of the Library of Congress

Religious differences among black people not-withstanding, the black churches, their parishioners, and clergymen would play a vital role in Reconstruction politics. More than one hundred black ministers were elected to political office after the Civil War.

EDUCATION

Freedom and education were inseparable. To remain illiterate after emancipation was to remain enslaved. One ex-slave master bluntly told his former slave, Charles Whiteside, "Charles, you is a free man they say, but Ah tells you now, you is still a slave and if you lives to be a hundred, you'll STILL be a slave, cause you got no education, and education is what makes a man free!"

Almost every freed black person—young or old—desperately wanted to learn. Elderly people were especially eager to read the Bible. Even before slavery ended, black people began to establish schools. In 1861 Mary Peake, a free black woman, opened a school in Hampton, Virginia. On South Carolina's Sea Islands, a black cabinetmaker began teaching openly after having covertly operated a school for years. In 1862 northern missionaries arrived on the Sea Islands to begin teaching. Laura Towne, a white woman, and Charlotte Forten, a black woman, opened a school on St. Helena's Island as part of the Port Royal Experiment. They enrolled 138 children and 58 adults. By 1863 there were 1,700 students and 45 teachers at 30 schools in the South Carolina low country.

With the end of the Civil War, northern religious organizations in cooperation with the Freedmen's Bureau organized hundreds of day and night schools. Classes were held in stables, homes, former slave cabins, taverns, churches, and even—in Savannah and New Orleans—in the old slave markets. Former slaves spent hours in the fields and then trudged to a makeshift school to learn the alphabet and arithmetic. In 1865 black ministers created the Savannah Educational Association, raised $1,000, employed fifteen black teachers, and enrolled six hundred students.

In 1866 the Freedmen's Bureau set aside $500,000 for education. The bureau furnished the buildings while former slaves hired, housed, and fed the teachers. By 1869 the Freedmen's Bureau was involved with 3,000 schools and 150,000 students. Even more impressive, by 1870 black people had contributed $1 million to educate their people.

Black Teachers

Although freedmen appreciated the dedication and devotion of the white teachers affiliated with the missionary societies, they usually preferred black teachers. The Reverend Richard H. Cain, an AME minister who came south from Brooklyn, New York, said that black people needed to learn to control their own futures. "We must take into our own hands the education of our race. . . . Honest, dignified whites may teach ever so well, but it has not the effect to exalt the black man's opinion of his own race, because they have always been in the habit of seeing white men in honored positions, and respected."

Black men and women responded to the call to teach. Virginia C. Green, a northern black woman, felt compelled to go to Mississippi. "Though I have never known servitude they are . . . my people. Born as far north as the lakes I have felt no freer because so many were less fortunate. . . . I look forward with impatience to the time when my people shall be strong, blest with education, purified and made prosperous by virtue and industry." Hezekiah Hunter, a black teacher from Brooklyn, New York, commented in 1865 on the need for black teachers. "I believe we best can instruct our own people, knowing our own peculiarities—needs—necessities. Further—I believe we that are competent owe it to our people to teach them our speciality." And in Malden, West Virginia, when black residents found that a recently arrived eighteen-year-old black man could read and write, they promptly hired him to teach.

In some areas of the South, the sole person available to teach was a poorly educated former slave equipped primarily with a willingness to teach his or her fellow freedmen. One such teacher explained, "I never had the chance of goen to school for I was a slave until freedom. . . . I am the only teacher because we can not doe better now." Many northern teachers, black and white, provided more than the basics of elementary education. Black life and history were occasionally read about and discussed. Abolitionist Lydia Maria Child wrote *The Freedmen's Book*, which offered short biographies of Benjamin Banneker, Frederick Douglass, and Toussaint Louverture. More often northern teachers, dismayed at the backwardness of the freedmen, struggled to modify behavior and to impart cultural values by teaching piety, thrift, cleanliness, temperance, and timeliness.

Many former slaves came to resent some of these teachers as condescending, self-righteous, and paternalistic. Sometimes the teachers, especially those who were white, became frustrated with recalcitrant students who did not readily absorb middle-class values. Others, however, derived enormous satisfaction from teaching freedmen. A Virginia teacher commented, "I think I shall stay here as long as I live and teach this people. I have no love or taste for any other work, and I am happy only here with them."

Black Colleges

Northern churches and religious societies established dozens of colleges, universities, academies, and institutes across the South in the late 1860s and the 1870s (see Map 12–1). Most of these institutions provided elementary and secondary education. Few black students were prepared for actual college or university work. The American Missionary Association—an abolitionist and Congregationalist organization—worked with the Freedmen's Bureau to establish Berea in Kentucky, Fisk in Tennessee, Hampton in Virginia, Tougaloo in Alabama, and Avery in South Carolina. The primary purpose of these schools was to educate black students to become teachers.

In Missouri, the black enlisted men and the white officers of the 62nd and 65th Colored Volunteers raised $6,000 to establish Lincoln Institute in 1866, which would become Lincoln University. The American Baptist Home Mission Society founded Virginia Union, Shaw in North Carolina, Benedict in South Carolina, and Morehouse in Georgia. Northern Methodists helped establish Claflin in South Carolina, Rust in Mississippi, and Bennett in North Carolina. The Episcopalians were responsible for St. Augustine's in North Carolina and St. Paul's in Virginia. These and many other similar institutions formed the foundation for the historically black colleges and universities.

MAP 12–1 The Location of Black Colleges Founded before and during Reconstruction. Three black colleges were founded before the Civil War. In Pennsylvania, Cheyney University opened in 1837, and it was followed by the establishment of Lincoln University in 1854. In 1856, Wilberforce University was founded in Ohio. After the Civil War, northern black and white missionary groups fanned out across the South and—frequently with the assistance of Freedmen's Bureau officials—founded colleges, institutes, and normal schools in the former slave states.

Response of White Southerners

White Southerners considered efforts by black people to learn absurd. For generations, white Americans had looked on people of African descent as abjectly inferior. When significant efforts were made to educate former slaves, white Southerners reacted with suspicion, contempt, and hostility. One white woman told a teacher, "I do assure you, you might as well try to teach your horse or mule to read, as to teach these niggers. They can't learn."

Most white people were well aware that black people could learn. Otherwise, the slave codes that prohibited educating slaves would have been unnecessary. After slavery's end, some white people went out of their way to prevent black people from learning. Countless schools were burned, mostly in rural areas. In Canton, Mississippi, black people collected money to open a school—only to have white residents inform them that the school would be burned and the prospective teacher lynched if it opened. The female teacher at a freedmen's school in Donaldsonville, Louisiana, was shot and killed.

Other white Southerners grudgingly tolerated the desire of black people to acquire an education. One planter bitterly conceded in 1870, "Every little negro in the county is now going to school and the public pays for it. This is one hell of [a] fix but we can't help it, and the best policy is to conform as far as possible to circumstances."

Most white people adamantly refused to attend school with black people. No integrated schools were established in the immediate aftermath of emancipation. Most black people were more interested in gaining an education than in caring whether white students attended school with them. When black youngsters tried to attend a white school in Raleigh, North Carolina, the white students stopped going to it. For a brief time in Charleston, South Carolina, black and white children attended the same school, but they were taught in separate classrooms.

VIOLENCE

In the days, weeks, and months after the end of the Civil War, an orgy of brutality and violence swept across the South. White Southerners—embittered by their crushing defeat and unable to adjust to the end of slave labor and the loss of millions of dollars worth of slave property—lashed out at black people. There were beatings, murders, rapes, and riots, often with little or no provocation.

Black people who demanded respect, wore better clothing, refused to step aside for white people, or asked to be addressed as "mister" or "missus" were attacked. In South Carolina, a white clergyman shot and killed a black man who protested when another black man was removed from a church service. In Texas, one black man was killed because he failed to remove his hat in the presence of a white man and another for refusing to relinquish a bottle of whiskey. A black woman was beaten for "using insolent language," and a black worker in Alabama was killed for speaking sharply to a white overseer. In Virginia, a black veteran was beaten after announcing he had been proud to serve in the Union Army.

In South Carolina, a white man asked a passing black man whom he belonged to. The black man replied that he no longer belonged to anybody. "I am free now." With that, the white man roared, "Sas me? You black devil!" He then slashed the freedman with a knife, seriously injuring him. The sheriff of DeWitt County, Texas, shot a black man who was whistling "Yankee Doodle." A Freedmen's Bureau agent in North Carolina explained the intense white hostility. "The fact is, it's the first notion with a great many of these people, if a Negro says anything or does anything that they don't like, to take a gun and put a bullet into him, or a charge of shot." In Texas another Freedmen's Bureau officer claimed that white people simply killed black people "for the love of killing."

There was also large-scale violence. In 1865 University of North Carolina students twice attacked peaceful meetings of black people. Near Pine Bluff, Arkansas, in 1866, a white mob burned a black settlement and lynched twenty-four men, women, and children. An estimated two thousand black people were murdered around Shreveport, Louisiana. In Texas, white people killed one thousand black people between 1865 and 1868.

In May 1866 in Memphis, white residents went on a brutal rampage after black veterans forced local police to release a black prisoner. The city was already beset with economic difficulties and racial tensions caused in part by an influx of rural refugees. White people, led by Irish policemen, invaded the black section of Memphis and destroyed hundreds of homes, cabins, and shacks as well as churches and schools. Forty-six black people and two white men died.

On July 30, 1866, in New Orleans, white people—angered that black men were demanding political rights—assaulted black people on the street and in a convention hall. City policemen, who were mostly Confederate veterans, shot down the black delegates as they fled in panic waving white flags in a futile attempt to surrender. Thirty-four black people and three of their white allies died. Federal troops eventually arrived and stopped the bloodshed. General Philip H. Sheridan characterized the riot as "an absolute massacre."

Little was done to stem the violence. Most Union troops had been withdrawn from the South and demobilized after the war. The Freedmen's Bureau was usually unwilling and unable to protect the black population. Black people left to defend themselves were usually in no position to retaliate. Instead, they sometimes attempted to bring the perpetrators to justice. In Orangeburg, South Carolina, armed black men brought three white men to the local jail who had been wreaking violence in the community. In Holly Springs, Mississippi, a posse of armed black men apprehended a white man who had murdered a freedwoman.

For black people, the system of justice was thoroughly unjust. Although black people could now testify against white people in a court of law, southern juries remained

Black and white land-grant colleges stressed training in agriculture and industry. In this late-nineteenth-century photograph, Hampton Institute students learn milk production. The men are in military uniforms, which was typical for males at these colleges. Military training was a required part of the curriculum.
Courtesy of Hampton University Archives

all white and refused to convict white people charged with harming black people. In Texas in 1865 and 1866, five hundred white men were indicted for murdering black people. Not one was convicted.

The Crusade for Political and Civil Rights

In October 1864 in Syracuse, New York, 145 black leaders gathered in a national convention. Some of the century's most prominent black men and women attended, including Henry Highland Garnet, Frances E. W. Harper, William Wells Brown, Francis L. Cardozo, Richard H. Cain, Jonathan J. Wright, and Jonathan C. Gibbs. They embraced the basic tenets of the American political tradition and proclaimed that they expected to participate fully in it.

Anticipating a future free of slavery, Frederick Douglass optimistically declared "that we hereby assert our full confidence in the fundamental principles of this government . . . the great heart of this nation will ultimately concede us our just claims, accord us our rights, and grant us our full measure of citizenship under the broad shield of the Constitution."

Even before the Syracuse gathering, northern Republicans met in Union-controlled territory around Beaufort, South Carolina, and nominated the state's delegates to the 1864 Republican national convention. Among those selected were Robert Smalls and Prince Rivers, former slaves who had exemplary records with the Union Army. The probability of black participation in postwar politics seemed promising indeed.

But northern and southern white leaders who already held power would largely determine whether black Americans would gain any political power or acquire the same rights as white people. As the Civil War ended, President Lincoln was more concerned with restoring the seceded states to the Union than in opening political doors for black people. Yet Lincoln suggested that at least some black men deserved the right to vote. On April 11, 1865, he wrote, "I would myself prefer that [the vote] were now conferred on the very intelligent, and on those who serve our cause as soldiers." Three days later Lincoln was assassinated.

Presidential Reconstruction under Andrew Johnson

Vice President Andrew Johnson then became president and initially seemed inclined to impose stern policies on the white South while befriending the freedmen. He announced that "treason must be made odious, and traitors must be punished and impoverished." In 1864 he had told black people, "I will be your Moses, and lead you through the Red Sea of War and Bondage to a fairer future of Liberty and Peace." Nothing proved to be further from the truth. Andrew Johnson was no friend of black Americans.

Born poor in eastern Tennessee and never part of the southern aristocracy, Johnson strongly opposed secession and was the only senator from the seceded states to remain loyal to the Union. He had nonetheless acquired five slaves and the conviction that black people were so thoroughly inferior that white men must forever govern them. In 1867 Johnson argued that black people could not exercise political power and they had "less capacity for government than any other race of people. No independent government of any form has ever been successful in their hands. On the contrary, wherever they have been left to their own devices they have shown a constant tendency to relapse into barbarism."

Johnson quickly lost his enthusiasm for punishing traitors. Indeed, he began to placate white Southerners. In May 1865 Johnson granted blanket amnesty and pardons to former Confederates willing to swear allegiance to the United States. The main exceptions were high former Confederate officials and those who owned property in excess of $20,000, a large sum at the time. Yet even these leaders could appeal for individual pardons. And appeal they did. By 1866 Johnson had pardoned more than seven thousand high-ranking former Confederates and wealthier Southerners. Moreover, he had restored land to those white people who had lost it to freedmen.

Johnson's actions blatantly encouraged those who had supported secession, owned slaves, and opposed the Union. He permitted longtime southern leaders to regain political influence and authority only months after the end of America's bloodiest conflict. As black people and radical Republicans watched in disbelief, Johnson appointed provisional governors in the former Confederate states. Leaders in those states then called constitutional conventions, held elections, and prepared to regain their place in the Union. Johnson merely insisted that each Confederate state formally accept the Thirteenth Amendment (ratified in December 1865, it outlawed slavery) and repudiate Confederate war debts.

The southern constitutional conventions gave no consideration to the inclusion of black people in the political system or to guaranteeing them equal rights. As one Mississippi delegate explained, "'Tis nature's law that the superior race must rule and rule they will."

Black Codes

After the election of state and local officials, white legislators gathered in state capitals across the South to determine the status and future of the freedmen. With little debate, the legislatures drafted the so-called black codes. Southern politicians gave no thought to providing black people with the political and legal rights associated with citizenship.

The black codes sought to ensure the availability of a subservient agricultural labor supply controlled by white people. They imposed severe restrictions on freedmen. Freedmen had to sign annual labor contracts with white landowners. South Carolina required black people who wanted to establish a business to purchase licenses costing from $10 to $100. The codes permitted black children ages two to twenty-one to be apprenticed to white people and spelled out their duties and obligations in detail. Corporal punishment was legal. Employers were designated "masters" and employees "servants." The black codes also restricted black people from loitering or vagrancy, using alcohol or firearms, hunting, fishing, and grazing livestock. The codes did guarantee rights that slaves had not possessed. Freedmen could marry legally, engage in contracts, purchase property, sue or be sued, and testify in court. But black people could not vote or serve on juries. The black codes conceded—just barely—freedom to black people.

Black Conventions

Alarmed by these threats to their freedom, black people met in conventions across the South in 1865 and 1866 to protest, appeal for justice, and chart their future. Men who had been free before the war dominated the conventions. Many were ministers, teachers, and artisans. Few had been slaves. Women and children also attended—as spectators, not delegates—but women often offered comments, suggestions, and criticism. These meetings were hardly militant or radical affairs. Delegates respectfully insisted that white people live up to the principles and rights embodied in the Declaration of Independence and the Constitution.

At the AME church in Raleigh, North Carolina, delegates asked for equal rights and the right to vote. At Georgia's convention they protested against white violence and appealed for leaders who would enforce the law without regard to color. "We ask not for a Black Man's Governor, nor a White Man's Governor, but for a People's Governor, who shall impartially protect the rights of all, and faithfully sustain the Union."

Delegates at the Norfolk meeting reminded white Virginians that black people were patriotic. "We are Americans. We know no other country. We love the land of our birth." But they protested that Virginia's black code caused "invidious political or legal distinctions, on account of color merely." They requested the right to vote and added that they might boycott the businesses of "those who deny to us our equal rights."

Two conventions were held in Charleston, South Carolina—one before and one after the black code was enacted. At the first, delegates stressed the "respect and affection" they felt toward white Charlestonians. They even proposed that only literate men be granted the right to vote if it were genuinely applied to both races. The second convention denounced the black code and insisted on its repeal. Delegates again asked for the right to vote and the right to testify in court. "These two things we deem necessary to our welfare and elevation." They also appealed for public schools and for "homesteads for ourselves and our children." White authorities ignored these and other black conventions and their petitions. Instead they were confident they had effectively relegated the freedmen to a subordinate role in society.

By late 1865 President Johnson's reconstruction policies had aroused black people. One black Union veteran summed up the situation. "If you call this Freedom, what do you call Slavery?" Republicans in Congress also opposed Johnson's policies toward the freedmen and the former Confederate states.

The Radical Republicans

Radical Republicans, as more militant Republicans were called, were especially disturbed that Johnson seemed to have abandoned the ex-slaves to their former masters. They considered white Southerners disloyal and unrepentant, despite their military defeat.

Moreover, radical Republicans—unlike moderate Republicans and Democrats—were determined to transform the racial fabric of American society by including black people in the political and economic system.

Among the most influential radical Republicans were Charles Sumner, Benjamin Wade, and Henry Wilson in the Senate and Thaddeus Stevens, George W. Julian, and James M. Ashley in the House. Few white Americans have been as dedicated to the rights of black people as these men. They had fought for the abolition of slavery. They were reluctant to compromise. They were honest, tough, and articulate but also abrasive, difficult, self-righteous, and vain. Black people appreciated them; many white people excoriated them. One black veteran wrote Charles Sumner in 1869, "Your name shall live in our hearts forever." A white Philadelphia businessman commented on Thaddeus Stevens, "He seems to oppose any measure that will not benefit the nigger."

Bearing a remarkable resemblance to a slave auction, this scene in Monticello, Florida, shows a black man auctioned off to the highest bidder shortly after the Civil War. Under the terms of most southern black codes, black people arrested and fined for vagrancy or loitering could be "sold" if they could not pay the fine. Such spectacles infuriated many Northerners and led to demands for more rigid Reconstruction policies.

The Granger Collection, New York

Radical Proposals

Stevens, determined to provide freedmen with land, introduced a bill in Congress in late 1865 to confiscate 400 million acres from the wealthiest 10 percent of Southerners and distribute it free to freedmen. The remaining land would be auctioned off in plots no larger than 500 acres. Few legislators supported the proposal. Even those who wanted fundamental change considered confiscation a gross violation of property rights.

Instead, radical Republicans supported voting rights for black men. They were convinced that black men—to protect themselves and to secure the South for the Republican Party—had to have the right to vote.

Moderate Republicans, however, found the prospect of black voting almost as objectionable as the confiscation of land. They preferred to build the Republican Party in the South by cooperating with President Johnson and attracting loyal white Southerners.

The thought of black suffrage appalled northern and southern Democrats. Most white Northerners—Republicans and Democrats—favored denying black men the right to vote in their states. After the war, proposals to guarantee the right to vote to black men were defeated in New York, Ohio, Kansas, and the Nebraska Territory. In the District of Columbia, a vote to permit black suffrage lost 6,951 to 35. However, five New England states as well as Iowa, Minnesota, and Wisconsin did allow black men to vote.

As much as they objected to black suffrage, most white Northerners objected even more strongly to defiant white Southerners. Journalist Charles A. Dana described the attitude of many Northerners. "As for negro suffrage, the mass of Union men in the Northwest do not care a great deal. What scares them is the idea that the rebels are all to be let back . . . and made a power in government again, just as though there had been no rebellion."

In December 1865 Congress created the Joint Committee on Reconstruction to determine whether the southern states should be readmitted to the Union. The committee investigated southern affairs and confirmed reports of widespread mistreatment of black people and white arrogance.

The Freedmen's Bureau Bill and The Civil Rights Bill

In early 1866 Senator Lyman Trumball, a moderate Republican from Illinois, introduced two major bills. The first was to provide more financial support for the Freedmen's Bureau and extend its authority to defend the rights of black people.

The second proposal was the first civil rights bill in American history. It made any person born in the United States a citizen (except Indians) and entitled them to rights protected by the U.S. government. Black people would possess the same legal rights as white people. The bill was clearly intended to invalidate the black codes.

Johnson's Vetoes

Both measures passed in Congress with nearly unanimous Republican support. President Johnson vetoed them. He claimed that the bill to continue the Freedmen's Bureau would greatly expand the federal bureaucracy and permit too "vast a number

FEDERAL RECONSTRUCTION LEGISLATION, 1865–1867	
1865	Freedmen's Bureau established
1865	Thirteenth Amendment passed and ratified
1866	Freedmen's Bureau Bill and the Civil Rights Act of 1866 passed over Johnson's veto
1866	Fourteenth Amendment passed (ratified 1868)
1867	Reconstruction Acts passed over Johnson's veto

of agents" to exercise arbitrary power over the white population. He insisted that the civil rights bill benefited black people at the expense of white people. "In fact, the distinction of race and color is by the bill made to operate in favor of the colored and against the white race."

The Johnson vetoes stunned Republicans. Although he had not meant to, Johnson drove moderate Republicans into the radical camp and strengthened the Republican Party. The president did not believe Republicans would oppose him to support the freedmen. He was wrong. Congress overrode both vetoes. The Republicans broke with Johnson in 1866, defied him in 1867, and impeached him in 1868 (failing to remove him from office by only one vote in the Senate).

THE FOURTEENTH AMENDMENT

To secure the legal rights of freedmen, Republicans passed the Fourteenth Amendment. This amendment fundamentally changed the Constitution by compelling states to accept their residents as citizens and to guarantee that their rights as citizens would be safeguarded.

Its first section guaranteed citizenship to every person born in the United States. This included virtually every black person. It made each person a citizen of the state in which he or she resided. It defined the specific rights of citizens and then protected those rights against the power of state governments. Citizens had the right to due process (usually a trial) before they could lose their life, liberty, or property.

> All persons born or naturalized in the United States, and subject to the jurisdiction thereof, are citizens of the United States and of the State wherein they reside. No State shall make or enforce any law which shall abridge the privileges or immunities of citizens of the United States; nor shall any State deprive any person of life, liberty, or property, without due process of law; nor deny to any person within its jurisdiction the equal protection of the laws.

Eleven years after Chief Justice Roger Taney declared in the Dred Scott decision that black people were "a subordinate and inferior class of beings" who had "no rights that white people were bound to respect," the Fourteenth Amendment vested them with the same rights of citizenship other Americans possessed.

The amendment also threatened to deprive states of representation in Congress if they denied black men the vote. The end of slavery had also made obsolete the three-fifths clause in the Constitution, which had counted slaves as only three-fifths (or 60 percent) of a white person in calculating a state's population and determining the number of representatives each state was entitled to in the House of Representatives. Republicans feared that southern states would count black people in their populations without permitting them to vote, thereby gaining more representatives than those states had had before the Civil War. The amendment mandated that the number of representatives each state would be entitled to in Congress (including northern states) would be reduced if that state did not allow adult males to vote.

Democrats almost unanimously opposed the Fourteenth Amendment. Andrew Johnson denounced it, although he had no power to prevent its adoption. Southern states refused to ratify it except for Tennessee. Women's suffragists felt badly betrayed because the amendment limited suffrage to males. Despite this opposition, the amendment was ratified in 1868.

Radical Reconstruction

By 1867 radical Republicans in Congress had wrested control over Reconstruction from Johnson, and they then imposed policies that brought black men into the political system as voters and officeholders. It was a dramatic development, second in importance only to emancipation and the end of slavery.

Republicans swept the 1866 congressional elections despite the belligerent opposition of Johnson and the Democrats. With two-thirds majorities in the House and Senate, Republicans easily overrode presidential vetoes. Two years after the Civil War ended, Republicans dismantled the state governments established in the South under President Johnson's authority. They instituted a new Reconstruction policy.

Republicans passed the First Reconstruction Act over Johnson's veto in March 1867. It divided the South into five military districts, each under the command of a general (see Map 12–2). Military personnel would protect lives and property while new civilian governments were formed. Elected delegates in each state would draft a new constitution and submit it to the voters.

Universal Manhood Suffrage

The Reconstruction Act stipulated that all adult males in the states of the former Confederacy were eligible to vote, except for those who had actively supported the Confederacy or were convicted felons. Once each state had formed a new government and approved the Fourteenth Amendment, it would be readmitted to the Union with representation in Congress.

The advent of radical Reconstruction was the culmination of black people's struggle to gain legal and political rights. Since the 1864 black national convention in Syracuse and the meetings and conventions in the South in 1865 and 1866, black leaders had argued that one of the consequences of the Civil War should be the inclusion of black men in the body politic. The achievement of that goal was due to their

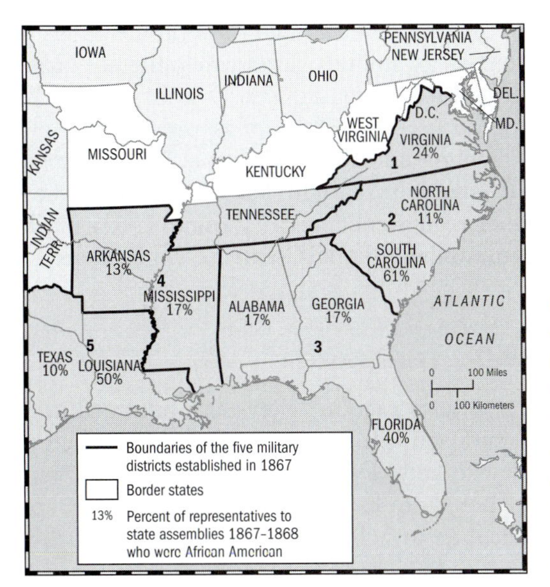

MAP 12–2 Congressional Reconstruction. Under the terms of the First Reconstruction Act of 1867, the former Confederate states (except Tennessee) were divided into five military districts and placed under the authority of military officers. Commanders in each of the five districts were responsible for supervising the reestablishment of civilian governments in each state.

persistent and persuasive efforts, the determination of radical Republicans, and, ironically, the obstructionism of Andrew Johnson who had played into their hands.

Black Politics

Full of energy and enthusiasm, black men and women rushed into the political arena in the spring and summer of 1867. Although women could not vote, they joined men at the meetings, rallies, parades, and picnics that accompanied political organizing in the South. For many former slaves, politics became as important as the church and religious activities. Black people flocked to the Republican Party and the new Union Leagues.

The Union Leagues had been established in the North during the Civil War, but they expanded across the South as quasi-political organizations in the late 1860s. The Leagues were social, fraternal, and patriotic groups in which black people often, but not always, outnumbered white people. League meetings featured ceremonies, rituals, initiation rites, and oaths. They gave people an opportunity to sharpen leadership skills and gain an informal political education by discussing issues from taxes to schools.

Sit-Ins and Strikes

Political progress did not induce apathy and a sense of satisfaction and contentment among black people. Gaining citizenship, legal rights, and the vote generated more expectations and demands for advancement. For example, black people insisted on equal access to public transportation. After a Republican rally in Charleston, South Carolina, in April 1867, several black men staged a "sit-in" on a nearby horse-drawn streetcar before they were arrested. In Charleston, black people were permitted to ride only on the outside running boards of the cars. They wanted to sit on the seats inside. Within a month, due to the intervention of military authorities, the streetcar company gave in. Similar protests occurred in Richmond and New Orleans.

Black workers also struck across the South in 1867. Black longshoremen in New Orleans, Mobile, Savannah, Charleston, and Richmond walked off the job. Black laborers were usually paid less than white men for the same work, and this led to labor unrest during the 1860s and 1870s. Sometimes the strikers won, sometimes they lost. In 1869 a black Baltimore longshoreman, Isaac Myers, organized the National Colored Labor Union.

THE REACTION OF WHITE SOUTHERNERS

White Southerners grimly opposed radical Reconstruction. They were outraged that black people could claim the same legal and political rights they possessed. Such a possibility seemed preposterous to people who had an abiding belief in the absolute inferiority of black people. A statement by Benjamin F. Perry, whom Johnson had appointed provisional governor of South Carolina in 1865, captures the depth of this

With the adoption of radical Republican policies, most black men eagerly took part in political activities. Political meetings, conventions, speeches, barbecues, and other gatherings also attracted women and children.

Courtesy of the Library of Congress

racist conviction. "The African," Perry declared, "has been in all ages, a savage or a slave. God created him inferior to the white man in form, color and intellect, and no legislation or culture can make him his equal. . . . His hair, his form and features will not compete with the caucasian race, and it is in vain to think of elevating him to the dignity of the white man. God created differences between the two races, and nothing can make him equal."

Some white people, taking solace in their belief in the innate inferiority of black people, concluded they could turn black suffrage to their advantage. White people, they assumed, should easily be able to control and manipulate black voters just as they had controlled black people during slavery. White Southerners who believed this, however, were destined to be disappointed, and their disappointment would turn to fury.

TIMELINE

AFRICAN-AMERICAN EVENTS	NATIONAL EVENTS
1862	
March 1862 The beginning of the Port Royal Experiment in South Carolina	**February 1862** Julia Ward Howe publishes the first version of "Battle Hymm of the Republic" in the "Atlantic Monthly" **July 1862** Morrell Land-Grant College Act signed into law by Abraham Lincoln
1864	
October 1864 Black national convention in Syracuse, New York	**November 1864** Abraham Lincoln reelected
1865	
January 1865 General Sherman's Special Field Order #15	**April 1865** Abraham Lincoln is assassinated; Andrew Johnson succeeds to presidency
March 1865 Freedmen's Bureau established	**May 1865** Andrew Johnson begins presidential Reconstruction
Sept.–Nov. 1865 Black codes enacted	**June–August 1865** Southern state governments are reorganized
	December 1865 Thirteenth Amendment to the Constitution is ratified

continued

AFRICAN-AMERICAN EVENTS	NATIONAL EVENTS
1866	
February 1866 Southern Homestead Act **March 1866** President Johnson's vetoes of bill to extend the Freedman's Bureau and the Civil Rights bill **April 1866** Override of Johnson's veto of the Civil Rights bill by Congress **May 1866** Memphis riot **July 1866** New Freedmen's Bureau bill enacted by Congress over Johnson's veto; New Orleans Riot	**November 1866** Republican election victories produce greater than two-thirds majorities in House and Senate
1867	
Spring–Summer 1867 Union Leagues and the Republican Party organized in southern states	**March 1867** The first Reconstruction Act passes over President Johnson's veto The United States agrees to buy Alaska from Russia
1868	
	February 1868 House impeaches President Johnson **May 1868** Senate acquits Johnson by one vote **July 1868** Fourteenth Amendment to the Constitution is ratified **November 1868** Ulysses S. Grant elected president
1869	
1869 The National Colored Labor Union established under the leadership of Isaac Myers	**May 1869** Transcontinental railroad completed

Conclusion

Why were black Southerners able to gain citizenship and access to the political system by 1868? Most white Americans did not suddenly abandon 250 years of deeply ingrained beliefs that people of African descent were their inferiors. The advances that African Americans achieved fit into a series of complex political developments after the Civil

War. Black people themselves had fought and died to preserve the Union, and they had earned the grudging respect of many white people and the open admiration of others. Black leaders in meetings and petitions insisted that their rights be recognized.

White Northerners—led by the radical Republicans—were convinced that President Andrew Johnson had made a serious error in supporting policies that permitted white Southerners to retain pre–Civil War leaders while the black codes virtually made freedmen slaves again. Republicans were determined that white Southerners realize their defeat had doomed the prewar status quo. Republicans established a Reconstruction program to disfranchise key southern leaders while providing legal rights to freedmen. The right to vote, they reasoned, would give black people the means to deal more effectively with white Southerners while simultaneously strengthening the Republican Party in the South.

The result was to make the mid to late 1860s one of the few high points in African-American history. During this period, not only was slavery abolished, but black Southerners were able to organize schools and churches, and black people throughout the South acquired legal and political rights that would have been incomprehensible before the war. Yet black people did not stand on the brink of utopia. Most freedmen still lacked land and had no realistic hope of obtaining much if any of it. White violence and cruelty continued almost unabated across much of the South. Still, for millions of African Americans, the future looked more promising than it had ever before in American history.

Review Questions

1. How did freedmen define their freedom? What did freedom mean to ex-slaves? How did their priorities differ from those of African Americans who had been free before the Civil War?
2. What did the former slaves and the former slaveholders want after emancipation? Were these desires realistic? How did former slaves and former slaveholders disagree after the end of slavery?
3. Why did African Americans form separate churches, schools, and social organizations after the Civil War? What role did the black church play in the black community?
4. How effective was the Freedmen's Bureau? How successful was it in assisting ex-slaves to live in freedom?
5. Why did southern states enact black codes?
6. Why did radical Republicans object to President Andrew Johnson's Reconstruction policies? Why did Congress impose its own Reconstruction policies?
7. Why were laws passed to enable black men to vote?
8. Why did black men gain the right to vote but not possession of land?
9. Did congressional Reconstruction secure full equality for African Americans as American citizens?

Recommended Reading

Ira Berlin and Leslie Rowland, eds. *Families and Freedom: A Documentary History of African-American Kinship in the Civil War Era.* New York: Cambridge University Press, 1997. A collection of documents that conveys the aspirations and frustrations of freedmen.

W. E. B. Du Bois. *Black Reconstruction in America: An Essay toward a History of the Part Which Black Folk Played in the Attempt to Reconstruct Democracy in America, 1860–1880.* New York: Russell & Russell, 1935. A classic account of Reconstruction challenging the traditional interpretation that it was a tragic era marked by corrupt and inept black rule of the South.

Eric Foner. *Reconstruction: America's Unfinished Revolution, 1863–1877.* New York: Harper & Row, 1988. The best and most comprehensive account of Reconstruction.

Herbert G. Gutman. *The Black Family in Slavery and Freedom, 1750–1925.* New York: Oxford University Press, 1976. An illustration of how African-American family values and kinship ties forged in slavery endured after emancipation.

Steven Hahn. *A Nation under Our Feet: Black Political Struggles in the Rural South from Slavery to the Great Migration.* Cambridge, MA: Harvard University Press, 2003. In a sophisticated analysis, Hahn explores the ways in which African Americans conceived of themselves as political people and organized from slavery through Reconstruction and disfranchisement to the growth of Marcus Garvey's Universal Negro Improvement Association in the 1920s.

Tera W. Hunter. *To 'Joy My Freedom: Southern Black Women's Lives and Labors after the Civil War.* Cambridge, MA: Harvard University Press, 1997. An examination of the interior lives of black women, their work, social welfare, and leisure.

Gerald D. Jaynes. *Branches without Roots: Genesis of the Black Working Class in the American South, 1862–1882.* New York: Pantheon, 1986. The changes in work and labor in the aftermath of slavery.

Leon F. Litwack. *Been in the Storm Too Long: The Aftermath of Slavery.* New York: Alfred A. Knopf, 1979. A rich and detailed account of the transition to freedom largely based on recollections of former slaves.

• CHAPTER THIRTEEN •

THE MEANING OF FREEDOM

THE FAILURE OF RECONSTRUCTION

CONSTITUTIONAL CONVENTIONS

Black men as a group first entered politics as delegates to constitutional conventions in the southern states in 1867 and 1868. Each of the former Confederate states, except Tennessee, which had already been restored to the Union, elected delegates to these conventions. Most southern white men were Democrats. They boycotted these elections to protest both Congress's assumption of authority over Reconstruction and the extension of voting privileges to black men. Thus the delegates to the conventions that met to frame new state constitutions to replace those drawn up in 1865 under President Johnson's authority were mostly Republicans joined by a few conservative southern Democrats. The Republicans represented three constituencies. One consisted of white northern migrants who moved to the South in the wake of the war. They were disparagingly called carpetbaggers, because they were said to have arrived in the South with all their possessions in a single carpetbag. A second group consisted of native white Southerners, mostly small farmers in devastated upland regions of the South who hoped for economic relief from Republican governments. This group was known derogatorily as scalawags, or scoundrels, by other southern white people. African Americans made up the third and largest Republican constituency.

Of the 1,000 men elected as delegates to the ten state conventions, 265 were black. Black delegates were a majority only in the South Carolina and Louisiana conventions. In most states, including Alabama, Georgia, Mississippi, Virginia, North Carolina, Arkansas, and Texas, black men made up 10 percent to 20 percent of the delegates. At least 107 of the 265 had been born slaves; about 40 had served in the Union Army. Several were well-educated teachers and ministers; others were tailors, blacksmiths, barbers, and farmers. Most went on to hold other political offices in the years that followed.

These delegates produced impressive constitutions. Unlike previous state constitutions in the South, the new constitutions ensured that all adult males could vote, and except in Mississippi and Virginia, they did not disfranchise large numbers of former Confederates. They conferred broad guarantees of civil rights. In several states they provided the first statewide systems of public education. These constitutions were progressive, not radical. Black and white Republicans hoped to attract support from white Southerners for the new state governments these documents created by encouraging state support for private businesses, especially railroad construction.

Southern black men cast ballots for the first time in 1867 in the election of delegates to state constitutional conventions. The ballots were provided by the candidates or political parties, not by state or municipal officials. Most nineteenth-century elections were not by secret ballot.
The Granger Collection, New York

Elections

Elections were held in 1868 to ratify the new constitutions and elect officials. The white Democratic response varied. In some states, Democrats boycotted the elections. In others, they participated, but voted against ratification, and in still other states they supported ratification and attempted to elect as many Democrats as possible to office. Congress required only a majority of those voting—not a majority of all registered voters—to ratify the constitutions. In each state a majority of those voting eventually did vote to ratify, and in each state, black men were elected to political offices.

Black Political Leaders

Over the next decade, 1,465 black men held political office in the South. Although black leaders individually and collectively enjoyed significant political leverage, white Republicans dominated politics during Reconstruction. In general the number of

Table 13–1
African-American Population and Officeholding during Reconstruction in the States Subject to Congressional Reconstruction

	African-American Population in 1870	African Americans as Percentage of Total Population	Number of African-American Officeholders during Reconstruction
South Carolina	415,814	58.9	314
Mississippi	444,201	53.6	226
Louisiana	364,210	50.1	210
North Carolina	391,650	36.5	180
Alabama	475,510	47.6	167
Georgia	545,142	46.0	108
Virginia	512,841	41.8	85
Florida	91,689	48.7	58
Arkansas	122,169	25.2	46
Texas	253,475	30.9	46
Tennessee	322,331	25.6	20

Source: Eric Foner, *Freedom's Lawmakers: A Directory of Black Officeholders during Reconstruction* (1993), xiv; The Statistics of the Population of the United States, Ninth Census (1873), xvii.

black officials in a state reflected the size of that state's African-American population. Black people were a substantial majority of the population in just Mississippi and South Carolina, and most of the black officeholders came from those two states and Louisiana, where black people were a bare majority. In most states, such as Arkansas, North Carolina, Tennessee, and Texas where black people made up between 25 percent and 40 percent of the population, far fewer black men were elected to office (see Table 13–1).

Initially, black men chose not to run for the most important political offices because they feared their election would further alienate already angry white Southerners. But as white Republicans swept into office in 1868, black leaders reversed their strategy, and by 1870 black men had been elected to many key political positions. No black man was elected governor, but Lieutenant Governor P. B. S. Pinchback served one month (from December 1872 to January 1873) as governor in Louisiana after the white governor was removed from office. Blanche K. Bruce and Hiram Revels represented Mississippi in the U.S. Senate. Beginning with Joseph Rainey in 1870 in South Carolina, fourteen black men served in the U.S. House of Representatives during Reconstruction. Six men served as lieutenant governors. In Mississippi and South Carolina, a majority of the representatives in state houses were black men, and each of these states had two black speakers of the house in the 1870s. Jonathan J. Wright served seven years as a state supreme court justice in South Carolina. Four black men served as state superintendents of education, and Francis L. Cardozo served as South Carolina's secretary of state and then treasurer. During Reconstruction,

112 black state senators and 683 black representatives were elected. There were also 41 black sheriffs, 5 black mayors, and 31 black coroners. Tallahassee, Florida, and Little Rock, Arkansas, had black police chiefs.

Many of these men—by background, experience, and education—were well qualified. Others were not. Of the 1,465 black officeholders, at least 378 had been free before the Civil War, 933 were literate, and 195 were illiterate (we lack information about the remaining 337). Sixty-four had attended college or professional school. In fact, 14 of the leaders had been students at Oberlin College in Ohio, which began admitting both black and female students before the Civil War.

Black farmers and artisans—tailors, carpenters, and barbers—were well represented among those who held political office. There were also 237 ministers and 172 teachers. At least 129 had served in the Union Army, and 46 had worked for the Freedmen's Bureau.

Several black politicians were wealthy, and a few were former slave owners. Antoine Dubuclet, who became Louisiana's treasurer, had owned more than one hundred slaves and land valued at more than $100,000 before the Civil War. Former slave Ferdinand Havis became a member of the Arkansas House of Representatives. He owned a saloon, a whiskey business, and two thousand acres near Pine Bluff, where he became known as "the Colored Millionaire."

Although black men did not dominate any state politically, a few did dominate districts with sizable black populations. Before he was elected to the U.S. Senate, Blanche K. Bruce all but controlled Bolivar County, Mississippi, where he served as sheriff, tax collector, and superintendent of education. Former slave and Civil War hero Robert Smalls was the political "kingpin" in Beaufort, South Carolina. He served successively in the South Carolina house and senate, and in the U.S. House of Representatives. He was also a member of the South Carolina constitutional conventions in 1868 and 1895. He was a major figure in the Republican Party and served as customs collector in Beaufort from 1889 to 1913.

THE ISSUES

Many, but not all, black and white Republican leaders favored increasing the authority of state governments to promote the welfare of all the state's citizens. Before the Civil War, most southern states did not provide schools, medical care, assistance for the mentally impaired, or prisons. Such concerns—if attended to at all—were left to local communities or families.

Education and Social Welfare

Black leaders were eager to increase literacy and promote education among black people. Republican politicians created statewide systems of public education throughout the South. It was a difficult and expensive task, and the results were only a limited success. Schools had to be built, teachers employed, and textbooks provided. To pay for it, taxes were increased in states still reeling from the war.

In some communities and in many rural areas, schools were not built. In other places, teachers were not paid. Some people—black and white—opposed compulsory education laws, preferring to let parents determine whether their children should attend school or work to help the family. Some black leaders favored a poll tax on voting if the funds it brought in were spent on the schools. Thus, although Reconstruction leaders established a strong commitment to public education, the results they achieved were uneven.

Furthermore, white parents refused to send their children to integrated schools. Although no laws required segregation, public schools during and after Reconstruction were invariably segregated. Black parents were usually more concerned that their children should have schools to attend than whether the schools were integrated. New Orleans, however, was an exception; it provided integrated schools.

Reconstruction leaders also supported higher education. In 1872 Mississippi legislators took advantage of the 1862 federal Morrill Land-Grant Act, which provided states with funds for agricultural and mechanical colleges, to found the first historically black state university: Alcorn A&M College. Although the university was named after a white Republican governor, James L. Alcorn, former U.S. senator Hiram Revels was its first president. The South Carolina legislature created a similar college and attached it to the Methodist-sponsored Claflin University.

Black leaders in the state legislature compelled the University of South Carolina, which had been all white, to admit black students and hire black faculty. Many, but not all, of the white students and faculty left. Several black politicians enrolled in the law and medical programs at the university. Richard Greener, a black Harvard graduate, served on the university's faculty and was its librarian.

Despite the costs, Reconstruction leaders also created the first state-supported institutions for the insane, the blind, and the deaf in the South. Some southern states during Reconstruction began to offer medical care and public health programs. Orphanages were established. State prisons were built. Black leaders also supported revising state criminal codes, eliminating corporal punishment for many crimes, and reducing the number of capital crimes.

Civil Rights

Black politicians were often the victims of racial discrimination when they tried to use public transportation and accommodations such as hotels and restaurants. Rather than provide separate arrangements for black customers, white-owned businesses simply excluded black patrons. This was true in the North as well as the South. Robert Smalls, for example, the Civil War hero who had commandeered a Confederate supply ship to escape from Charleston in 1862 (see Chapter 11), was unceremoniously ejected from a Philadelphia streetcar in 1864. After protests, the company agreed to accept black riders. In Arkansas, Mifflin Gibbs and W. Hines Furbish successfully sued a local saloon after they had been denied service. In South Carolina, Jonathan J. Wright won $1,200 in a lawsuit against a railroad after he had purchased a first-class ticket but had been forced to ride in the second-class coach.

Black leaders were determined to open public facilities to all people, in the process revealing deep divisions between themselves and white Republicans. In several southern states they introduced bills to prevent proprietors from excluding black people from restaurants, barrooms, hotels, concert halls, and auditoriums, as well as railroad coaches, streetcars, and steamboats. Many white Republicans and virtually every Democrat attacked such proposals as efforts to promote social equality and gain access for black people to places where they were not welcome. The white politicians blocked these laws in most states. Only South Carolina—with a black majority in the house and many black members in the senate—enacted such a law, but it was not effectively enforced. In Mississippi, the Republican governor James L. Alcorn vetoed a bill to outlaw racial discrimination by railroads. In Alabama and North Carolina, civil rights bills were defeated, and Georgia and Arkansas enacted measures that encouraged segregation.

Economic Issues

Black politicians sought to promote economic development in general and for black people in particular. For example, white landowners sometimes arbitrarily fired black agricultural laborers near the end of the growing season and then did not pay them. Some of these landowners were dishonest, but others were in debt and could not pay their workers. To prevent such situations, black politicians secured laws that required laborers to be paid before the crop was sold or at the time when it was sold. Some black leaders who had been slaves also wanted to regulate the wages of laborers, but these proposals invariably failed because most Republicans did not believe states had the right to regulate wages and prices.

Legislators also enacted measures that protected the land and property of small farmers against seizure for nonpayment of debts. Black and white farmers who lost land, tools, animals, and other property because they could not pay their debts were unlikely ever to recover financially. "Stay laws" prohibited, or "stayed," authorities from taking property. Besides affording financial protection to hard-pressed poor farmers, Republicans hoped these laws would attract political support from white yeomen and draw them away from their attachment to the Democratic Party.

Land

Black leaders were unable to initiate programs that would provide land to landless black and white farmers. Many black and white political leaders believed the state had no right to distribute land. Again, South Carolina was the exception. Its legislature created a state land commission in 1869.

The commission could purchase and distribute land to freedmen. It also gave the freedmen loans on generous terms to pay for the land. Unfortunately, the commission was corrupt, inefficiently managed, and it had little fertile land to distribute. However, despite its many difficulties, the commission enabled more than fourteen thousand black families and a few white families to acquire land in South Carolina. Their descendants still possess some of this land today.

Although some black leaders were reluctant to use the states' power to distribute land, others had no qualms about raising property taxes so high that large landowners would be forced to sell some of their property to pay their taxes. Abraham Galloway of North Carolina explained, "I want to see the man who owns one or two thousand acres of land, taxed a dollar on the acre, and if they can't pay the taxes, sell their property to the highest bidder . . . and then we negroes shall become the land holders."

Business and Industry

Black and white leaders had an easier time enacting legislation to support business and industry. Like most Americans after the Civil War, Republicans believed that expanding the railroad network would stimulate employment, improve transportation, and generate prosperity. State governments approved the sale of bonds supported by the authority of the state to finance railroad construction. In Georgia, Alabama, Texas, and Arkansas, the railroad network did expand. But the bonded debt of these states soared and taxes increased to pay for it. Moreover, railroad financing was often corrupt. Most of the illegal money wound up in the pockets of white businessmen and politicians. Black politicians rarely had access to truly large financial transactions.

So attractive were business profits that some black political leaders formed corporations. They invested modest sums and believed—like so many capitalists—that the rewards outweighed the risks. In Charleston, twenty-eight black leaders (and two white politicians) formed a horse-drawn streetcar line they called the Enterprise Railroad to carry freight between the city wharves and the railroad terminal. Black leaders in South Carolina also created a company to extract the phosphate used for fertilizer from riverbeds and riverbanks in the low country. Neither business lasted long. Black men found it far more difficult than white entrepreneurs to finance their corporations.

Black Politicians: An Evaluation

Southern black political leaders on the state level did create the foundation for public education, for providing state assistance for the blind, deaf, and insane, and for reforming the criminal justice system. They tried, but mostly failed, to outlaw racial discrimination in public facilities. They encouraged state support for economic revival and expansion.

But black leaders could not create programs that significantly improved the lives of their constituents. Because white Republicans almost always outnumbered them, they could not enact an agenda of their own. Moreover, black leaders often disagreed among themselves about specific issues and programs. Class and prewar status frequently divided them. Those leaders who had not been slaves and had not been raised in rural isolation were less likely to be concerned with land and agricultural labor. More prosperous black leaders showed more interest in civil rights and encouraging business. Even when they agreed about the need for public education, black leaders often disagreed about how to finance it and whether or not it should be compulsory.

Republican Factionalism

Disagreements among black leaders paled in comparison to the internal conflicts that divided the Republican Party during Reconstruction. Black and white Republicans often disagreed on political issues and strategy, but the lack of party cohesion and discipline was even more harmful. The Republican Party in the South constantly split into factions as groups fought with each other. Most disagreements were over who should run for and hold political office.

During Reconstruction, hundreds of would-be Republican leaders—black and white—sought public offices. If they lost the Republican nomination in county or state conventions, they often bolted and formed a competing slate of candidates. Then Republicans ran against each other and against the Democrats in the general election. It was not a recipe for political success.

These bitter and angry contests were based less on race and issues than on the desperate desire to gain an office that would pay even a modest salary. Most black and white Republicans were not well off; public office assured them a modicum of economic security.

Ironically, these factional disputes led to a high turnover in political leadership and the loss of that very economic security. It was difficult for black leaders (and white leaders too) to be renominated and reelected to more than one or two terms. Few officeholders served three or four consecutive terms in the same office during Reconstruction. This made for inexperienced leadership and added to Republican woes.

Opposition

Even if black and Republican leaders had been less prone to internecine conflict and more effective in adopting a political platform, they might still have failed to sustain themselves for long. Most white Southerners led by conservative Democrats remained absolutely opposed to letting black men vote or hold office. As a white Floridian put it, "The damned Republican Party has put niggers to rule us and we will not suffer it." Of course, because black people voted did not mean they ruled during Reconstruction, but many white people failed to grasp that. Instead, for most white Southerners, the only acceptable political system was one that excluded black men and the Republican Party.

As far as most white people were concerned, the end of slavery and the enfranchisement of black men did not make black people their equals. They did not accept the Fourteenth Amendment. They attacked Republican governments and their leaders unrelentingly. White Southerners blamed the Republicans for an epidemic of waste and corruption in state government. But most of all, they considered it preposterous and outrageous that former slaves could vote and hold political office.

James S. Pike spoke for many white people when he ridiculed black leaders in the South Carolina House of Representatives in 1873:

> The body is almost literally a Black Parliament. . . . The Speaker is black, the Clerk is black, the door-keepers are black, the little pages are black, the chairman of the Ways and Means is black, and the chaplain is coal-black. At some of the desks sit colored men whose types it would be hard to find outside of Congo; whose costume, visages, attitudes, and expression only befit the forecastle of a buccaneer. It must be remembered, also, that these men, with not more than a half a dozen exceptions, have been themselves slaves, and that their ancestors were slaves for generations.

Pike's observations circulated widely in both North and South.

White Southerners were determined to rid themselves of Republicans and the disgrace of having to live with black men who possessed political rights. White Southerners would "redeem" their states by restoring white Democrats to power. This did not simply mean defeating black and white Republicans in elections; it meant removing them from any role in politics. White Southerners believed any means—fair or foul—were justified in exorcising this evil.

THE KU KLUX KLAN

If black men in politics was illegitimate—in the eyes of white Southerners—then it was acceptable to use violence to remove them. This thinking gave rise to militant terrorist organizations, such as the Ku Klux Klan, the Knights of the White Camellia, the White Brotherhood, and the Whitecaps. Threats, intimidation, beatings, rapes, and murder

Head Quarters "Klu Klux"
Blood! Blood!! Blood!!!
First Quarter Bloody Moon
April 27 1868

To H. C. Warmouth

Villain Beware Your doom is sealed—Death now awaites you. The Midnight Owl Screames,

Revenge! Revenges!! Revenge!!!

Klu Klux Klan

By Order of Grand Giant
Bloody Knights
Klu Klux Klan

Prepare Death now awaits you

The flowing white robes and cone-shaped headdresses associated with the Ku Klux Klan today are mostly a twentieth-century phenomenon. The Klansmen of the Reconstruction era, like these two men in Alabama in 1868, were well armed, disguised, and prepared to intimidate black and white Republicans. The note is a Klan death threat directed at Louisiana's first Republican governor, Henry C. Warmoth.

Rutherford B. Hayes Presidential Center (left); from the Henry Clay Warmoth Papers #752, Southern Historical Collection, Wilson Library, University of North Carolina at Chapel Hill (right)

would restore conservative white Democratic rule and force black people back into subordination.

The Ku Klux Klan was founded in Pulaski, Tennessee, in 1866. It was originally a social club for Confederate veterans who adopted secret oaths and rituals—similar to the Union Leagues, but with far more deadly results. One of the key figures in the Klan's rapid growth was former Confederate general Nathan Bedford Forrest, who became its grand wizard. The Klan drew its members from all classes of white society, not merely from among the poor. Businessmen, lawyers, physicians, and politicians were active in the Klan as well as farmers and planters.

The Klan and other terrorist organizations functioned mainly where black people were a large minority and where their votes could affect the outcome of elections. Klansmen virtually took over areas of western Alabama, northern Georgia, and Florida's panhandle. The Klan controlled the up country of South Carolina and the area around Mecklenburg County, North Carolina. However, in the Carolina and Georgia low country where there were huge black majorities, the Klan never appeared.

Although the Klan and similar societies were neither well organized nor unified, they did reduce support for the Republican Party and helped eliminate its leaders. Often wearing hoods and masks to hide their faces, white terrorists embarked on a campaign of violence rarely matched and never exceeded in American history.

Mobs of marauding terrorists beat and killed hundreds of black people—and many white people. Black churches and schools were burned. Republican leaders were routinely threatened and often killed. The black chairman of the Republican Party in South Carolina, Benjamin F. Randolph, was murdered as he stepped off a train in 1868. Black legislator Lee Nance and white legislator Solomon G. W. Dill were murdered in 1868 in South Carolina. In 1870 black lawmaker Richard Burke was killed in Sumter County, Alabama, because he was considered too influential among "people of his color."

As his wife looked on, Jack Dupree—a local Republican leader—had his throat cut and was eviscerated in Monroe County, Mississippi. In 1870 North Carolina senator John W. Stephens, a white Republican, was murdered. After Alabama freedman George Moore voted for the Republicans in 1869, Klansmen beat him, raped a girl who was visiting his wife, and attacked a neighbor. An Irish-American teacher and four black men were lynched in Cross Plains, Alabama, in 1870. Notorious Texas outlaw John Wesley Hardin openly acknowledged he had killed several black Texas state policemen.

White men attacked a Republican campaign rally in Eutaw, Alabama, in 1870 and killed four black men and wounded fifty-four other people. After three black leaders were arrested in 1871 in Meridian, Mississippi, for delivering what many white people considered inflammatory speeches, shooting broke out in the courtroom. The Republican judge and two of the defendants were killed, and in a wave of violence, thirty black people were murdered, including every black leader in the small community. In the same year, a mob of five hundred men broke into the jail in Union County, South Carolina, and lynched eight black prisoners who had been accused of killing a Confederate veteran.

Nowhere was the Klan more active and violent than in York County, South Carolina. Almost the entire adult white male population joined in threatening, attacking, and murdering the black population. Hundreds were beaten and at least eleven killed. Terrified families fled from their homes into the woods. Appeals for help were sent to Governor Robert K. Scott.

But Scott did not send aid. He had already sent the South Carolina militia into areas of Klan activity, and even more violence had resulted. The militia was made up mostly of black men, and white terrorists retaliated by killing militia officers. Scott could not send white men to York County because most of them sympathized with the Klan. Thus Republican governors like Scott responded ineffectually. Republican-controlled legislatures passed anti-Klan measures that made it illegal to appear in public in disguises and masks, and they strengthened laws against assault, murder, and conspiracy. But enforcement was weak.

A few Republican leaders did deal harshly and effectively with terrorism. Governors in Tennessee, Texas, and Arkansas declared martial law and sent in hundreds of well-armed white and black men to quell the violence. Hundreds of Klansmen were arrested, many fled, and three were executed in Arkansas. But when Governor William W. Holden of North Carolina sent the state militia after the Klan, he succeeded only in provoking an angry reaction. Subsequent Klan violence in ten counties helped Democrats carry the 1870 legislative elections, and the North Carolina legislature then removed Holden from office.

Outnumbered and outgunned, black people in most areas did not retaliate against the Klan, and the Klan was rarely active where black people were in a majority and prepared to defend themselves. In the cause of white supremacy, the Klan usually attacked those who could not defend themselves.

The West

During the 1830s the U.S. government forced five tribes—the Cherokee, Chickasaw, Choctaw, Creek, and Seminole—from their southern homelands to Indian territory in what is now Oklahoma. By 1860 Native Americans held 7,367 African Americans in slavery. Many of the Indians fought for the Confederacy during the Civil War. Following the war, the former slaves encountered nearly as much violence and hostility from Native Americans as they did from southern white people. Indians were reluctant to share their land with freedmen, and they vigorously opposed policies that favored black voting rights.

Gradually and despite considerable Indian prejudice, some African Americans managed to acquire tribal land. Also, the Creeks and the Seminoles permitted former

Federal Reconstruction Legislation: 1868–1875

1869	Fifteenth Amendment passed (ratified 1870)
1870	Enforcement Act passed
1871	Ku Klux Klan Act passed
1875	Civil Rights Act of 1875 passed

slaves to take part in tribal government. Black men served in both houses of the Creek legislature—the House of Warriors and the House of Kings. An African American, Jesse Franklin, served as a justice on the Creek tribal court in 1876. In contrast, the Chickasaw and Choctaw were absolutely opposed to making concessions to freed people, and thus the U.S. government ordered federal troops onto Chickasaw and Choctaw lands to protect the former slaves.

Elsewhere on the western frontier, black people struggled for legal and political rights and periodically participated in territorial governments. In 1867 two hundred black men voted—although white men protested—in the Montana territorial election. In the Colorado territory, William Jefferson Hardin, a barber, campaigned with other black men for the right to vote, and they persuaded 137 African Americans (91 percent of Colorado's black population) to sign a petition in 1865 to the territorial governor appealing for an end to a white-only voting provision. In 1867 black men in Colorado finally did gain the right to vote. Hardin later moved to Cheyenne and was elected in 1879 to the Wyoming territorial legislature.

The Fifteenth Amendment

The federal government under Republican domination tried to protect black voting rights and defend Republican state governments in the South. In 1869 Congress passed the Fifteenth Amendment, which was ratified in 1870. It stipulated that a person could not be deprived of the right to vote because of race: "The right of citizens of the United States to vote shall not be denied or abridged by the United States or by any State on account of race, color, or previous condition of servitude." Black people, abolitionists, and reformers hailed the amendment as the culmination of the crusade to end slavery and give black people the same rights as white people.

Northern black men were the amendment's immediate beneficiaries because before its adoption, black men could vote in only eight northern states. Yet to the disappointment of many, the amendment said nothing about women voting and did not outlaw poll taxes, literacy tests, and property qualifications that could disfranchise citizens.

The Enforcement Acts

In direct response to the terrorism in the South, Congress passed the Enforcement Acts in 1870 and 1871, and the federal government expanded its authority over the states. The 1870 act outlawed disguises and masks and protected the civil rights of citizens. The 1871 act—known as the Ku Klux Klan Act—made it a federal offense to interfere with an individual's right to vote, hold office, serve on a jury, or enjoy equal protection of the law. Those accused of violating the act would be tried in federal court. For extreme violence, the act authorized the president to send in federal troops and suspend the writ of habeas corpus. (Habeas corpus is the right to be brought before a judge and not be arrested and jailed without cause.)

Black congressmen, who had long advocated federal action against the Klan, endorsed the Enforcement Acts. Representative Joseph Rainey of South Carolina wanted to suspend the Constitution to protect citizens. "I desire that so broad and liberal a construction be placed on its provisions, as will insure protection to the humblest citizen. Tell me nothing of a constitution which fails to shelter beneath its rightful power the people of a country."

Armed with this new legislation, the Justice Department and Attorney General Amos T. Ackerman moved vigorously against the Klan. Hundreds of Klansmen were arrested—seven hundred in Mississippi alone. Faced with a full-scale rebellion in late 1871 in South Carolina's up country, President Ulysses S. Grant declared martial law in nine counties, suspended the writ of habeas corpus, and sent in the U.S. Army. Mass arrests and trials followed, but federal authorities permitted many Klansmen to confess and thereby escape prosecution. The government lacked the human and financial resources to bring hundreds of men to court for lengthy trials. Some white men were tried, mostly before black juries, and were imprisoned or fined. Comparatively few Klansmen, however, were punished severely, especially considering the enormity of their crimes.

The North Loses Interest

Although the federal government did reduce Klan violence for a time, white Southerners remained convinced that white supremacy must be restored and Republican governments overturned. Klan violence did not overthrow any state governments, but it gravely undermined freedmen's confidence in the ability of these governments to protect them. Meanwhile, radical Republicans in Congress grew frustrated that the South and especially black people continued to demand so much of their time and attention year after year. There was less and less sentiment in the North to continue support for the freedmen and involvement in southern affairs.

Many Republicans in the North lost interest in issues and principles and became more concerned with elections and economic issues. By the mid-1870s there was more discussion in Congress of patronage, veterans' pensions, railroads, taxes, tariffs, the economy, and monetary policy than civil rights or the future of the South.

The American political system was awash in corruption by the 1870s, which detracted from concerns over the South. Although President Ulysses S. Grant was a man of integrity and honesty, many men in his administration were not. They were implicated in an assortment of scandals involving the construction of the transcontinental railroad, federal taxes on whiskey, and fraud within the Bureau of Indian Affairs. Nor was the dishonesty limited to Republicans. William Marcy "Boss" Tweed and the Democratic political machine that dominated New York City were riddled with corruption as well.

Many Republicans began to question the necessity for more moral, military, and political support for African Americans. Others, swayed by white Southerners' views of black people, began to doubt the wisdom of universal manhood suffrage. Many white people who had nominally supported black suffrage began to believe the exaggerated complaints about corruption among black leaders and the unrelenting claims that freedmen were incapable of self-government. Some white Northerners began to conclude that Reconstruction had been a mistake.

Economic conditions contributed to changing attitudes. A financial crisis—the Panic of 1873—sent the economy into a slump for several years. Businesses and financial institutions failed, unemployment soared, and prices fell sharply. In 1874 the Democrats recaptured a majority in the House of Representatives for the first time since 1860 and also took political control of several northern states.

The Freedmen's Bank

One of the casualties of the financial crisis was the Freedmen's Savings Bank, which failed in 1874. Founded in 1865 when hope flourished, the Freedmen's Savings and Trust Company had been chartered by Congress but was not connected to the Freedmen's Bureau. However, the bank's advertising featured pictures of Abraham Lincoln, and many black people assumed it was a federal agency. Freedmen, black veterans, black churches, fraternal organizations, and benevolent societies opened thousands of accounts in the bank. Most of the deposits totaled under $50, and some amounted to only a few cents.

Although the bank had many black employees, its board of directors consisted of white men. They unwisely invested the bank's funds in risky ventures, including Washington, D.C. real estate. With the Panic of 1873, the bank lost large sums in unsecured railroad loans. To restore confidence, its directors asked Frederick Douglass to serve as president and persuaded him to invest $10,000 of his own money to help shore up the bank. Douglass lost his money, and African Americans from across the South lost more than $1 million when the bank closed in June 1874. Eventually about half the depositors received three-fifths of the value of their accounts, but many African Americans believed the U.S. government owed them a debt. Well into the twentieth century, they wrote to Congress and the president to retrieve their hard-earned money.

The Civil Rights Act of 1875

Before Reconstruction finally expired, Congress made one final—some said futile—gesture to protect black people from racial discrimination when it passed the Civil Rights Act of 1875. Strongly championed by Senator Charles Sumner of Massachusetts, it was originally intended to open public accommodations including schools, churches, cemeteries, hotels, and transportation to all people regardless of race. It passed in the Republican-controlled Senate in 1874 shortly before Sumner died. But House Democrats held up passage until 1875 and deleted bans on discrimination in churches, cemeteries, and schools.

The act stipulated "That all persons . . . shall be entitled to the full and equal enjoyment of the accommodations, advantages, facilities, and privileges of inns, public conveyances on land or water, theaters, and other places of public amusement." After its passage, no attempt was made to enforce these provisions, and in 1883 the U.S. Supreme Court declared it unconstitutional. Justice Joseph Bradley wrote that the Fourteenth Amendment protected black people from discrimination by states but not by private businesses. Black newspapers likened the decision to the Dred Scott case a quarter century earlier.

As Reconstruction drew to an end in 1876, black men from across the country assembled in Nashville, Tennessee, for the Colored National Convention. They spent three days in April discussing their prospects for a future that did not look promising. Black and white Republican leaders had lost political control in each of the southern states except Florida, Louisiana, and South Carolina.
Corbis–NY

THE END OF RECONSTRUCTION

Reconstruction ended as it began—in violence and controversy. Democrats demanded "Redemption"—a word with biblical and spiritual overtones. They wanted southern states restored to conservative, white political control. By 1875 those Democrats had regained authority in all the former Confederate states except Mississippi, Florida, Louisiana, and South Carolina (see Map 13–1). Democrats had redeemed Tennessee in 1870 and Georgia in 1871. Democrats had learned two valuable lessons. First, few black men could be persuaded to vote for the Democratic Party—no matter how much white leaders wanted to believe former slaves were easy to manipulate. Second, intimidation and violence would win elections in areas where the number of black and white voters was nearly equal. The federal government had stymied Klan violence in 1871, but by the mid-1870s, the government had become reluctant to send troops to the South to protect black citizens.

Violent Redemption

In Alabama in 1874, black and white Republican leaders were murdered, and white mobs destroyed crops and homes. On Election Day in Eufaula, white men killed seven and injured nearly seventy unarmed black voters. Black voters were also driven from the polls in Mobile. Democrats won the election and redeemed Alabama.

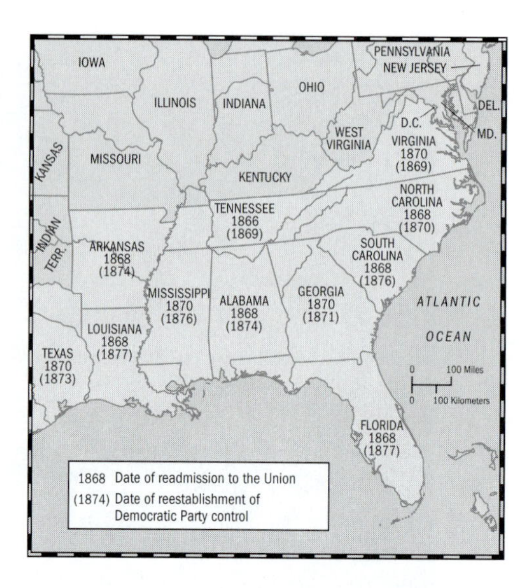

MAP 13–1 Dates of Readmission of Southern States to the Union and Reestablishment of Democratic Party Control. Once conservative white Democrats regained political control of a state government from black and white Republicans, they considered that state "redeemed." The first states the Democrats "redeemed" were Georgia, Virginia, and North Carolina. Louisiana, Florida, and South Carolina were the last. (Tennessee was not included in the Reconstruction process under the terms of the 1867 Reconstruction Act.)

White violence accompanied every election in Louisiana from 1868 to 1876. After Republicans and Democrats each claimed victory in the 1872 elections, black people seized the small town of Colfax along the Red River to protect themselves against a Democratic takeover. They held out for three weeks, and then on Easter Sunday in 1873, a well-armed white mob attacked the black defenders, killing 105 in the worst single day of bloodshed during Reconstruction. In 1874 the White League almost redeemed Louisiana in an astonishing wave of violence. Black people were murdered, courts were attacked, and white people refused to pay taxes to the Republican state government. Six white and two black Republicans were murdered at Coushatta. In September, President Grant finally sent federal troops to New Orleans after 3,500 White Leaguers attacked and nearly wiped out the black militia and the Metropolitan Police. But the stage had been set for the 1876 campaign.

The Shotgun Policy

In 1875 white Mississippians, no longer fearful the national government would intervene in force, declared open warfare on the black majority. The masks and hoods of the Klan were discarded. One newspaper publicly proclaimed that Democrats would carry the election, "peaceably if we can, forcibly if we must." Another paper carried a bold banner: "Mississippi is a white man's country, and by the eternal God we'll rule it."

White Mississippi unleashed a campaign of violence known as the "Shotgun Policy" that was extreme even for Reconstruction. Many Republicans fled and others were murdered. In late 1874 an estimated three hundred black people were hunted down outside Vicksburg after black men armed with inferior weapons had lost a "battle" with white men. In 1875 thirty teachers, church leaders, and Republican

Editorial cartoonist Thomas Nast chronicled the travails of freedmen during the twelve years of Reconstruction in the pages of *Harper's Weekly*. Here Nast deplores the violence and intimidation that accompanied the 1876 election campaign and questions the willingness of white Americans to respect the rights of black Americans.
Courtesy of the Library of Congress

officials were killed in Clinton. The white sheriff of Yazoo County, who had married a black woman and supported the education of black children, had to flee the state.

Mississippi governor Adelbert Ames appealed for federal help, but President Grant refused: "The whole public are tired out with these annual autumnal outbreaks in the South . . . [and] are ready now to condemn any interference on the part of the Government." No federal help arrived. The terrorism intensified, and many black voters went into hiding on Election Day, afraid for their lives and the lives of their families. Democrats redeemed Mississippi and prided themselves that they—a superior race representing the most civilized of all people—were back in control.

In Florida in 1876, white Republicans noted that support for black people in the South was fading. They nominated an all-white Republican slate and even refused to renominate black congressman Josiah Walls.

The Hamburg Massacre

South Carolina Democrats were divided between moderate and extreme factions, but they united to nominate former Confederate general Wade Hampton for governor after the Hamburg Massacre. The prelude to this event occurred on July 4, 1876—the nation's centennial—when two white men in a buggy confronted the black militia that was drilling on a town street in Hamburg, a small, mostly black town. Hot words were exchanged, and days later, Democrats demanded the militia be disarmed. White rifle club members from around the state arrived in Hamburg and attacked the armory, where forty black members of the militia defended themselves. The rifle companies brought up a cannon and reinforcements from nearby Georgia. After the militia ran low on ammunition, white men captured the armory. One white man was killed, twenty-nine black men were taken prisoner, and the other eleven fled. Five of the black men identified as leaders were shot down in cold blood. The rifle companies invaded and wrecked Hamburg. Seven white men were indicted for murder. All were acquitted.

The Hamburg Massacre incited South Carolina Democrats to imitate Mississippi's "Shotgun Policy." It also forced a reluctant President Grant to send federal troops to South Carolina. In the 1876 election campaign, hundreds of white men in red flannel shirts turned out on mules and horses to support Wade Hampton in his contest against incumbent Republican governor Daniel Chamberlain and his black and white allies. When Chamberlain and fellow Republicans tried to speak in Edgefield, they were ridiculed, threatened, and shouted down by six hundred Red Shirts, many of them armed.

Democrats attacked, beat, and killed black people to prevent them from voting. Democratic leaders instructed their followers to treat black voters with contempt. "In speeches to negroes you must remember that argument has no effect on them. They can only be influenced by their fears, superstition, and cupidity. . . . Treat them so as to show them you are a superior race and that their natural position is that of subordination to the white man."

As the election approached, black people in the up country of South Carolina knew it would be exceedingly dangerous if they tried to vote. But in the low country, black people went on the offensive and attacked Democrats. In Charleston, a white man was killed in a racial melee. At a campaign rally at Cainhoy, a few miles outside Charleston, armed black men killed five white men.

A few black men supported Wade Hampton and the Red Shirts. Hampton had a paternalistic view of black people and, although he considered them inferior to white people, promised to respect their rights. Martin Delany believed Hampton and the Democrats were more trustworthy than unreliable Republicans; Delany campaigned for Hampton and was later rewarded with a minor political post. A few genuinely conservative black men during Reconstruction also supported the Democrats and curried their favor and patronage. Most black people despised them. When one black man threw his support to the Democrats, his wife threw him and his clothes out, declaring she would prefer to "beg her bread" than live with a "Democratic nigger."

The "Compromise" of 1877

Threats, violence, and bloodshed accompanied the elections of 1876, but the results were confusing and contradictory. Samuel Tilden, the Democratic candidate, won the popular vote by more than 250,000, and he had a large lead over Republican Rutherford B. Hayes in the electoral vote. Hayes had won 167, but Tilden had 185, and the 20 remaining electoral college votes were in dispute. Both Democrats and Republicans claimed to have won in Florida, Louisiana, and South Carolina, the last three southern states that had not been redeemed. (There was also one contested vote from Oregon.) Whoever took the twenty electoral votes of the three contested states (and Oregon) would be the next president (see Map 13–2).

There was a prolonged controversy, and the constitutional crisis over the outcome of the 1876 election was not resolved until shortly before Inauguration Day in March 1877. Although not a formal compromise, an informal understanding ended the dispute. Democrats accepted a Hayes victory, but Hayes let southern Democrats know he would not support Republican governments in Florida, Louisiana, and South Carolina.

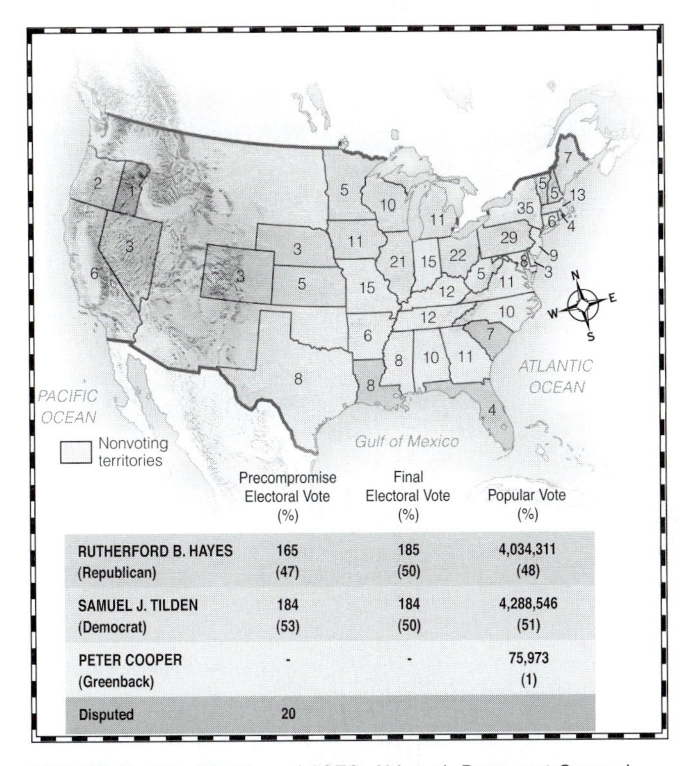

	Precompromise Electoral Vote (%)	Final Electoral Vote (%)	Popular Vote (%)
RUTHERFORD B. HAYES (Republican)	165 (47)	185 (50)	4,034,311 (48)
SAMUEL J. TILDEN (Democrat)	184 (53)	184 (50)	4,288,546 (51)
PETER COOPER (Greenback)	-	-	75,973 (1)
Disputed	20		

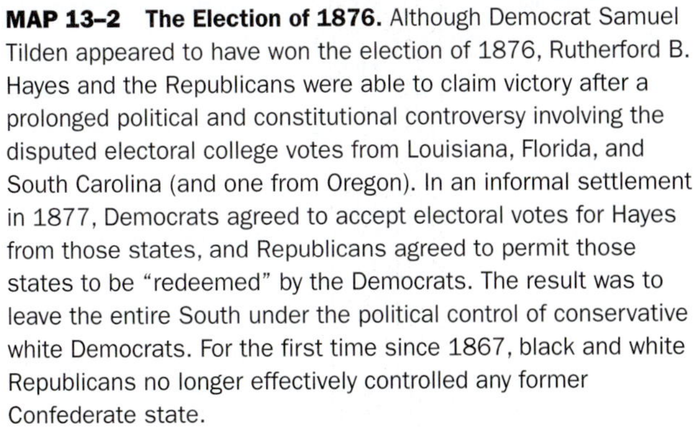

MAP 13–2 The Election of 1876. Although Democrat Samuel Tilden appeared to have won the election of 1876, Rutherford B. Hayes and the Republicans were able to claim victory after a prolonged political and constitutional controversy involving the disputed electoral college votes from Louisiana, Florida, and South Carolina (and one from Oregon). In an informal settlement in 1877, Democrats agreed to accept electoral votes for Hayes from those states, and Republicans agreed to permit those states to be "redeemed" by the Democrats. The result was to leave the entire South under the political control of conservative white Democrats. For the first time since 1867, black and white Republicans no longer effectively controlled any former Confederate state.

Hayes withdrew the last federal troops from the South, and the Republican administration in those states collapsed. Democrats immediately took control.

Redemption was now complete. Each of the former Confederate states was under the authority of white Democrats. Henry Adams, a black leader from Louisiana, explained what had happened. "The whole South—every state in the South had got into the hands of the very men that held us as slaves."

TIMELINE

AFRICAN-AMERICAN EVENTS	NATIONAL EVENTS
1865	
1865 The Freedmen's Savings Bank and Trust Company is established	**1865** Freedmen's Bureau established **1866** President Johnson vetoes Freedmen's Bureau Bill and civil rights bill. Congress overrides both vetoes Ku Klux Klan is founded in Pulaski, Tennessee
1867	
1867–1868 Ten southern states hold constitutional conventions **1867** Howard University established in Washington, DC **1868** Black political leaders elected to state and local offices across the South	**1867** Congress takes over Reconstruction and provides for universal manhood suffrage **1868** Fourteenth Amendment to the Constitution is ratified Ulysses S. Grant elected president
1869	
1870 Hiram R. Revels is elected to the U.S. Senate and Joseph H. Rainey is elected to the U.S. House of Representatives Congress passes the Enforcement Act	**1869** Knights of Labor founded in Philadelphia **1870** Fifteenth Amendment to the Constitution is ratified John D. Rockefeller incorporates Standard Oil Co. in Cleveland
1871	
1871 Congress passes the Ku Klux Klan Act	**1871** William Marcy "Boss" Tweed indicted for fraud in New York City Much of Chicago burns in a fire **1872** Ulysses S. Grant reelected Yellowstone National Park established

continued

AFRICAN-AMERICAN EVENTS	NATIONAL EVENTS
1873	
1873 The Colfax Massacre occurs in Louisiana	**1873** Financial panic and economic depression begin
1875	
1875 Blanche K. Bruce is elected to the U.S. Senate Congress passes the Civil Rights Act of 1875 Democrats regain Mississippi with the "Shotgun Policy" **1876** Hamburg Massacre occurs in South Carolina	**1875** Whiskey Ring exposes corruption in federal liquor tax collections **1876** Presidential election between Samuel J. Tilden and Rutherford B. Hayes is disputed Gen. George A. Custer and U.S. troops defeated by Sioux and Cheyenne in Battle of Little Big Horn
1877	
1877 Last federal troops withdrawn from South	**1877** The "Compromise of 1877" ends Reconstruction

CONCLUSION

The glorious hopes that emancipation and the Union victory in the Civil War had aroused among African Americans in 1865 appeared forlorn by 1877. To be sure, black people were no longer slave laborers or property. They lived in tightly knit families that white people no longer controlled. They had established hundreds of schools, churches, and benevolent societies. The Constitution now endowed them with freedom, citizenship, and the right to vote. Some black people had even acquired land.

But no one can characterize Reconstruction as a success. The epidemic of terror and violence made it one of the bloodiest eras in American history. Thousands of black people had been beaten, raped, and murdered since 1865, simply because they had acted as free people. Too many white people were determined that black people could not and would not have the same rights that white people enjoyed. White Southerners would not tolerate either the presence of black men in politics or white Republicans who accepted black political involvement. Gradually most white Northerners and even radical Republicans grew weary of intervening in southern affairs and became convinced again that black men and women were their inferiors and were not prepared to participate in government. Reconstruction, they concluded, had been a mistake.

Furthermore, black and white Republicans hurt themselves by indulging in fraud and corruption and by engaging in angry and divisive factionalism. But even if Republicans had been honest and united, white southern Democrats would never have accepted black people as worthy to participate in the political system.

Southern Democrats would accept black people in politics only if Democrats could control black voters. But black voters understood this, rejected control by former slave owners, and were loyal to the Republican Party—as flawed as it was.

But as grim a turn as life may have taken for black people by 1877, it would get even worse in the decades that followed.

Review Questions

1. What issues most concerned black political leaders during Reconstruction?
2. What did black political leaders accomplish and fail to accomplish during Reconstruction? What contributed to their successes and failures?
3. Were black political leaders unqualified to hold office so soon after the end of slavery?
4. To what extent did African Americans dominate southern politics during Reconstruction? Should we refer to this era as "Black Reconstruction"?
5. Why was it so difficult for the Republican Party to maintain control of southern state governments during Reconstruction?
6. What was "redemption"? What happened when redemption occurred? What factors contributed to redemption?
7. How did Reconstruction end?
8. How effective was Reconstruction in assisting black people to make the transition from slavery to freedom? How effective was it in restoring the southern states to the Union?

Recommended Reading

Eric Foner. *Freedom's Lawmakers: A Directory of Black Officeholders during Reconstruction.* New York: Oxford University Press, 1993. Biographical sketches of every known southern black leader during the era.

John Hope Franklin. *Reconstruction after the Civil War.* Chicago: University of Chicago Press, 1961. An excellent summary and interpretation of the postwar years.

William Gillette. *Retreat from Reconstruction, 1869–1879.* Baton Rouge: Louisiana State University Press, 1979. An analysis of how and why the North lost interest in the South.

Thomas Holt. *Black over White: Negro Political Leadership in South Carolina.* Urbana: University of Illinois Press, 1979. A masterful and sophisticated study of black leaders in the state with the most black politicians.

Michael L. Perman. *Emancipation and Reconstruction, 1862–1879.* Arlington Heights, IL: Harlan Davidson, 1987. Another excellent survey of the period.

Howard N. Rabinowitz, ed. *Southern Black Leaders of the Reconstruction Era.* Urbana: University of Illinois Press, 1982. A series of biographical essays on black politicians.

Frank A. Rollin. *Life and Public Services of Martin R. Delany.* Boston: Lee and Shepard, 1883. This is the first biography of a black leader by an African American. The author was Frances A. Rollin, but she used a male pseudonym.

Appendix

The Declaration of Independence

When in the course of human events it becomes necessary for one people to dissolve the political bands which have connected them with another and to assume, among the powers of the earth, the separate and equal station to which the laws of nature and of nature's God entitle them, a decent respect to the opinions of mankind requires that they should declare the causes which impel them to the separation.

We hold these truths to be self-evident, that all men are created equal; that they are endowed by their Creator with certain unalienable rights; that among these are life, liberty, and the pursuit of happiness. That, to secure these rights, governments are instituted among men, deriving their just powers from the consent of the governed; that, whenever any form of government becomes destructive of these ends, it is the right of the people to alter or to abolish it, and to institute a new government, laying its foundation on such principles, and organizing its powers in such form, as to them shall seem most likely to effect their safety and happiness. Prudence, indeed, will dictate that governments long established should not be changed for light and transient causes; and, accordingly, all experience hath shown that mankind are more disposed to suffer, while evils are sufferable, than to right themselves by abolishing the forms to which they are accustomed. But when a long train of abuses and usurpations, pursuing invariably the same object, evinces a design to reduce them under absolute despotism, it is their right, it is their duty, to throw off such government and to provide new guards for their future security. Such has been the patient sufferance of these colonies, and such is now the necessity which constrains them to alter their former systems of government. The history of the present King of Great Britain is a history of repeated injuries and usurpations, all having, in direct object, the establishment of an absolute tyranny over these States. To prove this, let facts be submitted to a candid world:

He has refused his assent to laws the most wholesome and necessary for the public good.

He has forbidden his governors to pass laws of immediate and pressing importance, unless suspended in their operation till his assent should be obtained; and, when so suspended, he has utterly neglected to attend to them.

He has refused to pass other laws for the accommodation of large districts of people, unless those people would relinquish the right of representation in the legislature, a right inestimable to them and formidable to tyrants only.

He has called together legislative bodies at places unusual, uncomfortable, and distant from the depository of their public records, for the sole purpose of fatiguing them into compliance with his measures.

He has dissolved representative houses, repeatedly for opposing, with manly firmness, his invasions on the rights of the people.

He has refused, for a long time after such dissolutions, to cause others to be elected; whereby the legislative powers, incapable of annihilation, have returned to the people at large for their exercise; the state remaining, in the meantime, exposed to all the danger of invasion from without and convulsions within.

He has endeavored to prevent the population of these States; for that purpose, obstructing the laws for naturalization of foreigners, refusing to pass others to encourage their migration hither, and raising the conditions of new appropriations of lands.

He has obstructed the administration of justice by refusing his assent to laws for establishing judiciary powers.

He has made judges dependent on his will alone for the tenure of their offices and the amount and payment of their salaries.

He has erected a multitude of new offices and sent hither swarms of officers to harass our people and eat out their substance.

He has kept among us, in time of peace, standing armies, without the consent of our legislatures.

He has affected to render the military independent of, and superior to, the civil power.

He has combined with others to subject us to a jurisdiction foreign to our Constitution and unacknowledged by our laws, giving his assent to their acts of pretended legislation—

For quartering large bodies of armed troops among us;

For protecting them, by mock trial, from punishment for any murders which they should commit on the inhabitants of these States;

For cutting off our trade with all parts of the world;

For imposing taxes on us without our consent;

For depriving us, in many cases, of the benefit of trial by jury;

For transporting us beyond seas to be tried for pretended offences;

For abolishing the free system of English laws in a neighboring province, establishing therein an arbitrary government, and enlarging its boundaries, so as to render it at once an example and fit instrument for introducing the same absolute rule into these colonies;

For taking away our charters, abolishing our most valuable laws, and altering, fundamentally, the powers of our governments.

For suspending our own legislatures and declaring themselves invested with power to legislate for us in all cases whatsoever.

He has abdicated government here by declaring us out of his protection and waging war against us.

He has plundered our seas, ravaged our coasts, burnt our towns, and destroyed the lives of our people.

He is, at this time, transporting large armies of foreign mercenaries to complete the works of death, desolation, and tyranny already begun with circumstances of cruelty and perfidy scarcely paralleled in the most barbarous ages, and totally unworthy the head of a civilized nation.

He has constrained our fellow citizens, taken captive on the high seas, to bear arms against their country, to become the executioners of their friends and brethren, or to fall themselves by their hands.

He has excited domestic insurrections amongst us and has endeavored to bring on the inhabitants of our frontiers, the merciless Indian savages, whose known rule of warfare is an undistinguished destruction of all ages, sexes, and conditions.

In every stage of these oppressions, we have petitioned for redress in the most humble terms; our repeated petitions have been answered only by repeated injury. A prince whose character is thus marked by every act which may define a tyrant is unfit to be the ruler of a free people.

Nor have we been wanting in attention to our British brethren. We have warned them, from time to time, of attempts made by their legislature to extend an unwarrantable jurisdiction over us. We have reminded them of the circumstances of our emigration and settlement here. We have appealed to their native justice and magnanimity, and we have conjured them, by the ties of our common kindred, to disavow these usurpations, which would inevitably interrupt our connections and correspondence. They, too, have been deaf to the voice of justice and consanguinity. We must, therefore, acquiesce in the necessity which denounces our separation, and hold them, as we hold the rest of mankind, enemies in war, in peace, friends.

We, therefore, the representatives of the United States of America, in general Congress assembled, appealing to the Supreme Judge of the world for the rectitude of our intentions, do, in the name and by the authority of the good people of these colonies, solemnly publish and declare, that these united colonies are, and of right ought to be, free and independent states: that they are absolved from all allegiance to the British Crown, and that all political connection between them and the state of Great Britain is, and ought to be, totally dissolved; and that, as free and independent states, they have full power to levy war, conclude peace, contract alliances, establish commerce, and to do all other acts and things which independent states may of right do. And, for the support of this declaration, with a firm reliance on the protection of Divine Providence, we mutually pledge to each other our lives, our fortunes, and our sacred honor.

Proposed clause on the slave trade omitted from the final draft of the Declaration

He has waged cruel war against human nature itself, violating its most sacred rights of life and liberty in the person of a distant people who never offended him; captivating and carrying them into slavery in another hemisphere, or to incur miserable death in their transportation thither. This piratical warfare, the opprobrium of infidel powers, is the warfare of the Christian king of Great Britain. Determined to keep open a market where men should be bought and sold, he has prostituted his negative for suppressing every legislative attempt to prohibit or restrain this execrable commerce.

Selected Articles and Amendments from The Constitution of the United States

The following selections from the Constitution are clauses and amendments that pertain specifically to the stature of African Americans within the United States.

The Preamble

We the people of the United States, in order to form a more perfect union, establish justice, insure domestic tranquility, provide for the common defense, promote the general welfare, and secure the blessings of liberty to ourselves and our posterity, do ordain and establish this Constitution for the United States of America. . . .

Article I

Section 2

3. Representatives and direct taxes shall be apportioned among the several States which may be included within this Union, according to their respective numbers, which shall be determined by adding to the whole number of free persons, including those bound to service for a term of years, and excluding Indians not taxed, three fifths of all other persons. The actual enumeration shall be made within three years after the first meeting of the Congress of the United States, and within every subsequent term of ten years, in such manner as they shall by law direct.

Section 9

1. The migration or importation of such persons as any of the States now existing shall think proper to admit, shall not be prohibited by the Congress prior to the year one thousand eight hundred and eight, but a tax or duty may be imposed on such importation, not exceeding ten dollars for each person.

Amendment XIII [Ratified December 6, 1865]

Section 1. Neither slavery nor involuntary servitude, except as punishment for crime whereof the party shall have been duly convicted, shall exist within the United States, or any place subject to their jurisdiction.

Section 2. Congress shall have power to enforce this article by appropriate legislation.

AMENDMENT XIV [RATIFIED JULY 9, 1868]

SECTION 1. All persons born or naturalized in the United States, and subject to the jurisdiction thereof, are citizens of the United States and of the State wherein they reside. No State shall make or enforce any law which shall abridge the privileges or immunities of citizens of the United States; nor shall any State deprive any person of life, liberty, or property, without due process of law; nor deny to any person within its jurisdiction the equal protection of the laws.

SECTION 2. Representatives shall be apportioned among the several States according to their respective numbers, counting the whole number of persons in each State, excluding Indians not taxed. But when the right to vote at any election for the choice of electors for President and Vice President of the United States, representatives in Congress, the executive and judicial officers of a State, or the members of the legislature thereof, is denied to any of the male inhabitants of such State, being twenty-one years of age, and citizens of the United States, or in any way abridged, except for participating in rebellion, or other crime, the basis of representation there shall be reduced in the proportion which the number of such male citizens shall bear to the whole number of male citizens twenty-one years of age in such State.

SECTION 3. No person shall be a senator or representative in Congress, or elector of President and Vice President, or hold any office, civil or military, under the United States, or under any State, who having previously taken an oath, as a member of Congress, or as an officer of the United States, or as a member of any State legislature, or as an executive or judicial officer of any State, to support the Constitution of the United States, shall have engaged in insurrection or rebellion against the same, or given aid or comfort to the enemies thereof. But Congress may by a vote of two thirds of each House, remove such disability.

SECTION 4. The validity of the public debt of the United States, authorized by law, including debts incurred for payment of pensions and bounties for services in suppressing insurrection or rebellion; shall not be questioned. But neither the United States nor any State shall assume or pay any debt or obligation incurred in aid of insurrection or rebellion against the United States, or any claim for the loss or emancipation of any slave; but all such debts, obligations, and claims shall be held illegal and void.

SECTION 5. The Congress shall have the power to enforce, by appropriate legislation, the provisions of this article.

AMENDMENT XV [RATIFIED FEBRUARY 30, 1870]

SECTION 1. The right of citizens of the United States to vote shall not be denied or abridged by the United States or by any State on account of race, color, or previous condition of servitude.

SECTION 2. The Congress shall have power to enforce this article by appropriate legislation.

AMENDMENT XXIV [RATIFIED JANUARY 23, 1964]

SECTION 1. The right of citizens of the United States to vote in any primary or other election for President or Vice President, for electors for President or Vice President, or for Senator or Representative in Congress, shall not be denied or abridged by the United States or any State by reason of failure to pay any poll tax or other tax.

SECTION 2. The Congress shall have power to enforce this article by appropriate legislation.

The Emancipation Proclamation

By the President of the United States of America

Whereas, on the twenty-second day of September, in the year of our Lord one thousand eight hundred and sixty-two, a proclamation was issued by the President of the United States, containing, among other things, the following, to wit:

> That on the first day of January, in the year of our Lord one thousand eight hundred and sixty-three, all persons held as slaves within any State or designated part of a State, the people whereof shall then be in rebellion against the United States, shall be then, thenceforward, and forever free; and the Executive Government of the United States, including the military and naval authority thereof, will recognize and maintain the freedom of such persons, and will do no act or acts to repress such persons, or any of them, in any efforts they may make for their actual freedom.
>
> That the Executive will, on the first day of January aforesaid, by proclamation, designate the States and parts of States, if any, in which the people thereof, respectively, shall then be in rebellion against the United States; and the fact that any State, or the people thereof, shall on that day be, in good faith, represented in the Congress of the United States by members chosen thereto at elections wherein a majority of the qualified voters of such State shall have participated, shall, in the absence of strong countervailing testimony, be deemed conclusive evidence that such State, and the people thereof, are not then in rebellion against the United States.

Now, therefore I, Abraham Lincoln, President of the United States, by virtue of the power in me vested as Commander-in-Chief, of the Army and Navy of the United States in time of actual armed rebellion against the authority and government of the United States, and as a fit and necessary war measure for suppressing said rebellion, do, on this first day of January, in the year of our Lord one thousand eight hundred and sixty-three, and in accordance with my purpose so to do publicly proclaimed for the full period of one hundred days, from the day first above mentioned, order and designate as the States and parts of States wherein the people thereof respectively, are this day in rebellion against the United States, the following, to wit:

Arkansas, Texas, Louisiana, (except the Parishes of St. Bernard, Plaquemines, Jefferson, St. John, St. Charles, St. James Ascension, Assumption, Terrebonne, Lafourche, St. Mary, St. Martin, and Orleans, including the City of New Orleans), Mississippi, Alabama, Florida, Georgia, South Carolina, North Carolina, and Virginia, (except the forty-eight counties designated as West Virginia, and also the counties of Berkley, Accomac, Northampton, Elizabeth City, York, Princess Ann, and Norfolk, including the cities of Norfolk and Portsmouth), and which excepted parts, are for the present, left precisely as if this proclamation were not issued.

And by virtue of the power, and for the purpose aforesaid, I do order and declare that all persons held as slaves within said designated States, and parts of States, are, and henceforward shall be free; and that the Executive government of the United States, including the military and naval authorities thereof, will recognize and maintain the freedom of said persons.

And I hereby enjoin upon the people so declared to be free to abstain from all violence, unless in necessary self-defense; and I recommend to them that, in all cases when allowed, they labor faithfully for reasonable wages.

And I further declare and make known, that such persons of suitable condition, will be received into the armed service of the United States to garrison forts, positions, stations, and other places, and to man vessels of all sorts in said service.

And upon this act, sincerely believed to be an act of justice, warranted by the Constitution, upon military necessity, I invoke the considerate judgment of mankind, and the gracious favor of Almighty God.

In witness whereof, I have hereunto set my hand and caused the seal of the United States to be affixed. Done at the City of Washington, this first day of January, in the year of our Lord one thousand eight hundred and sixty-three, and of the Independence of the United States of America the eighty-seventh.

By the President: Abraham Lincoln

William H. Seward, Secretary of State

KEY PROVISIONS OF THE CIVIL RIGHTS ACT OF 1964

AN ACT

To enforce the constitutional right to vote, to confer jurisdiction upon the district courts of the United States to provide injunctive relief against discrimination in public accommodations, to authorize the Attorney General to institute suits to protect constitutional rights in public facilities and public education, to extend the Commission on Civil Rights, to prevent discrimination in federally assisted programs, to establish a Commission on Equal Employment Opportunity, and for other purposes.

TITLE I—VOTING RIGHTS

SECTION 101. . . . (2) No person acting under color of law shall—

(A) In determining whether any individual is qualified under State law or laws to vote in any Federal election, apply any standard, practice, or procedure different from the standards, practices, or procedures applied under such law or laws to other individuals within the same county, parish, or similar political subdivision who have been found by State officials to be qualified to vote;

(B) deny the right of any individual to vote in any Federal election because of an error or omission on any record or paper relating to any application, registration, or other act requisite to voting, if such error or omission is not material in determining whether such individual is qualified under State law to vote in such election;

(C) employ any literacy test as a qualification for voting in any Federal election unless (i) such test is administered to each individual and is conducted wholly in writing, and (ii) a certified copy of the test and of the answers given by the individual is furnished to him within twenty-five days of the submission of his request made within the period of time during which records and papers are required to be retained and preserved . . .

TITLE II—INJUNCTIVE RELIEF AGAINST DISCRIMINATION IN PLACES OF PUBLIC ACCOMMODATION

SECTION 201. (a) All persons shall be entitled to the full and equal enjoyment of the goods, services, facilities, and privileges, advantages and accommodations of any place of public accommodation, as defined in this section, without discrimination or segregation on the ground of race, color, religion, or national origin. (b) Each of the following establishments which serves the public is a place of public accommodation within the meaning of this title if its operations effect commerce, or if discrimination or segregation by it is supported by State action:

(1) any inn, hotel, motel, or other establishment which provides lodging to transient guests, other than an establishment located within a building which contains not more than five rooms for rent or hire and which is actually occupied by the proprietor of such establishment as his residence;

(2) any restaurant, cafeteria, lunchroom, lunch counter, soda fountain, or other facility principally engaged in selling food for consumption on the premises, including, but not limited to, any such facility located on the premises of any retail establishment; or any gasoline station;

(3) any motion picture house, theater, concert hall, sports arena, stadium or other place of exhibition or entertainment;

(4) any establishment (A) (i) which is physically located within the premises of any establishment otherwise covered by this subsection, or (ii) within the premises of which is physically located any such covered establishment, and (B) which holds itself out as serving patrons of such covered establishment. . . .

(d) Discrimination or segregation by an establishment is supported by State action within the meaning of this title if such discrimination or segregation

(1) is carried on under color of any law, statute, ordinance, or regulation; or

(2) is carried on under color of any custom or usage required or enforced by officials of the State or political subdivision thereof; or

(3) is required by action of the State or political subdivision thereof. . . .

SECTION 202. All persons shall be entitled to be free, at any establishment or place, from discrimination or segregation of any kind on the ground of race, color, religion, or national origin, if such discrimination or segregation is or purports to be required by any law, statute, ordinance, regulation, rule, or order of a State or any agency or political subdivision thereof.

SECTION 203. No person shall (a) withhold, deny, or attempt to withhold or deny, or deprive or attempt to deprive, any person of any right or privilege secured by section 201 or 202, or (b) intimidate, threaten, or coerce, or attempt to intimidate, threaten, or coerce any person with the purpose of interfering with any right or privilege secured by section 201 or 202, or (c) punish or attempt to punish any person for exercising or attempting to exercise any right or privilege secured by section 201 or 202.

Title III—Desegregation of Public Facilities

Section 301. (a) Whenever the Attorney General receives a complaint in writing signed by an individual to the effect that he is being deprived of or threatened with the loss of his right to the equal protection of the laws, on account of his race, color, religion, or national origin, by being denied equal utilization of any public facility which is owned, operated, or managed by or on behalf of any State or subdivision thereof, other than a public school or public college as defined in section 401 of title IV hereof, and the Attorney General believes the complaint is meritorious and certifies that the signer or signers of such complaint are unable, in his judgment, to initiate and maintain appropriate legal proceedings for relief and that the institution of an action will materially further the orderly progress of desegregation in public facilities, the Attorney General is authorized to institute for or in the name of the United States a civil action in any appropriate district court of the United States against such parties and for such relief as may be appropriate. And such court shall have and shall exercise jurisdiction of proceedings instituted pursuant to this section. The Attorney General may implead as defendants such additional parties as are or become necessary to the grant of effective relief hereunder. . . .

Title VI—Nondiscrimination in Federally Assisted Programs

Section 601. No person in the United States shall, on the ground of race, color, or national origin, be excluded from participation in, be denied the benefits of, or be subjected to discrimination under any program or activity receiving Federal financial assistance.

Section 602. Each Federal department and agency which is empowered to extend Federal financial assistance to any program or activity, by way of grant, loan, or contract other than a contract of insurance or guaranty, is authorized and directed to effectuate the provisions of section 601 with respect to such program or activity by issuing rules, regulations, or orders of general applicability which shall be consistent with achievement of the objectives of the statute authorizing the financial assistance in connection with which the action is taken. No such rule, regulation, or order shall become effective unless and until approved by the President. Compliance with any requirement adopted pursuant to this section may be effected

> (1) by the termination of or refusal to grant or to continue assistance under such program or activity to any recipient as to whom there has been an express finding on the record, after opportunity for hearing, of a failure to comply with such requirement, but such termination or refusal shall be limited to the particular political entity, or part thereof, or other recipient as to whom such a finding has been made and, shall be limited in its effect to the particular program, or part thereof, in which such non-compliance has been so found . . .

TITLE VII—EQUAL EMPLOYMENT OPPORTUNITY . . .

Discrimination Because of Race, Color, Religion, Sex, or National Origin

SECTION 703. (a) it shall be an unlawful employment practice for an employer—

(1) to fail or refuse to hire or to discharge any individual, or otherwise to discriminate against any individual with respect to his compensation, terms, conditions, or privileges of employment, because of such individual's race, color, religion, sex, or national origin; or

(2) to limit, segregate, or classify his employees in any way which would deprive or tend to deprive any individual of employment opportunities or otherwise adversely affect his status as an employee, because of such individual's race, color, religion, sex, or national origin.

(b)it shall be an unlawful employment practice for an employment agency to fail or refuse to refer for employment, or otherwise to discriminate against, any individual because of his race, color, religion, sex, or national origin, or to classify or refer for employment any individual on the basis of his race, color, religion, sex, or national origin.

(c) it shall be an unlawful employment practice for a labor organization—

(1)to exclude or to expel from its membership, or otherwise to discriminate against, any individual because of his race, color, religion, sex, or national origin;

(2) to limit, segregate, or classify its membership, or to classify or fail or refuse to refer for employment any individual, in any way which would deprive or tend to deprive any individual of employment opportunities, or would limit such employment opportunities or otherwise adversely affect his status as an employee or as an applicant for employment, because of such individual's race, color, religion, sex, or national origin; or

(3) to cause or attempt to cause an employer to discriminate against an individual in violation of this section.

(d) It shall be an unlawful employment practice for any employer, labor organization, or joint labor-management committee controlling apprenticeship or other training or retraining, including on-the-job training programs to discriminate against any individual because of his race, color, religion, sex, or national origin in admission to, or employment in, any program established to provide apprenticeship or other training . . .

Other Unlawful Employment Practices

SECTION 704. (a) It shall be an unlawful employment practice for an employer to discriminate against any of his employees or applicants for employment, for an employment agency to discriminate against any individual, or for a labor organization to discriminate against any member thereof or applicant for membership, because he has opposed any practice made an unlawful employment practice by this title, or because he has made a charge, testified, assisted, or participated in any manner in an investigation, proceeding, or hearing under this title.

(b) It shall be an unlawful employment practice for an employer, labor organization, or employment agency to print or publish or cause to be printed or published any notice or advertisement relating to employment by such an employer or membership in or any classification or referral for employment by such a labor organization, or relating to any classification or referral for employment by such an employment agency, indicating any preference, limitation, specification, or discrimination, based on race, color, religion, sex, or national origin, except that such a notice or advertisement may indicate a preference, limitation, specification, or discrimination based on religion, sex, or national origin when religion, sex, or national origin is a bona fide occupational qualification for employment.

Equal Employment Opportunity Commission

SECTION 705. (a) There is hereby created a Commission to be known as the Equal Employment Opportunity Commission, which shall be composed of five members, not more than three of whom shall be members of the same political party, who shall be appointed by the President by and with the advice and consent of the Senate. One of the original members shall be appointed for a term of one year, one for a term of two years, one for a term of three years, one for a term of four years, and one for a term of five years, beginning from the date of enactment of this title, but their successors shall be appointed for terms of five years each, except that any individual chosen to fill a vacancy shall be appointed only for the unexpired term of the member whom he shall succeed. The President shall designate one member to serve as Chairman of the Commission, and one member to serve as Vice Chairman. The Chairman shall be responsible on behalf of the Commission for the administrative operations of the Commission, and shall appoint, in accordance with the civil service laws, such officers, agents, attorneys, and employees as it deems necessary to assist it in the performance of its functions and to fix their compensation in accordance with Classification Act of 1949, as amended. . . .

Key Provisions of the Voting Rights Act of 1965

An Act

To enforce the fifteenth amendment to the Constitution of the United States, and for other purposes.

Be it enacted by the Senate and House of Representatives of the United States of America in Congress assembled, That this Act shall be known as the "Voting Rights Act of 1965."

SECTION 2. No voting qualification or prerequisite to voting, or standard, practice, or procedure shall be imposed or applied by any State or political subdivision to deny or abridge the right of any citizen of the United States to vote on account of race or color.

SECTION 4. (a) To assure that the right of citizens of the United States to vote is not denied or abridged on account of race or color, no citizen shall be denied the right to vote in any Federal, State, or local election because of his failure to comply with any test or device in any State with respect to which the determinations have been made under subsection (b) . . . (1) demonstrate the ability to read, write, understand, or interpret any matter, (2) demonstrate any educational achievement or his knowledge of any particular subject, (3) possess good moral character, or (4) prove his qualifications by the voucher of registered voters or members of any other class. . . .

SECTION 10. (a) The Congress finds that the requirement of the payment of a poll tax as a precondition to voting (i) precludes persons of limited means from voting or imposes unreasonable financial hardship upon such persons as a precondition to their exercise of the franchise, (ii) does not bear a reasonable relationship to any legitimate State interest in the conduct of elections, and (iii) in some areas has the purpose or effect of denying persons the right to vote because of race or color. Upon the basis of these findings, Congress declares that the constitutional right of citizens to vote is denied or abridged in some areas by the requirement of the payment of a poll tax as a precondition to voting.

SECTION 11. (a) No person acting under color of law shall fail or refuse to permit any person to vote who is entitled to vote under any provision of this Act or is otherwise qualified to vote, or willfully fail or refuse to tabulate, count, and report such person's vote.

(b) No person, whether acting under color of law or otherwise, shall intimidate, threaten, or coerce, or attempt to intimidate, threaten, or coerce any person for voting or attempting to vote, or intimidate, threaten, or coerce, or attempt to intimidate, threaten, or coerce any person for urging or aiding any person to vote or attempt to vote, or intimidate, threaten, or coerce any person for exercising any powers or duties under section 3 (a), 6, 8, 9, 10, or 12 (e).

Additional Bibliography

Chapter 1 Africa

Prehistory, Egypt, and Kush

William Y. Adams, *Nubia—Corridor to Africa,* Princeton, NJ: Princeton University Press, 1984.

Martin Bernal. *Black Athena; The Afroasiatic Roots of Classical Civilization.* New Brunswick, NJ: Rutgers University, 1987.

Nicholas C. Grimal. *A History of Ancient Egypt.* Oxford, England: Blackwell, 1993.

Donald Johanson, Lenora Johanson, and Blake Edgar. *Ancestors: In Search of Human Origins.* New York: Villard Books, 1994.

Susan Kent. *Gender in African Prehistory.* Walnut Creek, CA: Altamira, 1998.

Mary R. Lefkowitz and Guy MacLean Rogers, eds. *Black Athena Revisited.* Chapel Hill, NC: University of North Carolina Press, 1996.

Michael Rice. *Egypt's Making: The Origins of Ancient Egypt, 5000–2000 B.C.* New York: Routledge, 1990.

Derek A. Welsby. *The Kingdom of Kush: The Napatan and Merotic Empires.* Princeton, NJ: Markus Wiener, 1998.

Western Sudanese Empires

Nehemiah Levtzion. *Ancient Ghana and Mali.* London: Methuen, 1973.

Nehemiah Levtzion and J. F. Hopkins, eds. *Corpus of Early Arabic Sources for West African History.* New York: Cambridge University Press, 1981.

Roland Oliver and Brian M. Fagan. *Africa in the Iron Age.* New York: Cambridge University Press, 1975.

Roland Oliver and Caroline Oliver, eds. *Africa in the Days of Exploration.* Englewood Cliffs, NJ: Prentice Hall, 1965.

J. Spencer Trimington. *A History of Islam in West Africa.* New York: Oxford University Press, 1962.

The Forest Region of the Guinea Coast

I. A. Akinjogbin. *Dahomey and Its Neighbors, 1708–1818.* New York: Cambridge University Press, 1967.

Daryll Forde, ed. *African Worlds.* New York: Oxford University Press, 1954.

Samuel Johnson. *History of the Yorubas.* Lagos: C.M.S., 1921.

Robert W. July. *Precolonial Africa.* New York: Scribner's, 1975.

Robin Law. *The Oyo Empire, c. 1600–c. 1836.* Oxford: Clarendon, 1977.

R. S. Rattray. *Ashanti.* Oxford: Clarendon, 1969.

Walter Rodney. *A History of the Upper Guinea Coast, 1545–1800.* Oxford: Clarendon, 1970.

Culture

Harold Courlander, ed. *A Treasury of African Folklore.* New York: Marlowe, 1996.

Susan Denyer. *African Traditional Architecture: An Historical and Geographical Perspective.* London: Heinemann, 1978.

Ruth Finnegan. *Oral Literature in Africa.* 1970; reprint, Nairobi: Oxford University Press, 1976.

Werner Gillon. *A Short History of African Art.* New York: Viking, 1984.

Paulin J. Hountondji. *African Philosophy: Myth and Reality.* Bloomington: University of Indiana Press, 1984.

John S. Mbiti. *An Introduction to African Religion.* London: Heinemann, 1975.

J. H. Kwabena Nketia. *The Music of Africa.* New York: Norton, 1974.

Oyekan Owomoyela. *Yoruba Trickster Tales.* Lincoln: University of Nebraska Press, 1977.

Chapter 2 Middle Passage

The Slave Trade in Africa

Bernard Lewis. *Race and Slavery in the Middle East: An Historical Enquiry.* New York: Oxford University Press, 1990.

Patrick Manning. *Slavery and African Life: Occidental, Oriental, and African Slave Trades.* New York: Cambridge University Press, 1990.

Suzanne Miers and Igor Kopytoff, eds. *Slavery in Africa.* Madison: University of Wisconsin Press, 1977.

Suzanne Miers and Richard Roberts. *The End of Slavery in Africa.* Madison: University of Wisconsin Press, 1988.

Claire C. Robertson and Martin A. Klein, eds. *Slavery in Africa.* Madison: University of Wisconsin Press, 1983.

Elizabeth Savage, ed. *The Human Commodity: Perspectives on the Trans-Saharan Slave Trade.* London: Frank Cass, 1992.

John K. Thornton. *The Kingdom of Kongo: Civil War and Transition, 1641–1718.* Madison: University of Wisconsin Press, 1983.

The Atlantic Slave Trade

Paul Edwards, ed. *Equiano's Travels.* London: Heinemann, 1967.

Herbert S. Klein. *The Middle Passage: Comparative Studies in the Atlantic Slave Trade.* Princeton, NJ: Princeton University Press, 1978.

Paul E. Lovejoy. *Africans in Bondage: Studies in Slavery and the Slave Trade.* Madison: University of Wisconsin Press, 1986.

Rosemarie Robotham, ed. *Spirits of the Passage: The Transatlantic Slave Trade in the Seventeenth Century.* New York: Simon & Schuster, 1997.

Lief Svalesen. *The Slave Ship Fredensborg.* Bloomington: Indiana University Press, 2000.

Hugh Thomas. *The Slave Trade: The Story of the Atlantic Slave Trade, 1440–1870.* New York: Simon & Schuster, 1997.

Vincent Bakpetu Thompson. *The Making of the African Diaspora in the Americas, 1441–1900.* New York: Longman, 1987.

John Vogt. *Portuguese Rule on the Gold Coast, 1469–1682.* Athens: University of Georgia Press, 1979.

James Walvin. *Making the Black Atlantic: Britain and the African Diaspora.* New York: Cassell, 2000.

The West Indies

Edward Brathwaite. *The Development of Creole Society in Jamaica, 1770–1820.* New York: Oxford University Press, 1971.

William Claypole and John Robottom. *Caribbean Story: Foundations.* Kingston: Longman, 1980.

Melville J. Herskovits. *The Myth of the Negro Past.* Boston: Beacon, 1941.

Clarence J. Munford. *The Black Ordeal of Slavery and Slave Trading in the French West Indies, 1625–1715.* Lewiston, NY: Mellen, 1991.

Keith Albert Sandiford. *The Cultural Politics of Sugar: Caribbean Slavery and Narratives of Colonialism.* New York: Cambridge University Press, 2000. The Granger Collection, New York.

Chapter 3 Black People in Colonial, North America

Colonial Society

Wesley Frank Craven. *The Southern Colonies in the Seventeenth Century, 1607–1689.* Baton Rouge: Louisiana State University Press, 1949.

Jack P. Greene. *Pursuits of Happiness: The Social Development of Early Modern British Colonies and the Formatiosn of American Culture.* Chapel Hill: University of North Carolina Press, 1988.

John J. McCusker and Russell R. Menard. *The Economy of British America, 1607–1789.* Chapel Hill: University of North Carolina Press, 1985.

Gary B. Nash. *Red, White, and Black: The Peoples of Early America,* 3d ed. Englewood Cliffs, NJ: Prentice Hall, 1992.

Origins of Slavery and Racism in the Western Hemisphere

David Brion Davis. *The Problem of Slavery in Western Culture.* Ithaca, NY: Cornell University Press, 1966.

Seymour Drescher. *From Slavery to Freedom: Comparative Studies of the Rise and Fall of Atlantic Slavery.* New York: New York University Press, 1999.

David Eltis. *The Rise of African Slavery in the Americas.* New York: Cambridge University Press, 2000.

Ronald Sanders. *Lost Tribes and Promised Lands: The Origins of American Racism.* Boston: Little, Brown, 1978.

Frank Tannenbaum. *Slave and Citizen: The Negro in the Americas.* New York: Knopf, 1946.

Betty Wood. *The Origins of American Slavery: Freedom and Bondage in the English Colonies.* New York: Hill and Wang, 1997.

The Chesapeake

Barbara A. Faggins. *Africans and Indians: An Afrocentric Analysis of Contacts between Africans and Indians in Colonial Virginia.* New York: Routledge, 2001.

Allan Kulikoff. *Tobacco and Slaves: The Development of Southern Cultures in the Chesapeake, 1680–1800.* Chapel Hill: University of North Carolina Press, 1986.

Gloria L. Main. *Tobacco Colony: Life in Early Maryland, 1650–1720.* Princeton, NJ: Princeton University Press, 1982.

Edmund S. Morgan. *American Slavery, American Freedom: The Ordeal of Colonial Virginia.* New York: Norton, 1975.

Isaac Rhys. *The Transformation of Virginia, 1740–1790.* New York: Norton, 1982.

Mechal Sobel. *The World They Made Together: Black and White Values in Eighteenth-Century Virginia.* Princeton, NJ: Princeton University Press, 1987.

The Carolina and Georgia Low Country

Judith Ann Carney. *Black Rice: The African Origins of Rice Cultivation in the Americas.* Cambridge, MA: Harvard University Press, 2001.

Alan Gallay. *The Indian Slave Trade: The Rise of the English Empire in the American South, 1670–1717.* New Haven: Yale University Press, 2002.

Daniel C. Littlefield. *Rice and Slaves: Ethnicity and the Slave Trade in Colonial South Carolina.* Baton Rouge: Louisiana State University Press, 1981.

Julia Floyd Smith. *Slavery and Rice Culture in Low Country Georgia, 1750–1860.* Knoxville: University of Tennessee Press, 1985.

Betty Wood. *Slavery in Colonial Georgia, 1730–1775.* Athens: University of Georgia Press, 1984.

The Northern Colonies

Lorenzo J. Greene. *The Negro in Colonial New England, 1620–1776.* 1942; reprint, New York: Atheneum, 1968.

Leslie M. Harris. *In the Shadow of Slavery: African Americans in New York City, 1626–1863.* Chicago: University of Chicago Press, 2003.

Graham R. Hodges. *Root and Branch: African Americans in New York and East Jersey, 1613–1863.* Chapel Hill: University of North Carolina Press, 1999.

Edgar J. McManus. *Black Bondage in the North.* Syracuse, NY: Syracuse University Press, 1973.

William D. Piersen. *Black Yankees: The Development of an Afro-American Subculture in Eighteenth-Century New England.* Amherst: University of Massachusetts Press, 1988.

Spanish Borderlands and Louisiana

Lynn Robinson Bailey. *Indian Slave Trade and the Southwest: A Study of Slave-Taking and the Traffic in Indian Captives.* Los Angeles: Westernlore, 1966.

Gwendolyn Midlo Hall. *Africans in Colonial Louisiana: The Development of Afro-Creole Culture in the Eighteenth Century.* Baton Rouge: Louisiana State University Press, 1992.

Thomas N. Ingersoll. *Mammon and Manon in Early New Orleans: The First Slave Society in the Deep South, 1718–1819.* Knoxville: University of Tennessee Press, 1999.

John L. Kessell. *Spain in the Southwest: A Narrative History of Colonial New Mexico, Arizona, Texas, and California.* Norman: University of Oklahoma Press, 2002.

Jane Landers. *Black Society in Spanish Florida.* Urbana: University of Illinois Press, 1999.

Michael M. Swann. *Migrants in the Mexican North: Mobility, Economy, and Society in a Colonial World.* Boulder, CO: Westview, 1989.

Quintard Taylor. *In Search of the Racial Frontier: African Americans in the American West, 1528–1990.* New York: Norton, 1998.

African-American Culture

John B. Boles. *Black Southerners, 1619–1869.* Lexington: University Press of Kentucky, 1983.

Joanne Brooks. *American Lazarus: Religion and the Rise of African American and Native American Literature.* New York: Oxford University Press, 2003.

Dickson D. Bruce. *The Origins of African American Literature, 1680–1865.* Charlottesville: University Press of Virginia, 2001.

Margaret W. Creel. *A Peculiar People: Slave Religion and Community Culture among the Gullahs.* New York: New York University Press, 1988.

Sylvaine A. Diouf. *Servants of Allah: African Muslims Enslaved in the Americas.* New York: New York University Press, 1998.

Michael Gomez. *Exchanging Our Country Marks: The Transformation of African Identities in the Colonial and Antebellum South.* Chapel Hill: University of North Carolina Press, 1998.

Melville J. Herskovits. *The Myth of the Negro Past.* 1941; reprint, Boston: Beacon, 1990.

Joseph E. Holloway, ed. *Africanisms in American Culture.* Bloomington: Indiana University Press, 1990.

Henry Mitchell. *Black Belief: Folk Beliefs of Blacks in America and West Africa.* New York: Harper & Row, 1975.

Sheila S. Walker, ed. *African Roots/American Culture: Africa and the Creation of the Americas.* Lanham: Rowman and Littlefield, 2001.

Joel Williamson. *New People: Miscegenation and Mulattoes in the United States.* New York: Free Press, 1980.

Black Women in Colonial America

Joan Rezner Gunderson, "The Double Bonds of Race and Sex: Black and White Women in a Colonial Virginia Parish," in Darlene Clark Hine, Wilma King, and Linda Reed, eds., *We Specialize in the Wholly Impossible: A Reader in Black Women's History*. Brooklyn, NY: Carlson, 1995.

Darlene Clark Hine and Kathleen Thompson. *A Shining Thread of Hope: The History of Black Women in America*. New York: Broadway, 1998, Chapter 1.

Jane Kamensky. *The Colonial Mosaic: American Women, 1600–1760: Rising Expectations from the Colonial Period to the American Revolution*. New York: Oxford University Press, 1995.

Jenny Sharpe. *Ghosts of Slavery: A Literary Archaeology of Black Women's Lives*. Minneapolis: University of Minnesota Press, 2003.

Resistance and Revolt

Herbert Aptheker. *American Negro Slave Revolts*. 1943; reprint, New York: International Publishers, 1974.

Thomas J. Davis. *A Rumor of Revolt: The "Great Negro Plot" in Colonial New York*. New York: Free Press, 1985.

Merton L. Dillon. *Slavery Attacked: Southern Slaves and Their Allies, 1619–1865*. Baton Rouge: Louisiana State University Press, 1990.

Eugene D. Genovese. *From Rebellion to Revolution: Afro-American Slave Revolts in the Making of the Modern World*. Baton Rouge: Louisiana State University Press, 1979.

Gerald W. Mullin. *Flight and Rebellion: Slave Resistance in Eighteenth-Century Virginia*. New York: Oxford University Press, 1972.

Michael Mullin. *Africa in America: Slave Aculturization and Resistance in the American South and the British Caribbean, 1736–1831*. Urbana: University of Illinois Press, 1992.

John K. Thornton. *African and Africans in the Making of the Atlantic World, 1400–1800*. New York: Cambridge University Press, 1992.

Chapter 4 Rising Expectations African Americans and the Struggle for Independence, 1763–1783

The Crisis of the British Empire

Stephen Conway. *The British Isles and the War of American Independence*. New York: Oxford University Press, 2000.

Edward Countryman. *The American Revolution*. New York: Hill and Wang, 1975.

Douglas E. Leach. *Roots of Conflict: British Armed Forces and Colonial Americans, 1677–1763*. Chapel Hill: University of North Carolina Press, 1986.

Pauline Maier. *From Resistance to Revolution: Colonial Radicals and the Development of American Opposition to Britain, 1765–1776*. New York: Knopf, 1972.

Peter David Garner Thomas. *Revolution in America: Britain and the Colonies, 1765–1776*. Cardiff, UK: University of Wales, 1992.

The Impact of the Enlightenment

Bernard Bailyn. *The Ideological Origins of the American Revolution*. Cambridge, MA: Harvard University Press, 1967.

Henry Steele Commager. *The Empire of Reason: How Europe Imagined and America Realized the Enlightenment*. Garden City, NY: Anchor, 1977.

Paul Finkelman. *Slavery and the Founders: Race and Liberty in the Age of Jefferson*. London: M. E. Sharpe, 1996.

J. G. A. Pocock. *The Machiavellian Moment: Florentine Political Thought and the Atlantic Republican Tradition*. Princeton, NJ: Princeton University Press, 1975.

Frank Shuffelton, ed. *The American Enlightenment*. Rochester, NY: University of Rochester Press, 1993.

African Americans and the American Revolution

Lerone Bennett Jr. *Before the Mayflower: A History of Black America*, 6th ed. Chicago: Johnson, 1987, Chapter 3.

Ira Berlin. "The Revolution in Black Life," in Alfred F. Young, ed., *The American Revolution: Explorations in the History of American Radicalism*. DeKalb: Northern Illinois University Press, 1976, 349–82.

Jeffrey J. Crow. *The Black Experience in Revolutionary North Carolina*. Raleigh: North Carolina Department of Cultural Resources, 1977.

Merton L. Dillon. *Slavery Attacked: Southern Slaves and Their Allies, 1619–1865*. Baton Rouge: Louisiana State University Press, 1990, Chapter 2.

Sylvia R. Frey. "Between Slavery and Freedom: Virginia Blacks in the American Revolution." *Journal of Southern History*, 69 (August 1983): 375–98.

Jack P. Greene. *All Men Are Created Equal: Some Reflections on the Character of the American Revolution*. Oxford: Clarendon, 1976.

Sidney Kaplan and Emma Nogrady Kaplan. *The Black Presence in the Era of the American Revolution*. Amherst: University of Massachusetts Press, 1989.

Peter Kolchin. *American Slavery, 1619–1877*. New York: Hill and Wang, 1993, Chapter 3.

Duncan McLeod. *Slavery, Race, and the American Revolution.* New York: Cambridge University Press, 1974.

Gary B. Nash. *Forging Freedom: The Formation of Philadelphia's Black Community, 1720–1840.* Cambridge, MA: Harvard University Press, 1988.

John W. Pulis. *Moving On: Black Loyalists in the Afro-Atlantic World.* New York: Garland, 1999.

Peter H. Wood. "'The Dream Deferred': Black Freedom Struggles on the Eve of White Independence," in Gary Y. Okihiro, ed., *In Resistance: Studies in African, Caribbean, and Afro-American History.* Amherst: University of Massachusetts Press, 1986, 166–87.

Antislavery and Emancipation in the North

Robin Blackburn. *The Overthrow of Colonial Slavery, 1776–1848.* New York: Verso, 1988, Chapter 3.

Merton L. Dillon. *The Abolitionists: The Growth of a Dissenting Minority.* New York: Norton, 1974, Chapter 1.

Dwight L. Dumond. *Antislavery: The Crusade for Freedom in America.* 1961; reprint, New York: Norton, 1966.

Joanne Pope Melish. *Disowning Slavery: Gradual Emancipation and "Race" in New England, 1780–1860.* Ithaca, NY: Cornell University Press, 1998.

Gary B. Nash. *Freedom by Degrees: Emancipation in Pennsylvania and Its Aftermath.* New York: Oxford University Press, 1991.

———. *Race and Revolution.* Madison, WI: Madison House, 1990.

James Brewer Stewart. *Holy Warriors: The Abolitionists and American Slavery.* Rev. ed. New York: Hill and Wang, 1997, Chapter 1.

Biography

Silvio A. Bedini. *The Life of Benjamin Banneker.* New York: Scribner, 1972.

Henry Louis Gates Jr. *The Trials of Phillis Wheatley.* New York: Basic Civitas Books, 2003.

William Henry Robinson. *Phillis Wheatley and Her Writings.* New York: Garland, 1984.

Chapter 5 African Americans in the New Nation, 1783–1820

Emancipation in the North

James D. Essig. *The Bonds of Wickedness: American Evangelicals against Slavery, 1770–1808.* Philadelphia: Temple University Press, 1982.

Joanne Pope Melish. *Disowning Slavery: Gradual Emancipation and "Race" in New England, 1780–1860.* Ithaca, NY: Cornell University Press, 1998.

Gary B. Nash and Jean R. Soderlund. *Freedom by Degrees: Emancipation in Pennsylvania and Its Aftermath.* New York: Oxford University Press, 1991.

Shane White. *Somewhat More Independent: The End of Slavery in New York City, 1770–1810.* Athens: University of Georgia Press, 1991.

Arthur Zilversmit. *The First Emancipation: The Abolition of Slavery in the North.* Chicago: University of Chicago Press, 1967.

Proslavery Forces

Paul Finkelman. *Slavery and the Founders: Race and Liberty in the Age of Jefferson.* Armonk: M. E. Sharpe, 1996.

Duncan J. MacLeod. *Slavery, Race, and the American Revolution.* New York: Cambridge University Press, 1974.

Donald G. Nieman. *Promises to Keep: African Americans and the Constitutional Order, 1776 to the Present.* New York: Oxford University Press, 1991.

Donald L. Robinson. *Slavery in the Structure of American Politics, 1765–1820.* New York: Harcourt Brace Jovanovich, 1971.

Larry E. Tise. *Proslavery: A History of the Defense of Slavery in America, 1701–1840.* Athens: University of Georgia Press, 1987.

Free Black Institutions and Migration Movements

Carol V. R. George. *Segregated Sabbaths: Richard Allen and the Emergence of Independent Black Churches, 1760–1840.* New York: Oxford University Press, 1973.

Eddie S. Glaude. *Exodus! Religion, Race, and Nation in Early Nineteenth-Century Black America.* Chicago: University of Chicago Press, 2000.

Sheldon H. Harris. *Paul Cuffe: Black America and the Africa Return.* New York: Simon & Schuster, 1972.

Leon Litwack. *North of Slavery: The Negro in the Free States.* Chicago: University of Chicago Press, 1961.

William A. Muraskin. *Middle-Class Blacks in a White Society: Prince Hall Freemasonry in America.* Berkeley: University of California Press, 1975.

Lamont D. Thomas. *Rise to Be a People: A Biography of Paul Cuffe.* Urbana: University of Illinois Press, 1986.

Julie Winch. *Philadelphia's Black Elite: Activism, Accommodation, and the Struggle for Autonomy,*

1787–1848. Philadelphia: Temple University Press, 1988.

———. *A Gentleman of Color: The Life of James Forten*. New York: Oxford University Press, 2002.

Carter G. Woodson. *The Education of the Negro Prior to 1861*. 1915; reprint, Brooklyn, NY: A&B Books, 1998.

The South

John Hope Franklin. *The Free Negro in North Carolina, 1790–1860*. 1943; reprint, New York: Russell and Russell, 1969.

Peter Kolchin. *American Slavery, 1619–1877*. New York: Hill and Wang, 1993.

John Chester Miller. *The Wolf by the Ears: Thomas Jefferson and Slavery*. 1977; reprint, Charlottesville: University Press of Virginia, 1991.

T. Stephen Whitman. *The Price of Freedom: Slavery and Manumission in Baltimore and Early National Maryland*. Lexington: University of Kentucky Press, 1997.

Slave Revolts, Resistance, and Escapes

Herbert Aptheker. *American Negro Slave Revolts*. 1943; reprint, New York: International, 1983.

Merton L. Dillon. *Slavery Attacked: Southern Slaves and Their Allies, 1619–1865*. Baton Rouge: Louisiana State University Press, 1990.

Eugene D. Genovese. *From Rebellion to Revolution: Afro-American Slave Revolts in the Making of the Modern World*. Baton Rouge: Louisiana State University Press, 1979.

John R. McKivigan and Stanley Harrold, eds. *Antislavery Violence: Sectional, Racial, and Cultural Conflict in Antebellum America*. Knoxville: University of Tennessee Press, 1999.

Gerald W. Mullin. *Flight and Rebellion: Slave Resistance in Eighteenth-Century Virginia*. New York: Oxford University Press, 1972.

James Sidbury. *Ploughshares into Swords: Race, Rebellion, and Identity in Gabriel's Virginia, 1730–1810*. New York: Cambridge University Press, 1998. The Library Company of Philadelphia.

Chapter 6 Life in the Cotton Kingdom

Slavery and Its Expansion

Stanley M. Elkins. *Slavery: A Problem in American Institutional and Intellectual Life*, 3d ed. Chicago: University of Chicago Press, 1976.

Eugene D. Genovese. *The Political Economy of Slavery: Studies in the Economy and Society of the Slave South*. 1961; reprint, New York: Random House, 1967.

Lewis C. Gray. *History of Agriculture in the Southern United States to 1860*. 1933; reprint, Clifton, NJ: A. M. Kelley, 1973.

Roger G. Kennedy. *Mr. Jefferson's Lost Cause: Land, Farmers, Slavery, and the Louisiana Purchase*. New York: Oxford University Press, 2003.

Larry Koger. *Black Slaveowners: Free Black Slave Masters in South Carolina, 1790–1860*. 1985; reprint, Columbia: University of South Carolina Press, 1994.

Donald P. McNeilly. *The Old South Frontier: Cotton Plantations and the Formation of Arkansas Society, 1819–1861*. Fayetteville: University of Arkansas Press, 2000.

John H. Moore. *The Emergence of the Cotton Kingdom in the Old Southwest*. Baton Rouge: Louisiana State University Press, 1988.

Larry Eugene Rivers. *Slavery in Florida: Territorial Days to Emancipation*. Gainsville: University Press of Florida, 2000.

Kenneth M. Stampp. *The Peculiar Institution: Slavery in the Antebellum South*. 1956; reprint, New York: Vintage Books, 1989.

Urban and Industrial Slavery

Ronald L. Lewis. *Coal, Iron, and Slaves: Industrial Slavery in Maryland and Virginia, 1715–1865*. Westport, CT: Greenwood, 1979.

Robert S. Starobin. *Industrial Slavery in the Old South*. New York: Oxford University Press, 1970.

Midori Takagi. *Rearing Wolves to Our Own Destruction: Slavery in Richmond, Virginia, 1782–1865*. Charlottesville: University Press of Virginia, 1999.

Richard C. Wade. *Slavery in the Cities: The South 1820–1860*. 1964; reprint, New York: Oxford University Press, 1967.

The Domestic Slave Trade

Frederic Bancroft. *Slave Trading in the Old South*. 1931; reprint, Columbia: University of South Carolina Press, 1996.

Walter Johnson. *Soul by Soul: Life inside the Antebellum Slave Market*. Cambridge, MA: Harvard University Press, 1999.

Michael Tadman. *Speculators and Slaves: Masters, Traders, and Slaves in the Old South*. 1989; reprint, Madison: University of Wisconsin Press, 1996.

The Slave Community

Ira Berlin. *Generations of Captivity: A History of African-American Slaves.* Cambridge, MA: Harvard University Press, 2003.

John W. Blassingame. *The Slave Community: Plantation Life in the Antebellum South,* 2d ed. New York: Oxford University Press, 1979.

Janet Duitsman Cornelius. *Slave Missions and the Black Church in the Antebellum South.* Columbia: University of South Carolina Press, 1999.

Wilma A. Dunaway. *The African-American Family in Slavery and Emancipation.* New York: Cambridge University Press, 2003.

Eugene D. Genovese. *Roll, Jordan, Roll: The World the Slave Made.* 1974; reprint, Vintage Books, 1976.

Herbert Gutman. *The Black Family in Slavery and Freedom.* 1976; reprint, Vintage Books, 1977.

Charles Joyner. *Down by the Riverside: A South Carolina Community.* Urbana: University of Illinois Press, 1984.

Ann Patton Malone. *Sweet Chariot: Slave Family and Household Structure in Nineteenth-Century Louisiana.* Chapel Hill: Univeristy of North Carolina Press, 1992.

Leslie Howard Owens. *This Species of Property: Slave Life and Culture in the Old South.* 1976; reprint, New York: Oxford University Press, 1977.

Todd L. Savitt. *Medicine and Slavery: The Diseases and Health Care of Blacks in Antebellum Virginia.* Urbana: University of Illinois Press, 1978.

Maria Jenkins Schwartz. *Born in Bondage: Growing Up Enslaved in the Antebellum South.* Cambridge, MA: Harvard University Press, 2000.

Enslaved Women

David Barry Gaspar and Darlene Clark Hine, eds. *More than Chattel: Black Women and Slavery in the Americas.* Bloomington: University of Indiana Press, 1996.

Darlene Clark Hine, Wilma King, and Linda Reed, eds. "*We Specialize in the Wholly Impossible": A Reader in Black Women's History.* Brooklyn, NY: Carlson, 1996.

Patricia Morton, ed. *Discovering the Women in Slavery: Emancipating Perspectives on the American Past.* Athens: University of Georgia Press, 1996.

Deborah Gray White. *Ar'n't I a Woman? Female Slaves in the Plantation South.* New York: Norton, 1985.

Jean Fagan Yellin. *Harriet Jacobs: A Life.* New York: Basic Civitas, 2003.

Slave Culture And Religion

John B. Boles, ed. *Masters and Slaves in the House of the Lord: Race and Religion in the American South, 1740–1870.* Lexington: University Press of Kentucky, 1988.

Janet Duitsman Cornelius. *When I Can Read My Title Clear: Literacy, Slavery, and Religion in the Antebellum South.* Columbia: University of South Carolina Press, 1991.

———. *Slave Missions and the Black Church in the Antebellum South.* Columbia: University of South Carolina Press, 1999.

Sharla M. Fett. *Working Cures: Healing, Health, and Power on Southern Slave Plantations.* Chapel Hill: University of North Carolina Press, 2002.

Lawrence W. Levine. *Black Culture and Black Consciousness: Afro-American Folk Thought from Slavery to Freedom.* New York: Oxford University Press, 1977.

Albert J. Raboteau. *Slave Religion: The "Invisible Institution" in the Antebellum South.* New York: Oxford University Press, 1978.

Chapter 7 Free Black People in Antebellum America

Community Studies

Tommy L. Bogger. *Free Blacks in Norfolk, Virginia, 1790–1860: The Darker Side of Freedom.* Charlottesville: University Press of Virginia, 1997.

Letitia Woods Brown. *Free Negroes in the District of Columbia, 1790–1846.* New York: Oxford University Press, 1972.

Leslie M. Harris. *In the Shadow of Slavery: African Americans in New York City, 1626–1863.* Chicago: University of Chicago Press, 2003.

Graham Russell Hodges. *Root and Branch: African Americans in New York and East Jersey, 1613–1863.* Chapel Hill: University of North Carolina Press, 1999.

———. *Slavery and Freedom in the Rural North: African Americans in Monmouth County, New Jersey, 1665–1865.* Madison, WI: Madison House, 1995.

James Oliver Horton. *Free People of Color: Inside the African-American Community.* Washington, DC: Smithsonian Institution Press, 1993.

James Oliver Horton and Lois E. Horton. *Black Bostonians: Family Life and Community Struggle in the Antebellum North.* New York: Holmes and Meier, 1979.

Gary B. Nash. *Forging Freedom: The Formation of Philadelphia's Black Community, 1720–1840.*

Cambridge, MA: Harvard University Press, 1988.

Christopher Phillips. *Freedom's Port: The African-American Community of Baltimore, 1790–1860.* Urbana: University of Illinois Press, 1997.

Bernard E. Powers Jr. *Black Charlestonians: A Social History, 1822–1885.* Fayetteville: University of Arkansas Press, 1994.

Harry Reed. *Platform for Change: The Foundations of the Northern Free Black Community, 1775–1865.* East Lansing: Michigan State University Press, 1994.

Judith Kelleher Schafer. *Becoming Free, Remaining Free: Manumission and Enslavement in New Orleans, 1846–1862.* Baton Rouge: Louisiana State University Press, 2003.

Julie Winch. *Philadelphia's Black Elite: Activism, Accommodation, and the Struggle for Autonomy, 1787–1848.* Philadelphia: Temple University Press, 1988.

State-Level Studies

Barbara Jeanne Fields. *Slavery and Freedom on the Middle Ground: Maryland during the Nineteenth Century.* New Haven, CT: Yale University Press, 1985.

John Hope Franklin. *The Free Negro in North Carolina, 1790–1860.* Chapel Hill: University of North Carolina Press, 1943.

John H. Russell. *The Free Negro in Viriginia, 1619–1865.* 1913; reprint, New York: Negro Universities Press, 1969.

H. E. Sterkx. *The Free Negro in Antebellum Louisiana.* Rutherford, NJ: Fairleigh Dickinson University Press, 1972.

Marina Wilkramangrake. *A World in Shadow—The Free Black in Antebellum South Carolina.* Columbia: University of South Carolina Press, 1973.

Race Relations

Francis D. Adams. *Alienable Rights: The Exclusion of African Americans in a White Man's Land, 1619–2000.* New York: Harper Collins, 2003.

Eugene H. Berwanger. *The Frontier against Slavery: Western Anti-Negro Prejudice and the Slavery Expansion Controversy.* Urbana: University of Illinois Press, 1967.

Phyllis F. Field. *The Politics of Race in New York: The Struggle for Black Suffrage in the Civil War Era.* Ithaca, NY: Cornell University Press, 1982.

Noel Ignatiev. *How the Irish Became White.* New York: Routledge, 1995.

David Roediger. *The Wages of Whiteness: Race and the Making of the American Working Class.* New York: Verso, 1991.

Joel Williamson. *New People: Miscegenation and Mulattoes in the United States.* New York: Free Press, 1980.

Carol Wilson. *Freedom at Risk: The Kidnapping of Free Blacks in America, 1780–1865.* Lexington: University Press of Kentucky, 1994.

Women and Family

Herbert G. Gutman. *The Black Family in Slavery and Freedom, 1750–1925.* New York: Pantheon Books, 1977.

Lynn M. Hudson. *The Making of "Mammy Pleasant": A Black Entrepreneur in Nineteenth-Century San Francisco.* Urbana: University of Illinois Press, 2003.

Jacqueline Jones. *Labor of Love, Labor of Sorrow: Black Women, Work and the Family from Slavery to the Present.* New York: Basic Books, 1985.

Suzanne Lebsock. *The Free Women of Petersburg: Status and Culture in a Southern Town, 1784–1860.* New York: Norton, 1984.

Bert James Loewenberg and Ruth Bogin, eds. *Black Women in Nineteenth-Century American Life.* University Park: Pennsylvania State University Press, 1976.

T. O. Madden Jr., with Ann L. Miller. *We Were Always Free: The Maddens of Culpeper County, Virginia, a 200 Year Family History.* New York: Norton, 1992.

Dorothy Sterling, ed. *We Are Your Sisters: Black Women in the Nineteenth Century.* New York: Norton, 1984.

Institutions and The Black Elite

Vincent P. Franklin. *The Education of Black Philadelphia.* Philadelphia: University of Pennsylvania Press, 1979.

Carlton Mabee. *Black Education in New York State.* Syracuse, NY: Syracuse University Press, 1979.

Eileen Southern. *The Music of Black America,* 2d ed. New York: Norton, 1983.

Loretta J. Williams. *Black Freemasonry and Middle-Class Realities.* Columbia: University of Missouri Press, 1980.

Chapter 8 Opposition to Slavery, 1800–1833

The Relationship Among Evangelicalism, Reform, and Abolitionism

Robert H. Abzug. *Cosmos Crumbling: American Reform and the Religious Imagination.* New York: Oxford University Press, 1994.

Gilbert H. Barnes. *The Antislavery Impulse, 1830–1844.* 1933; reprint, Gloucester, MA: Peter Smith, 1973.

Ronald G. Walters. *American Reformers, 1815–1860.* Baltimore: Johns Hopkins University Press, 1978.

American Abolitionism Before 1831

David Brion Davis. *The Problem of Slavery in the Age of Revolution.* Ithaca, NY: Cornell University Press, 1975.

———. *The Problem of Slavery in Western Culture.* Ithaca, NY: Cornell University Press, 1966.

———. *Slavery and Human Progress.* Ithaca, NY: Cornell University Press, 1987.

Merton L. Dillon. *The Abolitionists: The Growth of a Dissenting Minority.* New York: Norton, 1974.

———. *Benjamin Lundy and the Struggle for Negro Freedom.* Urbana: University of Illinois Press, 1966.

Richard S. Newman. *The Transformation of American Abolitionism: Fighting Slavery in the Early Republic.* Chapel Hill: University of North Carolina Press, 2002.

Sean Wilentz, ed. *David Walker's Appeal.* 1829; reprint, New York: Hill and Wang, 1995.

Slave Revolts and Conspiracies

Herbert Aptheker. *American Negro Slave Revolts.* 1943; new ed., New York: International Publishers, 1974.

Douglas R. Egerton. *Gabriel's Rebellion: The Virginia Slave Conspiracies of 1800 & 1802.* Chapel Hill: University of North Carolina Press, 1993.

———. *He Shall Go Out Free: The Lives of Denmark Vesey.* Madison, WI: Madison House, 1999.

David P. Feggus, ed. *The Impact of the Haitian Revolution on the Atlantic World.* Columbia: University of South Carolina Press, 2001.

Alfred N. Hunt. *Haiti's Influence on Antebellum America: Slumbering Volcano in the Caribbean.* Baton Rouge: Louisiana State University Press, 1988.

John Lofton. *Denmark Vesey's Revolt: The Slave Plot That Lit a Fuse to Fort Sumter.* Kent, OH: Kent State University Press, 1983.

Stephen B. Oates. *The Fires of the Jubilee: Nat Turner's Fierce Rebellion.* New York: Harper & Row, 1975.

Black Abolitionism and Black Nationalism

Eddie S. Glaude. *Exodus!: Religion, Race, and Nation in Early Nineteenth-Century Black America.* Chicago: Unversity of Chicago Press, 2000.

Leroy Graham. *Baltimore: Nineteenth-Century Black Capital.* Washington, DC: University Press of America, 1982.

Vincent Harding. *There Is a River: The Black Struggle for Freedom in America.* New York: Harcourt, Brace, Jovanovich, 1981.

Floyd J. Miller. *The Search for Black Nationality: Black Colonization and Emigration, 1787–1863.* Urbana: University of Illinois Press, 1975.

Marilyn Richardson. *Maria W. Stewart: America's First Black Woman Political Writer.* Bloomington: Indiana University Press, 1987.

Sterling Stuckey. *Slave Culture: Nationalist Theory and the Foundations of Black America.* New York: Oxford University Press, 1987.

Lamont D. Thomas. *Rise to Be a People: A Biography of Paul Cuffe.* Urbana: University of Illinois Press, 1986.

Julie Winch. *Philadelphia's Black Elite: Activism, Accommodation, and Struggle for Autonomy, 1787–1840.* Philadelphia: Temple University Press, 1988.

Chapter 9 Let Your Motto Be Resistance, 1833–1850

General Studies of the Antislavery Movement

Herbert Aptheker. *Abolitionism: A Revolutionary Movement.* Boston: Twayne, 1989.

Merton L. Dillon. *The Abolitionists: The Growth of a Dissenting Minority.* New York: Norton, 1974.

Lawrence J. Friedman. *Gregarious Saints: Self and Community in American Abolitionism, 1830–1870.* New York: Cambridge University Press, 1982.

Stanley Harrold. *American Abolitionists.* Harlow, England: Longman, 2001.

———. *The Rise of Aggressive Abolitionism: Addresses to the Slaves.* Lexington: University Press of Kentucky, 2004.

James Brewer Stewart. *Holy Warriors: The Abolitionists and American Slavery,* 2d ed. New York: Hill and Wang, 1997.

The Black Community

John Brown Childs. *The Political Black Minister: A Study in Afro-American Politics and Religion.* Boston: G. K. Hall, 1980.

Leonard P. Curry. *The Free Black in Urban America, 1800–1850: The Shadow of a Dream.* Chicago: University of Chicago Press, 1981.

Martin E. Dann. *The Black Press, 1827–1890.* New York: Capricorn, 1971.

James Oliver Horton and Lois E. Horton. *In Hope of Liberty: Culture, Community, and Protest among Northern Free Blacks, 1700–1860.* New York: Oxford University Press, 1997.

Patrick Rael. *Black Identity and Black Protest in the Antebellum North.* Chapel Hill: University of North Carolina Press, 2002.

David E. Swift. *Black Prophets of Justice: Activist Clergy before the Civil War.* Baton Rouge: Louisiana State University Press, 1989.

Black Abolitionists

Howard Holman Bell. *A Survey of the Negro Convention Movement, 1830–1861.* New York: Arno, 1969.

———, ed. *Minutes of the Proceedings of the National Negro Conventions, 1830–1864.* New York: Arno, 1969.

R. J. M. Blackett. *Building an Antislavery Wall: Blacks in the Atlantic Abolitionist Movement, 1830–1860.* Baton Rouge: Louisiana State University Press, 1983.

Women

Blanch Glassman-Hersh. *Slavery of Sex: Feminist-Abolitionists in Nineteenth-Century America.* Urbana: University of Illinois Press, 1978.

Darlene Clark Hine, ed. *Black Women in American History: From Colonial Times through the Nineteenth Century.* 4 vols. New York: Carlson, 1990.

Julie Roy Jeffrey. *The Great Silent Army of Abolitionism: Ordinary Women in the Antislavery Movement.* Chapel Hill: University of North Carolina Press, 1998.

Jean Fagan Yellin. *Women and Sisters: Antislavery Feminists in American Culture.* New Haven, CT: Yale University Press, 1990.

Biography

Catherine Clinton. *Harriet Tubman: The Road to Freedom.* New York: Little, Brown, 2003.

William S. McFeely. *Frederick Douglass.* New York: Simon & Schuster, 1991.

Nell Irvin Painter. *Sojourner Truth: A Life, A Symbol.* New York: Norton, 1996.

Joel Schor. *Henry Highland Garnet: A Voice of Black Radicalism in the Nineteenth Century.* Westport, CT: Greenwood, 1977.

James Brewer Stewart. *William Lloyd Garrison and the Challenge of Emancipation.* Arlington Heights, IL: Harlan Davidson, 1992.

Victor Ullman. *Martin R. Delany: The Beginnings of Black Nationalism.* Boston: Beacon, 1971.

Underground Railroad

Larry Gara. *The Liberty Line: The Legend of the Underground Railroad.* Lexington: University of Kentucky Press, 1961.

Stanley Harrold. *Subversives: Antislavery Community in Washington, D.C., 1828–1865.* Baton Rouge: Louisiana State University Press, 2003.

Wilbur H. Siebert. *The Underground Railroad from Slavery to Freedom.* 1898; reprint, New York: Arno, 1968.

William Still. *The Underground Railroad.* 1871; reprint, Chicago: Johnson Publishing, 1970.

Black Nationalism

Rodney Carlisle. *The Roots of Black Nationalism.* Port Washington, NY: Kennikat, 1975.

Floyd J. Miller. *The Search for Black Nationality: Black Emigration and Colonization, 1787–1863.* Urbana: University of Illinois Press, 1975.

Chapter 10 And Black People Were at the Heart of It: The United States Disunites over Slavery

California and the Compromise of 1850

Eugene H. Berwanger. *The Frontier against Slavery: Western Anti-Negro Prejudice and the Slave Extension Controversy.* Urbana: University of Illinois Press, 1967.

Holman Hamilton. *Prologue to Conflict: The Crisis and Compromise of 1850.* Lexington: University of Kentucky Press, 1964.

Rudolph M. Lapp. *Blacks in Gold Rush California.* New Haven, CT: Yale University Press, 1977.

The Fugitive Slave Law and Its Victims

Stanley W. Campbell. *The Slave Catchers: Enforcement of the Fugitive Slave Law, 1850–1860.* Chapel Hill: University of North Carolina Press, 1968.

Gary Collison. *Shadrach Minkins.* Cambridge, MA: Harvard University Press, 1998.

Albert J. von Frank. *The Trials of Anthony Burns.* Cambridge, MA: Harvard University Press, 1998.

Jonathan Katz. *Resistance at Christiana: The Fugitive Slave Rebellion at Christiana, Pennsylvania, September 11, 1851: A Documentary Account.* New York: Crowell, 1974.

Thomas P. Slaughter. *Bloody Dawn: The Christiana Riot and Violence in the Antebellum North.* New York: Oxford University Press, 1991.

The Late 1850s

Walter Ehrlich. *They Have No Rights: Dred Scott's Struggle for Freedom.* Westport, CT: Greenwood Press, 1979.

Don E. Fehrenbacher. *The Dred Scott Case: Its Significance in American Law and Politics.* New York: Oxford University Press, 1978.

Robert W. Johannsen. *Stephen A. Douglas.* New York: Oxford University Press, 1973.

Kenneth M. Stampp. *America in 1857: A Nation on the Brink.* New York: Oxford University Press, 1990.

John Brown and the Raid on Harpers Ferry

Paul Finkelman. *And His Soul Goes Marching On: Responses to John Brown and the Harpers Ferry Raid.* Charlottesville: University of Virginia Press, 1995.

Truman Nelson. *The Old Man John Brown at Harpers Ferry.* New York: Holt, Rinehart, & Winston, 1973.

Stephen Oates. *To Purge This Land with Blood: A Biography of John Brown.* New York: Harper & Row, 1970.

Benjamin Quarles. *Blacks on John Brown.* Urbana: University of Illinois Press, 1972.

Secession

William L. Barney. *The Road to Secession.* New York: Praeger, 1972.

Steven A. Channing. *Crisis of Fear: Secession in South Carolina.* New York: Simon & Schuster, 1970.

Kenneth M. Stampp. *And the War Came: The North and the Secession Crisis, 1860–1861.* Baton Rouge: Louisiana State University Press, 1950.

Abraham Lincoln

Gabor Boritt, ed. *The Lincoln Enigma.* New York: Oxford University Press, 2001.

David Herbert Donald. *Lincoln.* New York: Simon & Schuster, 1995.

Stephen B. Oates. *With Malice toward None: A Life of Abraham Lincoln.* New York: Harper & Row, 1977.

Benjamin Thomas. *Abraham Lincoln: A Biography.* New York: Alfred A. Knopf, 1952.

Novels

Martin R. Delany. *Blake or the Huts of America.* Boston: Beacon Press, 1970.

Harriet Beecher Stowe. *Uncle Tom's Cabin, or Life among the Lowly.* New York: Modern Library, 1985.

Chapter 11 Liberation: African Americans and the Civil War

Military

Joseph T. Glatthaar. *Forged in Battle: The Civil War Alliance of Black Soldiers and White Officers.* New York: The Free Press, 1990.

———. *The March to the Sea and Beyond: Sherman's Troops in the Savannah and Carolina Campaign.* New York: New York University Press, 1985.

Herman Hattaway and Archer Jones. *How the North Won: A Military History of the Civil War.* Urbana: University of Illinois Press, 1983.

Geoffrey Ward and Ken Burns. *The Civil War.* New York: Alfred A. Knopf, 1990.

Stephen R. Wise. *Gate of Hell: Campaign for Charleston Harbor, 1863.* Columbia: University of South Carolina Press, 1994.

African Americans and The War

Peter Burchard. *One Gallant Rush: Robert Gould Shaw and His Brave Black Regiment.* New York: St. Martin's Press, 1965.

Catherine Clinton. *Harriet Tubman: The Road to Freedom.* Boston: Little, Brown, 2004.

Ella Forbes. *African American Women during the Civil War.* New York: Garland, 1998.

Kate Clifford Larson. *Bound for the Promised Land: Harriet Tubman, Portrait of an American Hero.* New York: Ballantine, 2004.

Leon Litwack. *Been in the Storm So Long: The Aftermath of Slavery.* New York: Alfred A. Knopf, 1979.

Edward A. Miller. *Gullah Statesman: Robert Smalls from Slavery to Congress, 1839–1915.* Columbia: University of South Carolina Press, 1995.

Benjamin Quarles. *The Negro in the Civil War.* Boston: Little, Brown, 1953.

Willie Lee Rose. *Rehearsal for Reconstruction: The Port Royal Experiment.* Indianapolis: Bobbs Merrill, 1964.

Noah A. Trudeau. *Like Men of War: Black Troops in the Civil War, 1862–1865.* Boston: Little, Brown, 1998.

Bell I. Wiley. *Southern Negroes, 1861–1865.* New Haven, CT: Yale University Press, 1938.

Documents, Letters, and Other Sources

Virginia M. Adams, ed. *On the Altar of Freedom: A Black Soldier's Civil War Letters from the Front.* [Corporal James Henry Gooding]. Amherst: University of Massachusetts, 1991.

Ira Berlin et al., eds. "Freedom: A Documentary History of Emancipation, 1861–1867," Series 1, Volume I, *The Destruction of Slavery.* New York: Cambridge University Press, 1985.

———. "Freedom: A Documentary History of Emancipation, 1861–1867," Series 1, Volume III, *The Wartime Genesis of Free Labor: The Lower South.* New York: Cambridge University Press, 1990.

Robert F. Durden. *The Gray and the Black: The Confederate Debate on Emancipation.* Baton Rouge: Louisiana State University Press, 1972.

Michael P. Johnson and James L. Roark, eds. *No Chariot Letdown: Charleston's Free People of Color on the Eve of the Civil War.* Chapel Hill: University of North Carolina Press, 1984.

James McPherson. *The Negro's Civil War: How American Negroes Felt and Acted during the War for the Union.* New York: Pantheon, 1965.

Edwin S. Redkey, ed. *A Grand Army of Black Men: Letters from African American Soldiers in the Union Army, 1861–1865.* New York: Cambridge University Press, 1992.

Reminiscences

Thomas Wentworth Higginson. *Army Life in a Black Regiment.* Boston: Beacon Press, 1962.

Elizabeth Keckley. *Behind the Scenes: Or Thirty Years a Slave and Four Years in the White House.* New York: Oxford University Press, 1968.

Susie King Taylor. *Reminiscences of My Life in Camp.* Boston: Taylor, 1902.

Chapter 12 The Meaning of Freedom: The Promise of Reconstruction, 1865–1868

Education

James D. Anderson. *The Education of Blacks in the South, 1860–1935.* Chapel Hill: University of North Carolina Press, 1988.

Ronald E. Butchart. *Northern Schools, Southern Blacks, and Reconstruction: Freedmen's Education, 1862–1875.* Westport: Greenwood Press, 1981.

Edmund L. Drago. *Initiative, Paternalism, and Race Relations: Charleston's Avery Normal Institute.* Athens: University of Georgia Press, 1990.

Robert C. Morris. *Reading, 'Riting, and Reconstruction: The Education of the Freedmen in the South, 1861–1890.* Chicago: University of Chicago Press, 1981.

Joe M. Richardson. *Christian Reconstruction: The American Missionary Association and Southern Blacks, 1861–1890.* Athens: University of Georgia Press, 1986.

Willie Lee Rose. *Rehearsal for Reconstruction: The Port Royal Experiment.* Indianapolis: Bobbs Merrill, 1964.

Brenda Stevenson, ed. *The Journals of Charlotte Forten Grimke.* New York: Oxford University Press, 1988.

Land and Labor

Paul A. Cimbala and Randall M. Miller, eds. *The Freedmen's Bureau and Reconstruction.* New York: Fordham University Press, 1999.

Barbara J. Fields. *Slavery and Freedom on the Middle Ground: Maryland during the Nineteenth Century.* New Haven, CT: Yale University Press, 1985.

Jacqueline Jones. *Labor of Love, Labor of Sorrow: Black Women, Work and Family, from Slavery to the Present.* New York: Basic Books, 1985.

Edward Magdol. *A Right to the Land: Essays on the Freedmen's Community.* Westport, CT: Greenwood Press, 1977.

Claude F. Oubre. *Forty Acres and a Mule: The Freedmen's Bureau and Black Landownership.* Baton Rouge: Louisiana State University Press, 1978.

Dylan C. Penningroth. *The Claims of Kinfolk: African American Property and Community in the Nineteenth-Century South.* Chapel Hill: University of North Carolina Press, 2003.

Roger L. Ransom and Richard Sutch. *One Kind of Freedom: The Economic Consequences of Emancipation.* New York: Cambridge University Press, 1977.

Julie Saville. *The Work of Reconstruction: From Slave to Wage Labor in South Carolina, 1860–1870.* New York: Cambridge University Press, 1994.

James D. Schmidt. *Free to Work: Labor, Law, Emancipation, and Reconstruction, 1815–1880.* Athens: University of Georgia Press, 1998.

Leslie A. Schwalm. *A Hard Fight for We: Women's Transition from Slavery to Freedom in South Carolina.* Urbana: University of Illinois Press, 1997.

Black Communities

John W. Blassingame. *Black New Orleans, 1860–1880.* Chicago: University of Chicago Press, 1973.

Cyprian Davis. *The History of Black Catholics in the United States.* New York: Crossroad, 1990.

Robert F. Engs. *Freedom's First Generation: Black Hampton, Virginia, 1861–1890.* Philadelphia: University of Pennsylvania Press, 1979.

William E. Montgomery. *Under Their Own Vine and Fig Tree, The African American Church in the South 1865–1900.* Baton Rouge: Louisiana State University Press, 1993.

Bernard E. Powers, Jr. *Black Charlestonians: A Social History, 1822–1885.* Fayetteville: University of Arkansas Press, 1994.

Clarence E. Walker. *A Rock in a Weary Land: The African Methodist Episcopal Church during the Civil War and Reconstruction.* Baton Rouge: Louisiana State University Press, 1982.

James M. Washington. *Frustrated Fellowship: The Black Baptist Quest for Social Power.* Macon, GA: Mercer University Press, 1986.

Chapter 13 The Meaning of Freedom: The Failure of Reconstruction

Reconstruction in Specific States

Jane Dailey. *Before Jim Crow: The Politics of Race in Post Emancipation Virginia.* Chapel Hill: University of North Carolina Press, 2000.

Edmund L. Drago. *Black Politicians and Reconstruction in Georgia.* Athens: University of Georgia Press, 1982.

———. *Hurrah for Hampton: Black Red Shirts in South Carolina during Reconstruction.* Fayetteville: University of Arkansas Press, 1998.

Luther P. Jackson. *Negro Officeholders in Virginia, 1865– 1895.* Norfolk, VA: Guide Quality Press, 1945.

Peter Kolchin. *First Freedom: The Responses of Alabama's Blacks to Emancipation and Reconstruction.* Westport, CT: Greenwood, 1972.

Merline Pitre. *Through Many Dangers, Toils, and Snares: The Black Leadership of Texas, 1868–1900.* Austin, TX: Eakin Press, 1985.

Joe M. Richardson. *The Negro in the Reconstruction of Florida, 1865–1877.* Tallahassee: Florida State University Press, 1965.

Buford Stacher. *Blacks in Mississippi Politics, 1865–1900.* Washington, DC: University Press of America, 1978.

Ted Tunnell. *Crucible of Reconstruction: War, Radicalism and Race in Louisiana, 1862–1877.* Baton Rouge: Louisiana State University Press, 1984.

Charles Vincent. *Black Legislators in Louisiana during Reconstruction.* Baton Rouge: Louisiana State University Press, 1976.

Joel Williamson. *After Slavery: The Negro in South Carolina: 1861–1877.* Chapel Hill: University of North Carolina Press, 1965.

National Politics: Andrew Johnson and the Radical Republicans

Michael Les Benedict. *A Compromise of Principle: Congressional Republicans and Reconstruction.* New York: Norton, 1974.

Dan T. Carter. *When the War Was Over: The Failure of Self-Reconstruction in the South, 1865–1867.* Baton Rouge: Louisina State University Press, 1983.

Michael W. Fitzgerald. *The Union League Movement in the Deep South.* Baton Rouge: Louisiana State University Press, 1989.

Eric L. McKitrick. *Andrew Johnson and Reconstruction, 1865–1867.* Chicago: University of Chicago Press, 1960.

James M. McPherson. *The Struggle for Equality: Abolitionists and the Negro in the Civil War and Reconstruction.* Princeton, NJ: Princeton University Press, 1964.

Hans L. Trefousse. *The Radical Republicans: Lincoln's Vanguard for Racial Justice.* Baton Rouge: Louisiana State University Press, 1969.

Economic Issues: Land, Labor, and the Freedmen's Bank

Elizabeth Bethel. *Promiseland: A Century of Life in a Negro Community.* Philadelphia: Temple University Press, 1981.

Carol R. Bleser. *The Promised Land: The History of the South Carolina Land Commission, 1869–1890.* Columbia: University of South Carolina Press, 1969.

Sharon Ann Holt. *Making Freedom Pay: North Carolina Freed People Working for Themselves, 1865–1900.* Athens: University of Georgia Press, 2000.

Lynda J. Morgan. *Emancipation in Virginia's Tobacco Belt.* Athens: University of Georgia Press, 1992.

Donald G. Nieman. *To Set the Law in Motion: The Freedmen's Bureau and Legal Rights for Blacks, 1865–1869.* Millwood, NY: KTO, 1979.

Carl R. Osthaus. *Freedmen, Philanthropy and Fraud: A History of the Freedman's Savings Bank.* Urbana: University of Illinois Press, 1976.

Violence and The Ku Klux Klan

George C. Rable. *But There Was No Peace: The Role of Violence in the Politics of Reconstruction.* Athens: University of Georgia Press, 1984.

Allen W. Trelease. *White Terror: The Ku Klux Klan Conspiracy and Southern Reconstruction.* New York: Harper & Row, 1973.

Lou Falkner Williams. *The Great South Carolina Ku Klux Klan Trials, 1871–1872.* Athens: University of Georgia Press, 1996.

Autobiography and Biography

Mifflin Wistar Gibbs. *Shadow & Light: An Autobiography.* Lincoln: University of Nebraska Press, 1995.
Peter D. Klingman. *Josiah Walls.* Gainesville: University Presses of Florida, 1976.
Peggy Lamson. *The Glorious Failure: Black Congressman Robert Brown Elliott and Reconstruction in South Carolina.* New York: Norton, 1973.
Edward A. Miller. *Gullah Statesman: Robert Smalls: From Slavery to Congress, 1839–1915.* Columbia: University of South Carolina Press, 1995.
Loren Schweninger. James T. *Rapier and Reconstruction.* Chicago: University of Chicago Press, 1978.
Okon E. Uya. *From Slavery to Public Service: Robert Smalls, 1839–1915.* New York: Oxford University Press, 1971.

Chapter 14 White Supremacy Triumphant: African Americans in the South in the Late Nineteenth Century

State and Local Studies

Eric Anderson. *Race and Politics in North Carolina, 1872–1901: The Black Second.* Baton Rouge: Louisiana State University Press, 1981.
David Cecelski and Timothy B. Tyson, eds. *Democracy Betrayed: The Wilmington Race Riot and Its Legacy.* Chapel Hill: University of North Carolina Press, 1998.
Helen G. Edmonds. *The Negro and Fusion Politics in North Carolina, 1894–1901.* Chapel Hill: University of North Carolina Press, 1951.
William Ivy Hair. *Carnival of Fury: Robert Charles and the New Orleans Riot of 1900.* Baton Rouge: Louisiana State University Press, 1976.
Neil R. McMillen. *Dark Journey: Black Mississippians in the Age of Jim Crow.* Urbana: University of Illinois Press, 1989.
H. Leon Prather. *We Have Taken a City: Wilmington Racial Massacre and Coup of 1898.* Rutherford: Fairleigh Dickinson University Press, 1984.
David M. Oshinsky. *"Worse Than Slavery": Parchman Farm and the Ordeal of Jim Crow Justice.* New York: The Free Press, 1999.
George B. Tindall. *South Carolina Negroes, 1877–1900.* Columbia: University of South Carolina Press, 1952.
Vernon Wharton. *The Negro in Mississippi, 1865–1890.* Chapel Hill: University of North Carolina Press, 1947.

Biographies and Autobiographies

Albert S. Broussard. *African-American Odyssey: The Stewarts, 1853–1963.* Lawrence: University Press of Kansas, 1998.
Alfreda Duster, ed. *Crusade for Justice: The Autobiography of Ida B. Wells.* Chicago: University of Chicago Press, 1972.
Henry O. Flipper. *The Colored Cadet at West Point.* New York: Arno Press, 1969.
John F. Marszalek Jr. *Court Martial: The Army vs. Johnson Whittaker.* New York: Scribner, 1972.
Linda McMurry. *To Keep the Waters Troubled: The Life of Ida B. Wells.* New York: Oxford University Press, 1998.
Patricia A. Schechter. *Ida B. Wells-Barnett and American Reform, 1882–1930.* Chapel Hill: University of North Carolina Press, 2001.

Politics and Segregation

Grace Hale. *Making Whiteness: The Culture of Segregation in the South, 1890–1940.* New York: Pantheon Books, 1998.
J. Morgan Kousser. *The Shaping of Southern Politics: Suffrage Restriction and the Establishment of the One-Party South, 1880–1910.* New Haven, CT: Yale University Press, 1974.
Michael Perman. *Struggle for Mastery: Disfranchisement in the South, 1888–1908.* Chapel Hill: University of North Carolina Press, 2001.

Lynching

James Allen, Hinton Als, John Lewis, and Leon F. Litwack. *Without Sanctuary: Lynching Photography in America.* Santa Fe, NM: Twin Palms Books, 2000.
W. Fitzhugh Brundage, ed. *Under Sentence of Death: Lynching in the South.* Chapel Hill: University of North Carolina Press, 1997.
W. Fitzhugh Brundage. *Lynching in the New South: Georgia and Virginia, 1880–1930.* Urbana: University of Illinois Press, 1993.
Sandra Gunning. *Race, Rape, and Lynching: The Red Record of American Literature, 1890–1912.* New York: Oxford University Press, 1996.
National Association for the Advancement of Colored People. *Thirty Years of Lynching in the United States, 1889–1918.* New York: NAACP, 1919.

The West

Robert G. Athearn. *In Search of Canaan: Black Migration to Kansas, 1879–80.* Lawrence: Regents Press of Kansas, 1978.

Jacob U. Gordon. *Narratives of African Americans in Kansas, 1870–1992.* Lewiston, NY: Edward Mellon Press, 1993.

Nell Irvin Painter. *Exodusters: Black Migration to Kansas after Reconstruction.* New York: Alfred A. Knopf, 1977.

Quintard Taylor. *In Search of the Racial Frontier: African Americans in the American West, 1528–1990.* New York: Norton, 1998.

Migration, Mobility, and Land Ownership

William Cohen. *At Freedom's Edge: Black Mobility and the Southern White Quest for Racial Control, 1861–1915.* Baton Rouge: Louisiana State University Press, 1991.

Pete Daniel. *The Shadow of Slavery: Peonage in the South, 1901–1969.* Urbana: University of Illinois Press, 1972.

Edward Royce. *The Origins of Southern Sharecropping.* Philadelphia: Temple University Press, 1993.

Loren Schweninger. *Black Property Owners in the South, 1790–1915.* Urbana: University of Illinois Press, 1990.

Chapter 15 Black Southerners Challenge White Supremacy

Education

Eric Anderson and Alfred A. Moss Jr. *Dangerous Donations: Northern Philanthropy and Southern Black Education, 1902–1930.* Columbia: University of Missouri Press, 1999.

James D. Anderson and V. P. Franklin, eds. *New Perspectives on Black Education.* Boston: G. K. Hall, 1978.

Henry A. Bullock. *A History of Negro Education in the South from 1619 to the Present.* Cambridge, MA: Harvard University Press, 1967.

Religion

Stephen W. Angell. *Bishop Henry McNeal Turner and African American Religion in the South.* Knoxville: University of Tennessee Press, 1992.

Cyprian Davis. *The History of Black Catholics in the United States.* New York: Crossroad, 1990.

Harold T. Lewis. *Yet with a Steady Beat: The African American Struggle for Recognition in the Episcopal Church.* Valley Forge, PA: Trinity Press International, 1996.

Iain MacRobert. *The Black Roots and White Racism of Early Pentecostalism in the USA.* Basingstoke, England: Macmillan, 1988.

James M. O'Toole. *Passing for White: Race, Religion, and the Healy Family, 1820–1920.* Amherst: University of Massachusetts Press, 2002.

Edwin S. Redkey, ed. *The Writings and Speeches of Henry McNeal Turner.* New York: Arno Press, 1971.

Clarence E. Walker. *A Rock in a Weary Land: The African Methodist Episcopal Church during the Civil War and Reconstruction.* Baton Rouge: Louisiana State University Press, 1982.

The Military and the West

John M. Carroll, ed. *The Black Military Experience in the American West.* New York: Liveright, 1973.

Willard B. Gatewood, ed. *Smoked Yankees and the Struggle for Empire: Letters from Negro Soldiers, 1898–1902.* Urbana: University of Illinois Press, 1971.

William Loren Katz. *The Black West.* New York: Touchstone Books, 1996.

William H. Leckie. *The Buffalo Soldiers: A Narrative of the Negro Cavalry in the West.* Norman: University of Oklahoma Press, 1967.

Paul W. Stewart and Wallace Yvonne Ponce. *Black Cowboys.* Broomfield, CO: Phillips, 1986.

John D. Weaver. *The Brownsville Raid.* New York: Norton, 1971.

Labor

Tera W. Hunter. *To 'Joy My Freedom: Southern Black Women's Lives and Labors after the Civil War.* Cambridge, MA: Harvard University Press, 1997.

Gerald D. Jaynes. *Branches without Roots: Genesis of the Black Working Class in the American South, 1862–1882.* New York: Oxford University Press, 1986.

The Professions

V. N. Gamble. *The Black Community Hospital: Contemporary Dilemmas in Historical Perspective.* New York: Garland, 1989.

Darlene Clark Hine. *Speak Truth to Power: Black Professional Class in United States History.* Brooklyn, NY: Carlson, 1996.

J. Clay Smith Jr. *Emancipation: The Making of the Black Lawyer, 1844–1944.* Philadelphia: University of Pennsylvania Press, 1993.

J. Clay Smith Jr., ed. *Rebels in Law: Voices in History of Black Women Lawyers.* Ann Arbor: University of Michigan Press, 1998.

Susan L. Smith. *Sick and Tired of Being Sick and Tired: Black Women's Health Activism in America, 1890–1950.* Philadelphia: University of Pennsylvania Press, 1995.

Thomas J. Ward Jr. *Black Physicians in the Jim Crow South.* Fayetteville: University of Arkansas Press, 2003.

Music

W. C. Handy. *Father of the Blues: An Autobiography.* New York: Macmillan, 1941.

John Edward Hasse, ed. *Ragtime, Its History, Composers, and Music.* London: Macmillan, 1985.

Alan Lomax. Mr. *Jelly Roll: The Fortunes of Jelly Roll Morton, New Orleans Creole and "Inventor of Jazz."* New York: Grove Press, 1950.

Gunther Schuller. *Early Jazz: Its Roots and Musical Development.* New York: Oxford University Press, 1968.

Sports

Ocania Chalk. *Black College Sport.* New York: Dodd, Mead, 1976.

Neil Lanctot. *Negro League Baseball: The Rise and Ruin of a Black Institution.* Philadelphia: University of Pennsylvania Press, 2004.

Robert W. Peterson. *Only the Ball Was White: Negro Baseball: A History of Legendary Black Players and All-Black Professional Teams before Black Men Played in the Major Leagues.* New York: Prentice-Hall, 1970.

Andrew Ritchie. *Major Taylor: The Extraordinary Career of a Championship Bicycle Racer.* San Francisco: Bicycle Books, 1988.

Randy Roberts. *Papa Jack: Jack Johnson and the Era of White Hopes.* New York: Free Press, 1983.

Chapter 16 Conciliation, Agitation, and Migration: African Americans in the Early Twentieth Century

Leadership Conflicts and the Emergence of African-American Organizations

Charles F. Kellogg. *NAACP: A History of the National Association for the Advancement of Colored People.* Baltimore: Johns Hopkins University Press, 1967.

August Meier. *Negro Thought in America, 1880–1915.* Ann Arbor: University of Michigan Press, 1967.

Alfred A. Moss Jr. *American Negro Academy: Voice of the Talented Tenth.* Baton Rouge: Louisiana State University Press, 1981.

B. Joyce Ross. *J. E. Spingarn and the Rise of the N.A.A.C.P.* New York: Atheneum, 1972.

Lawrence C. Ross Jr. *The Divine Nine: The History of African-American Fraternities and Sororities.* New York: Kensington Books, 2000.

Elliott Rudwick. *W. E. B. Du Bois.* New York: Atheneum, 1968.

Nancy Weiss. *The National Urban League, 1910–1940.* New York: Oxford University Press, 1974.

Shamoon Zamir. *Dark Voices: W. E. B. Du Bois and American Thought, 1888–1903.* Chicago: University of Chicago Press, 1995.

African-American Women in the Early Twentieth Century

Elizabeth Clark-Lewis. *Living In, Living Out: African American Domestics in Washington, D.C., 1910–1940.* Washington, DC: Smithsonian Institution Press, 1994.

Anna Julia Cooper. *A Voice from the South.* New York: Oxford University Press, 1988.

Cynthia Neverdon-Morton. *Afro-American Women of the South and the Advancement of the Race, 1895–1925.* Knoxville: University of Tennessee Press, 1998.

Jacqueline A. Rouse. *Lugina Burns Hope: A Black Southern Reformer.* Athens: University of Georgia Press, 1989.

Stephanie J. Shaw. *What a Woman Ought to Be and to Do: Black Professional Women Workers during the Jim Crow Era.* Chicago: University of Chicago Press, 1996.

Rosalyn Terborg-Penn. *African American Women in the Struggle for the Vote, 1850–1920.* Bloomington: Indiana University Press, 1998.

African Americans in the Military in the World War I Era

Arthur E. Barbeau and Florette Henri. *Black American Troops in World War I.* Philadelphia: Temple University Press, 1974.

Edward M. Coffman. *The War to End All Wars: The American Military Experience in World War I.* Madison: University of Wisconsin Press, 1986.

Arthur W. Little. *From Harlem to the Rhine: The Story of New York's Colored Volunteers.* New York: Covici, Friede, 1936.

Bernard C. Nalty. *Strength for the Fight: A History of Black Americans in the Military.* New York: Free Press, 1986.

Cities and Racial Conflict

Michael D'Orso. *Rosewood.* New York: Boulevard Press, 1996.

St. Clair Drake and Horace R. Clayton. *Black Metropolis: A Study of Negro Life in a Northern City.* 2 vols. Chicago: Harcourt, Brace and Co., 1945.

Sherry Sherrod Dupree. *The Rosewood Massacre at a Glance.* Gainesville, FL: Rosewood Forum, 1998.

Scott Ellsworth. *Death in a Promised Land: The Tulsa Race Riot of 1921.* Baton Rouge: Louisiana State University Press, 1982.

Robert V. Haynes. *A Night of Violence: The Houston Riot of 1917.* Baton Rouge: Louisiana State University Press, 1976.

Hannibal Johnson. *Black Wall Street, From Riot to Renaissance in Tulsa's Historic Greenwood District.* Austin, TX: Eakin Press, 1998.

David M. Katzman. *Before the Ghetto: Black Detroit in the Nineteenth Century.* Urbana: University of Illinois Press, 1973.

Kenneth L. Kusmer. *A Ghetto Takes Shape: Black Cleveland, 1870–1930.* Urbana: University of Illinois Press, 1976.

Gilbert Osofsky. *Harlem: The Making of a Ghetto, 1890–1930.* New York: Harper & Row, 1966.

Christopher Reed. *The Chicago NAACP and the Rise of Black Professional Leadership, 1910–1966.* Bloomington: Indiana University Press, 1997.

Elliott M. Rudwick. *Race Riot at East St. Louis, July 2, 1917.* Cleveland: World Publishing, 1966.

Roberta Senechal. *The Sociogenesis of a Race Riot: Springfield, Illinois, in 1908.* Urbana: University of Illinois Press, 1990.

Allan H. Spear. *Black Chicago: The Making of a Negro Ghetto, 1890–1920.* Chicago: University of Chicago Press, 1967.

Joe William Trotter Jr. *Black Milwaukee: The Making of an Industrial Proletariat, 1915–1945.* Urbana: University of Illinois Press, 1985.

William Tuttle. *Chicago in the Red Summer of 1919.* New York: Atheneum, 1970.

Lee E. Williams. *Anatomy of Four Race Riots: Racial Conflict in Knoxville, Elaine (Arkansas), Tulsa, and Chicago, 1919–1921.* Hattiesburg: University and College Press of Mississippi, 1972.

The Great Migration

Peter Gottlieb. *Making Their Own Way: Southern Blacks' Migration to Pittsburgh, 1916–1930.* Urbana: University of Illinois Press, 1987.

James R. Grossman. *Land of Hope: Chicago, Black Southerners, and the Great Migration.* Chicago: University of Chicago Press, 1989.

Florette Henri. *Black Migration, 1900–1920.* Garden City, NY: Anchor Press, 1975.

Carole Marks. *Farewell—We're Good and Gone: The Great Black Migration.* Bloomington: Indiana University Press, 1989.

Milton C. Sernett. *Bound for the Promised Land: African American Religion and the Great Migration.* Durham, NC: Duke University Press, 1997.

Joe William Trotter Jr., ed. *The Great Migration in Historical Perspective.* Bloomington: Indiana University Press, 1991.

Autobiography and Biography

W. E. B. Du Bois. *Dusk of Dawn.* New York: Harcourt, Brace & Co., 1940.

———. *The Autobiography: A Soliloquy on Viewing My Life from the Last Decade of Its First Century.* New York: International Publishers, 1968.

Stephen R. Fox. *The Guardian of Boston: William Monroe Trotter.* New York: Atheneum, 1970.

Kenneth R. Manning. *Black Apollo of Science: The Life of Ernest Everett Just.* New York: Oxford University Press, 1983.

Linda O. McMurry. *George Washington Carver: Scientist and Symbol.* New York: Oxford University Press, 1981.

Arnold Rampersad. *The Art and Imagination of W. E. B. Du Bois.* Cambridge, MA: Harvard University Press, 1976.

Mary Church Terrell. *A Colored Woman in a White World.* New York: Arno Press reprint, 1940.

Emma Lou Thornbrough. *T. Thomas Fortune.* Chicago: University of Chicago Press, 1970.

Booker T. Washington. *Up from Slavery.* New York: Doubleday, 1901.

Chapter 17 African Americans and the 1920s

The Ku Klux Klan

David M. Chalmers. *Hooded Americanism: A History of the Ku Klux Klan.* New York: Franklin Watts, 1965.

Kenneth T. Jackson. *The Ku Klux Klan in the City.* New York: Oxford University Press, 1967.

The NAACP

Charles F. Kellogg. *NAACP: A History of the National Association for the Advancement of Colored People.* Baltimore: Johns Hopkins University Press, 1967.

Robert L. Zangrando. *The NAACP Campaign against Lynching, 1909–1950.* Philadelphia: Temple University Press, 1980.

Black Workers, A. Philip Randolph, and the Brotherhood of Sleeping Car Porters

Jervis B. Anderson. *A. Philip Randolph: A Biographical Portrait.* New York: Harcourt, Brace, Jovanovich, 1973.

Beth Tompkins Bates. *Pullman Porters and the Rise of Protest Politics in Black America, 1925–1945.* Chapel Hill: University of North Carolina Press, 2001.

David E. Bernstein. *Only One Place of Redress: African Americans, Labor Regulations and the Courts from Reconstruction to the New Deal.* Durham, NC: Duke University Press, 2001.

Jack Santino. *Miles of Smiles, Years of Struggle: Stories of Black Pullman Porters.* Urbana: University of Illinois Press, 1989.

Marcus Garvey and the Universal Negro Improvement Association

Randall K. Burkett. *Garveyism as a Religious Movement: The Institutionalization of a Black Civil Religion.* Metuchen, NJ: Scarecrow Press, 1978.

E. David Cronon. *Black Moses: The Story of Marcus Garvey and the Universal Negro Improvement Association.* Madison: University of Wisconsin Press, 1955.

Marcus Garvey. *Philosophy and Opinions of Marcus Garvey.* New York: Atheneum, 1969.

Theodore Kornweibel, Jr. *Seeing Red: Federal Campaigns against Black Militancy, 1919–1925.* Bloomington: Indiana University Press, 1998.

The Harlem Renaissance

Arna W. Bontemps, ed. *The Harlem Renaissance Remembered.* New York: Dodd, Mead, 1972.

Nathan Huggins. *Harlem Renaissance.* New York: Oxford University Press, 1971.

Bruce Kellner, ed. *The Harlem Renaissance: A Historical Dictionary of the Era.* Westport, CT: Greenwood Press, 1984.

Steven Watson. *The Harlem Renaissance: Hub of African American Culture, 1920–1930.* New York: Pantheon, 1995.

Biographies and Autobiographies

Pamela Bordelon, ed. *Go Gator and Muddy the Water: Writings by Zora Neale Hurston from the Federal Writers Project.* New York: Norton, 1999.

Robert C. Cottrell. *The Best Pitcher in Baseball: The Life of Rube Foster; Negro League Giant.* New York: New York University Press, 2001.

Thadious M. Davis. *Nella Larsen: Novelist of the Harlem Renaissance.* Baton Rouge: Louisiana State University Press, 1994.

Wayne F. Cooper. *Claude McKay, Rebel Sojourner in the Harlem Renaissance: A Biography.* Baton Rouge: Louisiana State University Press, 1987.

Robert Hemenway. *Zora Neale Hurston: A Literary Biography.* Urbana: University of Illinois Press, 1977.

Gloria T. Hull. *Color, Sex, and Poetry: Three Women Writers of the Harlem Renaissance.* Bloomington: Indiana University Press, 1987.

James Weldon Johnson. *Along the Way.* New York: Viking Press, 1933.

Cynthia E. Kerman. *The Lives of Jean Toomer: A Hunger for Wholeness.* Baton Rouge: Louisiana State University Press, 1987.

Eugene Levy. *James Weldon Johnson: Black Leader, Black Voice.* Chicago: University of Chicago Press, 1973.

Chapter 18 Black Protest, the Great Depression, and the New Deal

Politics

Adam Fairclough. *Better Day Coming: Blacks and Equality, 1890–2000.* New York: Viking, 2001.

Kenneth W. Goings. *"The NAACP Comes of Age": The Defeat of Judge John J. Parker.* Bloomington: Indiana University Press, 1990.

Charles V. Hamilton. *Adam Clayton Powell, Jr., the Political Biography of an American Dilemma.* New York: Atheneum, 1991.

Darlene Clark Hine. *Black Victory: The Rise and Fall of the White Primary in Texas.* New edition with essays by Darlene Clark Hine, Steven F. Lawson, and Merline Pitre. Columbia: University of Missouri Press, 2003.

John B. Kirby. *Black Americans in the Roosevelt Era: Liberalism and Race.* Knoxville: University of Tennessee Press, 1980.

Christopher R. Reed. *The Chicago NAACP and the Rise of Black Professional Leadership, 1910–1966.* Bloomington: Indiana University Press, 1997.

Bernard Sternsher, ed. *The Negro in Depression and War: Prelude to Revolution, 1930–1945.* Chicago: Quadrangle Books, 1969.

Mark V. Tushnet. *The NAACP's Legal Strategy against Segregated Education, 1925–1950.* Chapel Hill: University of North Carolina Press, 1987.

Nancy J. Weiss. *Farewell to the Party of Lincoln: Black Politics in the Age of Lincoln.* Princeton, NJ: Princeton University Press, 1983.

Labor

Lizabeth Cohen. *Making a New Deal: Industrial Workers in Chicago, 1919–1939.* New York: Cambridge University Press, 1990.

Dennis C. Dickerson. *Out of the Crucible: Black Steelworkers in Western Pennsylvania, 1875–1980.* Albany, NY: SUNY Press, 1986.

William H. Harris. *The Harder We Run: Black Workers since the Civil War.* New York: Oxford University Press, 1982.

August Meier and Elliott Rudwick. *Black Detroit and the Rise of the UAW.* New York: Oxford University Press, 1979.

Daryl Michael Scott. *Contempt and Pity: Social Policy and the Image of the Damaged Black Psyche, 1880–1996.* Chapel Hill: University of North Carolina Press, 1997.

Mark Solomon. *The Cry Was Unity: Communists and African Americans, 1917–1936.* Jackson: University Press of Mississippi, 1998.

Richard W. Thomas. *Life for Us Is What We Make It: Building Black Community in Detroit, 1915–1945.* Bloomington: Indiana University Press, 1992.

Thomas J. Ward Jr. *Black Physicians in the Jim Crow South.* Fayetteville: University of Arkansas Press, 2003.

Education

James D. Anderson. *The Education of Blacks in the South, 1860–1935.* Chapel Hill: University of North Carolina Press, 1988.

Horace M. Bond. *The Education of the Negro in the American Social Order.* New York: Octagon Books, 1934; rev. 1966.

Richard Kluger. *Simple Justice: The History of Brown v. Board of Education and Black America's Struggle for Equality,* 1976; new rev. ed., 2004. With a new chapter assessing the 50th year impact of *Brown.*

Mark V. Tushnet. *Making Civil Rights Law: Thurgood Marshall and the Supreme Court, 1935–1961.* New York: Knopf, 1994.

Black Radicalism

Dan Carter. *Scottsboro: A Tragedy of the American South.* Baton Rouge: Louisiana State University Press, 1969.

Vanessa Northington Gamble. *Making a Place for Ourselves: The Black Hospital Movement, 1920–1945.* New York: Oxford University Press, 1995.

Kenneth W. Goings. *Mammy and Uncle Mose: Black Collectibles and American Stereotyping.* Bloomington: Indiana University Press, 1994.

Michael K. Honey. *Southern Labor and Black Civil Rights: Organizing Memphis Workers.* Urbana: University of Illinois Press, 1993.

Jacqueline Jones. *Labor of Love, Labor of Sorrow: Black Women, Work, and the Family from Slavery to the Present.* New York: Basic Books, 1985.

Nicholas Natanson. *The Black Image in the New Deal: The Politics of FSA Photography.* Knoxville: University of Tennessee Press, 1992.

Richard H. Pells. *Radical Visions and American Dreams: Culture and Social Thought in the Depression Years.* New York: Harper & Row, 1973.

Economics

Charles T. Banner-Haley. *To Do Good and to Do Well: Middle Class Blacks and the Depression, Philadelphia, 1929–1941.* New York: Garland, 1993.

Abram L. Harris. *The Negro as Capitalist: A Study of Banking and Business among American Negroes.* Originally published by the American Academy of Political and Social Sciences, 1936; reprint, Chicago: Urban Research Press, 1992.

Alexa Benson Henderson. *Atlanta Life Insurance Company: Guardian of Black Economic Dignity.* Tuscaloosa: University of Alabama Press, 1990.

Robert E. Weems Jr. *Black Business in the Black Metropolis: The Chicago Metropolitan Assurance Company, 1924–1985.* Bloomington: Indiana University Press, 1996.

Biography and Autobiography

Andrew Buni. *Robert L. Vann of the Pittsburgh Courier.* Pittsburgh: University of Pittsburgh Press, 1974.

Henry Louis Gates, Jr. and Evelyn Brooks Higginbotham, eds. *African American Lives.* New York: Oxford University Press, 2004.

Wil Haywood. *King of the Cats: The Life and Times of Adam Clayton Powell, Jr.* Boston: Houghton Mifflin, 1993.

Spencie Love. *One Blood: The Death and Resurrection of Charles R. Drew.* Chapel Hill: University of North Carolina Press, 1996.

Genna Rae McNeil. *Groundwork: Charles Hamilton Houston and the Struggle for Civil Rights.* Philadelphia: University of Pennsylvania Press, 1983.

Nell Irvin Painter. *The Narrative of Hosea Hudson: His Life as a Negro Communist in the South.* Cambridge, MA: Harvard University Press, 1979.

Paula F. Pfeffer. *A. Philip Randolph, Pioneer of the Civil Rights Movement.* Baton Rouge: Louisiana State University Press, 1990.

Barbara Ransby. *Ella Baker and the Black Freedom Movement.* Chapel Hill: University of North Carolina Press, 2003.
George S. Schuyler. *Black and Conservative: The Autobiography of George S. Schuyler.* New Rochelle, NY: Arlington House, 1966.
Gilbert Ware. *William Hastie: Grace under Pressure.* New York: Oxford University Press, 1984.
Roy Wilkins with Tom Mathews. *Standing Fast: The Autobiography of Roy Wilkins.* New York: Da Capo Press, 1994.

Chapter 19 Meanings of Freedom: Culture and Society in the 1930s and 1940s

Art

Michael D. Harris and Moyo Okediji. *Colored Pictures: Race and Visual Representation.* Chapel Hill: University of North Carolina Press, 2003.
Sharon F. Patton. *African-American Art.* New York: Oxford University Press, 1998.
Richard J. Powell. *Black Art and Culture in the 20th Century.* New York: Thames and Judson, 1997.
William E. Taylor and Harriet G. Warkel. *A Shared Heritage: Art by Four African Americans.* Bloomington: Indiana University Press, 1996.

Black Chicago Renaissance

Robert Bone. "Richard Wright and the Chicago Renaissance." *Callaloo,* 9, no. 3 (1986): 446–68.
Craig Werner. "Leon Forrest, the AACM and the Legacy of the Chicago Renaissance." *The Black Scholar,* 23, no. 3/4 (1993): 10–23.

Culture

St. Clair Drake and Horace R. Cayton. *Black Metropolis: A Study of Negro Life in a Northern City.* New York: Harper & Row, 1962.
Gerald Early, ed. *"Ain't But a Place": An Anthology of African American Writing about St. Louis.* St. Louis: Missouri Historical Society Press, 1998.
Geneviève Fabre and Robert O'Meally, eds. *History and Memory in African-American Culture.* New York: Oxford University Press, 1994.
Kenneth W. Goings. *Mammy and Uncle Mose: Black Collectibles and American Stereotyping.* Bloomington: Indiana University Press, 1994.
Joseph E. Harris, ed. *Global Dimensions of the African Diaspora.* Washington, DC: Howard University Press, 1993.
Robin D. G. Kelley. *Race Rebels: Culture, Politics, and the Black Working Class.* New York: Free Press, 1994.
Lawrence Levine. *Black Culture and Black Consciousness: Afro-American Folk Thought from Slavery to Freedom.* New York: Oxford University Press, 1977.
Tommy L. Lott. *The Invention of Race: Black Culture and the Politics of Representation.* Malden, MA: Blackwell, 1999.
Daryl Scott. *Contempt and Pity: Social Policy and Image of the Damaged Black Psyche, 1880–1996.* Chapel Hill: University of North Carolina Press, 1997.
Mel Watkins. *On the Real Side: Laughing, Lying, and Signifying.* New York: Simon & Schuster, 1994.
Robert E. Weems Jr. *Desegregating the Dollar: African American Consumerism in the Twentieth Century.* New York: New York University Press, 1998.

Dance

Katherine Dunham. *A Touch of Innocence.* London: Cassell, 1959.
Terry Harnan. *African Rhythm–American Dance.* New York: Knopf, 1974.

Films

Donald Bogle. *Brown Sugar: Eighty Years of America's Black Female Superstars.* New York: Crown, 1980.
Thomas Cripps. *Making Movies Black: The Hollywood Message Movie from World War II to the Civil Rights Era.* New York: Oxford University Press, 1993.
Jane M. Gaines. *Fire and Desire: Mixed-Race Movies in the Silent Era.* Chicago: University of Chicago Press, 2001.

Literature

Ralph Ellison. "The World and the Jug." In Joseph F. Trimmer, ed., *A Casebook on Ralph Ellison's Invisible Man* (pp. 172–200). New York: T. Y. Crowell, 1972.
Michael Fabre. *The Unfinished Quest of Richard Wright.* Iowa City: University of Iowa Press, 1973.
Henry Louis Gates and Nellie Y. McKay, eds. *Norton Anthology of African American Literature.* New York: Norton, 1997.
Joyce Ann Joyce. *Richard Wright's Art of Tragedy.* New York: Warner Books, 1986.
Robert G. O'Meally. *The Craft of Ralph Ellison.* Cambridge, MA: Harvard University Press, 1980.
Arnold Rampersad. *The Life of Langston Hughes.* New York: Oxford University Press, 1986.

Margaret Walker. *Richard Wright, Daemonic Genius: A Portrait of the Man, a Critical Look at His Work.* New York: Morrow, 1988.

Music and Radio

William Barlow. *Looking Up at Down: The Emergence of Blues Culture.* Philadelphia: Temple University Press, 1989.

Thomas Brothers, ed. *Louis Armstrong: In His Own Words.* New York: Oxford University Press, 1999.

Jack Chalmers. *Milestones I: The Music and Times of Miles Davis to 1960.* Toronto, Canada: University of Toronto Press, 1983.

John Chilton. *The Song of the Hawk: The Life and Recordings of Coleman Hawkins.* Ann Arbor: University of Michigan Press, 1990.

Donald Clarke. *Wishing on the Moon: The Life and Times of Billie Holiday.* New York: Viking Penguin, 1994.

Linda Dahl. *Morning Glory: A Biography of Mary Lou Williams.* New York: Pantheon Books, 2000.

Miles Davis and Quincy Troupe. *Miles: The Autobiography.* New York: Simon & Schuster, 1989.

Duke Ellington. *Music Is My Mistress.* New York: Da Capo Press, 1973.

John Birks Gillespie and Wilmot Alfred Fraser. *To Be or Not . . . to Bop: Memoirs/Dizzy Gillespie with Al Fraser.* New York: Doubleday, 1979.

Michael Harris. *The Rise of Gospel Blues: The Music of Thomas Andrew Dorsey in the Urban Church.* New York: Oxford University Press, 1992.

Allan Keiler. *Marian Anderson: A Singer's Journey.* New York: Scribner, 2000.

Robert G. O'Meally. *Lady Day: The Many Faces of Billie Holiday.* New York: Arcade Publishers, 1991.

Thomas Owens. *Bebop: The Music and Its Players.* New York: Oxford University Press, 1955.

Barbara Dianne Savage. *Broadcasting Freedom: Radio, War, and the Politics of Race, 1938–1948.* Chapel Hill: University of North Carolina Press, 1999.

Jules Schwerin. *Got to Tell It: Mahalia Jackson, Queen of Gospel.* New York: Oxford University Press, 1992.

Alyn Shipton. *Groovin' High: The Life of Dizzy Gillespie.* New York: Oxford University Press, 1999.

Eileen Southern. *The Music of Black Americans: A History,* 2d ed. New York: Norton, 1983.

Quintard Taylor. *In Search of the Racial Frontier: African Americans in the American West, 1528–1900.* New York: Norton, 1998.

J. C. Thomas. *Chasin' the Trane: The Music and Mystique of John Coltrane.* Garden City, NY: Doubleday, 1975.

Dempsey J. Travis. *Autobiography of Black Jazz.* Chicago: Urban Research Press, 1983.

Sports

Arthur Ashe, with the assistance of Kip Branch, Ocania Chalk, and Francis Harris. *A Hard Road to Glory: A History of the African-American Athlete.* New York: Warner Books, 1988.

Richard Bak. *Joe Louis: The Great Black Hope.* New York: Da Capo Press, 1998.

Robert Peterson. *Only the Ball Was White: A History of Legendary Black Players and All-Black Professional Teams.* New York: McGraw-Hill, 1984.

Arnold Rampersad. *Jackie Robinson: A Biography.* New York: Alfred A. Knopf, 1997.

Jackie Robinson. *I Never Had It Made.* New York: G. P. Putnam's Son, 1972.

Jeffrey T. Sammons. *Beyond the Ring: The Role of Boxing in American Society.* Urbana: University of Illinois Press, 1988.

Religion

Claude Andrew Clegg III. *An Original Man: The Life and Times of Elijah Muhammad.* New York: St. Martin's Griffin, 1997.

C. Eric Lincoln and Lawrence H. Mamiya. *The Black Church in the African American Experience.* Durham, NC: Duke University Press, 1990.

Elijah Muhammad. *The True History of Elijah Muhammad: Autobiographically Authoritative.* Atlanta: Secretrius Publications, 1997.

Jill Watts. *God, Harlem USA: The Father Divine Story.* Berkeley: University of California Press, 1992.

Robert Weisbrot. *Father Divine and the Struggle for Racial Equality.* Urbana: University of Illinois Press, 1983.

Chapter 20 The World War II Era and the Seeds of a Revolution

African Americans and the Military

Robert Allen. *Port Chicago Mutiny: The Story of the Largest Mass Mutiny in U.S. Naval History.* New York: Warner Books-Amistad Books, 1989.

Richard Dalfiume. *Desegregation of the U.S. Armed Forces: Fighting on Two Fronts 1939–1953.* Columbia: University of Missouri Press, 1969.

Charles W. Dryden. *A-Train: Memoirs of a Tuskegee Airman.* Tuscaloosa: University of Alabama Press, 1997.

Charity Adams Earley. *One Woman's Army: A Black Officer Remembers the WAC.* College Station: Texas A & M University Press, 1989.

Darlene Clark Hine. *Black Women in White: Racial Conflict and Cooperation in the Nursing Profession,*

1890–1950. Bloomington: Indiana University Press, 1989.

Ulysses Lee. *The Employment of Negro Troops.* Washington, DC: Center of Military History, 1990.

Neil McMillen, ed. *Remaking Dixie: The Impact of World War II on the American South.* Jackson: University Press of Mississippi, 1997.

Mary Penick Motley. *The Invisible Soldier: The Experience of the Black Soldier, World War Two.* Detroit: Wayne State University Press, 1975.

Alan M. Osur. *Blacks in the Army Air Forces during World War II: The Problem of Race Relations.* Washington, DC: Office of Air Force History, 1977.

Lou Potter. *Liberators: Fighting on Two Fronts in World War II.* New York: Harcourt Brace Jovanovich, 1992.

Stanley Sandler. *Segregated Skies: All-Black Combat Squadrons of WWII.* Washington, DC: Smithsonian Institution Press, 1992.

Howard Sitkoff. "Racial Militancy and Interracial Violence in the Second World War," *Journal of American History,* 58, no. 3 (1971): 663–83.

Paul Stillwell, ed. *The Golden Thirteen: Recollections of the First Black Naval Officers.* Annapolis, MD: Naval Institute Press, 1993.

Black Urban Studies

Albert Broussard. *Black San Francisco: The Struggle for Racial Equality in the West, 1900–1954.* Lawrence: University of Kansas Press, 1993.

Dominic Capeci. *The Harlem Riot of 1943.* Philadephia: Temple University Press, 1977.

Dominic Capeci. *Race Relations in Wartime Detroit: The Sojourner Truth Housing Controversy of 1942.* Philadelphia: Temple University Press, 1984.

Dominic Capeci and Martha Wilkerson. *Layered Violence: The Detroit Rioters of 1943.* Jackson: University Press of Mississippi, 1991.

Lawrence B. DeGraaf. "Significant Steps on an Arduous Path: The Impact of World War II on Discrimination Against African Americns in the West." *Journal of the West,* 35, no. 1 (1996): 24–33.

St. Clair Drake and Horace R. Cayton. *Black Metropolis: A Study of Negro Life in a Northern City.* New York: Harcourt Brace, 1945.

August Meier and Elliott Rudwick. *Black Detroit and the Rise of the UAW.* New York: Oxford University Press, 1979.

Robert Shogan and Tom Craig. *The Detroit Race Riot: A Study in Violence.* New York: Chilton Books, 1964.

Richard W. Thomas. *Life for Us Is What We Make It: Building Black Community in Detroit, 1915–1945.* Bloomington: Indiana University Press, 1992.

Black Americans, Domestic Radicalism, and International Affairs

William C. Berman. *The Politics of Civil Rights in the Truman Administration.* Columbus: Ohio State University Press, 1970.

John Morton Blum. *V Was for Victory: Politics and American Culture during World War II.* New York: Harcourt Brace Jovanovich, 1996.

Richard M. Freeland. *The Truman Doctrine and the Origins of McCarthyism.* New York: New York University Press, 1985.

Herbert Garfinkel. *When Negroes March: The March on Washington Movement in the Organizational Politics for FEPC.* New York: Atheneum, 1973.

Joseph Harris. *African American Reactions to War in Ethiopia, 1936–1941.* Baton Rouge: Louisiana State University Press, 1994.

Gerald Horne. *Black and Red: W. E. B. Du Bois and the Afro-American Response to the Cold War.* Albany: State University of New York Press, 1986.

Sudarshan Kapur. *Raising Up a Prophet: The Afro-American Encounter with Gandhi.* Boston: Orbis, 1992.

Andrew Edmund Kersten. *Race and War: The FEPC in the Midwest, 1941–46.* Urbana: University of Illinois Press, 2000.

George Lipsitz. *Rainbow at Midnight: Labor and Culture in the 1940s.* Urbana: University of Illinois Press, 1994.

August Meier and Elliott Rudwick. *CORE: A Study in the Civil Rights Movement, 1942–1968.* Urbana: University of Illinois Press, 1975.

Gail Williams O'Brien. *The Color of the Law: Race, Violence and Justice in the Post–World War II South.* Chapel Hill: University of North Carolina Press, 1999.

Brenda Gayle Plummer. *Rising Wind: Black Americans and U.S. Foreign Affairs, 1935–1960.* Chapel Hill: University of North Carolina Press, 1996.

Linda Reed. *Simple Decency and Common Sense: The Southern Conference Movement, 1938–1963.* Bloomington: Indiana University Press, 1991.

Patricia Scott Washburn. *A Question of Sedition: The Federal Government's Investigation of the Black Press during World War II.* New York: Oxford University Press, 1986.

Autobiography and Biography

Andrew Buni. *Robert Vann of the Pittsburgh Courier.* Pittsburgh: University of Pittsburgh Press, 1974.

Martin Bauml Duberman. *Paul Robeson: A Biography.* New York: Ballantine Press, 1989.

Shirley Graham Du Bois. *His Day Is Marching On: A Memoir of W. E. B. Du Bois.* New York: Lippincott, 1971.

Kenneth R. Janken. *Rayford W. Logan and the Dilemma of the African-American Intellectual.* Amherst: University of Massachusetts Press, 1993.

Spencie Love. *One Blood: The Death and Resurrection of Charles Drew.* Chapel Hill: University of North Carolina Press, 1996.

Manning Marable. *W. E. B. Du Bois: Black Radical Democrat.* Boston: Twayne, 1986.

Constance Baker Motley. *Equal Justice under Law: An Autobiography.* New York: Farrar, Straus and Giroux, 1998.

Pauli Murray. *Song in a Weary Throat: An American Pilgrimage.* New York: Harper & Row, 1987.

Bayard Rustin. *Troubles I've Seen.* New York: HarperCollins, 1996.

Studs Terkel, ed. *The Good War.* New York: Pantheon, 1984.

Brian Urquhart. *Ralph Bunche: An American Life.* New York: Norton, 1993.

Gilbert Ware. *William Hastie: Grace under Pressure.* New York: Oxford University Press, 1984.

Roy Wilkins with Tom Mathews. *Standing Fast: The Autobiography of Roy Wilkins.* New York: Da Capo Press, 1994.

Chapter 21 The Freedom Movement, 1954–1965

General Overviews of Civil Rights Movement and Organizations

Robert Fredrick Burk. *The Eisenhower Administration and Black Civil Rights.* Knoxville: University of Tennessee Press, 1984.

Stewart Burns. *Daybreak of Freedom: The Montgomery Bus Boycott.* Chapel Hill: University of North Carolina Press, 1997.

John Dittmer. *Local People: The Struggle for Civil Rights in Mississippi.* Urbana: University of Illinois Press, 1994.

Adam Fairclough. *To Redeem the Soul of America: The Southern Christian Leadership Conference and Martin Luther King, Jr.* Athens: University of Georgia Press, 1987.

David R. Goldfield. *Black, White and Southern: Race Relations and the Southern Culture, 1940 to the Present.* Baton Rouge: Louisiana State University Press, 1991.

Martin Luther King Jr. *Stride Towards Freedom: The Montgomery Story.* New York: Harper, 1958.

Michael J. Klarman. *From Jim Crow to Civil Rights: The Supreme Court and the Struggle for Racial Equality.* New York: Oxford University Press, 2003.

Steven F. Lawson. *Black Ballots: Voting Rights in the South, 1944–1969.* New York: Columbia University Press, 1976.

Manning Marable. *Race, Reform, and Rebellion: The Second Reconstruction in Black America, 1945–1982.* Jackson: University Press of Mississippi, 1984.

August Meier and Elliot Rudwick. *CORE: A Study of the Civil Rights Movement, 1942–1968.* New York: Oxford University Press, 1973.

Anne Moody. *Coming of Age in Mississippi.* New York: Dial Press, 1968.

Donald G. Nieman. *Promises to Keep: African-Americans and the Constitutional Order, 1776 to the Present.* New York: Oxford University Press, 1991.

Robert J. Norrell. *Reaping the Whirlwind: The Civil Rights Movement in Tuskegee.* New York: Alfred A. Knopf, 1985.

James T. Patterson. *Brown v. Board of Education: A Civil Rights Milestone and Its Troubled Legacy.* New York: Oxford University Press, 2000.

Charles M. Payne. *I've Got the Light of Freedom: The Organizing Tradition and the Mississippi Freedom Struggle.* Berkeley: University of California Press, 1995.

Fred Powledge. *Free at Last? The Civil Rights Movement and the People Who Made It.* Boston: Little, Brown, 1991.

Howell Raines. *My Soul Is Rested: Movement Days in the Deep South Remembered.* New York: Putnam, 1977.

Belinda Robnett. *How Long? How Long? African-American Women in the Struggle for Civil Rights.* New York: Oxford University Press, 1997.

Juan Williams. *Eyes on the Prize: America's Civil Rights Years, 1954–1965.* New York: Viking, 1987.

Black Politics/White Resistance

Numan V. Bartley. *The Rise of Massive Resistance: Race and Politics in the South during the 1950's.* Baton Rouge: Louisiana State University Press, 1969.

Elizabeth Jacoway and David R. Colburn. *Southern Businessmen and Desegregation.* Baton Rouge: Louisiana State University Press, 1982.

Darlene Clark Hine. *Black Victory: The Rise and Fall of the White Primary in Texas* (Columbia: University of Missouri Press, 2nd ed. 2003.)

Doug McAdam. *Freedom Summer.* New York: Oxford University Press, 1988.

Neil R. McMillen. *The Citizen's Council: A History of Organized Resistance to the Second Reconstruction.* Urbana: University of Illinois Press, 1971.

Frank R. Parker. *Black Votes Count: Political Empowerment in Mississippi after 1965.* Chapel Hill: University of North Carolina Press, 1990.

Autobiography and Biography

Daisy Bates. *The Long Shadow of Little Rock: Memoir.* New York: David McKay Co., 1962.

Taylor Branch. *Pillar of Fire: America in the King Years, 1963–65.* New York: Simon & Schuster, 1998.

Eric R. Burner. *And Gently He Shall Lead Them: Robert Parris Moses and Civil Rights in Mississippi.* New York: New York University Press, 1994.

Septima Clark. *Ready from Within: Septima Clark and the Civil Rights Movement.* Navarro, CA: Wild Tree Press, 1986.

Robert S. Dallek. *Flawed Giant: Lyndon Johnson and His Times, 1961–1973.* New York: Oxford University Press, 1998.

Dennis C. Dickerson. *Militant Mediator: Whitney M. Young, Jr., 1921–1971.* Lexington: University Press of Kentucky, 1998.

James Farmer. *Lay Bare the Heart: An Autobiography of the Civil Rights Movement.* New York: Arbor House, 1985.

Cynthia Griggs Fleming. *Soon We Will Not Cry: The Liberation of Ruby Doris Smith Robinson.* Lanham, MD: Rowman & Littlefield, 1998.

David J. Garrow. *Bearing the Cross: Martin Luther King, Jr., and the Southern Christian Leadership Conference.* New York: William Morrow & Company, 1986.

———. *The FBI and Martin Luther King, Jr.* New York: Penguin Books, 1981.

Chana Kai Lee. *For Freedom's Sake: The Life of Fannie Lou Hamer.* Urbana: University of Illinois Press, 1999.

David Levering Lewis. *King: A Critical Biography.* New York: Praeger, 1970.

Genna Rae McNeil. *Groundwork: Charles Hamilton Houston and the Struggle for Civil Rights.* Philadelphia: University of Pennsylvania Press, 1983.

Barbara Ransby. *Ella Baker and the Black Freedom Movement.* Chapel Hill: University of North Carolina Press, 2003.

Jo Ann Gibson Robinson, with David Garrow. *The Montgomery Bus Boycott and the Women Who Started It.* Knoxville: University of Tennessee Press, 1987.

Mark V. Tushnet. *Making Civil Rights Law: Thurgood Marshall and the Supreme Court, 1936–1961.* New York: Oxford University Press, 1994.

Timothy B. Tyson. *Radio Free Dixie: Robert F. Williams and the Roots of Black Power.* Chapel Hill: University of North Carolina Press, 1999.

Juan Williams. *Thurgood Marshall: American Revolutionary.* New York: Times Books, 1998.

Reference Works

Charles Eagles, ed. *The Civil Rights Movement in America.* Jackson: University Press of Mississippi, 1986.

Charles S. Lowery and John F. Marszalek, eds. *Encyclopedia of African-American Civil Rights: From Emancipation to the Present.* New York: Greenwood Press, 1992.

Chapter 22 The Struggle Continues, 1965–1980

Black Panthers

Philip S. Foner, ed. *The Black Panther Speaks.* Philadelphia: Lippincott, 1970.

Toni Morrison, ed. *To Die for the People: The Writings of Huey P. Newton.* New York: Writers and Readers Publishing, 1995.

Kenneth O'Reilly. *Racial Matters: The FBI's Secret File on Black America, 1960–1972.* New York: Free Press, 1989.

Robert Scheer, ed. *Eldridge Cleaver: Post-Prison Writings and Speeches.* New York: Random House, 1969.

Black Power and Politics

Robert L. Allen. *Black Awakening in Capitalist America.* Trenton, NJ: Africa World Press, 1990.

Elaine Brown. *A Taste of Power: A Black Woman's Story.* New York: Pantheon, 1992.

James H. Cone. *Martin & Malcolm & America: A Dream or a Nightmare.* Maryknoll, NY: Orbis, 1991.

Sidney Fine. *Violence in the Model City: The Cavanagh Administration, Race Relations and the Detroit Riot of 1967.* Ann Arbor: University of Michigan Press, 1989.

James F. Finley Jr. *Church People in the Struggle: The National Council of Churches and the Black Freedom Movement, 1950–1970.* New York: Oxford University Press, 1993.

Frye Gaillard. *The Dream Long Deferred.* Chapel Hill: University of North Carolina Press, 1988.

B. I. Kaufman. *The Presidency of James E. Carter, Jr.* Lawrence: University of Kansas Press, 1993.

Steven Lawson. *In Pursuit of Power: Southern Blacks and Electoral Politics, 1965–1982.* New York: Columbia University Press, 1985.

C. Eric Lincoln. *The Black Muslims in America.* Boston: Beacon Press, 1961.

J. Anthony Lukas. *Common Ground.* New York: Knopf, 1985.

John T. McCartney. *Black Power Ideologies: An Essay in African-American Thought.* Philadelphia: Temple University Press, 1992.

William B. McClain. *Black People in the Methodist Church.* Cambridge, MA: Schenkman, 1984.

Larry G. Murphy. *Down by the Riverside: Readings in African American Religion.* New York: New York University Press, 2000.

William E. Nelson Jr. and Philip J. Meranto. *Electing Black Mayors: Political Action in the Black Community.* Columbus: Ohio State University Press, 1977.

Gary Orfield. *Must We Bus? Segregated Schools and National Policy.* Washington, DC: Brookings Institution, 1978.

Robert A. Pratt. *The Color of Their Skin: Education and Race in Richmond, Virginia, 1954–89.* Charlottesville: University Press of Virginia, 1992.

James R. Ralph Jr. *Northern Protest: Martin Luther King, Jr., Chicago, and the Civil Rights Movement.* Cambridge, MA: Harvard University Press, 1993.

Diane Ravitch. *The Great School Wars.* New York: Basic Books, 1974.

Wilbur C. Rich. *Coleman Young and Detroit Politics.* Detroit, MI: Wayne State University Press, 1989.

Bobby Seale. *Seize the Time.* New York: Random House, 1970.

James Melvin Washington. *Frustrated Fellowship: The Black Baptist Quest for Social Power.* Macon, GA: Mercer University Press, 1986.

Delores S. Williams. *Sisters in the Wilderness: The Challenge of Womanist God-Talk.* Maryknoll, NY: Orbis, 1993.

Gayraud S. Wilmore. *Black Religion and Black Radicalism.* New York: Anchor Press, 1973.

Black Studies and Black Students

Talmadge Anderson, ed. *Black Studies: Theory, Method, and Cultural Perspectives.* Pullman: Washington State University Press, 1990.

Jack Bass and Jack Nelson. *The Orangeburg Massacre.* Cleveland, OH: Word Publishing, 1970.

William H. Exum. *Paradoxes of Protest: Black Student Activism in a White University.* Philadelphia: Temple University Press, 1985.

Richard P. McCormick. *The Black Student Protest Movement at Rutgers.* New Brunswick, NJ: Rutgers University Press, 1990.

Cleveland Sellers, with Robert Terrell. *The River of No Return: The Autobiography of a Black Militant and the Life and Death of SNCC.* New York: William Morrow, 1987.

Class and Race

Jack M. Bloom. *Class, Race, and the Civil Rights Movement.* Bloomington: Indiana University Press, 1987.

Martin Gilens. *Why Americans Hate Welfare: Race, Media, and the Politics of Antipoverty Policy.* Chicago: University of Chicago Press, 1999.

Michael Katz. *The Undeserving Poor: From the War on Poverty to the War on Welfare.* New York: Pantheon Books, 1989.

Bart Landry. *The New Black Middle Class.* Berkeley: University of California Press, 1987.

William Julius Wilson. *The Truly Disadvantaged: The Inner City, the Underclass, and Public Policy.* Chicago: University of Chicago Press, 1987.

Black Arts and Black Consciousness Movements

William L. Andrews, Frances Smith Foster, and Trudier Harris, eds. *The Oxford Companion to African American Literature.* New York: Oxford University Press, 1997.

James Baldwin. *Notes of a Native Son.* New York: Dial Press, 1955.

———. *Nobody Knows My Name.* New York: Dial Press, 1961.

———. *The Fire Next Time.* New York: Dial Press, 1963.

———. *No Name in the Street.* New York: Dial Press, 1972.

Imamu Amiri Baraka. *Dutchman and the Slave, Two Plays by LeRoi Jones.* New York: William Morrow, 1964.

Samuel A. Hay. *African American Theater: An Historical and Critical Analysis.* Cambridge, MA: Cambridge University Press, 1994.

LeRoi Jones and Larry Neal, eds. *Black Fire: An Anthology of Afro-American Writing.* New York: William Morrow, 1968.

LeRoi Jones. *Blues People: Negro Music in White America.* New York: William Morrow, 1963.

Frank Kofsky. *Black Nationalism and the Revolution in Music.* New York: Pathfinder Press, 1970.

Larry Neal. *Visions of a Liberated Future: Black Arts Movement Writings.* New York: Thunder's Mouth Press, 1989.

Leslie Catherine Sanders. *The Development of Black Theater in America: From Shadow to Selves.* Baton Rouge: Louisiana State University Press, 1988.

Suzanne E. Smith. *Dancing in the Streets: Motown and the Cultural Politics of Detroit.* Cambridge, MA: Harvard University Press, 2000.

Autobiography and Biography

Imamu Amiri Baraka. *The Autobiography of LeRoi Jones.* New York: Freundlich Books, 1984.

Dennis C. Dickerson. *Militant Mediator: Whitney M. Young, Jr.* Lexington: University Press of Kentucky, 1998.

James Farmer. *Lay Bare the Heart: An Autobiography of the Civil Rights Movement.* New York: Arbor House, 1985.

Jimmie Lewis Franklin. *Back to Birmingham: Richard Arrington, Jr., and His Times.* Tuscaloosa: University of Alabama Press, 1989.

Elliott J. Gorn, ed. *Muhammad Ali: The People's Champ.* Urbana: University of Illinois Press, 1995.

Charles V. Hamilton. *Adam Clayton Powell, Jr.: The Political Biography of an American Dilemma.* New York: Atheneum, 1991.

Hil Haygood. *King of the Cats: The Life and Times of Adam Clayton Powell, Jr.* Boston: Houghton Mifflin, 1993.

David Remnick. *King of the World: Muhammad Ali and the Rise of an American Hero.* New York: Random House, 1998.

Mary Beth Rogers. *Barbara Jordan: American Hero.* New York: Bantam Books, 1998.

Kathleen Rout. *Eldridge Cleaver.* Boston: Twayne Publishers, 1991.

Bobby Seale. *Seize the Time.* New York: Random House, 1970.

Nancy J. Weiss. *Whitney M. Young, Jr., and the Struggle for Civil Rights.* Princeton, NJ: Princeton University Press, 1989.

Chapter 23 Black Politics, White Backlash, 1980 to the Present

Culture and Race Studies

Molefi Kete Asante. *Erasing Racism: The Survival of the American Nation.* New York: Prometheus Books, 2003.

Robin D. G. Kelley. *Race Rebels: Culture, Politics, and the Black Working Class.* New York: Free Press, 1994.

Jacob Levenson. *The Secret Epidemic: The Story of AIDS and Black America.* New York: Pantheon, 2004.

Manning Marable. *The Great Wells of Democracy: The Meaning of Race in American Life.* New York: Basic Books, 2002.

Terry McMillan. *Five for Five: The Films of Spike Lee.* New York: Stewart, Tabori & Chang, 1991.

Nikhil Pal Singh. *Black Is a Country: Race and the Unfinished Struggle for Democracy.* Cambridge: Harvard University Press, 2004.

Black Politics and Economics

Andrew Billingsley. *Climbing Jacob's Ladder: The Enduring Legacy of African-American Families.* New York: Simon & Schuster, 1993.

Barry Bluestone and Bennett Harrison. *The Deindustrialization of America: Plant Closings, Community Abandonment, and the Dismantling of Basic Industry.* New York: Basic Books, 1982.

Donna Brazile. *Cooking with Grease: Stirring the Pot in American Politics.* New York: Simon & Schuster, 2004.

Michael K. Brown. *Race, Money, and the American Welfare State.* Ithaca, NY: Cornell University Press, 1999.

Robert D. Bullard, Glenn S. Johnson, and Angel O. Torres, eds. *Highway Robbery: Transportation Racism and New Routes to Equity.* Cambridge, MA: South End Press, 2004.

Martin Carnoy. *Faded Dreams: The Politics and Economics of Race in America.* Cambridge, England: Cambridge University Press, 1994.

Dalton Conley. *Being Black, Living in the Red: Race, Wealth, and Social Policy in America.* Berkeley: University of California Press, 1999.

Robert Dallek. *Ronald Reagan: The Politics of Symbolism.* Cambridge, MA: Harvard University Press, 1984.

W. Avon Drake and Robert D. Holsworth. *Affirmative Action and the Stalled Quest for Black Progress.* Urbana: University of Illinois Press, 1996.

Robert Gooding-Williams, ed. *Reading Rodney King: Reading Urban Uprising.* New York: Routledge, 1993.

Lani Guinier. *Tyranny of the Majority: Fundamental Fairness and Representative Democracy.* New York: Free Press, 1995.

Andrew Hacker. *Two Nations: Black and White, Separate, Hostile, Unequal.* New York: Ballantine Books, rev., 1995.

Melissa Victoria Harris-Lacewell. *Barbershops, Bibles, and Bet: Everyday Talk and Black Political Thought.* Princeton: Princeton University Press, 2004.

Charles P. Henry. *Jesse Jackson: The Search for Common Ground.* Oakland, CA: Black Scholar Press, 1991.

Anita Faye Hill and Emma Coleman Jordan, eds. *Race, Gender, and Power in America: The Legacy of the Hill–Thomas Hearings.* New York: Oxford University Press, 1995.

James Jennings. *Welfare Reform and the Revitalization of Inner City Neighborhoods.* East Lansing: Michigan State University Press, 2003.
Norman Kelley. *The Head Negro in Charge Syndrome: The Dead End of Black Politics.* New York: Nation Books, 2004.
Douglas S. Massey and Nancy A. Denton. *American Apartheid: Segregation and the Making of the Underclass.* Cambridge, MA: Harvard University Press, 1993.
Adolph Reed Jr. *The Jesse Jackson Phenomenon: The Crisis in Afro-American Politics.* New Haven, CT: Yale University Press, 1986.
Condoleezza Rice. "Why We Know Iraq Is Lying," *New York Times,* January 23, 2003.
Andrea Y. Simpson. *The Tie That Binds: Identity and Political Attitudes in the Post–Civil Rights Generation.* New York: New York University Press, 1998.
Special Issue on Affirmative Action. *The Western Journal of Black Studies,* 27, no. 1 (Spring 2003).
William Julius Wilson. *The Bridge over the Racial Divide: Rising Inequality and Coalition Politics.* Berkeley: University of California Press, 1999.

Liberation Studies

Derrick Bell. *Faces at the Bottom of the Well: The Permanence of Racism.* New York: Basic Books, 1992.
Michael C. Dawson. *Behind the Mule: Race and Class in African-American Politics.* Princeton, NJ: Princeton University Press, 1994.
W. Marvin Dulaney. *Black Police in America.* Bloomington: Indiana University Press, 1996.
Henry Hampton and Steve Fayer. *Voices of Freedom: An Oral History of the Civil Rights Movement from the 1950s through the 1980s.* New York: Bantam Books, 1990.
Randall Robinson. *The Debt: What America Owes to Blacks.* New York: Plume, 2000.
Cornel West. *Democracy Matters: Wining the Fight Against Imperialism.* New York: The Penguin Press, 2004.

Black Conservatives

Thomas Sowell. *Preferential Policies: An International Perspective.* New York: William Morrow, 1990.
Shelby Steele. *A Dream Deferred: The Second Betrayal of Black Freedom in America.* New York: HarperCollins, 1998.
Shelby Steele/CCC. *The Content of Our Character: A New Vision of Race in America.* New York: St. Martin's Press, 1990.

Autobiography and Biography

Marshall Frady. *Jesse: The Life and Pilgrimage of Jesse Jackson.* New York: Random House, 1996.
Barack Obama, *Dreams from My Father: A Story of Race and Inheritance.* New York: Three Rivers Press, 1995, 2004.
Rev. Al Sharpton (with Karen Hunter). *Al on America.* New York: Kensington, 2002.

Chapter 24 African Americans at the Dawn of a New Millennium

Black Culture Studies

Anthony Bogues. *Black Heretics, Black Prophets: Radical Political Intellectuals.* New York: Doubleday, 2003.
Brian Cross. *It's Not about a Salary . . . Rap, Race and Resistance in Los Angeles.* London: Verso, 1993.
Michael Eric Dyson. *Between God and Gangsta Rap: Bearing Witness to Black Culture.* New York: Oxford University Press, 1996.
Patricia Liggins Hill, gen. ed. Call and Response: The Riverside Anthology of the African American Literary Tradition. New York: Houghton Mifflin, 1969.
bell hooks. *Outlaw Culture: Resisting Representations.* New York: Routledge, 1994.
Robin D. G. Kelley. *Race Rebels: Culture, Politics, and the Black Working Class.* New York: Free Press, 1994.
Terry McMillan. *Five for Five: The Films of Spike Lee.* New York: Stewart, Tabori & Chang, 1991.
Joan Morgan. *When Chickenheads Come Home to Roost: My Life as a Hip-Hop Feminist.* New York: Simon & Schuster, 1999.
Tricia Rose. *Black Noise: Rap Music and Black Culture in Contemporary America.* Hanover, NH: Wesleyan University Press, 1994.
Greg Tate. *Flyboy in the Buttermilk.* New York: Fire-side, 1992.
Deborah Willis. *Reflections in Black: A History of Black Photographers, 1840 to the Present.* New York: Norton, 2000.

Identity Studies

K. Anthony Appiah and Amy Guttman. *Color Conscious: The Political Morality of Race.* Princeton: Princeton University Press, 1996.
Molefi Kete Asante. *The Afrocentric Idea.* Philadelphia: Temple University Press, 1987.
Martin Bernal. *Black Athena: The Afroasiatic Roots of Classical Civilization: The Fabrication of Ancient*

Greece, 1785–1985. New Brunswick, NJ: Rutgers University Press, 1987.

Jonathan Betsch Cole and Beverly Guy Sheftall. *Gender Talk: The Struggle for Women's Equality in African-American Communities.* New York: Ballantine Books, 2003.

F. James Davis. *Who Is Black? One Nation's Definition.* University Park: Pennsylvania State University Press, 1991.

Charles Harmon, ed. *Double Exposure: Poverty and Race in America.* Armonk, NY: M. E. Sharpe, 1997.

Tsehloane Keto. *Vision, Identity and Time: The Afrocentric Paradigm and the Study of the Past.* Dubuque, IA: Kendall/Hunt, 1995.

Wilson Jeremiah Moses. *Afrotopia: The Roots of African American Popular History.* Cambridge, MA: Cambridge University Press, 1998.

Arthur M. Schlesinger Jr. *The Disuniting of America.* New York: Norton, 1992.

Clarence Walker. *You Can't Go Home Again.* New York: Oxford University Press, 2001.

Cornel West. *Race Matters.* Boston: Beacon Press, 1993.

Race, Gender, and Class

Paul M. Barrett. *The Good Black: A True Story of Race in America.* New York: Dutton, 1999.

Lois Benjamin. *The Black Elite: Facing the Color Line in the Twilight of the Twentieth Century.* Chicago: Nelson-Hall, 1991.

Douglas G. Glasgow. *The Black Underclass: Poverty, Unemployment, and Entrapment of Ghetto Youth.* New York: Random House, 1981.

Christopher Jencks. *Rethinking Social Policy: Race, Poverty, and the Underclass.* Cambridge, MA: Harvard University Press, 1992.

Jonathan Kozel. *Savage Inequalities: Children in America's Schools.* New York: Crown, 1991.

Haki R. Madhubuti. *Black Men—Obsolete, Single, Dangerous? Afrikan American Families in Transition: Essays in Discovery, Solution, and Hope.* Chicago: Third World Press, 1990.

Leith Mullings. *On Our Own Terms: Race, Class, and Gender in the Lives of African American Women.* New York: Routledge, 1997.

Autobiography and Biography

Amy Alexander, ed. *The Farrakhan Factor: African-American Writers on Leadership, Nationhood and Minister Louis Farrakhan.* New York: Grove Press, 1998.

E. Lynn Harris. *What Becomes of the Broken Hearted?* New York: Doubleday, 2003.

Randall Robinson. *Defending the Spirit: A Black Life in America.* New York: NAL/Dutton, 1998.

Index